MW00339278

Entrepreneurship

Second Edition

Brenda Clark
MBA Research and Curriculum Center
Columbus, OH

Judy Commers
Ivy Tech Community College
Michigan City, Indiana

Publisher
The Goodheart-Willcox Company, Inc.
Tinley Park, Illinois
www.g-w.com

Copyright © 2018
by
The Goodheart-Willcox Company, Inc.

Previous edition copyright 2013

All rights reserved. No part of this work may be reproduced, stored, or transmitted in any form or by any electronic or mechanical means, including information storage and retrieval systems, without the prior written permission of The Goodheart-Willcox Company, Inc.

Manufactured in the United States of America.

ISBN 978-1-63126-635-5

1 2 3 4 5 6 7 8 9 – 18 – 21 20 19 18 17 16

The Goodheart-Willcox Company, Inc. Brand Disclaimer: Brand names, company names, and illustrations for products and services included in this text are provided for educational purposes only and do not represent or imply endorsement or recommendation by the author or the publisher.

The Goodheart-Willcox Company, Inc. Safety Notice: The reader is expressly advised to carefully read, understand, and apply all safety precautions and warnings described in this book or that might also be indicated in undertaking the activities and exercises described herein to minimize risk of personal injury or injury to others. Common sense and good judgment should also be exercised and applied to help avoid all potential hazards. The reader should always refer to the appropriate manufacturer's technical information, directions, and recommendations; then proceed with care to follow specific equipment operating instructions. The reader should understand these notices and cautions are not exhaustive.

The publisher makes no warranty or representation whatsoever, either expressed or implied, including but not limited to equipment, procedures, and applications described or referred to herein, their quality, performance, merchantability, or fitness for a particular purpose. The publisher assumes no responsibility for any changes, errors, or omissions in this book. The publisher specifically disclaims any liability whatsoever, including any direct, indirect, incidental, consequential, special, or exemplary damages resulting, in whole or in part, from the reader's use or reliance upon the information, instructions, procedures, warnings, cautions, applications, or other matter contained in this book. The publisher assumes no responsibility for the activities of the reader.

The Goodheart-Willcox Company, Inc. Internet Disclaimer: The Internet resources and listings in this Goodheart-Willcox Publisher product are provided solely as a convenience to you. These resources and listings were reviewed at the time of publication to provide you with accurate, safe, and appropriate information. Goodheart-Willcox Publisher has no control over the referenced websites and, due to the dynamic nature of the Internet, is not responsible or liable for the content, products, or performance of links to other websites or resources. Goodheart-Willcox Publisher makes no representation, either expressed or implied, regarding the content of these websites, and such references do not constitute an endorsement or recommendation of the information or content presented. It is your responsibility to take all protective measures to guard against inappropriate content, viruses, or other destructive elements.

Cover image: MikaelDamkier/Shutterstock.com
Image p. v: iStock.com/DeanDrobot

Introduction

In today's fast-paced economy, investigating multiple career options is more challenging than ever. *Entrepreneurship* helps you meet that challenge. By providing a comprehensive framework to learn about a career as an entrepreneur, you can explore what it is like to be a business owner.

One of the major goals of this text is to provide direction to create a business plan. To help accomplish this, each chapter concludes with a project-based activity designed to lead you through this process. A template is available on the companion website to assist in writing a customized business plan.

It is important to understand how our free enterprise system plays a role in business. Each unit starts with an Entrepreneurs and the Economy feature article discussing important economic concepts that relate to entrepreneurship.

The step-by-step narrative leads you through selecting an idea for a business, social and ethical responsibilities, start-up options for the new business, operating the business, and exiting the business. Separate chapters on funding the business and financial management of the business add clarity to the two separate finance functions.

A new learning tool has been included to help you study. QR codes are provided for use with your smartphone to go directly to selected activities. In addition, the G-W Learning Companion Website makes it easy for you to study on the go!

About the Authors

Brenda Clark is a retired CTE director, marketing and business instructor, SBE advisor, and DECA advisor for Jenison, Michigan Public Schools. She was named Marketing Teacher of the Year at state and national levels, and her marketing program was named Business of the Year by the Jenison Chamber of Commerce. She received the Outstanding Service Award from DECA and was given the Honorary Life Membership Award for Michigan. Brenda currently serves as the Professional Development Manager for MBA Research and Curriculum Center and is a coauthor of *Marketing Dynamics* and *Principles of Business, Marketing, and Finance*. She earned a bachelor degree in marketing education, a master degree in educational leadership, and an EdD in educational leadership with a concentration in career and technical education from Western Michigan University.

Judy Commers has been a marketing teacher-coordinator and DECA advisor in Indiana for 40 years. For 24 years, she supervised a DECA School-Based Enterprise at Porter County Career and Technical Center in Valparaiso, Indiana. She currently teaches business and marketing at Ivy Tech Community College. She has been an instructor for the Indiana Marketing Academy, instructing high school business and marketing teachers. She received her bachelor degree in business and distributive education and an MAE in vocational business and distributive education from Ball State University.

Copyright Goodheart-Willcox Co., Inc.

Reviewers

Goodheart-Willcox Publisher would like to thank the following instructors and professionals who reviewed selected manuscript chapters and provided input for the development of *Entrepreneurship*.

Dr. Cathy Ashmore
Executive Director
Consortium for Entrepreneurship Education
Columbus, Ohio

Barbara J. Bielenberg
Head Teacher, Business Education (retired)
Sioux City Community Schools
Sioux City, Iowa

Melissa P. Bourgeois, MAEd, NBCT
Business Educator
Richlands High School
Richlands, North Carolina
President, North Carolina Business
    Education Association

Debra C. Carter
Entrepreneurship Academy Lead Teacher
Spanish River High School
Boca Raton, Florida

Sharon A. Casbon
AVP Human Resources, Retired
Ivy Tech Community College of Indiana
Valparaiso, Indiana

Greg R. Chapman
CFO/Member
Aerotek Design Labs, LLC
Plainfield, Illinois

John E. Clarkin, PhD
Associate Professor of Entrepreneurship
Northern Kentucky University
Highland Heights, Kentucky

Jeff Cook
Partner
Redsock Advisors LLC
Germantown, Tennessee

Dana T. Dingell
CTE Department Chair
James Madison High School
Vienna, Virginia

Dwionne R. Freeman
Business Teacher
Atlanta Public Schools
Atlanta, Georgia
President, Georgia Business Educators
    Association

Kimberly Guest
Marketing Teacher
Kearsley High School
Flint, Michigan

Delda L. Hagin
Business Education Teacher
Ware County High School
Waycross, Georgia

Amy Holbrook
Associate Attorney
Parent & Parent, LLP
Wallingford, Connecticut

Joseph Incrocci
CEO and President
Incrocci Financial Solutions Consulting, LLC
Chicago, Illinois

Liz Lancaster
Marketing Education/DECA Advisor
Creekview High School
Carrollton, Texas

Donna W. Martin
Director, Academy of Entrepreneurship
Buchholz High School
Gainesville, Florida

Yvonne J. Mullins
Business and Marketing Teacher
Midlothian High School
Chesterfield County Public Schools
Midlothian, Virginia

Lots Pinnyei
Jimtown High School DECA
Jimtown High School
Elkhart, Indiana

Copyright Goodheart-Willcox Co., Inc.

Stuart Slippen
President
Stuart Slippen & Associates, LLC
McKinney, Texas

Georgann Smith
AD Business
Human Resources Generalist
Ivy Tech Community College of Indiana
Valparaiso, Indiana

Pamela J. Varnish
Chef Instructor
Dixie High School
Due West, South Carolina

Gwendolyn Wells, NBCT
Business Education Teacher and BPA
    Advisor
Naperville Central High School
Naperville, Illinois

Marysusan Williamson
Business and Marketing Teacher/DECA
    Advisor
Brookland-Cayce High School
Cayce, South Carolina

Charisse Woodward
Business Teacher
Sherando High School
Stephens City, Virginia

Precision Exams Certification

Goodheart-Willcox is pleased to partner with Precision Exams by correlating *Entrepreneurship* to the Standards, Objectives, and Indicators for Precision Exams Entrepreneurship Exam. Precision Exams were created in concert with industry and subject matter experts to match real-world job skills and marketplace demands. Students who pass the exam and performance portion of the exam can earn a Career Skills Certification™. To see how *Entrepreneurship* correlates to the Precision Exam Standards, please visit www.g-w. com/entrepreneurship-2018 and click on the Correlations tab. For more information on Precision Exams, please visit www.precisionexams.com.

I earned a CAREER SKILLS™ Certificate in Entrepreneurship. You can earn one, too!

Ask your instructor how you can earn a

CAREER SKILLS™ Certificate for your résumé.

800.470.1215   PRECISION EXAMS   precisionexams.com

Copyright Goodheart-Willcox Co., Inc.

Contents in Brief

Copyright Goodheart-Willcox Co., Inc.

Expanded Table of Contents

Copyright Goodheart-Willcox Co., Inc.

Copyright Goodheart-Willcox Co., Inc.

Copyright Goodheart-Willcox Co., Inc.

Features

Picture Yourself Here

Social Entrepreneurs

Copyright Goodheart-Willcox Co., Inc.

Global Entrepreneurs

Focus on Finance

You Do the Math

Green Entrepreneurs

Copyright Goodheart-Willcox Co., Inc.

Prepare for Your Future

Looking for a career that gives you independence? Envision your career as an entrepreneur!

Entrepreneurship was designed with you, the student, in mind. Contemporary issues and a fresh new presentation of concepts make this text inviting for you to use.

Did you know that the economy plays an important role in becoming a business owner? To highlight the importance of the economy on business, economic concepts are integrated throughout the text. Also, to address specific current economic events, each unit of the text opens with an **Entrepreneurs and the Economy** feature article. These articles highlight information about the economy that is helpful to small business owners.

One of the goals of an entrepreneurship course is to create a complete business plan. The ongoing **Building Your Business Plan— Putting the Puzzle Together** feature provides a project-based, hands-on learning experience. Starting in the first chapter, you will begin creating a business plan for your own business. By the end of the text, you will have completed your own plan. The **Building Your Business Plan—Putting the Puzzle Together** project addresses 21st-century learning skills.

- Creativity and Innovation
- Critical Thinking and Problem Solving
- Communication and Collaboration

It is all about getting ready for college and a career. College and Career Readiness activities address literacy skills to help prepare you for the real world. Standards for English Language Arts for reading, writing, speaking, and listening are incorporated in a **Reading Prep** activity as well as end-of-chapter **Communication Skills** activities.

Copyright Goodheart-Willcox Co., Inc.

Amplify Your Learning

Content is presented in an easy-to-comprehend and relevant format. Practical activities relate everyday learning to enable you to experience real-life communication situations and challenges.

- Each chapter opens with a **pretest** and concludes with a **posttest**. The pretest will help evaluate your prior knowledge of chapter content. The posttest will help evaluate what you have learned after studying the chapter.

- The **Essential Question** at the beginning of each section engages you with the important points presented in the content.

- A **You Do the Math** activity in each chapter focuses on skills that are important to your understanding of math for business.

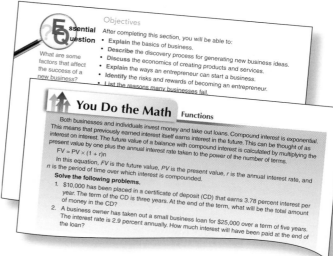

- **Event Prep–CTSOs** features present information to use when preparing for the competitive activities and events of career and technical student organizations (CTSOs).

- The **Math Skills Handbook** provides you with a quick reference for basic math functions and helps clarify business math that is presented in the chapters.

Ever wonder how other people with an idea started a business? The entrepreneurial experience comes to life through stories about real-life entrepreneurs.

- **Picture Yourself Here** highlights entrepreneurs who got an early start on becoming business owners.

- **Chapter introductions** present entrepreneurs who overcame challenges as small-business owners.

- **Global Entrepreneurs** features entrepreneurs who took a local business to an international location.

- **Social Entrepreneurs** demonstrates how business owners can be socially and ethically responsible within their communities.

Copyright Goodheart-Willcox Co., Inc.

Assess Your Progress

It is important to assess what you learn as you progress through the text. Multiple opportunities are provided for self-assessment to confirm learning as the content is explored. **Formative assessment** includes the following.

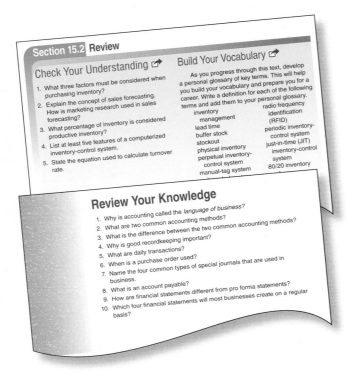

- **Checkpoint** activities at the end of each main chapter section provide you with an opportunity to review what you have learned before moving on to the remaining content.

- **Review Your Knowledge** covers basic entrepreneurial concepts to help you evaluate your understanding of the main points presented in the chapter.

- **Apply Your Knowledge** challenges you to begin the planning process and prepare your business plan.

- **Teamwork** encourages a collaborative experience to help you learn to interact with others in a productive manner.

- **College and Career Readiness** activities provide real-world literacy skills to prepare for life outside of school.

- Research skills are critical for success in college and career. **Internet Research** activities at the end of each chapter provide opportunities to put them to work.

- **Building Your Business Plan–Putting the Puzzle Together** is an ongoing project-based activity that guides you through preparing a complete business plan.

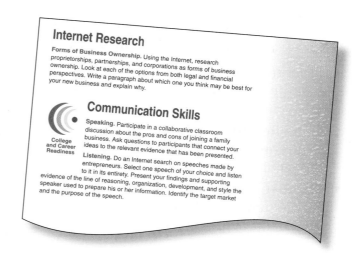

Copyright Goodheart-Willcox Co., Inc.

Maximize the Impact

G-W Learning Companion Website

Technology is an important part of your world. So, it should be part of your everyday learning experiences. G-W Learning for Entrepreneurship is a study reference that contains activity files, vocabulary exercises, interactive quizzes, and more. Visit www.g-wlearning.com/marketing.

G-W Learning provides you with opportunities for hands-on interactivity so you can study on the go. Look for the activity icon in the text next to the following activities:

- Chapter **pretests** and **posttests** allow you to assess what you know before you begin the chapter, as well as evaluate what you have learned upon completion of your study.

- **E-flash cards** and **matching activities** for the key terms in each chapter reinforce the vocabulary learned in the text and enable you to study on the go.

- Data files for **Building Your Business Plan—Putting the Puzzle Together** are downloadable, hands-on activities that include a business plan template and a sample business plan to assist you in creating plans for your own business.

Goodheart-Willcox QR Codes

This Goodheart-Willcox product contains QR codes*, or quick response codes. These codes can be scanned with a smartphone bar code reader to access chapter pretests. For more information on using QR codes and a recommended QR code reader, visit G-W Learning. www.g-wlearning.com

*An Internet connection is required to access the QR code destination. Data-transfer rates may apply. Check with your Internet service provider for information on your data-transfer rates.

Copyright Goodheart-Willcox Co., Inc.

G-W Integrated Learning Solution

The G-W Integrated Learning Solution offers easy-to-use resources for both students and instructors. Digital and blended learning content can be accessed through any Internet-enabled device, such as a computer, smartphone, or tablet. Students spend more time learning, and instructors spend less time administering.

G-W Learning Companion Website/Student Textbook

The G-W Learning companion website is a study reference that contains e-flash cards, vocabulary exercises, interactive quizzes and more! Accessible from any digital device, the G-W Learning companion website complements the textbook and is available to students at no charge.

Visit www.g-wlearning.com.

Online Learning Suite

Available as a classroom subscription, the Online Learning Suite provides the foundation of instruction and learning for digital and blended classrooms. An easy-to-manage, shared classroom subscription makes it a hassle-free solution for both students and instructors. An online student text and workbook, along with rich supplemental content, bring digital learning to the classroom. All instructional materials are found on a convenient online bookshelf and are accessible at home, at school, or on the go.

Copyright Goodheart-Willcox Co., Inc.

Assess Your Progress

Online Learning Suite/Student Textbook Bundle

Looking for a blended solution? Goodheart-Willcox offers the Online Learning Suite bundled with the printed text in one easy-to-access package. Students have the flexibility to use the print version, the Online Learning Suite, or a combination of both components to meet their individual learning styles. The convenient packaging makes managing and accessing content easy and efficient.

Online Instructor Resources

Online Instructor Resources provide all the support needed to make preparation and classroom instruction easier than ever. Available in one accessible location, support materials include Answer Keys, Lesson Plans, Instructor's Presentations for PowerPoint®, ExamView® Assessment Suite, and more! Online Instructor Resources are available as a subscription and can be accessed at school or at home.

G-W Integrated Learning Solution

For the Student:

Student Textbook (print)
Student Workbook (print)
G-W Learning Companion Website (free)
Online Learning Suite (subscription)
Online Learning Suite/Student Textbook bundle

For the Instructor:

Instructor's Presentations for PowerPoint® (CD)
ExamView® Assessment Suite (CD)
Instructor's Resources (CD)
Online Instructor Resources (subscription)

Copyright Goodheart-Willcox Co., Inc.

StockLite/Shutterstock.com

Unit 1
Entrepreneurship

Your Business Plan—
Putting the Puzzle Together

As part of the *Entrepreneurship* text, you will develop a business plan. Writing a business plan can be overwhelming unless you approach it like a puzzle. Think about how you put a puzzle together—one piece at a time. Your business plan will evolve as each chapter is covered. In this unit, you will:

Set goals for your business.

Create vision and mission statements.

Write an overview of your business.

Investigate how ethics and social responsibility fit into your business plan.

Unit Overview

Exploring career opportunities is an important step as the choices are endless. In this text, you will have an opportunity to investigate the career choice to become an entrepreneur and run your own business. Successful entrepreneurs develop an idea and then create a solid business plan to serve as a road map. Unit 1 guides you through the steps of developing new business ideas. It outlines the basic parts of a good business plan, which is critical to the success of any new business. Ethics and social responsibility are also presented as a foundation for becoming an entrepreneur.

Chapters

1. Entrepreneurial Careers
2. Business Plan
3. Ethics and Social Responsibility

Entrepreneurs and the Economy

The term *new economy* was coined in the late 1990s to describe the impact of information technology on the economy. The Internet and affordable personal computers changed how business was conducted—and made it much easier to become an entrepreneur. Because entrepreneurs are often also innovators, their impact on the US economy is great. Some entrepreneurs are creating new technology, while others are using existing technology to develop faster, more efficient business processes.

Entrepreneurs are nimble—meaning their businesses start out small, so they can act quickly to take advantage of new opportunities. Entrepreneurial businesses do not have the red tape and long approval processes of larger companies. In effect, entrepreneurs are starting to create small businesses that can now compete with big business.

While entrepreneurs have always been the backbone of the US economy, they are even more important since the recession of 2008. High unemployment and forced early retirements have made going into business for yourself more attractive than ever. Carl Schramm, president and chief executive officer of the Kauffman Foundation said, "Americans in big numbers are looking to entrepreneurs to rally the economy. More than 70 percent of voters say the health of the economy depends on the success of entrepreneurs. And a full 80 percent want to see the government use its resources to actively encourage entrepreneurship in America."

The ability to raise start-up capital is a critical issue for most entrepreneurs. Many states and the federal government now have policies designed to assist entrepreneurial efforts. These policies include incentives for banks to increase lending to start-up companies—as well as tax breaks for entrepreneurs. According to the Small Business Administration (SBA), over 50 percent of US

alphaspirit/Shutterstock.com

employees work for a small business. *Small businesses* are defined as those businesses independently owned and operated, organized for profit, and not dominant in their fields. In the United States, 99.7 percent of businesses are classified as small, and most of them were started by entrepreneurs. Successful entrepreneurs create new jobs and provide social benefits in every region. For all of these reasons, it has never been a better time to become an entrepreneur.

G-WLEARNING.com

While studying, look for the activity icon 🔗 for:

- Chapter pretests and posttests
- Key terms activities
- Section reviews
- Building Your Business Plan activities

1 Entrepreneurial Careers

What might Oprah Winfrey, Steven Spielberg, Paul Allen, Larry Page, Sergey Brin, and you have in common? *Entrepreneurship.* They are all entrepreneurs, and you may be an entrepreneur, too. Each of these entrepreneurs sat where you are now sitting at one point in his or her life—thinking about becoming an entrepreneur. Oprah began her career by learning to perform at age three and entered broadcasting at age 17. By age 12, Steven Spielberg had created his first movie and charged admission to showings of it. Microsoft cofounder Paul Allen began programming computers when he was 15. Larry Page loved working with computers by the time he had reached the age of six. In college, he met Sergey Brin and together they created Google. What will you do?

> *"I had to make my own living and my own opportunity! But I made it! Don't sit down and wait for the opportunities to come. Get up and make them!"*
>
> —Madam C.J. Walker, creator of a popular line of African-American hair-care products and America's first African-American female millionaire

College and Career Readiness

Reading Prep. Review the table of contents for this text. Trace the development of the content that is being presented from simple to complex ideas.

Sections

Picture Yourself Here
Tim O'Shaughnessy

In 2007 at the age of 25, Tim O'Shaughnessy, together with Val Aleksenko, Aaron Batalion, and Eddie Frederick, started a company called Hungry Machine. The company began as a business consultancy and Facebook-application developer. As the business evolved, it began focusing on how to bridge the gap between online and offline business. Two years later, LivingSocial was born.

While serving as LivingSocial's chief executive officer, Tim was responsible for setting the company's strategies and overseeing its growth. Tim has earned degrees in marketing, operations, and information management from Georgetown University. Degrees like the ones Tim has are invaluable when starting your own business.

Today, LivingSocial has become the online source for discovering valuable local experiences in the United States and worldwide. LivingSocial members receive daily e-mails offering big discounts for new experiences, such as excursions, meals, and getaways, in their area.

Photo © Doug Sonders

Check Your Entrepreneurship IQ

Before you begin the chapter, see what you already know about entrepreneurship by taking the chapter pretest. The pretest is available at www.g-wlearning.com

Your Career

Essential Question

How can research and planning contribute to career success?

Objectives

After completing this section, you will be able to:

- **Identify** some of the resources available to explore career opportunities.
- **Explain** the purpose and process of creating a career plan.

Key Terms

career clusters
career pathways
career and technical student
  organization (CTSO)
career plan
aptitude

skill
attitude
values
goal
SMART goals

Critical Thinking

Write about where you see yourself in five, ten, or even twenty years. What type of career will you have? Will you own your own business? Even if you become a doctor, lawyer, or pharmacist, you can still own your own business; many do.

Explore Your Career Options

The average worker spends 36 percent of his or her day working, as shown in Figure 1-1. This means a choice of career is one of the most important decisions a person will make as an adult. There are many potential careers from which to choose, so it is important to explore and research the career that is the best fit for you.

Career Clusters

The workplace is changing rapidly, and researching a career can be somewhat overwhelming. Studying the career clusters is a good starting point to see where your interests lie. The **career clusters** are 16 groups of occupational and career specialties, as shown in Figure 1-2. Each cluster has specific career pathways that range from entry-level jobs to more advanced positions. **Career pathways** are subgroups within the career clusters that reflect occupations requiring similar knowledge and skills. By exploring the career clusters, you can gain information about various career choices.

Copyright Goodheart-Willcox Co., Inc.

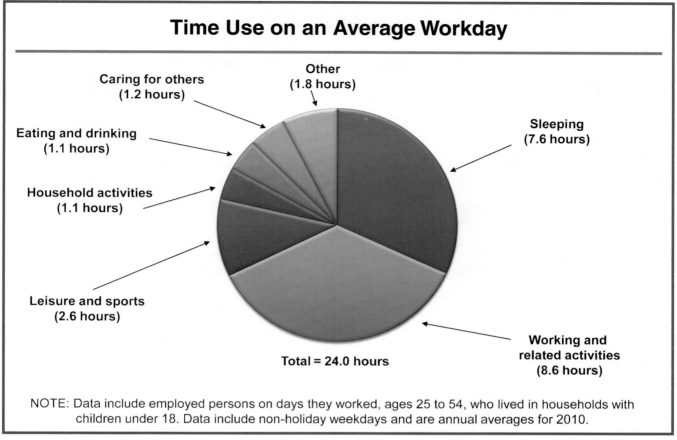

Time Use on an Average Workday

Caring for others
(1.2 hours)

Other
(1.8 hours)

Eating and drinking
(1.1 hours)

Sleeping
(7.6 hours)

Household activities
(1.1 hours)

Leisure and sports
(2.6 hours)

Working and
related activities
(8.6 hours)

Total = 24.0 hours

NOTE: Data include employed persons on days they worked, ages 25 to 54, who lived in households with children under 18. Data include non-holiday weekdays and are annual averages for 2010.

Source: US Department of Labor; Goodheart-Willcox Publisher

Figure 1-1. Average workday for working adults with children.

Career exploration can be an exciting time in your life. Will you choose a traditional career or a nontraditional career? Will you work for a company or own your own business?

No matter what direction you choose, education and training will be necessary to be successful. There are many foundation skills that are necessary for success in any career. Some of those skills include:

- basic skills—reading, writing, listening, speaking, and math;

- thinking skills—decision making, creative thinking, problem solving, visualization, reasoning;

- personal qualities—self-management, integrity, honesty, sociability, responsibility;

- technology skills—social media knowledge, software skills, systems skills; and

- business skills—planning, organizing, negotiating, leadership, communication.

Strengthen the skills that you have and set a goal to improve those that need additional work.

Copyright Goodheart-Willcox Co., Inc.

The 16 Career Clusters

Careers involving the production, processing, marketing, distribution, financing, and development of agricultural commodities and resources. *Agriculture, Food & Natural Resources*	Careers involving management, marketing, and operations of foodservice, lodging, and recreational businesses. *Hospitality & Tourism*
Careers involving the design, planning managing, building, and maintaining of buildings and structures. *Architecture & Construction*	Careers involving family and human needs. *Human Services*
Careers involving the design, production, exhibition, performance, writing, and publishing of visual and performing arts. *Arts, A/V Technology & Communications*	Careers involving the design, development, support, and management of software, hardware, and other technology-related materials. *Information Technology*
Careers involving the planning, organizing, directing, and evaluation of functions essential to business operations. *Business Management & Administration*	Careers involving the planning, management, and providing of legal services, public safety, protective services, and homeland security. *Law, Public Safety, Corrections & Security*
Careers involving the planning, management, and providing of training services. *Education & Training*	Careers involving the planning, management, and processing of materials to create completed products. *Manufacturing*
Careers involving the planning and providing of banking, insurance, and other financial-business services. *Finance*	Careers involving the planning, management, and performance of marketing and sales activities. *Marketing*
Careers involving governance, national security, foreign service, revenue and taxation, regulation, and management and administration. *Government & Public Administration*	Careers involving the planning, management, and providing of scientific research and technical services. *Science, Technology, Engineering & Mathematics*
Careers involving planning, managing, and providing health services, health information, and research and development. *Health Science*	Careers involving the planning, management, and movement of people, materials, and goods. *Transportation, Distribution & Logistics*

Source: States' Career Clusters Initiative 2008; Goodheart-Willcox Publisher

Figure 1-2. There are 16 career clusters. Each cluster contains several career pathways.

Copyright Goodheart-Willcox Co., Inc.

Career and Technical Student Organizations

Career and technical student organizations (CTSOs) are national student organizations with local school chapters that are related to career and technical education (CTE) courses. CTSO programs are tied to various course areas. Internships and other cooperative work experiences may be a part of the CTSO experience. CTSOs can help prepare high school graduates for their next step, whether it is college or a job.

The goal of CTSOs is to help students acquire knowledge and skills in different career and technical areas. Participating in career and technical student organizations (CTSOs) can also help develop leadership skills that are important in the success of future entrepreneurial activities. These organizations offer many opportunities to develop leadership skills and perform as a leader, including various chapter events and CTSO competitions. Assuming a leadership role helps build confidence and provides opportunities to practice and strengthen leadership skills. To demonstrate your leadership skills, consider running for president of a CTSO or volunteering to chair an event.

Research Career Opportunities

There are many resources available to help discover and develop your career interests. The school guidance counselor is always a good first stop for career resource recommendations. Guidance counselors have reference guides, books, and self-assessment tests that provide in-depth information about many types of careers.

The US Department of Labor is a reliable source of career information that is updated regularly. The website of the College Board is an informational resource about colleges, student life, and other important facts about higher education.

Career fairs are another great opportunity to meet recruiters from a variety of different companies. These career fairs are typically held at local convention centers. Students and potential employees can visit companies at their respective booths and ask questions about careers and employment. Professionals who are working these booths can provide a wealth of information about careers and necessary education for positions in the company. Of course, you can always search the Internet for career resources and get the most up-to-date information.

Make a Career Plan

When evaluating career options, consider how a career will fit your lifestyle. Developing a plan will help you reach your goals. A **career plan** is a list of steps on a time line to reach each of your career goals. It is also known as a *postsecondary plan*. Your career goals will probably change during different stages of life. The plan you start now will lay the foundation and guide you through the decision-making process for deciding on your first career.

Copyright Goodheart-Willcox Co., Inc.

Selecting a career is a major decision. Using the decision-making process, as shown in Figure 1-3, can help.

1. Define the challenge. It is always important to define the challenge or problem in clear terms before trying to solve it. This model can work for anything that needs to be solved. If creating a career plan, the challenge or problem is selecting a career path.

2. Gather the facts. What careers are available that match your interests? What careers would provide the income for the lifestyle you want?

3. Analyze the situation. What are your goals? Do you want to select a career path now to help guide your education?

4. Generate ideas. Write down all the career opportunities that fit your interests and meet your goals.

5. Consider the alternatives. Now that you have a list of career options, consider how each would meet your goals.

6. Make a decision. Decide which career path to take. You can always change your decision as your interests change.

7. Implement your decision. Start planning for the necessary education. Enroll in courses that will help you meet your career goals and save money for your education.

Once you understand the decision-making process, you can apply what you have learned to creating a career plan. The first step is to complete a self-assessment. It is important to learn about yourself—your likes and dislikes, your abilities, and what you want from a career.

Figure 1-3. Use this process when making important decisions.

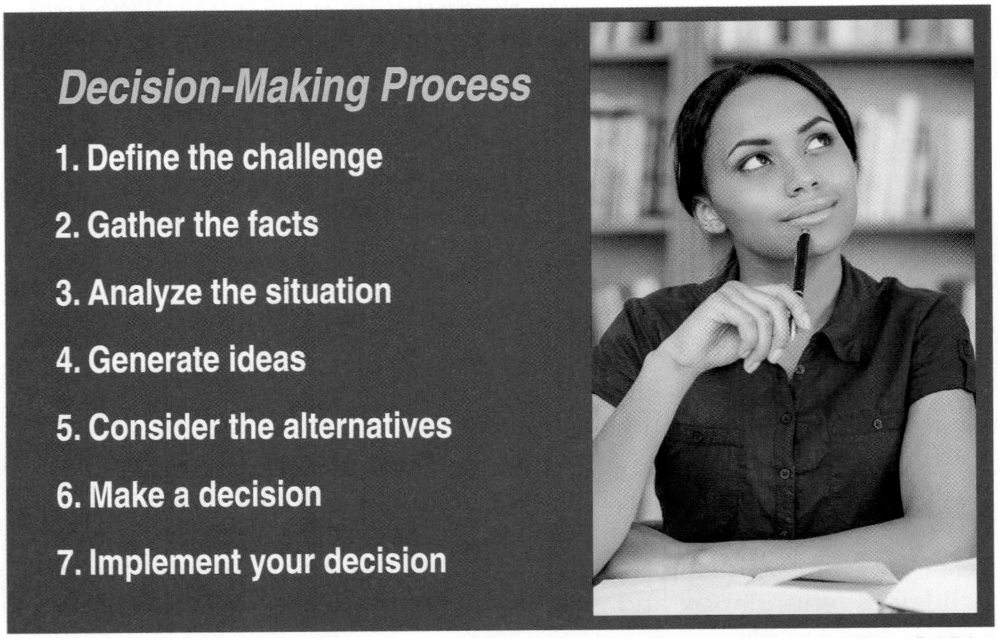

Decision-Making Process

1. Define the challenge

2. Gather the facts

3. Analyze the situation

4. Generate ideas

5. Consider the alternatives

6. Make a decision

7. Implement your decision

g-stockstudio/Shutterstock.com; Goodheart-Willcox Publisher

Copyright Goodheart-Willcox Co., Inc.

Aptitude

Aptitude is the natural ability to do or learn something. Aptitudes are also called *talents*. Your aptitudes will influence your career choices. A fashion designer can look at a piece of material and visualize the finished shirt, dress, or sport jacket. He or she may have a natural aptitude for creating clothing without using patterns. A cabinetmaker may have realized he or she had a natural aptitude for it when taking a woodworking class in school. This may lead to a kitchen remodeling business.

Skills

A **skill** is an ability that a person has learned over time and can do well. What skills do you have? Can you repair a car, analyze a spreadsheet, or create a website? These are all specific skills. You will use learned skills in a career and continue acquiring new skills as you advance in your career.

Attitude

You may have heard the saying, "Do you look at the glass as half full or half empty?" **Attitude** is the feelings a person has about people or things. Attitude will make a huge difference in a future career and in your life. A positive attitude can help you get a job, make new friends, and get involved in activities and organizations. A negative attitude may result in a dismissal from a job, losing friends, or being asked to leave an organization.

FYI

Employees' attitudes can directly affect both the quality of the work they do and the overall productiveness of a business.

A positive attitude is important for an entrepreneur.

arek_malang/Shutterstock.com

Copyright Goodheart-Willcox Co., Inc.

Your attitude also impacts your work ethic. Those with a strong work ethic place high importance on working hard, being productive, creating positive interactions, and efficiently performing assigned tasks as directed. Building and maintaining a strong work ethic will contribute to your professional success.

Values

Values are the beliefs of a person or a culture. Personal values are sometimes called *core values*. What do you value? Values guide a person when making decisions and choices. Therefore, a person who understands and clarifies his or her personal values has a better sense of purpose. For example, a teacher values education and wants to make sure that students learn while in class. You may value a clean, healthy environment and join the school's environmental club.

Goals

A **goal** is something a person wants to achieve in a specified time period. We all have goals. You may have a goal to get a good grade on your next test. Your friend may have a goal to save enough money to take a trip over spring break. Well-defined goals follow the SMART goal process. **SMART goals** are specific, measurable, attainable, realistic, and timely, as illustrated in Figure 1-4.

Specific

How will you know if you have reached your career goal? You must be specific about it. For example, "I want to be rich" is not a very specific goal. Instead, you might say, "I want to have $100,000 in a savings account."

Entrepreneur Ethics

Ethics is a set of rules that define what is wrong and right. Ethics helps people make good decisions in both personal and professional lives. *Business ethics* is a set of rules that help define appropriate behavior in the business setting. It is important for an entrepreneur to set the example of ethical behavior for the business.

Figure 1-4. Set SMART career goals.

SMART Goals

S	Are my short- and long-term goals **specific**? Exactly what do I want to achieve?
M	Are my goals **measurable**? How will I know when a goal is achieved?
A	Are my goals **attainable**? Am I setting goals that can be achieved?
R	Are my goals **realistic**? Have I set goals that are practical?
T	Are my goals **timely**? Are the dates for achieving my goals appropriate?

Goodheart-Willcox Publisher

Copyright Goodheart-Willcox Co., Inc.

Measurable

For a goal to be measurable, the progress should be able to be tracked. Many people say, "My goal is to…" but never figure out how or when they will reach their goal. Measuring goals is like keeping track of mileage on a trip. Following the map helps to know how much farther a destination is at any point in time.

Attainable

Is the goal actually attainable? For example, a student may want to be an electrical engineer. Engineers, however, need very strong math and science skills. The goal becomes more attainable with a plan to obtain the necessary aptitudes and skills.

Realistic

For a goal to be realistic, it must also be practical. High goals can be achieved if the person is highly motivated and has a plan to achieve them. Sometimes several shorter, more realistic goals are necessary to reach a final goal. For example, your final goal may be to own a clothing store. Your first goal might be to become a manager in the store where you currently work. After learning how to manage that store, perhaps the next goal could be to open your own store.

Timely

Setting a time for achieving a goal is the step most often overlooked. A goal needs an end date for progress to stay on track. For example, you may have a goal to find a summer job. If you do not set a firm date for starting the job search, summer might come without you applying for a job. However, if you decide to apply to three businesses every week—with the goal of having a job by May 15—you now have an end date. This helps you remain motivated to reach your goal on time.

Copyright Goodheart-Willcox Co., Inc.

Section 1.1   Review

Check Your Understanding ➦

1. How can you demonstrate leadership skills as a member of a CTSO?
2. List two sources for researching career opportunities.
3. What is the purpose of creating a career plan?
4. List the steps in the decision-making process.
5. What is the difference between an aptitude and a skill?

Build Your Vocabulary ➦

As you progress through this text, develop a personal glossary of key terms. This will help you build your vocabulary and prepare you for a career. Write a definition for each of the following terms and add them to your personal glossary.

career clusters
career pathways
career and
   technical student
   organization
   (CTSO)
career plan

aptitude
skill
attitude
values
goal
SMART goals

Copyright Goodheart-Willcox Co., Inc.

Becoming an Entrepreneur

How do the qualities common to many entrepreneurs help them succeed?

Objectives

After completing this section, you will be able to:

- **Explain** what an entrepreneur does.
- **Describe** the qualities and characteristics common to entrepreneurs.

Key Terms

entrepreneur
intrapreneur
entrepreneurship
start-up companies

leader
interpersonal skills
traits
self-assessment

Critical Thinking

Think about businesses in your community. Identify four that were started by entrepreneurs. List the attitudes and aptitudes these entrepreneurs probably possess. Now make a list of the attitudes and aptitudes that you possess. Circle the ones that you think would be critical to your success as an entrepreneur.

What Is an Entrepreneur?

You may have been talking all of your life about what you want to be when you grow up. Now the time is here, and you are creating career plans. It is an exciting time in your life. There are many traditional careers you could pursue. Are you a person who likes to take a chance? Do you prefer independence to working for someone else? Are you always coming up with ideas for new goods or services? Then being an entrepreneur may be a career choice for you.

An **entrepreneur** is a person who starts a new business. The word entrepreneur comes from the French word *entreprendre,* or to undertake. These individuals were willing to take risks by literally undertaking new ventures. If you have ever mowed lawns, started a babysitting service, or sold lemonade on hot days, then you are an entrepreneur.

An **intrapreneur** is a person who works for a company and uses skills, knowledge, and company resources to create new products, make improvements, or develop ideas that benefit the company. Is it possible to be an employee, an intrapreneur, and an entrepreneur?

Focus on Finance

Business Accounts

When starting a new business, it is wise to keep personal finances separate from business finances. New entrepreneurs sometimes make the mistake of combining personal finance records with business finance records. When it comes time to evaluate business expenses, it can be challenging to separate them from personal expenses. In addition, keeping separate bank accounts makes it easier to complete your taxes.

During your lifetime, you might be all three. Your could be an employee working for a business. You report to work, do your job, and go home at the end of the day. After you have experience working and creating products for your employer, you might decide to become an entrepreneur and operate your own business.

Entrepreneurship is taking on both the risks and responsibilities of starting a new business. It also includes learning about how to run a business and manage other people. Activities involved in entrepreneurship include deciding the type of business to open, identifying customers, developing a marketing plan, managing finances, and hiring qualified employees.

More people than ever are thinking about starting their own business. Newly created businesses are sometimes called **start-up companies**, especially if they are high-growth or technology businesses. According to the Small Business Administration (SBA), there are an estimated 28.2 million small businesses and start-ups in the United States. These businesses have a huge impact on the economy. Small businesses employ more than half of the private-sector employees in the country and hire 37 percent of all high-tech workers. Even more amazing is the fact that small businesses export 98 percent of all exported goods and represent 99.7 percent of all employer firms.

FYI

During tough economic times, people begin to rely on themselves for their income. In 2009, more new businesses were started than in the previous 14 years.

Who Can Be an Entrepreneur?

Have you ever thought about becoming an entrepreneur? You, your classmates, relatives, neighbors, and friends can all be entrepreneurs. In the United States, a person is only limited by his or her creativity, drive, and desire to start a business as illustrated in Figure 1-5. Everyone is free to start a legal business in this country. According to the US Census Bureau, over 677,000 new US businesses are started each year. That is an average of just under 1,855 per day. Will you start a new business today, next month, or next year?

Many people have business ideas, and many have a dream or goal to start a business. Entrepreneurs, however, take steps to make their dreams come true. The road to creating a business can be difficult and full of risk. Successful entrepreneurs will tell you it is worth it.

Copyright Goodheart-Willcox Co., Inc.

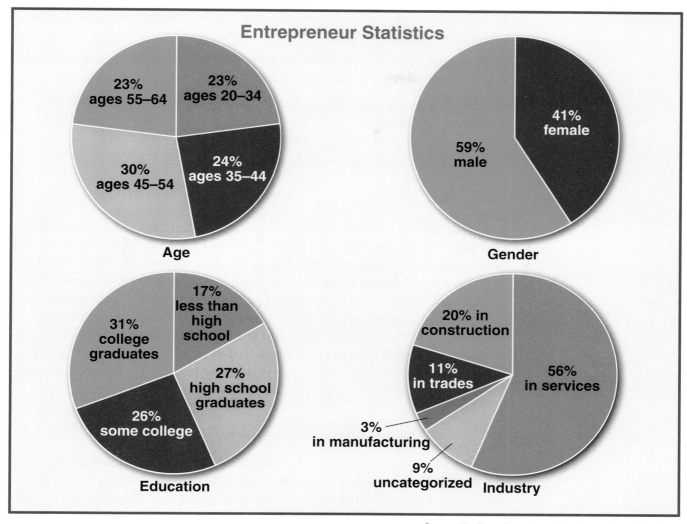

Entrepreneur Statistics

Age
- 23% ages 55–64
- 23% ages 20–34
- 30% ages 45–54
- 24% ages 35–44

Gender
- 59% male
- 41% female

Education
- 17% less than high school
- 31% college graduates
- 27% high school graduates
- 26% some college

Industry
- 20% in construction
- 11% in trades
- 3% in manufacturing
- 9% uncategorized
- 56% in services

Source: Kauffman Foundation; Goodheart-Willcox Publisher

Figure 1-5. Anyone can become an entrepreneur.

Entrepreneurs are creative people who have an idea to start a business. However, starting a business and keeping the business going are two different things. A **leader** is someone who influences others in a positive way and makes things different or makes things better. Most entrepreneurs are natural leaders; that is, they motivate and inspire others to do great things. Think about the entrepreneurs you know or have read about. Do they ever give up? Are they excited about what they do? Is the next challenge for them just around the corner?

To be a successful entrepreneur, you must lead your employees, vendors, and customers. Good leaders make others believe in what they are doing by selling their ideas and sharing their visions. Effective entrepreneurs

- establish and manage relationships by spending time and energy with peers, suppliers, and customers;

- empower others to act and allow capable people to make appropriate decisions;

Copyright Goodheart-Willcox Co., Inc.

- lead by example; a leader does not just tell people what to do, but models the behavior;

- encourage others; leaders show appreciation, provide rewards, and motivate others in positive ways; and

- communicate their ideas; leaders are good speakers as well as good listeners.

Aptitudes and Attitudes of Successful Entrepreneurs

Aptitudes and attitudes are important when creating a career plan. Did you know that these are also important traits for an entrepreneur? Successful entrepreneurs have the aptitude to open a business and complete the work in their chosen fields. For example, a student with an aptitude for styling hair might open a salon. A student with an aptitude for cooking might open a restaurant. A student with an aptitude for writing might edit and proofread papers as their business. Your attitude will also make a huge difference in your success as an entrepreneur. Starting a business is no easy task, but with an aptitude for it and the right attitude, you can be successful.

Values and Goals of Successful Entrepreneurs

Entrepreneurs know their values and can establish realistic goals for their businesses. For example, some entrepreneurs may value the freedom of being their own boss. Others may value the ability to make a difference in another person's life.

Without establishing individual values and goals, it will be difficult to be a successful entrepreneur. You will need to set SMART goals so that you are able to open and operate a profitable business.

Green Entrepreneurs

Green Certification

Many businesses are focused on offering goods and services that respect the environment. If you are an entrepreneur selling retail products, consider having your products certified as sustainable. There are various organizations, such as Green Seal, that use rigid criteria to evaluate products for sustainability. If a product meets all of the requirements, it earns an official green seal of approval. A product with a seal of approval sends the message that your company values preserving the environment.

Copyright Goodheart-Willcox Co., Inc.

Skills of Successful Entrepreneurs

What are your talents? Are you a good storyteller or can you fix things without having to follow instructions? Are you a good artist, a great cook, or a talented debater? These skills can help you build your own company. As an artist, you might decide to open a graphic illustration firm, design your own line of clothing, or sell art in your own gallery. As a cook, you could start a restaurant, a pastry shop, or an online candy company. As a debater, you might decide to open your own law firm or become an independent political consultant.

The list of effective entrepreneurship skills is endless, but there are some skills that every good leader must possess. These skills are discussed in the following sections.

Interpersonal Skills

Have you heard the phrase *people skills?* People skills are **interpersonal skills**—ones you use to communicate with those around you. Effective leaders have good listening and communication skills, as well as the ability to work well with people to get the job done.

Problem-Solving Skills

Leaders have many challenges that require negotiation as well as problem-solving skills. Daily business activities require the ability to take charge and keep things running smoothly.

Business Skills

In order to run a business, it is important for a leader to have basic business skills. Basic record-keeping skills, business-letter writing skills, and math skills are just some of the business skills important for an entrepreneur to master.

Planning Skills

Effective leaders know how to create a plan and engage others to follow a plan and get the job done. Planning skills are critical to entrepreneurs.

Leadership Skills

Entrepreneurs take responsibility for leading the business and their teams. Owners with good leadership skills have the ability to support team members and grow the business.

SBA Tips

The SBA recommends that entrepreneurs consult with a mentor when starting a business. A *mentor* is an experienced, successful business person who is willing to provide advice and guidance—for no personal gain. The SBA can provide names of government-sponsored mentor organizations that provide resources both online and locally. www.sba.gov

Copyright Goodheart-Willcox Co., Inc.

Traits of Successful Entrepreneurs

Some say that entrepreneurs are *born*. Others say that entrepreneurs are *made*. Both theories are correct. Some research shows that entrepreneurship runs in families. Most people who start their own businesses, however, are the first in their family to take the risk of becoming an entrepreneur.

Do you have what it takes to start a business? There are many traits that entrepreneurs have in common. Numerous studies have been done to identify personality traits of successful entrepreneurs. **Traits** are behavioral and emotional characteristics that make each person unique. Have you thought about what your unique traits might be?

Personality traits include the *five Ps of entrepreneurship*—passion, perseverance, persistence, planning, and problem solving, as shown in Figure 1-6. There are many more traits commonly associated with successful entrepreneurs. Look at the list in Figure 1-7. How many of these traits could describe you?

You do not need to be at work 24 hours a day, 7 days a week to be a business owner. However, you do need to enjoy the work and have the ability to sell your products, ideas, or services. It is important that you evaluate your aptitudes, attitudes, traits, and skills as you consider starting your own business.

Social Entrepreneurs

Jim Fruchterman

For some entrepreneurs, the American Dream does not involve simply starting a business, the business must have socially responsible goals. These social entrepreneurs dream of improving living or economic conditions with the business they create. Jim Fruchterman is a social entrepreneur. He always felt that there was an equity gap for those with disabilities and that by applying technology, those with disabilities could be helped. Fruchterman founded Arkenstone in 1989 as a nonprofit social enterprise organization that uses technology to help address social needs. Arkenstone created a reading machine for the blind, which has delivered reading tools in a dozen languages to over 50,000 disabled people living in 60 countries. The Arkenstone product line was sold and the nonprofit organization renamed Benetech. One of the products Benetech has developed is Bookshare, an online library of over 80,000 books and periodicals for people with disabilities such as blindness or low vision.

Copyright Goodheart-Willcox Co., Inc.

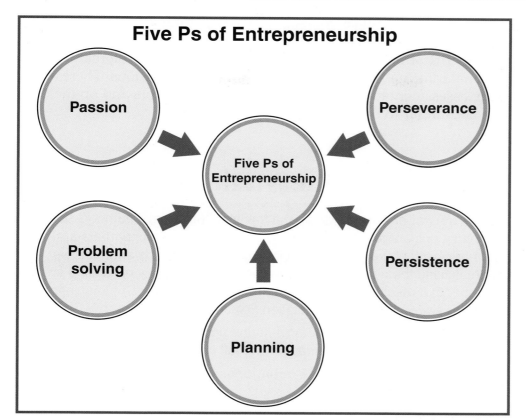

Five Ps of Entrepreneurship

- Passion
- Perseverance
- Five Ps of Entrepreneurship
- Problem solving
- Persistence
- Planning

Goodheart-Willcox Publisher

Figure 1-6. The five Ps are common qualities of successful entrepreneurs.

Entrepreneurial Traits and Skills

• Achievement-oriented	• Good with money	• Perseverance
• Adaptable	• Honest	• Plans ahead
• Competitive	• Independent	• Positive attitude
• Creative	• Intuitive	• Resourceful
• Disciplined	• Learns quickly	• Risk-tolerant
• Empathetic	• Motivated	• Self-confident
• Energetic	• Nonjudgmental	• Self-starter
• Goal-oriented	• Organized	• Visionary

Goodheart-Willcox Publisher

Figure 1-7. Successful entrepreneurs possess common traits and skills.

Copyright Goodheart-Willcox Co., Inc.

One way to evaluate yourself is by completing a **self-assessment**, which is a tool that helps a person understand personal preferences and identify strengths and weaknesses. The goal is to use that personal information when making your career decisions. There are many assessment tools available from your counselors and on the Internet similar to the one shown in Figure 1-8.

 # You Do the Math   Numeric Reasoning

Real numbers are all whole and fractional or decimal numbers on a continuous number line that are not imaginary. *Whole numbers* are numbers with no fractional or decimal portion. *Decimals* are numbers with digits to the right of the decimal point. An *imaginary number* is any number that results in a negative number when squared. An imaginary number always includes the notation *i*, such as *2i*.

To add a positive number, move to the right on the number line. To subtract a positive number, move to the left on the number line.

Find the solution to these equations.

1. $5.87 + 4.956 + 2.011 + 4 =$
2. $34 + 9 - 127 + 783 =$

Section 1.2 Review

Check Your Understanding ↗

1. Clarify the differences between the terms *entrepreneur* and *entrepreneurship*.
2. What role do entrepreneurship and small businesses play in the US economy?
3. Explain the importance of leadership in being a successful entrepreneur.
4. List the five Ps of entrepreneurship. Give an example of each.
5. Identify three skills common to successful entrepreneurs and explain how they contribute to success.

Build Your Vocabulary ↗

As you progress through this text, develop a personal glossary of key terms. This will help you build your vocabulary and prepare you for a career. Write a definition for each of the following terms and add them to your personal glossary.

entrepreneur   leader
intrapreneur   interpersonal skills
entrepreneurship   traits
start-up companies   self-assessment

Copyright Goodheart-Willcox Co., Inc.

Are You Ready to Be an Entrepreneur?				
Does this sound like you?	**No, definitely not me.**	**Occasionally.**	**This describes me most of the time.**	**This describes me all of the time.**
	1 point	**2 points**	**3 points**	**4 points**
1. Others consider me to be a leader.			3	
2. I want control of whatever job, project, or work I am doing.				4
3. Others turn to me for help when making decisions.			3	
4. I am willing to commit long hours and work seven days a week to make my business a success.		2		
5. I am a team player.			3	
6. I enjoy tackling a challenge with a group of people.		2		
7. When I hear the word *impossible,* I begin to think of how it can be done.				4
8. I want to change things for the better. I am not satisfied with the way things are.				4
9. I enjoy the freedom, power, and ability to make money based on my decisions and talents.				4
10. I would like being my own boss.				4
11. I am persistent and will rarely take *no* for an answer.			3	
12. I have always been good at selling things, whether it was for a student fund-raiser or selling an idea to a teacher.			3	
13. I take responsibility for my actions. When I am wrong, I am willing to admit it. When I am right, I want to be recognized.			3	
14. My teachers and friends know they can count on me to get work done.				4
15. I am a risk taker.		2		
16. I am willing to invest my own money to start a business.			3	
17. I am confident in my ability to make good decisions.			3	
TOTAL = 54		6	24	24
A score of 60–85: High likelihood of being an entrepreneur. A score of 35–60: Needs to develop more entrepreneurial skills. A score of 0–35: Not yet ready to be an entrepreneur.				

Goodheart-Willcox Publisher

Figure 1-8. Entrepreneur Self-Assessment Checklist

Copyright Goodheart-Willcox Co., Inc.

Chapter Summary

Section 1.1 Your Career

- There are many resources available to help you explore different career paths and develop foundation skills, including the career clusters and the opportunities provided by CTSOs.
- Developing a career plan early lays the foundation of your career goals and can guide career decisions in different stages of your life.

Section 1.2 Becoming an Entrepreneur

- An entrepreneur is someone who takes on the risks and responsibilities of starting a new business.
- Anyone can become an entrepreneur as long as he or she has the drive and desire to start up a new company. Certain values, skills, and traits are needed to be successful.

Online Activities

Complete the following activities to help you learn, practice, and expand your knowledge and skills.

Posttest. Now that you have finished the chapter, see what you learned by taking the chapter posttest.

Key Terms. Practice vocabulary for this chapter using the e-flash cards, matching activity, and vocabulary game until you are able to recognize their meanings.

Review Your Knowledge

1. Review the 16 career clusters. List five careers that interest you. Indicate the related career cluster for each.
2. What is the goal of career and technical student organizations?
3. Explain what it means to define the challenge in the career decision-making process.
4. What must students evaluate about themselves in the process of creating a career plan?
5. How do SMART goals apply to creating a career plan?
6. Describe the impact of start-up companies on the economy.
7. Who can be an entrepreneur?
8. List five leadership activities of effective entrepreneurs.
9. Identify some skills that every good leader must possess.
10. Identify ten common traits of successful entrepreneurs.

Copyright Goodheart-Willcox Co., Inc.

Apply Your Knowledge

1. Identify one of the career clusters that most interests you. List the entry-level jobs you might have, followed by the more advanced jobs within that career. Why are you interested in this career choice?

2. Write down your SMART goals for the next six months. These could be about your education or your career. What did you learn from this?

3. List some of the aptitudes you have. Next to each aptitude, list how each one can help you pursue the career you have chosen.

4. Describe how the five Ps of entrepreneurship match your personality.

5. In starting an entrepreneurial venture, what values would be important to you? What values would you want your employees to have?

6. Outline your current career plan. Where do you see yourself in five years?

7. Make a list of the skills you possess that would make you an effective entrepreneur.

8. Make a list of five people whom you consider entrepreneurs and strong leaders. These leaders do not need to be famous or public figures. Next to each name, list at least three characteristics that you believe make the person a strong leader. How do each of these people demonstrate a positive, productive work ethic?

9. Create a two-column chart. In column one, write down ten traits that you think make a strong leader. Identify a businessperson in your community whom you consider to be a strong leader, and interview that person. Ask that person to list the ten traits that she or he thinks makes a strong leader. Write those traits in column two of your chart. Compare your list with that of the person you interviewed. What did you learn from the interview?

10. Review the list of common personality traits of successful entrepreneurs in Figure 1-7. Create a document that lists the personality traits you feel you already have and those that you need to develop before becoming an entrepreneur. How do you plan to develop them?

Teamwork

This chapter discusses personality traits that help define an entrepreneur. Working with a teammate, make a list of personality traits that you observe in your teammate. Have your teammate make a list of personality traits you possess. Discuss your opinions with each other. What did you learn from this experience?

Copyright Goodheart-Willcox Co., Inc.

Internet Research

SBA Resources. Plan to become familiar with business resources available for entrepreneurs on the Internet. A good source of information is the US Small Business Administration (SBA) website, which is a government resource to help small businesses succeed. Visit the SBA website and research data trends and statistics that could help you as you establish a business.

College and Career Readiness

Communication Skills

Reading. Research an entrepreneur that you know personally or one who is well known. List the person's name, business, and when the business was organized. Cite specific evidence that supports the person's entrepreneurial spirit.

Writing. Conduct a short research project to answer questions about the history of entrepreneurship. Use multiple authoritative print and digital sources. Where did the idea of entrepreneurship originate? Write several paragraphs about your findings to demonstrate your understanding of entrepreneurship.

CTSOs

Student Organizations. Career and Technical Student Organizations (CTSOs) are a valuable asset to any educational program. These organizations support student learning and application of skills learned to be applied in real-world situations. Also, participation in career and technology education student organizations can promote lifelong responsibility for community service and professional development.

There are a variety of organizations from which to select, depending on the goals of your educational programs.

To prepare for any competitive event:

1. Contact the organization before the next competition. This gives you time to review and decide which competitive events are correct for you or your team.

2. Read all the guidelines closely. These rules and regulations must be strictly adhered to or disqualification can occur.

3. Competitive events may be written, oral, or a combination of both.

4. Communication plays a role in all the competitive events, so read which communication skills are covered for the event you select. Research and preparation are important keys to successful competition.

5. Go to the website of your organization for specific information for the events. Visit the site often as information changes quickly.

6. Select one or two events that are of interest to you. Print the information for the events and discuss your interest with your instructor.

Copyright Goodheart-Willcox Co., Inc.

Building Your Business Plan—Putting the Puzzle Together

Entrepreneurial Careers

You have sixty seconds. Sixty seconds to tell your story, convince an investor your business is worth funding, and explain your background and skills as an entrepreneur. How will you use those sixty seconds? As an entrepreneur, your audience may be investing money in or lending money to your business. You must be able to convince them of your ability to make that business successful. They want to be sure that you have the skills or are willing to learn the skills necessary to become a successful entrepreneur.

Goals

- Set personal and business goals.
- Assess your aptitude and attitude as a potential entrepreneur.
- Create business plan notes.

Directions

Access the *Entrepreneurship* companion website at www.g-wlearning.com ➡. Download each data file for the following activities. A complete sample business plan is available on the companion website to use as a reference. The name of the file is BusPlan_Sample.RetroAttire.docx.

Preparation

Activity 1-1. SMART Goals. Practice setting SMART personal and professional goals.

Activity 1-2. Self-Assessment. Complete a self-analysis of your skills, abilities, experiences, work ethic, strengths, and weaknesses.

Activity 1-3. Business Plan Notes. Create notes about how you plan to gain the additional skills you will need to become an entrepreneur.

Business Plan—Management Team

You are in the beginning stages of creating a business plan. In chapter 2, you will learn about a business plan and how to write one for your new business. In this first activity, you will preview the business plan template and become acquainted with each section.

1. Open the data file called Business Plan Template.docx.

2. Preview each section of the document. To familiarize yourself with the business plan, read the instructions and questions that will guide you to complete each section. As you progress through the chapters, you will be directed to complete each section. However, the sections that you complete in each activity may not be in the order listed in the document.

3. Locate the Operations section of the business plan and start to write the second subsection called Management Team. If you are the sole owner/manager of the business, then *you* are the management team. The Operations section is an extensive one that will be completed as you progress through this text. Use the suggestions and questions listed in the template to help you generate ideas. Delete the instructions and questions when you are finished writing the section. Proofread your document and correct any errors in keyboarding, spelling, and grammar.

4. Save your document as FirstnameLastname_BusPlan.docx (i.e., JohnSmith_BusPlan.docx). Ask your instructor where to save your documents.

CHAPTER

2 Business Plan

Unable to find a recipe for the perfect chocolate chip cookie, Judith Moore decided to create her own. Her cookies soon had a loyal following, and her son-in-law suggested she start her own business. Judith contacted the local SCORE chapter for assistance with a business plan. SCORE is a nonprofit association that helps small businesses get started. Her SCORE counselor helped her to focus the vision she had for the business. He recommended she create a spreadsheet to produce three years of cash-flow projections. Judith credits her counselor's guidance as crucial to the development of her business plan. The business, Charleston Cookie Company, opened in 2003. In 2011, her company was named a Dream Big Small Business of the Year by the US Chamber of Commerce.

"A business has to be involving, it has to be fun, and it has to exercise your creative instincts."

—Sir Richard Branson, founder of Virgin Records, Virgin Airways, Virgin Galactic, and many other companies

College and Career Readiness

Reading Prep. Before reading, observe the objectives for each section in this chapter. Keep these in mind as you read, and focus on the structure of the author's writing—was the information presented in a way that was clear and engaging?

Sections

2.1 Business Ideas

2.2 Business Plan Puzzle

Picture Yourself Here
Krystal Harrell

Create Exposure, located in Charlotte, North Carolina, is a marketing and communication company that provides marketing research, public relations, and design services for a variety of clients including the Susan G. Komen for the Cure® foundation. Its founder and managing partner is Krystal Harrell. This entrepreneur got her start at the age of 13 with a $20 loan from her mother. Krystal's Lucky You Designs began by selling pajamas and moved on to other apparel and accessories. Krystal sold Lucky You Designs in 2009 and used the profits to start Create Exposure, which specializes in designing marketing campaigns that target younger consumers.

Krystal attended Columbia College where she studied communications and The Art Institute of Charlotte where she studied fashion marketing and management. She also served in the US Army Reserve as a broadcast journalist. What Krystal shares with most successful entrepreneurs is a strong entrepreneurial spirit and a willingness to try something new.

Photo © Krystal Harrell

Check Your Entrepreneurship IQ

Before you begin the chapter, see what you already know about entrepreneurship by taking the chapter pretest. The pretest is available at www.g-wlearning.com

SECTION 2.1 Business Ideas

What are some factors that affect the success of a new business?

Objectives

After completing this section, you will be able to:

- **Explain** the basics of business.
- **Describe** the discovery process for generating new business ideas.
- **Discuss** the economics of creating products and services.
- **Explain** the ways an entrepreneur can start a business.
- **Identify** the risks and rewards of becoming an entrepreneur.
- **List** the reasons many businesses fail.

Key Terms

business	want	wholesaler
revenue	good	retailer
expenses	service	opportunity cost
small business	product	market structure
functions of business	economics	cash flow
production	supply and demand	franchise
finance	economic resources	
need	manufacturer	

Critical Thinking

Think about the activities you enjoy most. You are probably good at them as well. Take time to observe needs in the community that also tie into your favorite activities. This could lead to a potential entrepreneurial idea. List four activities and how they could become ideas for businesses.

Business Basics

The term **business** includes all the activities involved in developing and exchanging products. The primary goal of business is to generate revenue. **Revenue** is the earnings that a business receives for the goods and services it sells. Revenue is also called *income*. In order to generate enough revenue to maintain operations, a business must control expenses. **Expenses** are the costs involved in operating a business. Rent and employee wages are examples of expenses. *Profit* is the difference between the income earned and expenses incurred by a business during a specific period of time.

Successful businesses have three core goals. Each relate to generating adequate revenue:

- *Pay debts.* Banks, vendors, and any individuals who have extended loans to the business must be paid. These debts must be paid on time.

- *Provide returns for investors.* Those who have made a financial investment in the business expect to receive a return on that investment.

- *Finance business growth.* In order for a business to continue, money must be available to finance future growth.

The first endeavor of most entrepreneurs is a small business. The SBA defines a **small business** as "one that is independently owned and operated, organized for profit, and not dominant in its field." However, certain principles apply to businesses of any type. For example, all businesses perform basic functions in order to remain in operation. The four **functions of business** are production, finance, marketing, and management. All the functions of business, shown in Figure 2-1, must work together if a business is to be successful.

Production

Production is all activities required to make a product. It applies to goods, services, and ideas. Production of goods may include farming, mining, construction, or manufacturing activities. Production also includes the work performed at a television station in preparing a program for broadcast. For services, production is often the service itself. For example, the activities of cutting and styling hair produce the service.

Figure 2-1. Each of the four functions of business work together to create business success.

Goodheart-Willcox Publisher

Copyright Goodheart-Willcox Co., Inc.

Finance

Businesses handle a large amount of money. As a function of business, **finance** includes all the business activities that involve money. Businesses handle the money that customers pay them. Businesses pay for raw materials and business services. Businesses also pay their employees and taxes. Sometimes businesses borrow money from banks.

An important task of the finance function is planning. The people who work in finance are often responsible for developing budgets. A *budget* is a spending plan for a fixed period of time. Budgets help a business ensure there is enough money to cover expenses. Budgets also help guide the business in handling its money wisely and making a profit. If a business decides to take out a loan, the financing function must plan for the repayment of the loan.

Accounting is one part of finance. Accounting handles paying bills, receiving payments, and keeping track of all money that enters or leaves the business.

Marketing

Marketing is the part of the business that focuses on the customer. Marketers are responsible for helping the entire business focus on the needs and wants of customers. The marketing function includes learning about customers so that the business can develop products that customers want and are able and willing to buy. Marketing then promotes and sells the products to customers. Marketing also follows up to find out how satisfied customers are with their products.

Management

Management is the process of controlling and making decisions about a business. It includes all the activities required to plan, coordinate, and monitor a business. The managers look at the big picture and lead workers to make changes to make the business better. A manager plans, implements plans, and controls. In business, control means to monitor and evaluate results. Managers also hire, train, and supervise employees.

Discovery Process

You know you want to start your own business some day. Your personality and career goals are a perfect match for becoming an entrepreneur. But how do you come up with an idea that will work? Entrepreneurs are always thinking. They are thinking about new and innovative ways to use products and the creation of new products. Finding business opportunities requires that you actively engage with other people and organizations.

The discovery process begins. In its simplest form, the entrepreneurial *discovery process* is about finding a need for a good or service. However, it is also much more than that. History has shown

Copyright Goodheart-Willcox Co., Inc.

repeatedly that many people have found a need for a product that did not yet exist. For whatever reasons, they chose not to pursue the idea. The entrepreneurial discovery process actually consists of two parts:

- identifying the marketplace needs and recognizing a need or want that is not being met

- the willingness to take the risk to exploit the opportunity

Recognition of Marketplace Needs and Wants

A **need** is something necessary for survival, such as food, clothing, and shelter. A need can also be defined as something necessary to function in society, such as schoolbooks, transportation, and electricity. A **want** is something that a person desires, but could function without, such as a new cell phone or a vacation.

In the marketplace, needs and wants are fulfilled by goods and services. **Goods** are physical, or *tangible*, items that can be touched and used. Examples include food, clothing, and toothpaste. **Services** are *intangible* actions or tasks that are performed, usually for a fee. These may include cleaning services, preparing tax returns, and delivery services. A **product** is anything that can be bought or sold, which includes both goods and services. An important part of the discovery process is to identify and list the marketplace needs. This will help define the product and help your business succeed.

Abraham Maslow, a famous psychologist, developed a theory of human needs. He believed that each person has the same basic physical needs. Maslow also believed that people must first meet their physical needs before they fulfill any other needs and wants, as shown in Figure 2-2. Many of the most successful products meet both needs and wants at the same time.

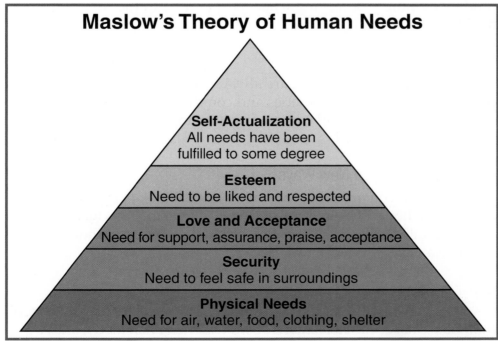

Maslow's Theory of Human Needs

Self-Actualization
All needs have been
fulfilled to some degree

Esteem
Need to be liked and respected

Love and Acceptance
Need for support, assurance, praise, acceptance

Security
Need to feel safe in surroundings

Physical Needs
Need for air, water, food, clothing, shelter

Goodheart-Willcox Publisher

Figure 2-2. Abraham Maslow believed physical needs must be met before all other needs and wants.

Copyright Goodheart-Willcox Co., Inc.

Microsoft cofounder Bill Gates grew up in Seattle, Washington. He began programming computers at age 13 and sold his first program to a large Seattle business several years later while still in high school.

Recognition of Opportunity

If you think about it carefully, you probably have had some great ideas for a business, but did not act on them. *Business opportunities* are those ideas that have potential to become successful commercial ventures. Many people have good ideas, but most do not turn into businesses. Why not? Perhaps the ideas did not appeal to a large enough market or they were not cost-effective at the time. Or, maybe the people simply did not want to put the necessary time, effort, and money into starting a business.

For those entrepreneurs who do act on their ideas, success can be fleeting, or long lasting, or even have a global impact. For example, Thomas Edison, Bill Gates, and Mark Zuckerberg turned their ideas to businesses that changed the world. You do not have to actually invent a new good or service to be an entrepreneur, though. In fact, you might be more successful by drawing on several already-existing products or ideas.

Generate Ideas

There are as many business ideas as there are people to think of them. Your challenge is finding the best ideas. Start close to home: what is going on in the local community? There may be a demand for goods or services that is not being met.

Environmental Observation

Environmentally conscious people are always looking for new ways to protect the environment. You may come up with ideas for a product by simply observing what is happening in the community, nationally, or globally.

Social Observation

Socially conscious people are always looking for ways to solve problems faced daily by societies and communities. Make a list of the social challenges the local community is facing and see if any ideas for products come to mind.

Look at Old Things in New Ways

Next time you are shopping, take a critical look at the products offered. See how companies take one popular staple product and expand it into a dozen varieties. This may spark an idea about how to improve an existing product.

Capitalize on Your Hobbies

Many hobbies turn into successful businesses. Do you like to work on computers? bake? provide lawn care for your neighbors? free run? Any one of these hobbies could turn into a business under the right conditions.

Copyright Goodheart-Willcox Co., Inc.

Identify One Problem Each Day

Read the newspaper; search the Internet; watch TV news programs; listen to your teachers, your parents, and your friends discuss problems and issues. Identify at least one problem each day and think creatively about different ways that problem could be solved.

Brainstorm

Ideas are the result of creative thinking. *Brainstorming* is a group discussion where individuals generate as many ideas as possible within a set amount of time. It is one of the most creative ways to generate ideas. A key part of brainstorming is to consider all suggestions as a possible solution. Brainstorming is valuable for a variety of activities, such as the following:

- expanding the creative thinking of an individual or group
- generating new ideas
- identifying issues and opportunities
- identifying possible causes of a problem
- identifying potential solutions to a problem
- identifying types of data needed and how to get the data
- seeing other points of view

Brainstorming is a creative way to come up with business ideas. Get a group of your friends or family together to help you brainstorm. The brainstorming process is illustrated in Figure 2-3.

Is My Idea Feasible?

One of the biggest challenges an entrepreneur will face is determining the feasibility of a business idea. *Feasible* means that something can be done successfully. Successful entrepreneurs and businesses conduct some form of feasibility analysis, often called a

Brainstorming Process
Step 1. Clearly define the topic. Be precise in defining the question.
Step 2. Generate as many ideas as possible within a 20–30 minute time limit. Have someone write every idea on a white board or paper.
Step 3. Set the ground rules that no one can comment on, change, or criticize an idea during the brainstorming session. No idea is bad.
Step 4. Make sure every person is presenting as many ideas as possible. Call on those not contributing.
Step 5. Do not stop until all ideas are presented. Even if you go over your time limit, let everyone share their ideas.
Step 6. Evaluate the results when the session is over. Choose the best ones.

Figure 2-3. Follow these steps for successful brainstorming sessions.

Goodheart-Willcox Publisher

Copyright Goodheart-Willcox Co., Inc.

Entrepreneur Ethics

Most companies establish a set of ethics that employees must follow. The code of ethics outlines acceptable behavior when interacting with coworkers, suppliers, and customers. As an entrepreneur and potential employer, creating a code of ethics can help employees make correct decisions for the business. Some businesses even post their code of ethics on their websites.

feasibility study, before starting a new business. The analysis helps them determine if their new product idea is worth pursuing. This requires some research to determine if customers will buy the good or service and if investors would be likely to fund the business. Feasibility studies must be based on reality, not theory.

First, the business idea must be well defined. Without product details, feasibility is hard to determine. Spend time learning who is most likely to want or need your product. Find a way to survey a large enough number of potential customers about your proposed business. For example, five is probably not enough, but 20 may be good. Ask them what they like and do not like about the product, if they would buy it, how often, and what they would pay. These responses will give you a good idea if you are headed in the right direction or if you need to make changes. All first-hand information is valuable and will be useful when actually creating your business plan to solicit funding.

There is a wealth of research on the Internet. Look at chambers of commerce, industry organizations, and government resources, such as the Small Business Administration (SBA). *Industry* refers to a group of businesses that provide a particular good or service. Local and large-market newspapers can also be useful sources of information. Find statistics about the industry, good business locations, and who the customers are. Will the time, effort, and money that would go into starting a venture be worthwhile?

Only a small percentage of business ideas and new products achieve long-term success. Business failure rates are high for new businesses. Some of those failures could have been prevented if the owners had studied the feasibility of their businesses *before* starting them.

Economics of Creating Product

Economics is a science that deals with examining how goods and services are produced, sold, and used. Economics is how people, governments, and companies make choices about using limited resources to satisfy unlimited wants. Consumers can purchase goods and services from whomever they choose.

Entrepreneurs have two challenges. They must create a desirable good or service and then determine the reasons for customers to buy it from them. **Supply and demand** is the economic principle relating the quantity of products available to meet consumer demand. When demand is higher than the available resources, it is called *scarcity*.

Economies

Depending on where a business operates, the economics of creating goods and services may differ. A *market economy* is a system that allows privately owned businesses to operate and make a profit

Copyright Goodheart-Willcox Co., Inc.

with limited government regulation. It is also referred to as a free enterprise system. Businesses must follow the laws of the country, but other than that, government is not overly involved.

In a *command economy,* the government determines what goods are produced, how much is produced, and the prices. Most industries are owned by the government, and shortages of products may occur.

A *mixed economy* is one in which both the government and the private sector make decisions about providing goods and services. Most developed countries have some form of a mixed economy, with the market economy form as the dominant factor.

A *traditional economy* is one in which citizens have just enough to survive. There is little to no manufacturing. Countries with traditional economies often have primarily rural populations.

Economic Resources

Every country has limited **economic resources** with which to create goods and provide services. Economic resources are also called *factors of production,* which are defined as follows:

- *natural resources,* or land, water, minerals, forests, sunlight, etc.; these are not made by man

- *human resources,* or the work performed by people

- *capital resources,* or money, supplies, buildings, vehicles, etc.; these are man-made

A **manufacturer** turns raw materials from natural resources or product components into new products for sale. Manufactured products fall into two categories: industrial and consumer. *Industrial goods* are products or components made for manufacturing other products, such as steel beams, computer hardware, or fabrics. *Consumer goods* are the end products bought by the public for personal use, such as clothing, appliances, or sporting equipment. The demand for industrial goods is usually based on the demand for the consumer goods they help produce.

Green Entrepreneurs

Paper Products

Businesses use a lot of paper, so look for paper products that are safe for the environment. Paper manufacturers are always looking for new ideas to produce paper products from renewable sources. Currently, some paper is made from by-products of sugar cane instead of wood. Sugar cane biodegrades faster than wood, is less expensive, and is cleaner to use in the production process. Many office supply companies are now carrying sugar cane paper with more new products to come. Other companies use recycled paper to create new paper products.

Copyright Goodheart-Willcox Co., Inc.

A **wholesaler** purchases large amounts of goods directly from manufacturers. It stores the products and then resells them in smaller amounts to various retailers. Wholesalers do not sell directly to the consumers. A **retailer** buys products either from wholesalers or directly from manufacturers and resells them to consumers. A *service business* earns income by providing its services and expertise to businesses or consumers.

As an entrepreneur, your resources will be limited. You cannot provide every product to meet every want or need. So, which ones should your business offer? An **opportunity cost** is the cost of passing up the next best choice when making a decision. For example, you just purchased some wood at a lumber store. You have enough wood to make a chair or a table, but you decide to make the table. The opportunity cost is the chair you did not make. In entrepreneurship, opportunity costs are often defined in terms of time and money lost or risk versus reward.

It is important to recognize your opportunity costs and make calculated decisions about which products will be most profitable. Identifying and analyzing the many opportunity costs and then making the best decisions are critical processes. In fact, they are necessary for the long-term success of any business.

Market Structure

Market structure is how a market is organized and is based on the number of businesses competing for sales in an industry. The four basic market structures are oligopoly, monopoly, perfect competition, and monopolistic competition. The main difference among them is the number operating on the supply, or selling, side of a market.

An *oligopoly* is a market structure with a small number of large companies selling the same or similar products. A *monopoly* is a market structure with one business that has complete control of a market's entire supply of goods or services.

Perfect competition is a market structure characterized by a large number of small businesses selling identical products for the same prices. It is the ideal market structure, but is unrealistic.

Monopolistic competition is a market structure in which a large number of small businesses sell similar, but not identical, products at different prices. It is also known as *imperfect competition*. This is the actual market structure under which many small businesses operate.

Take Your Idea to the Next Level

Once you have decided on a business and determined its feasibility, the next step is to think about the type of business start-up. Business decisions will be influenced by your lifestyle, access to factors of production, and the type of goods or services you will offer.

Copyright Goodheart-Willcox Co., Inc.

Focus on Finance

Cash Flow

Cash flow is important to the success of any business. As a business owner, it is important to monitor how much money is coming in and going out of the business. It is a common error for new businesses to start off with too little cash. It may take some time for sales to get to the level you want. Make sure to plan for enough money to cover at least the first six months of expenses. If there is not enough available cash, you may have to borrow money to pay your debts.

Starting any type of business is a courageous move that involves many risks. Some businesses fail no matter how much effort is put into them. Most likely, you will invest some of your own money. You may also borrow money that must be repaid whether the business succeeds or not. Many business owners work long hours and six or seven days a week, especially in their first few years of operation. However, the risks and hard work can pay off with much higher profits and satisfaction than you may find working for someone else. There are several ways to start a new business. You can open a new business, buy an existing business, or buy a franchise.

Open a New Business

A new business could be a storefront for providing existing products or services to consumers. Examples of this type of business include a day spa, boutique, car repair garage, or restaurant. Another alternative is to create and offer a new good or service that does not exist yet. Research the ideas, design the product, get a patent to protect the ownership, manufacture, and sell it.

Buy an Existing Business

Owners sell their individual businesses for a variety of reasons. Research thoroughly why an owner is selling before buying a business. The owner may simply want to retire, move, or begin a different business or job. If the owner is selling because the business is struggling, has legal problems, or is near bankruptcy, these are red flags that should be investigated.

A wiser decision may be to buy an existing business that is already successful. These businesses usually come with a solid client base, employees, a good location, necessary equipment, and operations in place. The new owner would enjoy immediate cash flow and may have easier access to loans. **Cash flow** is the money flowing into and out of a business. Businesses for sale can be found in the local classifieds, on the Internet, or by networking with other business owners.

Copyright Goodheart-Willcox Co., Inc.

Buy a Franchise

A **franchise** is the right to sell a company's goods or services in a particular area. The *franchisor* is the parent company that owns the chain and the brand. Examples of well-known franchisors include Subway, H&R Block, and Snap-on Tools corporations. The many individual business owners are the *franchisees,* or the people who bought the rights to use that brand.

The franchisor provides a business model, training and other help, the goods or services, some marketing support, and brand recognition. It is up to the franchisee, however, to provide the entrepreneurial spirit and uphold the brand's success to make a profit.

Rewards and Risks of Being an Entrepreneur

Why would a person want to be an entrepreneur? Many people would respond, "Because you can make a lot of money!" Money is not the only reason to start a business, though. The reasons for starting a business are countless. Controlling your destiny is an exciting reason to be an entrepreneur. Other rewards include the following.

- being your own boss; determine your own work schedule, set your own prices, and see the hard work pay off

- taking advantage of your earning potential; with high unemployment and global issues, an entrepreneur can continue working and not depend on someone else for an income

- enjoying your career; as an entrepreneur, you can do something you truly like, are good at, and believe in; you can apply your creativity with no limits and start a business you are passionate about

Every new venture comes with risks. In general, the higher the risk, the greater potential for reward—but also the greater potential for loss. Being aware of the risks makes you better prepared for entrepreneurship. For example, a profit may not be realized for many months, so you will not collect a regular paycheck. It is important to be financially prepared as an uncertain income may be a hardship for an owner. Other risks include the following.

- being responsible; you make all the decisions, reap all the rewards, and take responsibilities for the good and bad decisions you might make

- working long hours; as an owner of a new business, you will probably work long days that can put stress on personal health and emotions as well as affect the family

- risking personal finances; money is needed for start-up costs and expenses which may come from your personal funds; new businesses often do not make a profit for several months to several years

Copyright Goodheart-Willcox Co., Inc.

There are other risks that are associated with creating a new business. Creating a thorough business plan will identify the risks so you can overcome them.

Businesses That Fail

According to Benjamin Franklin, the only things certain in life are death and taxes. Starting a business does not guarantee success. In fact, starting a new business can be risky. According to the SBA, 69 percent of all new business will survive the first two years. On average, a business has a 50 percent chance of surviving the first five years of operation. Only 34 percent survive 10 years or more.

Only you can decide if you have the personality, drive, and risk tolerance to be an entrepreneur. The rewards can be big and the work fulfilling. At the same time, the risks of starting a new business are also great, and the consequences of failure affect more people than just the owner.

There are many reasons any given business fails. The following sections discuss some of the most common ones:

Failure to Complete a Feasibility Analysis

Do *not* rely on friends and family members to decide if your business idea is a good one. Get some professional help and advice when researching an idea to make sure it is feasible. Contact the SBA, the local chamber of commerce, do some industry research, or find a mentor who owns a similar business.

Working nontraditional hours can be enjoyable for some entrepreneurs.

Ollyy/Shutterstock.com

Copyright Goodheart-Willcox Co., Inc.

Lack of Planning

Not having a business plan can ruin the chances for success. Think about taking a cross-country trip. Would you leave home without a map or GPS? Starting a new business without a business plan would be like attempting to travel across the country without a map. You will end up somewhere, but probably not where you were headed. Determine your business goals and the strategies for reaching them before you ever open the doors.

Insufficient Start-Up Capital

Determining realistic start-up costs and securing proper funding are vital to survival. Unexpected expenses can catch a new business short of cash. A business owner may have higher shipping charges, need more employees, or have higher materials costs than expected. New business owners, in the excitement of starting a business, often overspend on equipment or a building. Equipment and buildings are not easy to sell if money gets tight. Get help from a knowledgeable mentor in the industry and an accountant to avoid those pitfalls.

Location, Location, Location

Many people locate a new business near their homes because it is convenient. Depending on the type of business and customers, however, being close to home may not be the best location. For example, starting a business that sells ice skates and downhill skis in Florida may not make good business sense. The location of your business can make or break it.

Underestimating the Competition

It is important to know and understand the competition in order to create a product or service that will take business away from them. What makes the competition strong? What makes your business unique and able to compete with them?

Poor Management Decisions

A business owner manages people, money, inventory, and marketing efforts. His or her decisions will directly affect the business either positively or negatively. Stick to the budget to avoid overspending. Do not make business decisions in haste. Learn from previous mistakes. If a decision needs to be made about something you have little experience with, get advice from a professional or a mentor.

Copyright Goodheart-Willcox Co., Inc.

Ineffective Marketing Strategies

Good marketing strategies lead to sales, which will help to keep the business going. Obviously, the lack of sales will make a business more likely to fail. Set a realistic marketing budget and make sure the promotions are reaching the people most likely to buy the products. In today's digital world, the lack of a website, social networking sites, and consistent marketing efforts on the Internet can affect the bottom line. Potential customers are constantly swamped with sales messages. Make sure your message is meaningful and stands out.

Unexpected Growth

Managing rapid growth sounds like a good problem to have. However, if growth happens too quickly and the business cannot fulfill orders or manage quality, customers will disappear. Overexpanding before an economic downturn may also cause a business to fail. It is important to understand both the market and the economy before making any big, hard-to-reverse decisions.

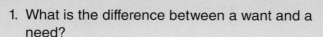

Section 2.1 Review

Check Your Understanding

1. What is the difference between a want and a need?
2. List and describe the factors of production.
3. What are the different types of businesses that you can consider?
4. Give an example of opportunity cost.
5. It is a known fact that many businesses fail. What are five of the reasons that they fail?

Build Your Vocabulary

As you progress through this text, develop a personal glossary of key terms. This will help you build your vocabulary and prepare you for a career. Write a definition for each of the following terms and add them to your personal glossary.

business
revenue
expenses
small business
functions of
    business
production
finance
need
want
good
service
product

economics
supply and
    demand
economic
    resources
manufacturer
wholesaler
retailer
opportunity cost
market structure
cash flow
franchise

SECTION 2.2 Business Plan Puzzle

What are the benefits of writing a thorough business plan?

Objectives

After completing this section, you will be able to:

- **Describe** the process of building the business plan.
- **Outline** the necessary sections of the business plan and describe the information contained in them.

Key Terms

business plan
vision statement
mission statement
nature of business
product mix

business operations
business risk
risk management
start-up capital
sources of funds

pro forma financial
statements
contingency plan

Critical Thinking

Some believe the only reason to write a business plan is to obtain a business loan or investor funding. There are entrepreneurs who already have the money to start a business, however, and they still write business plans. Why do you think they choose to write and use one?

Build the Plan

Think about a puzzle. If you attempt to solve a puzzle without organizing the pieces, you may waste valuable time and become frustrated. Ultimately, without an organized strategy, the puzzle will take you much longer to solve. To be successful at solving puzzles, you will need to

- develop a strategy for solving the puzzle; decide which pieces you will tackle first;

- decide how much time you think it will take to solve; and

- learn if you need additional resources or research to complete the puzzle.

These are all important planning tools—organization and a concrete plan of action are necessary for success. Writing a business plan is much like solving a large puzzle. A **business plan** is a written document that describes in detail the strategy for creating a new business. A business plan is the road map for starting a new endeavor.

Copyright Goodheart-Willcox Co., Inc.

A well-orchestrated plan outlines the steps needed to guide the business through the first few years of operation. It includes revenue projections and financial milestones. A well-written business plan helps you:

- *determine* if the business is feasible

- *understand* your customers and competition

- *create* a realistic picture of what is necessary to start your business

Most businesses need start-up capital during the first years of operation. Lenders and investors require a detailed business plan when a business seeks funding. Take the time to create a comprehensive, detailed business plan. Business plan resources and suggestions can be found on the *Small Business Administration (SBA)* website.

Writing a business plan is one of the most challenging activities an entrepreneur will face when creating a business. It is also the most important one.

Research

Research is vital to completing a business plan. Without research, the plan will not be valid. It will be necessary to spend time researching the
- industry

- current economy

- good or service

- people most likely to buy your product

- competition

- potential location of the business

Plan to use the research you collected for the feasibility analysis and other parts of the business plan. Make sure that the resources used are reliable. Websites ending in .gov and .edu are generally reliable. When citing websites ending in .com or .net, use only well-known companies or experts in the field. Do not use blogs or websites that allow anyone to post information.

Consider the following as reliable research sources, although there are certainly many more:
- Small Business Administration (SBA)

- US government websites, such as those for the Bureau of Labor Statistics, the Department of Commerce, and the Census Bureau

- state economic websites

- local chambers of commerce

- Service Corps of Retired Executives (SCORE)

- banks and venture capital companies

Copyright Goodheart-Willcox Co., Inc.

- professional trade organizations in your business' industry
- entrepreneurial organization websites, such as the National Federation of Independent Business and the National Association of Small Business Owners

Writing and Presentation Tips

A good business plan helps you stay focused and on track as you open and grow your business. It is a *living document*, meaning it will be updated regularly as your business evolves. Your plan will be shared with others interested in the venture. Most entrepreneurs need funding at some point in the start-up of their businesses. A well-written and researched business plan helps to secure funding. Investors and lenders read many business plans with requests for funding or loans, so it is important that your plan stand out from the many others crossing their desks. The best business plans are

- well-written; the sentences and paragraphs make sense and accurately describe your plans;
- grammatically correct; the words selected must be appropriate with correct spelling, punctuation, and grammar; use a dictionary and writing style guide;
- unique; your plan must be compelling; show an interesting plan that is worthy of investment;
- viable; the business opportunity must clearly show the ability to achieve long-term success; and
- attractive; it is acceptable to use the styles in Microsoft Word to create the headings and subheadings of the plan, or create your own individual style.

At some point, you will be asked to present your business plan to investors and lenders. The layout of the document should be professional and uncluttered. Be prepared to give a copy to interested parties. Business plans are often bound to make them look more professional. You should also provide a digital version in a file format that can be opened by various types of devices and operating systems, such as Portable Document Format (PDF) and DOCX.

In addition to providing a copy of the business plan, it is common to make a presentation that includes slides. A business plan presentation should last approximately 15 minutes. Use only 10 to 12 slides and limit the use of animation to keep the presentation focused. Practice the presentation several times before the actual presentation day to build your confidence and ensure a smooth delivery. Review the business plan and become familiar with the details it contains so that you are prepared for questions.

SBA Tips

The SBA recommends writing a business plan as the first step to creating a business. A business plan is an important road map leading to success. This document generally projects three to five years ahead in the business. It outlines the plans to reach, maintain, and grow revenues. A well-thought-out business plan helps an entrepreneur to think objectively about key elements of the business venture. www.sba.gov

Copyright Goodheart-Willcox Co., Inc.

Sections of the Business Plan

There is no right or wrong way to write a business plan. Using a template can help make the writing process easier. A *template* is a document containing a basic format that can be used many times. There are many organizations that provide free business plan templates online. The SBA offers detailed templates and information for writing a business plan. The *Service Corps of Retired Executives (SCORE)* also offers resources at no charge. SCORE is a "nonprofit association dedicated to helping small businesses get off the ground, grow, and achieve their goals through education and mentorship." Many nonprofit organizations have an abundance of resources for writing business plans in addition to offering entrepreneurs advice and mentorship.

As you progress through this text, you will be writing your own business plan. The business plan outline you will use includes the following sections: Title Page, Table of Contents, Executive Summary, Business Description, Market Evaluation, Operations, Financial Plans, Conclusion, Bibliography, and Appendices.

Title Page

All formal reports include a title page that shows the name of the company, owner, and date the plan is presented. The title page makes the first impression of what will follow in the business plan.

 You Do the Math   Numeric Reasoning

To multiply whole numbers and decimals, place the numbers, called the *factors*, in pairs in a vertical list. When multiplying a percentage, move the decimal two places to the left. To find the number of decimal places needed in the final product, add the number of places in each number. Two decimal places plus three decimal places means the product must have five decimal places.

Solve the following problems.

1. You have hired an employee who earns $12 an hour and earns time and a half (1.5×) for hours worked over 40. Last week, she worked a total of 42 hours. What is her gross pay?

2. Your business must pay a 2 percent fee on all credit card transactions. What is the total fee for all of these transactions: $24.76, $52.76, and $29.35?

Copyright Goodheart-Willcox Co., Inc.

Table of Contents

A table of contents is necessary so that the reader knows what will be included in the business plan and where each section is located. Prepare the table of contents after the business plan is completed.

Executive Summary

An executive summary provides the overview of the business by highlighting the main points from the business plan. Your business plan will be read by people interested in investing in or lending money to your business, such as investors or bankers. This is your opportunity to show them that the business plan is worth reading. The goal is to provide a snapshot that will entice the reader to review the entire document. Even though the executive summary will be positioned at the beginning of the business plan, write it last. After all of the other parts have been written, you will be able to summarize everything in this section.

Keep the summary succinct and to the point, not exceeding two pages. A partial example of an executive summary is shown in Figure 2-4. Start the executive summary with a sentence that describes the problem solved by the creation of the business. Next, address the following topics:

- List the owners and business type.

- Describe the good or service.

Executive Summary

While at Butler University in Indianapolis earning my bachelor's degree in merchandising management, I was an assistant manager in the student store for two years. I was in charge of inventory and noticed that the fastest sellers were the higher-quality clothing items with retro designs. They consistently flew out of the store and we were always taking special orders. On further research, I found there was no supplier in the Midwest offering custom clothing with specifically retro designs. I started RetroAttire when I found an old warehouse in New York City by accident. It was full of old iron-on designs from the 1970s and 1980s. The owner was willing to almost give the iron-ons away. The only catch was I had to remove them from the warehouse before it was demolished. RetroAttire was born in my basement and immediately took off. With Butler and six area high schools as my initial customers, I managed sales of $20,000 in the first quarter. My personal initial investment was $300. I am currently the only employee.

RetroAttire is taking advantage of the growing interest in all things retro by providing quality retro T-shirts at reasonable prices through our website, www.RetroAttire.com. Our current supply of retro iron-ons is vast. However, I want to expand the business to offer customers more clothing choices.

Goodheart-Willcox Publisher

Figure 2-4. The executive summary should be written last.

Copyright Goodheart-Willcox Co., Inc.

- Summarize the competition.
- Identify what makes your business different from the competition.
- Describe why your business will be profitable.
- Briefly describe the promotional plans.
- Briefly explain the operations processes.
- Explain how and when investors or lenders will get their money back.

Business Description

The business description includes the goals, a vision statement, a mission statement, a business overview, a description of the good or service, and the business location. Here, you can show your entrepreneurial spirit and explain in more detail why you think the business will succeed, as illustrated in Figure 2-5.

BUSINESS DESCRIPTION

Goals

It has always been my goal to start a business that also has socially conscious values. As a student in an Entrepreneurship class, I set a goal to have my first business up and running by the age of 24. I am currently 23 years old and have met that goal by opening RetroAttire, a custom retro clothing venture. Sales in the first quarter of RetroAttire's operation were $20,000. My goal for sales growth is at least 20% each year. The storefront will open in year three.

Vision Statement

RetroAttire will become the most sought after provider of personalized, quality retro clothing in the Midwest.

Mission Statement

RetroAttire is a socially conscious company providing personalized retro clothing printed on demand at reasonable prices. Our products are available through a fun, hip, and retro website and store for anyone who craves quality and style.

Business Overview

RetroAttire is currently taking advantage of the growing interest in retro clothing. We provide quality retro-look T-shirts at reasonable prices through our website, www.RetroAttire.com. Our current supply of iron-ons is vast. However, we want to expand the business to offer customers more retro clothing choices and ways to customize their items. Therefore, we plan to purchase commercial silk-screening and embroidery equipment. I will start the process to acquire suitable retro storefront space in the Broad Ripple neighborhood. This unique space will reinforce our retro brand. It will also give us another distribution avenue and provide more room to produce, inventory, and sell the new products.

Goodheart-Willcox Publisher

Figure 2-5. The business description should explain, in detail, why you will succeed.

Copyright Goodheart-Willcox Co., Inc.

Goals

Use this section to describe the goals for your business. Write two to four SMART goals that describe what the business aims to accomplish on a short-term and long-term basis.

Vision Statement

A **vision statement** is the overall goal for the company's future. It should not be longer than one sentence, preferably fewer than ten words. The vision statement is like looking into a crystal ball and seeing the future of your company. One example of a vision statement is, "To become the safest, most customer-focused manufacturer in the world." A good vision statement should inspire employees and help drive the business.

Mission Statement

The **mission statement** is your message to the customer as to why the business exists. It describes the business, identifies the customers, and shows how the business adds value to the customers' lives. Develop the mission statement from the *customer's perspective*. One example is, "Providing the most fuel-efficient cars to help you save money and the environment." It should answer the following three questions:

- What does the business do?

- How is it done?

- Who benefits from it?

Business Overview

Provide a brief overview of the business and identify the nature of your business. The **nature of business** is the general category of operations that generates profit. Is your business a service business, retail business, or manufacturing business? Is the business online, brick-and-mortar store, or a combination? What are your hours of operation? If the location is important to customers, explain why you chose it. Identify what makes the company unique and which factors will make the company successful. Describe your major competitive strengths.

Goods or Services

Describe the products that will be offered to customers. Identify the **product mix**, which is all the goods or services the business will sell. Your business may have only one good or service or may offer multiple products. Identify how your product fulfills a recognized need in the marketplace.

Copyright Goodheart-Willcox Co., Inc.

Business Location

Explain why you selected this location. If the business requires a brick-and-mortar location, explain its layout and the plan to acquire the space. If the business will be operating from a home office, describe the working space. In later chapters, demographic, geographic, and economic factors will be described. These factors will help you decide the best location for your business.

Market Evaluation

The *market evaluation*, also called *market analysis*, explains the industry and knowledge of the market gained through research. Performing detailed market research forces entrepreneurs to analyze all aspects of their markets as well as the competition, as shown in Figure 2-6. This is a necessary step to position a business for getting its share of sales. In addition, a thorough analysis of the business situation provides an indication of the growth potential within the industry. Market evaluation includes information on industry conditions, economic conditions, trade area analysis, target market, and competition.

Market Evaluation

Industry Conditions

Most major multi-store retail chains had sales declines in the first part of 20xx. However, they saw improvements toward the end of that year, and the upward trend has continued into this year. The retail industry continues to show weak, yet positive, signs of growth. Sales of retail clothing topped $75 billion nationwide in the past year. Custom and imprinted clothing accounted for just under 5%, or $375 million of these sales.

According to *Internet Retailer*, e-commerce retail sales were up by 15% over the previous year. In fact, any growth in the retail industry is attributed to online sales increases. Analysts at *eMarketer* forecast continued growth in American e-commerce sales of between 13% and 18% yearly, much of it spurred by social media.

Economic Conditions

During the past five years, the US economy has experienced the worst recession since the Great Depression in the 1930s. According to the US Bureau of Labor Statistics, the average unemployment rate hovers around 8.3% (down from a high of 10.9%). Businesses that are hiring have decreased by over 30%. The US Department of Housing and Urban Development (HUD) indicates that home foreclosures are dropping. However, the overall 20% foreclosure rate is still the highest the country has experienced in 75 years.

Goodheart-Willcox Publisher

Figure 2-6. Market research will reveal how the business can succeed in its industry.

Copyright Goodheart-Willcox Co., Inc.

Industry Conditions

Describe the overall industry that you have chosen, and explain how your business fulfills market needs. Investors will want to know the strength of the industry, opportunity for growth, and details of competition within the industry.

Economic Conditions

Explain how the current economic conditions will affect your business. Economic conditions influence funding, employment, and other important factors that determine if a business can be a success. Describe the current economy and how it will impact your business.

Trade Area Analysis

The trade area analysis is a geographic and economic look at where you will be selling your product. For example, your trade area may be a town, city, county, state, or country.

Target Market

Identify the customers most likely to buy your products. Create a customer profile based on gender, age, education, income level, or lifestyle. Knowing this information about your current and potential customers helps you determine the best strategies for reaching them effectively.

Competition

List and describe your competitors and their physical locations in relation to your business. Analyze their strengths and weaknesses. Explain how you will compete with others in the business to gain your share of the sales.

Operations

Business operations are the day-to-day activities necessary to keep a business up and running. The business' organizational structure and management team are described in this section, as illustrated in Figure 2-7. In addition, how your goods or services are created and sold is also detailed. Operations also include managing employees and protecting the business from potential risks.

Organizational Structure

Describe the organizational structure of your business. Are you a sole proprietorship, partnership, limited liability company (LLC), or corporation? It is important that the reader understand how the business is organized.

Copyright Goodheart-Willcox Co., Inc.

OPERATIONS

Organizational Structure

I started RetroAttire as a sole proprietorship. A sole proprietorship offers the following advantages for RetroAttire: a low entry cost (my DBA license costs less than $50); the business is not taxed, only my personal income; any losses are tax deductible; and I have control over how the business is run. I am also taking advantage of the State of Indiana Incubators Program, which helps new companies grow during the start-up phase to reduce the risk of small business failures.

Management Team

My experience as the assistant manager of the Butler University student store gives me management experience. I worked in the store for two years while earning a bachelor's degree in Merchandising Management. I currently assume all functions within the business and make all decisions. My grandfather is a CPA and serves as RetroAttire's accountant. I am also utilizing my college mentors for advice.

I anticipate hiring my next employee in year two at the latest. He or she will have a bachelor's degree in graphic design. This person will serve as the company's graphic designer and production assistant. The graphic designer will create our own unique, proprietary retro designs. The designer will help expand the business into also offering customer-created retro designs through our website. After year three, I will hire more production and sales staff as needed.

Marketing Strategies

Product:

RetroAttire's value proposition is to provide the highest-quality retro clothing for the best prices both online and eventually through a hip storefront. We offer uncompromising customer service, rapid turnaround times on shipping and delivery, as well as fun, unique products.

Goodheart-Willcox Publisher

Figure 2-7. The operations section will outline the day-to-day activities of the business.

Management Team

Include your self-assessment and information about the other principals and key players in the business. Provide specific examples of your willingness to take risks, and include a brief plan for personal development in your field. Include the experience, titles, and job responsibilities for other key players. Reference the team's résumés, which are included in the appendices. If any expertise is missing from your team, outline plans for continuing education or outside consulting help.

Marketing Strategies

Marketing is an important function of any business. Marketing strategies will come from researching your target markets. They will cover the *four Ps of marketing*—product, price, place, and promotion. Marketing strategies will reflect your research to create short-term and long-term goals for marketing your products.

Copyright Goodheart-Willcox Co., Inc.

Marketing is getting customers interested in what the business is selling. Marketing efforts are most successful when they focus on what the customers *really* want or need—not on what you *think* they want or need.

Human Resources

Provide the company's job descriptions and how you plan to hire, train, and manage the necessary employees. If you have more than five employees, create an organizational chart and include it in the appendices. Explain who will run the business on a daily basis.

Risk Management Evaluation

Business risk is the possibility of loss or injury that might occur while running a business. Depending on the business, risks may include workplace accidents, natural disasters, potential lawsuits, or economic problems. **Risk management** is a process for identifying, assessing, and reducing risks of different kinds. Determine the necessary types of insurance and identify other ways to reduce business risks.

Financial Plans

Potential investors and loan officers analyze financial plans carefully. Financial plans play a large part in the decision to invest in or lend money to a start-up business. Investors want a good return on their investment. Bankers want to know you will make enough money and stay in business long enough to pay back a loan. Refer to chapter 9 for more details.

Capital

Start-up capital is the initial sum of money needed to open the business and cover start-up expenses. It is also called *seed money.* It may come from you, business loans, or investors who want to know that your business is a solid investment. A **sources of funds** document summarizes where the start-up funding comes from for a new business.

Financial Statements

Pro forma financial statements are financial statements based on the best estimate of the business' future sales and expenses. These include a pro forma cash flow, balance sheet, and income statement. Also required will be a sales forecast and a break-even analysis. When applying for a loan, you will also need a personal financial statement.

Future Plans

Investors expect to see your future business plans for at least three to five years. Describe the growth goals and strategies, how growth will affect the business, and what you will do to accommodate and sustain the business. Include a **contingency plan**, which is a written plan of action to ensure a positive and rapid response to a changing situation. What is the plan for continuation if you or your top manager leaves or is incapacitated? This section should also include an exit strategy for selling or closing the business.

Conclusion

The conclusion summarizes why your business will be successful and ends with a specific request for financing. Write your conclusion so it is easy to read and highlights all the points important to potential investors and lenders.

Bibliography

The bibliography lists all of the resources used to develop the business plan, as shown in Figure 2-8. This might include interviews you conducted; books, periodicals, and websites cited; or other information you gathered while researching your business plan.

Appendices

This may include résumés, financial statements, promotional plans, and other documents that support your plan. Arrange these documents in a logical order and list each in the table of contents.

Bibliography

Internet Retailer. "Sales." Trends & Data. Accessed May 9, 2012. http://www.internetretailer.com/trends/sales/.

eMarketer. "Social Media Key Influencer in Multi-Exposure Purchase Path." Last modified February 16, 2012. Accessed May 9, 2012. http://www.emarketer.com/Article.aspx?R=1008845.

US Bureau of Labor Statistics. "Employment Situation Summary." Economic News Release. Last modified May 4, 2012. Accessed May 9, 2012. http://www.bls.gov/news.release/empsit.nr0.htm.

Goodheart-Willcox Publisher

Figure 2-8. The bibliography is an important record of the sources used to write the business plan.

Copyright Goodheart-Willcox Co., Inc.

Global Entrepreneurs

Cecil Altmann, Robert S. Mackay, and John F. Herminghaus

For many people, starting a business is the American Dream. But, for some Americans, that dream involves a country other than the United States. Some Americans vacation in another country, fall in love with the country, and decide to open a business there. Other entrepreneurs have an idea and look to other countries for a new market or opportunities.

Global entrepreneurship is not a new phenomenon. In the late 1950s, Americans Robert S. Mackay and John F. Herminghaus and Austrian Cecil Altmann, who were all in their twenties, were interested in opening bowling alleys. They wanted to open bowling alleys only in locations that had a large, growing middle-class population. Across America at that time, the middle-class population was growing, but there were already around 10,000 bowling alleys in the United States. What about going global?

In the 1950s, Western Europe was in the midst of an economic boom as it rebuilt after World War II. The middle-class population was growing across France, West Germany, Italy, Switzerland, and other western European countries. Robert, John, and Cecil formed the Overseas Bowling Corporation and began opening bowling alleys in Europe. They would have bowling alleys in Munich, Basel, Strasbourg, Milan, and other cities.

Section 2.2   Review

Check Your Understanding 🔗

1. Describe the process of writing and presenting a business plan.
2. Describe the difference between a vision statement and a mission statement.
3. What information needs to be included in the market evaluation?
4. Give an example of the type of business operations you will include in your business plan.
5. Why is the financial plans section of the business plan important?

Build Your Vocabulary 🔗

As you progress through this text, develop a personal glossary of key terms. This will help you build your vocabulary and prepare you for a career. Write a definition for each of the following terms and add them to your personal glossary.

business plan
vision statement
mission statement
nature of business
product mix
business
   operations

business risk
risk management
start-up capital
sources of funds
pro forma financial
   statements
contingency plan

Copyright Goodheart-Willcox Co., Inc.

Chapter Summary

Section 2.1 Business Ideas

- The primary goal of business is to generate revenue. All businesses perform four basic functions in order to remain in operation: production, finance, marketing, and management.
- The discovery process helps identify wants and needs that could be met by a new business.
- The two goals of an entrepreneur are to create a desirable product and develop reasons why a customer should purchase it from you. Economic factors will have a big impact on how these goals are met.
- Once you decide what type of business to open, analyze the best form for it to take. There are many rewards of being an entrepreneur, but there are also many risks.
- There are many rewards, other than money, to becoming an entrepreneur. Entrepreneurs enjoy independence, being their own boss, and doing something they are passionate about. However, every entrepreneurial venture comes with risks. Entrepreneurs are responsible for all the decisions they make about the business and risk personal finances.
- Businesses fail for a variety of reasons, and it is important to consider and accept this possibility before beginning.

Section 2.2 Business Plan Puzzle

- Creating a successful business plan involves a lot of research about the industry, current economy, the good or service, potential customers, competition, and potential location. The best business plans are carefully researched and well written.
- The business plan should include a title page, table of contents, executive summary, business description, market evaluation, business operations, financial plans, and a conclusion. A bibliography and appendices will include sources and additional information or documents.

Online Activities

Complete the following activities to help you learn, practice, and expand your knowledge and skills.

Posttest. Now that you have finished the chapter, see what you learned by taking the chapter posttest.

Key Terms. Practice vocabulary for this chapter using the e-flash cards, matching activity, and vocabulary game until you are able to recognize their meanings.

Review Your Knowledge

1. Identify and analyze each of the four functions of business.
2. Discuss the importance of budgeting.
3. List the two parts of the discovery process.
4. Explain how the goods and services of a business meet the needs of the market.
5. After you have completed your feasibility study, you will need to think about the type of business start-up you will choose. Identify three options for starting your business.
6. In which section of the business plan is the nature of business addressed?
7. Discuss the rewards and risks of being an entrepreneur.
8. Describe the characteristics of and need for a well-orchestrated business plan.
9. List three topics you will need to research when writing your business plan.
10. What sources are available for you to use when creating your business plan?

Apply Your Knowledge

1. In the Building Your Business Plan project at the end of each unit, you will be writing a complete plan for a business of your choice. The plan should be clear in purpose and the details of each section should be critically explained. When the plan is finished and ready for submission, it should be well-written, organized, and as perfect as possible. Make a list of items you should incorporate that will add clarity and critical explanations to each section of the plan. In addition, create a checklist that you will use as you write the business plan throughout this course. This list should include tasks you will complete that will result in an outstanding business plan.
2. Select one of the methods of generating ideas for a business covered in this chapter. Once you have an idea for a product, the next step is to conduct a feasibility study. Explain how your business' goods or services meet the needs of the market. Conduct a survey of your classmates to find out how many people would be interested in your product.
3. Franchises are one way to become an entrepreneur. Make a list of franchise businesses in your community. Would any of these franchises be opportunities that you would like to consider? Why or why not?
4. You identified a good or service that holds potential for creating a new business. If you create a business, what are some of the risks you might face as an entrepreneur? Brainstorm ways you could overcome each risk.
5. Failure to do research is one of the reasons some businesses fail. List the ways you would research your idea for a business. How can you ensure that your business will not fail?

Copyright Goodheart-Willcox Co., Inc.

6. List one or two businesses that you would consider creating. What would the nature of your business be? Would it be a service, retail, or manufacturing business? List the marketplace needs satisfied by your business. Is it a new business, an established business you would purchase, a franchise, or an invention?

7. Create a title page and a business description for a business you might like to start.

8. Many people confuse the vision and the mission statements. Create a vision statement and a mission statement for a business you might want to start. How do they differ?

9. In the Market Evaluation section of the business plan, you will evaluate industry and economic conditions. Using the Internet, research the current conditions of the industry you want to be in. Write an example of how a business you want to create fulfills market needs.

10. In the Operations sections of your business plan, you will identify the management team. If you were to start the business tomorrow, make a list of experts or people that you would want to have help you and why you would need them.

Teamwork

Contact a business in your community that would allow you and your team to make an after-school visit. The business may be a franchise or an independently-owned small business. Create a list of questions to ask the manager or owner about how the functions of business are carried out within the business. Ask questions that specifically pertain to production, finance, marketing, and management. Make notes on the information you receive and compare your team's experience with other teams in the class.

Internet Research

Business Plan Templates. Numerous business plan templates, outlines, and sample plans are available at no charge on the Internet. Conduct a search for *business plan templates* and compare the results with the one you will use in this text. Compare and contrast the section names and locations within the different documents.

Business Plan Resources. There are many business plan resources available online. Search *business plan resources* on the Internet. Record three different websites that provide business plan resources. Identify the related organizations for each of the online resources you find. Which one would you recommend?

Copyright Goodheart-Willcox Co., Inc.

Communication Skills

College and Career Readiness

Listening. Research the positives and negatives of opening a new business. Find video footage of at least three speeches or news broadcasts that discuss the opportunities for opening a business. Compare and contrast the speakers' information, points of view, and opinions. Create a list of positives and negatives that you might encounter when starting a business.

Speaking. Develop a list of regulations that you would like to have in your classroom and your reasoning for each one. Develop a presentation in which you attempt to persuade your classmates to adopt your regulations. Develop a separate presentation in which you attempt to persuade your teacher. How will you alter your presentations for these two different audiences?

CTSOs

Written Business Plan. Writing a business plan is a competitive entrepreneurship event that may be offered by your Career and Technical Student Organization (CTSO). This may be an individual or team event. There may be two parts to this event: the written business plan and the oral presentation of the plan.

The event calls for the development of a written proposal to start a new business. Students are given an opportunity to present an idea for a business and how the business will be created, marketed, and financed.

Students who participate are required to write a plan and submit it either before the competition or on arrival at the event. Written events can be lengthy and take a lot of time to prepare. Therefore, it is important to start early.

To prepare for writing a business plan, complete the following activities.

1. Read the guidelines provided by your organization. Specific directions will be given as to the parts of the business plan and how each should be presented. All final formatting guidelines will be given, including how to organize and submit the final plan.

2. Select a business that interests you for which you will write a business plan. Do your research early. Research may take days or weeks.

3. Study chapter 2 to learn about the steps for writing a comprehensive plan. Review the Putting the Puzzle Together activities at the end of each chapter.

4. Visit your CTSO's website and create a checklist of the guidelines for the event. Set a deadline for yourself.

5. After you write your first draft, ask a teacher to review it and give you feedback.

6. Once you have the final version of your business plan, review your checklist. Make sure you have addressed all the requirements. You will be penalized on your score if a direction is not followed exactly.

Copyright Goodheart-Willcox Co., Inc.

Building Your Business Plan—Putting the Puzzle Together

Business Plan

As a famous philosopher said, "A journey of a thousand miles begins with a single step." The first step of your journey as an entrepreneur is your business plan. There will be many revisions, so there are no right or wrong answers to any of the activities that you complete. You are now ready to begin writing your own plan. Keep in mind that you are writing a draft as you complete each section of your business plan. You will revise each section or subsection multiple times as you conduct more research and learn more about your business and industry.

Goals

- Identify the type of business you want to operate.
- Determine the feasibility of your business.
- Create business plan notes.

Directions

Access the *Entrepreneurship* companion website at www.g-wlearning.com ➦. Download each data file for the following activities. A complete sample business plan is available on the companion website to use as a reference. The name of the file is BusPlan_Sample.RetroAttire.docx.

Preparation

Activity 2-1. Entrepreneurial Assessment. Identify the type of business you want to open and the specific skills you have that will make you successful in that business.

Activity 2-2. Feasibility Checklist. Use the checklist to determine if your idea is a good one. Conduct some preliminary research about the business or industry. You must determine this *before* you spend the time, energy, and money to write a business plan. You may want to conduct a feasibility study for two or three different businesses.

Activity 2-3. Business Plan Rubric. View the rubric for the final business plan to see how the plan will be assessed.

Activity 2-4. Business Plan Notes. Create notes about the business that you are interested in starting. Keep your notes and research sources here. What are you learning about the industry and the competition?

Business Plan—Business Description

By starting your business plan now, you will have a head start on creating the final plan. It is never too early to start making notes and keeping track of your progress. Continually list the sources of your information, which will be used in the Bibliography section. In this activity, you are starting to develop the Business Description section of the business plan.

1. Open your business plan document that you saved in chapter 1.

2. Locate the Business Description section of the plan. Begin writing the Goals, Vision Statement, Mission Statement, and Business Overview subsections. Use the suggestions and questions listed in each section of the template to help generate ideas. Delete the instructions and questions when you are finished writing each section.

3. Save your document.

CHAPTER

3 Ethics and Social Responsibility

Burt's Bees began with selling honey off the back of a pickup truck and selling beeswax candles at a local craft show. The partnership between Roxanne Quimby and Burt Shavitz has become an international company. It is ranked as one of the best socially responsible businesses worldwide. Burt's Bees helped develop the Natural Standard for Personal Care Products and follows the highest possible standards for sustainable packaging. The company has a strong commitment to give back to the community and created The Greater Good Foundation. Through the foundation, Burt's Bees donates 10 percent of its online sales to social and environmental causes. Part of employee bonuses is based on the company meeting its energy-conservation goals. What started as a $200 sale at a local craft show has grown into a multimillion-dollar business. Profit, ethics, and social responsibility are good for business.

"You can have everything in life you want, if you will just help other people get what they want."

—Zig Ziglar, salesman and author of See You at the Top

College and Career Readiness

Reading Prep. Before reading the chapter, skim the photos and their captions. As you are reading, determine how these concepts contribute to the ideas presented in the text.

Sections

3.1 Ethics

3.2 Social Responsibility

Picture Yourself Here
Justin Gold

Justin Gold founded Justin's Nut Butter in 2002, just two years after graduating from Dickinson College. Located in Boulder, Colorado, Justin's Nut Butter specializes in creating different types of nut butter using organic and all-natural ingredients. Flavors include chocolate almond, honey peanut, and maple almond to name a few. All of the nut butter flavors are made in small batches and are available in squeezable packs as well as traditional jars.

The idea for different nut butters came to Justin while grocery shopping one day. He noticed the lack of peanut butter variety. He began making his own flavored peanut butter. It was a hit with his roommates, and Justin knew he had a great idea. He also knew he needed more than just an idea—he needed a business plan, a mentor, and investors. Justin researched how to start a business, then began selling his nut butters at farm stands. The products were a success. Today, the nut butters are available online as well as at major retailers.

Photo © Justin Gold

Check Your Entrepreneurship IQ

Before you begin the chapter, see what you already know about entrepreneurship by taking the chapter pretest. The pretest is available at www.g-wlearning.com

SECTION 3.1 Ethics

Essential Question

How does a code of conduct help guide entrepreneurs through ethical issues?

Objectives

After completing this section, you will be able to:

- **Explain** the importance of a code of ethics.
- **Describe** ethical issues that most entrepreneurs face.

Key Terms

ethics
integrity
code of ethics
code of conduct
proprietary information
confidentiality agreement
conflict of interest
insider trading

digital communication
digital citizen
digital citizenship
plagiarism
shareware
freeware
digital literacy
spam

Critical Thinking

Why is it important to let your customers know that you, personally, are ethical and run an ethical business? Write a paragraph about the importance of ethics to a business' long-term success.

Ethics

You probably hear the word *ethics* every day. But what does it really mean? **Ethics** are rules of behavior based on ideas about what is right and wrong. *Business ethics* are rules related to professional standards of conduct and integrity to all areas of business. **Integrity** is the quality of being honest and fair. As an entrepreneur, ethics will play an important role in how you create and run your business.

A successful entrepreneur leads by example. Setting the bar high inspires others. Many businesses publish guidelines for their employees' values and behavior at work. A company's **code of ethics** provides general principles or values, often social or moral, that guide the organization.

A code of ethics may or may not be written. Certain behaviors, such as honesty, are expected in the business environment and may not be written down. However, as the business grows, a written code of ethics can help employees understand the company's values. Figure 3-1 illustrates a partial code of ethics for a business.

SBA Tips

The SBA has a very detailed code of ethics. The first statement summarizes the code of ethics document: "Our goal is to treat others as we would like to be treated—honestly, and with integrity."
www.sba.gov

Copyright Goodheart-Willcox Co., Inc.

RetroAttire
CODE OF ETHICS

The RetroAttire is committed to putting customers first and being responsible members of the community. RetroAttire will create meaningful work, protect the environment, be socially responsible, produce a solid return for our owners and employees, and provide an important service to society.

Our company's core values are built on trust. Trust is fragile. It takes many years to build, but can disappear in an instant due to one missed deadline, one broken promise, or one disappointed customer. Our company will have a well-earned reputation of meeting deadlines, keeping promises, and maintaining the highest level of integrity and honesty. At times, you may be tempted to ignore or circumvent our values. However, one thing is certain—violating the Code of Conduct and ignoring the rules is unacceptable.

Integrity

Integrity is at the core of everything we do at RetroAttire. We are an honest, ethical, and trustworthy organization. Integrity is the foundation of our relationship with our clients, our communities, and each other. We will never record hours not worked or bill a client for hours that were not spent directly on their work. Confidentiality is critical in our business. We are committed to maintaining the highest degree of confidentiality for our clients, employees, suppliers, and associates.

Respect

Respect is the foundation of any good relationship. Discrimination or harassment based on age, race, ethnicity, gender, or any other legally protected status is not tolerated. RetroAttire values each individual; embraces diversity; and listens to clients and employees as we continue to build on the foundation of respect. RetroAttire is focused on sustainability and minimizing our long-term impact on the environment. We seek to reduce our carbon footprint on the environment by finding ways to use fewer raw materials and less energy by increasing our recycling and reuse of materials.

Goodheart-Willcox Publisher

Figure 3-1. Some ethical standards are implied in business and may not be written down.

Copyright Goodheart-Willcox Co., Inc.

A **code of conduct** lists the acceptable behavior for specific business situations. It is based on a company's code of ethics. The code of conduct is a standard for all employees and those representing the business. It may also be written or implied. For example, stating that it is unacceptable for an employee to take a gift from a vendor is a specific code of conduct. Figure 3-2 illustrates a partial code of conduct for a business.

Employment relationships between an employer and employee are important to the success of a business. Employers must be able to trust their employees. Employees must manage relationships with fellow employees, as well as external relationships with customers and competitors.

Ethical Issues

As an entrepreneur, you should demonstrate integrity by choosing ethical courses of action and complying with all applicable business rules, laws, and regulations. Business rules, laws, and regulations are discussed in more detail in chapter 8.

What are some ethical issues that entrepreneurs might face? When starting a business, there are many details that need attention. Time and money are usually scarce. It may be tempting to cut corners

RetroAttire
Code of Conduct

The RetroAttire Code of Conduct sets specific expectations and rules to guide our employees' actions when conducting business. We expect our employees to conduct themselves appropriately. Employees or contractors who violate this Code of Conduct are subject to dismissal.

Company Assets

No employee shall use company assets such as computers, telephones, copiers, or the like for personal use. If a situation warrants personal use of company assets, written permission must be granted by a supervisor.

Gifts

From time to time, vendors may offer our employees gifts. Employees may not accept gifts that have a value of more than $25. Gifts over $25 must be politely declined.

Confidentiality

Employees are required to keep all information about RetroAttire confidential. No information will be shared with any individual or organization outside of the company without a written signature from an officer of the company or the human resources manager.

Goodheart-Willcox Publisher

Figure 3-2. A code of conduct will provide employees with clear guidelines for acceptable behavior.

Copyright Goodheart-Willcox Co., Inc.

at various stages to make things happen faster. For example, when applying for your first loan, it might seem like a good idea to project higher-than-realistic sales figures. However, inflating your plans to a loan officer is unethical. Intentionally misrepresenting your company can hurt, rather than help, your business in the long term.

As a business grows, ethical issues will arise when working with employees, customers, and the community. When faced with making a difficult decision, ask yourself the questions listed in the *ethics checklist* shown in Figure 3-3. The three questions are easy to remember and may help make ethical decisions. You can also use them to create a business code of ethics.

Legal

Businesses must comply with local, state, and federal laws. Part of the commitment a business makes to its customers is to operate within the legal system. Business owners who misrepresent their goods or services—or run an illegal operation—risk losing customers, at the very least. There are legal consequences when businesses break laws. These can include lawsuits, fines, jail time for the owners and managers, or even having the business closed. Ethical entrepreneurs run businesses that do not break any laws.

Privacy

Human resources are the people, or employees, who work for an organization. They are one of the most important assets of a business. Internal relationships between the owner of the business and employees must be managed so that positive interaction can occur.

Employees have the right to expect their employers to keep all their personal information confidential. This includes information on employment applications and medical information.

When a potential employee completes a job application, it is your responsibility to keep all information private. If you interview that person, any information you gain must also be kept confidential.

All medical records of employees must be confidential. The federal government established the HIPAA Privacy Rule to protect individuals' medical records. More details about HIPAA are found in a later chapter.

Employees are also obligated to keep information about other employees confidential. Employees should never share information

FYI

For more information on trade secrets, conduct an Internet search for the federal *Uniform Trade Secrets Act.* Most states also have their own laws on trade secrets modeled on the federal act.

Ethics Checklist
❑ **Is it legal?** Am I breaking any laws or rules by doing this?
❑ **Is it a balanced decision?** Do both parties in this agreement win?
❑ **How will it make me feel about myself?** Will this decision make me proud?

Goodheart-Willcox Publisher

Figure 3-3. Asking these questions will help you determine what is ethical.

Copyright Goodheart-Willcox Co., Inc.

about others without written permission from that person. In addition, any private information about customers, such as their addresses and credit card numbers, must remain private by law.

Proprietary Information

Workplace regulations, also known as rules, are necessary to protect the interest of a business. Employee relationships must be managed, in addition to external business relationships. An example of a workplace rule that must be adhered to is protecting proprietary information.

Proprietary information, sometimes referred to as *trade secrets*, is information a company wishes to keep private. It is not for public knowledge. Proprietary information can include many things, such as product formulas, financial information, customer lists, or manufacturing processes. All employees must understand the importance of keeping the company's information confidential. The code of conduct should explain that company information may only be shared with your permission. Employees who share proprietary information with outsiders are unethical and, possibly, breaking the law.

Before hiring employees, you may want them to sign a confidentiality agreement, as shown in Figure 3-4. A **confidentiality agreement** typically states that the employee will not share any company information with outsiders. A confidentiality agreement is important when a business has product information that would benefit competitors if they had it. These agreements can also prevent former employees from working for a competitor for a certain time period. As an entrepreneur, it is important to safeguard your products and business. Always seek legal advice when creating any type of agreement.

RetroAttire
Confidentiality Agreement

THIS AGREEMENT made on ___, 20___, between RetroAttire, a place of business at 101 Main Street, Anytown, IL, and _____, an employee of RetroAttire.

As an employee of RetroAttire, we require nondisclosure of any proprietary information about our products, employees, or business plans. This confidential information may include, but is not limited to, patents, trademarks, research, market analyses, or any other information concerning RetroAttire.

All work contributed by the employee as part of the employee's paid position remains the property of RetroAttire.

The obligations of this agreement shall continue two (2) years after employee leaves RetroAttire.

Goodheart-Willcox Publisher

Figure 3-4. A confidentiality agreement will help protect your business and your ideas.

Copyright Goodheart-Willcox Co., Inc.

Focus on Finance

Identity Theft

Someone is using your personal information without your permission, or in effect, stealing your identity. As an entrepreneur, it is important to protect both personal accounts and business accounts from potential identity theft. As the business grows, you will be dealing with people by phone, Internet, and mail. Never give anyone your social security number. If a bank requests it, get a copy of its privacy policy. Shred all documents with any trace of personal information. Use virus and malware software protection on your computers to decrease potential theft by hackers. Many good anti-virus programs are available at no cost.

Conflict of Interest

A **conflict of interest** exists when an employee has competing interests or loyalties. For example, an employee tells you about a great opportunity to sell a new barbeque sauce in your store. The employee convinces you the product will be a big seller, and your cost of carrying the product will be low. What the employee did *not* tell you is that he or she gets a percentage of every sale made in your store from the manufacturer. This is known as a kickback. A *kickback* is an amount of money given to someone in return for providing help in a business deal. This is clearly a conflict of interest.

Conflicts of interest can take many forms and harm a business. Some are illegal; others are unethical, yet legal. Be aware of how specific conflicts of interest could negatively impact your business. These situations should be addressed in the code of conduct.

Insider Trading

You have probably heard the term insider trading. **Insider trading** is when an employee uses private company information to purchase company stock or other securities for personal gain. Using company information for personal gain is both unethical and illegal. While it may be hard to control information, employees must know the legal consequences of insider trading.

Internet

Digital communication is the exchange of information through electronic means. Using technology to communicate in the workplace, as well as in one's personal life, requires users to be responsible. A **digital citizen** is someone who regularly and skillfully engages in the use of technology, such as the Internet, computers, and other digital devices. **Digital citizenship** is the standard of appropriate behavior

Entrepreneur Ethics

It is unethical to use something created or written by another person. Under copyright law, as soon as something is in tangible form, it is automatically copyrighted. Anything in print, including music, images on television or movie screens, or the Internet is copyrighted. If any material is copied or used without the copyright holder's permission, a theft has occurred.

Copyright Goodheart-Willcox Co., Inc.

when using technology to communicate. Good digital citizenship focuses on using technology in a positive manner rather than using it for negative or illegal purposes.

Any information on the Internet belongs to the person who wrote and posted it. Even though there may not be a copyright notice, the material legally belongs to that person. All documents, art, photos, and music are protected under copyright law. Therefore, do not copy something from the Internet and use it without permission. It is important that employees understand that copyright infringement is a crime.

Plagiarism is using another's words without giving credit to the person who wrote them. Plagiarism is a form of copyright infringement. It is unethical and illegal.

Downloading software from the Internet without permission is also unethical and illegal. It is important to know the rules of downloading software. **Shareware** is copyrighted software that is available free of charge on a trial basis. Users pay a fee for continued use when the trial period is over. **Freeware** is software available at no charge. It can be used at any time. *For-purchase software* is software that you must buy to use.

Many codes of conduct have guidelines for visiting websites and rules for downloading to company computers. This is to protect the business' computer system and its private information. Some downloaded files and software contain computer viruses or other harmful *malware* designed to damage or disrupt a computer or network. Any person who purposefully introduces a virus to a computer or network has broken the law.

Using company equipment for personal reasons is unethical and should be addressed in the company's code of conduct.

lightpoet/Shutterstock.com

Copyright Goodheart-Willcox Co., Inc.

Company Equipment

Company equipment is for performing business-related functions. Using company equipment for personal tasks is unethical. This may include sending personal e-mails, copying personal documents, and using the company telephone for personal calls. Some personal uses of company equipment add costs; others may take employees' time away from their job duties. The code of conduct should outline expected employee behavior while at work.

Promotions

Digital communication requires digital literacy skills. **Digital literacy** is the ability to use technology to locate, evaluate, communicate, and create information.

As you begin marketing your business, you will create marketing pieces to promote it. It is important to show the business in the best light. However, be honest in the messages. Do not overstate the features and benefits of goods or services or say things that are not true. This is known as *false advertising,* and it is both unethical and illegal.

It is unethical to send spam when promoting a business electronically. **Spam** is electronic messages sent in bulk to people who did not give a company permission to e-mail them. Sending spam can reflect poorly on an entrepreneur's business. Marketing efforts should include sending e-mails only to customers who have given that permission.

Section 3.1 Review

Check Your Understanding

1. Describe the importance of a business code of ethics.
2. What is the difference between a code of ethics and a code of conduct?
3. Why is it important to have employees sign a confidentiality agreement?
4. What is a conflict of interest?
5. Describe why it is important not to send spam.

Build Your Vocabulary

As you progress through this text, develop a personal glossary of key terms. This will help you build your vocabulary and prepare you for a career. Write a definition for each of the following terms and add them to your personal glossary.

ethics
integrity
code of ethics
code of conduct
proprietary
    information
confidentiality
    agreement
conflict of interest
insider trading

digital
    communication
digital citizen
digital citizenship
plagiarism
shareware
freeware
digital literacy
spam

Social Responsibility

Objectives

?ssential **Q**uestion

In what ways do businesses demonstrate social responsibility?

After completing this section, you will be able to:

- **Discuss** what it means to be a socially responsible entrepreneur.
- **Explain** how corporate culture affects social responsibility.

Key Terms

socially responsible
corporate social responsibility
goodwill
philanthropy

Environmental Protection Agency
  (EPA)
corporate culture

Critical Thinking

Many businesses are socially responsible and give back to their communities. For example, a business may support a particular charitable organization or give employees paid time off to perform volunteer activities of their choosing. Why would companies want to be involved in activities that are not obviously profitable?

Socially Responsible Entrepreneurs

Being **socially responsible** means behaving with sensitivity to social, economic, and environmental issues, as shown in Figure 3-5. **Corporate social responsibility** is the actions of a business to further social good. It goes beyond a business' profit interests and legal requirements. Examples include donating to nonprofits, recycling, supporting local businesses, using nonanimal testing, or supporting a cause like cancer research.

Entrepreneurs are in business to make money. So, why is social responsibility important when it does not help make a profit? Aside from the obvious reason of promoting society's welfare, it can also help a business grow.

For-profit businesses have to make money to stay open. Customers are necessary to generate sales, and they can choose to buy from any business. Being a good corporate citizen promotes goodwill and may encourage customers to buy from a business. **Goodwill** is the advantage a business has due to its good reputation; it cannot be bought. Goodwill creates customer loyalty and is vitally important to

Copyright Goodheart-Willcox Co., Inc.

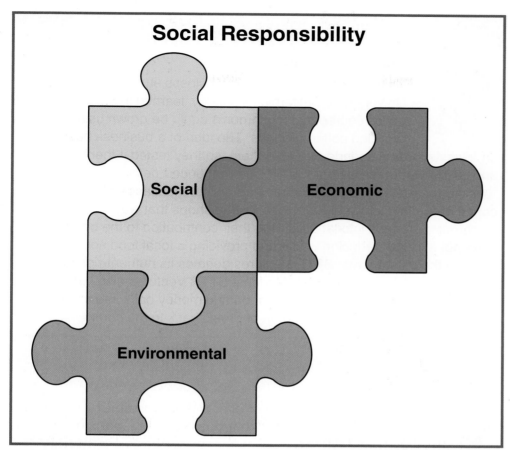

Social Responsibility

Social

Economic

Environmental

Goodheart-Willcox Publisher

Figure 3-5. Think of the components of social responsibility as the pieces of a puzzle.

any business' success. Customer-oriented businesses know that people are more likely to buy from businesses that reflect their own values.

Social Issues

Businesses have a responsibility to help society achieve its basic goals. **Philanthropy** is promoting the welfare of others—usually through volunteering, protecting resources, or donating money or products. Giving back when you can is the basis of creating goodwill for your business. There are many ways for entrepreneurs to give back.

Many businesses support a charity or social cause on a regular basis. Social responsibility does not always mean giving money, however. You or your employees could volunteer your time. For example, some businesses allow employees paid time off work to volunteer at local schools. It could be reading to preschoolers, mentoring a high school student, or even speaking about entrepreneurship on career day. Companies can adopt a school and may help reward children for reading, getting good grades, or having good attendance.

Consider supporting a cause that fits in with your goods or services. For example, a children's clothing store might help fund children's diabetes research. Another option is to consider supporting those causes important to your customers. Some businesses donate $1 to a local nonprofit for each purchase a customer makes.

Social Entrepreneurs

Nikhil Arora and Alex Velez

Nikhil Arora and Alex Velez, business students at the University of California at Berkley, learned in a business ethics course that mushrooms could be grown using recycled coffee grounds. The idea of a business based on a waste stream sounded good to them, so they tested it themselves, and BTTR Ventures was born. BTTR is pronounced *better* and stands for "back to the roots." These entrepreneurs collect thousands of pounds of coffee grounds each week from local coffee shops that would normally discard the grounds into landfills. But, their contribution to the community does not end with reducing waste and providing a local food source. After growing the mushrooms, BTTR Ventures donates its nutrient-rich compost to local schools and community gardens. BTTR Ventures also hires local people to work in their business, putting money back into the local community. It also donates a portion of profits back to the community.

Economic Issues

There is also an economic aspect of social responsibility that goes beyond volunteering or donating. What does social responsibility have to do with economics? All businesses operate within a community. It is important for any business to put money back into its community and support the local economy. You may wonder how this can be done. A socially responsible business owner hires local people whenever possible. Those employees will spend some of their earnings in other community businesses. After all, individuals in a community depend on each other for their livelihoods.

Using local vendors whenever possible also supports the local economy. For example, a restaurant purchases produce and meat from local farmers. That helps the local community and lowers its cost of doing business, which can increase the profit. Transportation costs are low and the restaurant has the freshest supplies. The farmers, in turn, spend their money locally and may eat at the restaurant. It is a system that benefits everyone.

Environmental Issues

Protecting the environment directly affects society as a whole. There are many ways for socially responsible business owners to conserve natural resources and reduce pollution. Use environmentally friendly or *green* products—both in the business and when packaging products. Provide customers with reusable shopping bags or those made from recycled materials. Recycle everything the business uses, such as paper, printer cartridges, or glass bottles. Look for other ways your business can help protect the environment.

FYI

Warren Buffet, the famous head of Berkshire Hathaway, pledged to give away 99 percent of his wealth during his lifetime. Buffet's philanthropy supports numerous charities and causes. He is widely considered to be one of the most successful businessmen in the world.

Copyright Goodheart-Willcox Co., Inc.

©Peaces by Amanda Taylor

Sometimes protecting the environment can become a business itself, such as for these young entrepreneurs, Amanda Erickson and Taylor Brychell, who create and sell recycled and repurposed items through Peaces by Amanda Taylor.

Become familiar with government resources that help businesses with their green practices. The **Environmental Protection Agency (EPA)** provides information about environmental compliance rules and regulations. These laws vary by business sector. The website of the EPA also has a vast amount of information devoted to environmental law and sustainable business practices. Basic activities, such as recycling, using energy-efficient lightbulbs, and turning off lights save money and conserve resources. As you progress through this text, notice the **Green Entrepreneurs** features. These features highlight different ways for businesses to go green.

Corporate Culture

The term **corporate culture** describes how a company's owners and employees think, feel, and act as a business. As an entrepreneur and business owner, you will set your company's corporate culture. A company's level of social responsibility is part of its corporate culture.

When creating the business plan, make social responsibility an important part of the corporate culture. You may also want to include it in the company's written code of ethics. Start small and create a plan for corporate culture using SMART goals. Will the business support a particular cause or nonprofit? How will it recycle or reduce pollution? Explain how your socially responsible choices will impact the community and the business as a whole.

Copyright Goodheart-Willcox Co., Inc.

Recognizing employees for a job well done creates a positive corporate culture.

Franz Pfluegl/Shutterstock.com

Many companies discuss their socially responsible activities on their websites and through social media. This makes a statement about the business and its dedication to the community. It is good for public relations and makes the company visible to current and potential customers as well as employees. Post your successes on a regular basis, and recognize individual contributors when appropriate.

A positive corporate culture includes employee recognition. Showing employees they are valued for the jobs they perform is often as important as the paycheck. Listen to them, their ideas, and their priorities. They may be your greatest asset for spreading the good word about the company.

Green Entrepreneurs

Energy Savings

Entrepreneurs make many buying decisions. They range from expensive purchases to low-dollar purchases, such as the type of lightbulbs used in the business. Compact fluorescent lamps (CFL) can save up to 80 percent of the energy used by a regular incandescent lightbulb. By using bulbs that last longer, the business will save money by saving energy. A CFL lasts up to 10 times longer than an incandescent bulb. However, CFLs contain mercury, so they must be disposed of properly.

Copyright Goodheart-Willcox Co., Inc.

You Do the Math   Problem Solving and Reasoning

Word problems are exercises in which the problem is set up in text, rather than as a mathematical notation. Many word problems tell a story. You must identify the elements of the math problem and solve it. There are several strategies for solving word problems. Some of the common strategies include making a list or table, working backward, making a guess and then checking and revising, and substituting simpler numbers to solve the problem.

Solve the following problems.

1. An online bookseller must earn a profit of 27 percent on each book it sells. The bookseller's cost for each book is $5.58. How much must the bookseller charge to make the required profit?

2. A delivery service charges a fuel surcharge whenever the price of gasoline exceeds $4 per gallon. The surcharge is 45 percent of the amount over $4 for each gallon of gasoline used. The current price of gasoline is $4.32 per gallon. If the price of the delivery service is $6.95 and the driver uses 5.25 gallons of gasoline for the delivery, what is the total charged for the delivery?

Section 3.2 Review

Check Your Understanding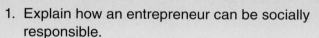

1. Explain how an entrepreneur can be socially responsible.

2. Socially responsible entrepreneurs are aware of which three categories of issues?

3. What is philanthropy?

4. Name three ways business owners can protect the environment.

5. How might companies use the Internet to discuss their socially responsible efforts?

Build Your Vocabulary

As you progress through this text, develop a personal glossary of key terms. This will help you build your vocabulary and prepare you for a career. Write a definition for each of the following terms and add them to your personal glossary.

socially responsible
corporate social responsibility
goodwill
philanthropy
Environmental Protection Agency (EPA)
corporate culture

Copyright Goodheart-Willcox Co., Inc.

Chapter Summary

Section 3.1 Ethics

- Ethics are rules of behavior based on ideas about right and wrong that are important for individuals and businesses alike. Creating guidelines about ethics and conduct make it easier to determine what business practices are acceptable.

- Employers are faced with many ethical challenges with issues of laws, privacy, intellectual property, employee conduct, company equipment, and advertising.

Section 3.2 Social Responsibility

- Social responsibility is behaving ethically and being sensitive to social, economic, and environmental issues. Being a socially responsible entrepreneur means being aware of all the social, economic, and environmental issues that may affect your business.

- Corporate culture refers to the way a business and its employees think, feel, and act. Entrepreneurs need to be socially responsible when developing their business' corporate culture.

Online Activities

Complete the following activities to help you learn, practice, and expand your knowledge and skills.

Posttest. Now that you have finished the chapter, see what you learned by taking the chapter posttest.

Key Terms. Practice vocabulary for this chapter using the e-flash cards, matching activity, and vocabulary game until you are able to recognize their meanings.

Review Your Knowledge

1. What are business ethics?
2. Discuss the importance of the ethics checklist, shown in Figure 3-3.
3. Explain the importance of respecting the private information of employees and customers.
4. Why is a confidentiality agreement important to a business?
5. Give examples of corporate responsibility.
6. Explain how an employer can manage employee interactions with external customers.
7. Describe social responsibility.
8. How can a business promote goodwill with its customers? Why is this important?

Copyright Goodheart-Willcox Co., Inc.

9. What information can a business obtain by contacting the EPA?

10. How can a positive corporate culture benefit the employees and the business?

Apply Your Knowledge

1. As an entrepreneur, which ethical issues do you think will be most important for your business? List and explain your reasoning for each.

2. Describe the plagiarism policies that you will create for your employees.

3. You have started your business and realize the importance of having a code of ethics. Write a one-page summary describing the important topics that you will include in your code of ethics.

4. A code of conduct is necessary to guide employee behavior while representing your business both internally and externally. What will your code of conduct include? How would you expect your employees to demonstrate integrity? Why are workplace regulations necessary to manage internal employee relationships, as well as external business relationships?

5. You have started your business and are creating a new product with a formula that needs to remain secret. Several employees will be working on this product and need to sign a confidentiality statement. Create a confidentiality agreement for your new business. Search the Internet for examples of confidentiality agreements.

6. As a new business owner, you need additional employees and are concerned with a process to keep all records, including health information, confidential. Research your responsibility as a business owner in protecting individuals' privacy. Write a one-page report on your obligations. What rules or legislation must be followed?

7. As a new business owner, you understand the value of being socially responsible. List and describe three activities that your business can undertake to show your responsibility to the community.

8. Look around your community and select an entrepreneur who you think is socially responsible. What is this entrepreneur's business doing to support the community?

9. Research proprietary information. What proprietary information might your company possess?

10. As an entrepreneur, what activities could increase your business' environmental responsibility?

Teamwork

Ethics and integrity in business are discussed in this chapter. Working with your team, discuss ethics and integrity in business. Explain how a business owner can demonstrate integrity by choosing an ethical course of action and complying with all applicable rules, laws, and regulations.

Copyright Goodheart-Willcox Co., Inc.

Internet Research

Patents and Trademarks. If you decide to create a new product as an entrepreneur, it is wise to obtain a patent and protect your idea. Visit the website of the US Patent and Trademark Office and research the differences between patents and trademarks.

Business Ethics and Legal Responsibilities. Using the Internet, research ethical actions in business operations. Summarize what you find about managing internal employee relationships, as well as external business relationships and the ethical issues that may occur.

College
and Career
Readiness

Communication Skills

Reading. Read a magazine, newspaper, or online article about a recent unethical business situation. Determine the central issues and conclusions of the article. Provide an accurate summary of the article, making sure to incorporate who, what, when, and how the unethical situation happened.

Writing. Go to the Environmental Protection Agency website. How does the EPA help businesses protect the environment? Write an informative report consisting of several paragraphs to describe your findings.

CTSOs

Ethics. Business ethics may be a competitive event you might enter with your Career and Technical Student Organization (CTSO). The competitive event may include an objective test that covers multiple topics. However, business ethics may be one part of another event that may include objective questions or a presentation. Ethics will also be a part of your business plan presentation.

To prepare for an ethics event, complete the following activities.

1. Read the guidelines provided by your organization. Make certain that you ask any questions about points you do not understand. It is important you follow each specific item that is outlined in the competition rules.

2. Review this chapter about ethics and social responsibility. Make notes on index cards about important points to remember. Use these notes to study.

3. To get an overview of various ethical situations that entrepreneurs encounter, read each of the Entrepreneur Ethics features that appear throughout this text.

4. Ask someone to practice role-playing with you by asking questions or taking the other side of an argument.

5. Use the Internet to find more information about ethics and social responsibility. Find and review ethics cases that involve small businesses.

Copyright Goodheart-Willcox Co., Inc.

Building Your Business Plan—Putting the Puzzle Together

Ethics and Social Responsibility

While they may seem like the buzz words of entrepreneurs today, ethics and social responsibility are serious business. An ethical business is one that does the right thing because it is the right thing to do, not just because there are laws or regulations requiring it. Many companies support local or national charities. One national chain sells specific merchandise that supports children's literacy programs; another is dedicated to raising money for those with muscular dystrophy. Any company, however, can be both ethical and socially responsible. What will your business do?

Goals

- Discover your personal ethics.
- Create a code of ethics for your business.
- Create business plan notes.

Directions

Access the *Entrepreneurship* companion website at www.g-wlearning.com 📲 . Download each data file for the following activities. A complete sample business plan is available on the companion website to use as a reference. The name of the file is BusPlan_Sample.RetroAttire.docx.

Preparation

Activity 3-1. Ethics Self-Assessment. Take time to complete an ethics self-assessment to help clarify your ethics. You will also use the self-assessment to develop your code of ethics.

Activity 3-2. Code of Ethics. Create a code of ethics for your new business. If you need examples, conduct Internet research on *code of ethics.* Include your finished document in the appendices of the business plan.

Activity 3-3. Business Plan Notes. Create notes about organizations or causes you are interested in supporting. The organizations that you choose should reflect a personal interest or be related to the business you are starting. Conduct some preliminary research about different organizations, and keep your notes and resources here for further reference. Your decision to support a cause or organization may change as you continue writing your business plan.

Business Plan—Business Description

You have now written a code of ethics and examined ways to incorporate social responsibility into your business. In this activity, you will refine the portion of the Business Description section you created in the previous chapter.

1. Open your saved business plan document.

2. Review the part of the Business Description section you wrote for chapter 2. Now that you know more about ethics and social responsibility, you may want to update your business' Goals, Vision, Mission Statement, and Business Overview. Use the suggestions and questions listed in each section of the template to help you generate ideas. Delete the instructions and questions when you are finished writing each section. Make sure to proofread your document and correct any errors in keyboarding, spelling, and grammar.

3. Save your document.

elwynn/Shutterstock.com

Unit 2
Explore the Opportunities

Your Business Plan—Putting the Puzzle Together

You are making some important decisions that affect the pieces of your business plan puzzle. Will you locate the business near or far, and who will buy your products? How will you find your customers? Continue to look at each chapter as a puzzle piece that is important to the finished puzzle. In this unit, you will:

Identify local and global opportunities for your business.

Research your target market and the competition.

Determine the type of business ownership.

Unit Overview

Learning about the many business opportunities and choices available to entrepreneurs is exciting. If you ever dreamed about doing business locally or in another country, there has never been a better time. However, before making important business decisions, market research is necessary. Conducting research gives you the necessary knowledge to locate, start, and run a successful new business. Research will also help determine start-up strategies and different ownership options.

Chapters

4 Local and Global Opportunities
5 Market Research
6 Business Ownership

Entrepreneurs and the Economy

Technology has removed many barriers to doing business around the world. This is great for entrepreneurs and the opportunities are endless. You can sell goods to New Zealand or Morocco from the comfort of your own home. All you need is a computer and the products to sell. However, the competition has also increased dramatically. In the 21st century, Brazil, Russia, India, and China (BRIC) are becoming new sources of global economic growth. Learning how to compete in different countries is critical for global entrepreneurs.

Depending on whether you launch a local or global business, you may encounter a market, command, mixed, or traditional economy. Wise entrepreneurs study the economies of the countries in which they do business to ensure their success.

A *market economy* allows individuals to own private property and do what they want with it. The goods and services offered are determined by what customers choose to buy. Buying and selling with relatively few restrictions defines a market economy. In a total market economy, no businesses would be owned by the government.

In a *command economy,* however, the government regulates what goods are produced, how much is produced, and the prices. Most industries are publically owned. Communist countries, such as North Korea and Cuba, have command economies.

A *mixed economy* is one in which both the government and the private sector make decisions about providing goods and services. Most developed countries have some form of a mixed economy. Most businesses are privately owned. However, some are publicly owned for the citizens' welfare. Some examples of publicly owned institutions in a mixed economy include the US Post Office, the French national health system, and public education systems.

A *traditional economy* is one in which most citizens have just enough to survive.

alphaspirit/Shutterstock.com

There is little to no manufacturing. Countries with traditional economies often have primarily rural populations and are farm based. Most people trade or barter for needed goods and services. Money is scarce and property is held by families to be passed down every generation.

Business is not always conducted the same in every country. Entrepreneurs can succeed in most economies simply by learning the rules for doing business in each country.

While studying, look for the activity icon for:

- Chapter pretests and posttests
- Key terms activities
- Section reviews

G-WLEARNING.com • Building Your Business Plan activities

4 Local and Global Opportunities

Eduardo Cuneo owns a small business in Birmingham, Alabama, named Old Iron Doors. When he started his business, Cuneo sent his designs and orders to a supplier in Mexico. The supplier shaped iron into doors and shipped the doors to Cuneo in the United States for distribution. Cuneo's sales grew every year, and he soon had fourteen distributors around the country. As his business grew, he was able to secure a loan so that he could begin producing doors in the United States, rather than importing them from Mexico. By producing doors locally, Cuneo is able to save money on shipping costs, hire more employees, and improve the quality of the doors. Old Iron Doors is now one of the top companies in the custom wrought iron business.

"If you are not willing to risk the unusual, you will have to settle for the ordinary."

—*Jim Rohn, author and personal development expert*

College and Career Readiness

Reading Prep. As you read this chapter, determine the point of view or purpose of the author. What aspects of the text help to establish this purpose or point of view?

Sections

4.1 Local Opportunities

4.2 Go Global

Picture Yourself Here
Jessica Mah

Jessica Mah and her classmate Andy Su launched their company, inDinero, in 2010 when Mah was just 20. inDinero offers small businesses a money-management tool that they can use online. Clients enter account information and inDinero organizes transactions, updates budgets, and provides a financial dashboard.

A major hurdle when starting a business is getting the needed funds. Mah was able to raise $1 million in two months from investors including YouTube cofounder Jawed Karim and Y Combinator, a venture capital fund for technology start-ups.

inDinero currently has six employees and over 20,000 clients. Its plan for the future is to gain more publicity through a variety of means including social media marketing. inDinero is not Mah's first entrepreneurial leap. In 2008, she created Anapata to match college students to law-related jobs.

Photo © Jessica Mah

Check Your Entrepreneurship IQ

Before you begin the chapter, see what you already know about entrepreneurship by taking the chapter pretest. The pretest is available at www.g-wlearning.com

Local Opportunities

?Essential **Q**uestion

How do small businesses impact the local economy?

Objectives

After completing this section, you will be able to:

- **Explain** how small businesses contribute to the local economy.
- **Identify** resources available to entrepreneurs when developing a local business.

Key Terms

chamber of commerce
Better Business Bureau (BBB)
enterprise zone
Small Business Administration (SBA)
small business development center (SBDC)
Service Corps of Retired Executives (SCORE)

Critical Thinking

Take a look at the small, independent businesses in your community. Why do you think these businesses are important to the people who live there? List a service business you could start with little money to provide a needed service to the local area.

Local Economic Benefits

You may have heard the term *mom-and-pop stores*, which is one way to describe small businesses. The SBA defines a *small business* as "one that is independently owned and operated, is organized for profit, and is not dominant in its field." The SBA has established guidelines to define a small business based on the number of employees and yearly revenues. These guidelines vary by industry.

Small businesses play an important role in a local economy. They both create American-made products and often use products from local suppliers. This practice keeps more production and manufacturing in the United States. Buying local saves transportation costs so the owner then has more money to spend locally. In addition, small businesses create local jobs. Those employees also spend money in their community. Local hiring policies also boost payroll taxes and support local government. Figure 4-1 shows the positive impact of small business on a local economy.

Copyright Goodheart-Willcox Co., Inc.

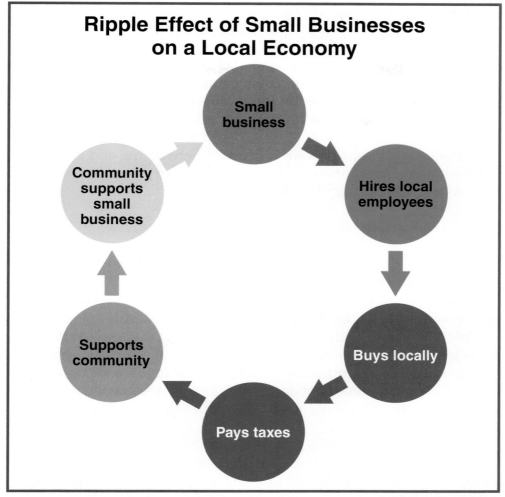

Ripple Effect of Small Businesses on a Local Economy

Small business → Hires local employees → Buys locally → Pays taxes → Supports community → Community supports small business

Goodheart-Willcox Publisher

Figure 4-1. Small businesses are at the heart of a local community.

It is estimated that for every dollar customers spend in a locally owned small business, 73 cents stays in the community. For every dollar spent in a national business, only 43 cents stays in the community.

However, one small business closure can have a negative ripple effect on a local economy. Businesses depend on each other to keep a local economy functioning. If one local business closes, people may have to go outside of the community to fulfill their needs. The remaining local businesses may struggle to keep their customers, which can negatively impact a community.

Local Resources

Like many entrepreneurs, you may want to open a business in your own town or community. Opening a business in a familiar area can be a good idea. You may have contacts or family in town to more quickly create a customer base to purchase your products. There are many local organizations and people who can help with your ideas for starting a business.

Copyright Goodheart-Willcox Co., Inc.

Chamber of Commerce

A **chamber of commerce** is an association of business people that promote the commercial interests of a community. The local chamber of commerce consists of entrepreneurs, business owners, government leaders, and others interested in the community. Many chambers have incentives for new business start-ups because new businesses help the economy.

Attending a chamber event is good for networking and getting to know other entrepreneurs. This is a supportive group and a good place to ask for advice and feedback on ideas.

FYI

Networking is developing personal and professional relationships that may lead to new business opportunities. Successful entrepreneurs are always networking.

Better Business Bureau

The **Better Business Bureau (BBB)** was established in 1912 as a nonprofit organization to provide services to both businesses and consumers. It evaluates and monitors more than three million businesses and charities that earn its stamp of approval.

The BBB helps businesses by providing programs encouraging firms to maintain truth-in-advertising and ethical selling policies. It also gives valuable information about potential fraud to local, state, and federal law enforcement agencies. As a business owner, it is wise to obtain information about potential competitors and suppliers from the BBB.

For consumers, the BBB provides *reliability reports* about companies. These reports help consumers make informed decisions about which businesses to use. Consumers can also file complaints with the BBB related to a business to get help resolving issues.

Enterprise Zone

An **enterprise zone** is a geographic area in which businesses receive favorable tax credits, financing, or other incentives. Enterprise zones are created to help stimulate rural or urban disadvantaged economies. For example, California established its first enterprise zones in 1984. The state now has over 42 enterprise zones helping those local economies.

Small Business Administration (SBA)

The **Small Business Administration (SBA)** is a governmental agency dedicated to helping small businesses and entrepreneurs succeed. The SBA provides help for doing feasibility studies and developing business plans both online and in SBA offices across the country.

The SBA also administers the **small business development center (SBDC)** program giving a wide variety of information and small business guidance. There are now 63 lead SBDCs with easily accessible branch locations. These branches are located at colleges, universities,

Kenneth Sponsler/Shutterstock.com

Opening a business in your community has many benefits.

community colleges, vocational schools, and chambers of commerce. The program is a joint effort of private businesses; the educational community; and federal, state, and local economic development corporations.

Service Clubs

Many entrepreneurs and business people belong to local chapters of service clubs, such as the Jaycee's, Rotary, Lions, and Kiwanis. Service club members volunteer in local communities in numerous ways. Service clubs also provide good networking opportunities for small business owners.

State Websites

State websites have valuable help and information for entrepreneurs. Some states have even created their own entrepreneurship websites. Depending on the site, new entrepreneurs can find resources, register a business, or identify the permits needed to operate a business. Check out your state's website to find help for starting a business.

SBA Tips

Each year more than 10 million people in the United States consider opening a business. However, only 3 million will actually carry out the idea and start a business. The SBA offers online courses for aspiring entrepreneurs. Courses include *How to Start and Grow an Online Business* and *How to Prepare a Business Plan.* The website also has links to other useful government websites for entrepreneurs.
www.sba.gov

Copyright Goodheart-Willcox Co., Inc.

Green Entrepreneurs

Energy-Saving Policies

It is a common practice in Europe to unplug equipment that is not in use, including lights and computers. A business owner can *save some green,* as in dollars, by going green. Up to 25 percent can be saved on energy costs by just turning off and unplugging equipment at the end of the day. Less energy usage also reduces negative effects on the environment. Consider creating a policy regarding electrical use or hold an employee contest to implement energy-saving techniques in the business.

SCORE

Service Corps of Retired Executives (SCORE) is a nonprofit association helping small business start-ups and entrepreneurs. SCORE provides many services including personal mentoring, local and online workshops, and business templates and tools. SCORE is supported by the SBA and has 13,000 volunteers in many varied industries at no charge.

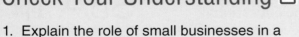

Section 4.1   Review

Check Your Understanding

1. Explain the role of small businesses in a local economy.
2. Describe how the closing of a small business affects the local economy.
3. How can the local chamber of commerce be a resource for entrepreneurs?
4. What is the purpose of enterprise zones?
5. What are some of the services provided by SCORE volunteers?

Build Your Vocabulary

As you progress through this text, develop a personal glossary of key terms. This will help you build your vocabulary and prepare you for a career. Write a definition for each of the following terms and add them to your personal glossary.

chamber of commerce
Better Business Bureau (BBB)
enterprise zone
Small Business Administration (SBA)
small business development center (SBDC)
Service Corps of Retired Executives (SCORE)

Copyright Goodheart-Willcox Co., Inc.

Go Global

What are some of the challenges involved in doing business in foreign countries?

Objectives

After completing this section, you will be able to:

- **Describe** some of the challenges faced by global entrepreneurs.
- **Explain** strategies for creating a global business.
- **Describe** government regulations for international business.

Key Terms

exchange rate
logistics
exporting
importing
supply chain
licensing

joint venture (JV)
trade barriers
tariff
administrative law
regulation

Critical Thinking

Businesses selling products in foreign countries may have to make adjustments for the products to be used. For example, US car manufacturers may have to adjust some equipment to meet other countries' safety standards. Research a company that expanded globally. List the changes that were necessary to sell the products in other countries.

Entrepreneurship Has No Boundaries

You might dream of traveling the world and learning how business is done in other countries. The world's population is over seven billion and growing fast. With that many potential customers, entrepreneurs are only limited by their imaginations.

In today's global market, goods, services, labor, and money easily cross most borders. For those with adventurous spirits, great business opportunities exist outside of the United States. You might sell products to, or actually start a business in, one or more countries. Just look for the possibilities. There are many benefits to operating a business in the global market. Entering a new market or creating new products to meet different demands helps businesses grow.

Technology has changed the way business is done around the world. Conducting business in a foreign country may be easier today than in previous times. However, there are some challenges for global entrepreneurs. The next sections discuss some of these challenges.

Copyright Goodheart-Willcox Co., Inc.

The terms *global trade* and *international trade* mean the same thing.

Cultural Differences

Cultural beliefs, customs, and social behaviors often differ from those in the United States. When doing business in a foreign country, it is important to fully understand its culture. For example, in some Asian countries, a business card must be treated with utmost respect. It should be taken with both hands, carefully reviewed for a few seconds, and put in a shirt pocket or business card holder. Never put someone's business card in your pants pocket. Doing so would offend your counterpart since you would be sitting on his or her card.

Communication

Even though English is considered a universal business language, not every person speaks it. It is important to learn the country's language or have a reliable interpreter. Patience is needed when communicating with somebody who does not speak the same language as you. Incorrect word choice or even a different inflection can send the wrong message. Nonverbal communication may also be different. In the United States, nodding your head up and down means *yes*. In some countries, nodding is a nonverbal greeting. In countries like Greece and Turkey, a single upward nod of the head means *no*. It is important to understand accepted body language for the countries in which you are doing business.

Exchange Rates

The **exchange rate** is the rate at which one currency can be converted to another. For example, $40 in the United States may be worth only €35 (euros) in Europe. Exchange rates change daily and are based on the strength of a country's economy. Activity in the economy has a direct impact on exchange rates. Because the exchange rates change daily, it is important to take advantage of the rates when they are in your favor. When traveling to a foreign country, it is recommended to change your US currency into the local currency, as shown in Figure 4-2. Keep in mind there may also be a conversion fee that adds to the cost.

Focus on Finance

Professional Guidance

Being an entrepreneur means taking some financial risk for your personal assets as well as your business assets. Consider hiring professional help, such as an attorney or accountant, during the business planning stage. The old saying "penny wise, but pound foolish" is good advice. Spending money to hire professional help could save you from making expensive mistakes in the long run.

Copyright Goodheart-Willcox Co., Inc.

International Currencies	
Country	**Currency**
United States	Dollar
European Union	Euro
United Kingdom	Pound
Australia	Australian dollar
Canada	Canadian dollar
Mexico	Peso
Japan	Yen
South Korea	Won
China	Yuan Renminbi
Brazil	Real
Saudi Arabia	Riyal
Venezuela	Bolivar
India	Rupee
South Africa	Rand

Figure 4-2. International currencies are varied and the exchange rate changes daily.

Goodheart-Willcox Publisher

Legal Documents

Certain legal documents are needed to do business in a foreign country. For example, an exporting business may require an invoice, packing list, weight certificate, insurance certificate, and the certificate of origin. The US Department of Commerce can help you get the proper documents for your type of business.

Logistics

Logistics is planning and managing the flow of goods, services, and people to a destination. There are companies whose business is the logistics related to international shipping. Shipments can be by air, rail, or water. It is best to use a professional transportation company to ship products. Use a company that guarantees its shipments.

Labor Laws

The United States has labor laws that apply to doing business in foreign countries. For example, US laws on child labor do not allow children under age 14 to work. In addition, other countries have their own labor laws that must be followed. The Bureau of International Labor Affairs (ILAB) and the Office of International Relations (OIR) help small businesses with labor laws.

Copyright Goodheart-Willcox Co., Inc.

Global Entrepreneurs

Mark Secchia

Some American entrepreneurs find international success without selling globally. Mark Secchia was born in the United States, raised in Grand Rapids, Michigan. He attended high school in Italy. While completing coursework for his MBA at China Europe International Business School in 1999, he and two classmates launched a call center and delivery service in Shanghai to complete their course's requirement of practical business experience. With $50,000 in loans, Sherpa's Delivery Service Company was incorporated at the end of 1999.

Who knew food delivery could become a business opportunity? Secchia evidently did and now owns a food-delivery business headquartered in Shanghai, China. Within nine months after launching the business, it had a positive cash flow. What started with six people now has grown into a business with over 200 employees throughout four Chinese cities: Beijing, Shanghai, Suzhou, and Hangzhou.

The unique selling point of Sherpa's Delivery Service Company is that it caters to people who are not native Chinese speakers. The call-center is always staffed with employees who speak fluent English. Additionally, the company's website is in English. Even after more than a decade, the company has almost no competitors serving the non-Chinese-speaking market in the cities where it does business.

Strategies to Enter the Global Market

Doing business in another country is more difficult than opening a small business in your town. There are many great global business opportunities, though. If you decide to do business outside the country, include a global strategy in the business plan.

Start a Business in a Foreign Country

You may choose to start a business in another country and actually live there. There are generally two options: create a new business or buy a franchise. If you already have a US business, you may be able to recreate it in another country. Even though there will be different laws and practices in the new country, the good or service is familiar to the business. Duplicating that business in another country may be manageable.

Copyright Goodheart-Willcox Co., Inc.

Did you know that you could also buy a franchise in another country? Many well-known US franchises have foreign stores. Some of the products may differ from those in the United States, but the branding is the same. For example, food-service franchises modify their menus to appeal to foreign customers. US franchises in other countries are often very profitable business ventures.

Exporters

Exporting is shipping products made in one country to another country for future sale. Exporting is one of the most widely used ways to have a global business. Historically, exports are important to the overall economy. For example, in 2014, the United States exported $2.35 trillion to other countries, as shown in Figure 4-3. The federal government offers many financial and tax incentives to companies that export.

Many US businesses use *export management companies* to help them find global buyers. They are also called *export trading companies.* These companies help US businesses with foreign customs offices; documentation; and sizing, weights, and measurement conversions. Export management companies can be either locally or foreign owned,

US Export Totals for 2014		
Country/Region	Export Dollar Amount	Percent of Total US International Exports
Canada	$287,818,800,000	19.3%
Mexico	221,437,000,000	14.8%
China	111,792,500,000	7.5%
Japan	61,185,700,000	4.1%
United Kingdom	49,031,300,000	3.3%
Germany	45,668,000,000	3.0%
South Korea	40,720,800,000	2.7%
Netherlands	40,031,300,000	2.6%
Brazil	39,280,900,000	2.6%
Hong Kong	37,578,800,000	2.5%

Source: US Dept. of Commerce: International Trade Administration; Goodheart-Willcox Publisher

Figure 4-3. The countries included in this list represent the top ten US exports in 2014.

Copyright Goodheart-Willcox Co., Inc.

and are paid by commission or a fee. The US Bureau of Industry and Security under the US Department of Commerce and the SBA also assist exporters. Other government agencies that help exporters can be found on the website of the US Export Assistance Center.

Importers

Importing is bringing products made in one country into another country for future sale. It is the opposite of exporting. Importing is also subject to government rules and regulations. Importers may sell the products in their businesses or serve as part of the supply chain. A **supply chain** is the businesses, people, and activities involved in turning raw materials into products and delivering them to end users. For example, both a shipping company and a retail store are part of a supply chain. A good way to learn about importing opportunities is to attend a trade show for importers.

anekoho/Shutterstock.com

Many entrepreneurs start businesses involved in importing or exporting.

Copyright Goodheart-Willcox Co., Inc.

Licensing

Licensing is when a business sells the right to manufacture its products or use its trademark. An entrepreneur may decide to license a product or trademark in another country. The foreign company pays a licensing fee and royalties to the entrepreneur for those rights. The seller of the license is the *licensor* and the buyer is the *licensee.* The licensor may help the licensee with operations, sales, promotions, and consulting. This works much like franchising.

A licensing arrangement can be profitable for the licensor. The licensor receives income and spends little time or money producing the products. However, allowing a foreign company to use licensed products or trademarks also has risks. The licensee may not follow the agreement for payment and distribution. Trying to resolve issues with someone in another country can be time-consuming and costly.

International Joint Ventures

Another way of doing business globally is to work with a business already established in another country. A **joint venture (JV)** is a partnership in which two or more companies work together for a specific business purpose. The companies remain independent, but share in their joint venture's profits or losses.

In some countries, foreign businesses cannot create independent companies. They must join a business already established in that country. For example, the Chinese government does not allow foreign-owned businesses. However, a foreign business can set up a joint venture with a Chinese company.

There are advantages to joint ventures. One partner already knows the market, the culture, and how to do business in that country. The other partner can provide the goods or services needed in the country. A JV may provide a business opportunity that cannot be opened any other way.

The downside to JVs is that the partners may do business very differently. In addition, one partner may want to be on site to have an equal say. Like any partnership, the agreement must be understood before the JV begins. Always seek legal advice before signing any agreement.

Government Regulations

Every country has some rules and regulations to protect their import and export operations. Some countries, however, create barriers designed to reduce importing. **Trade barriers** are governmental regulations that restrict trade with other countries. One common trade barrier is a **tariff**, which is a tax on imported goods. Placing tariffs on certain imported products results in higher prices for those

Entrepreneur Ethics

One way an entrepreneur can show that he or she runs an ethical business is to join the Better Business Bureau (BBB) and prominently display the BBB plaque. Joining the BBB is a proactive way for businesses to help build a positive reputation in the community. The BBB has high standards of conduct for businesses that join the network.

Copyright Goodheart-Willcox Co., Inc.

products than the same products made within the country. There are many reasons countries create trade barriers, but most of them involve protecting their own industries.

Not all countries have trade barriers, though. These countries believe that free trade benefits every country's economy. The *World Trade Organization (WTO)* was formed in 1995 to work to reduce trade barriers. The WTO is an organization of 153 countries that helps members solve any trade problems with each other. Another example of removing barriers is the *North American Free Trade Agreement (NAFTA)* of 1994. NAFTA removed all tariffs between Canada, the United States, and Mexico. The United States also has free trade agreements with other countries. In addition, the European Union consists of many of the countries in Europe that choose to trade freely between member countries, as shown in Figure 4-4.

mart/Shutterstock.com

Figure 4-4. The 28 countries of the European Union have no trade barriers with each other.

Copyright Goodheart-Willcox Co., Inc.

Administrative law is the body of law that governs the activities of administrative agencies of government. It is considered a branch of public law. The role of administrative law is to grant governmental agencies, departments, and commissions the ability to create and enforce rules and regulations. A **regulation** is a rule that has the force of law and is issued by an agency of government. These regulations apply to all businesses. However, they can be particularly important to companies that operate globally in order to protect their businesses.

The governmental agencies that create and enforce rules and regulations are created by Congress or by state legislatures. Examples include the Federal Trade Commission (FTC), the US Department of Labor (DOL), and state transportation departments.

It is important to know that some countries have poor working conditions. Some countries employ children or have businesses that pay extremely low wages. There are US laws and policies to prohibit imported products from countries abusing human rights. In addition, some products are simply against the law to import from certain countries. Consult the Bureau of International Labor Affairs under the DOL. It is also wise to seek advice from attorneys and others specializing in international business. Because importing and exporting is important to the US economy, there are many agencies to provide support, as shown in Figure 4-5. These agencies can also help you understand global labor issues.

Governmental Agency Resources	
Agency	**Function**
US Department of Commerce (DOC)	The DOC promotes US interests by helping businesses export US goods and services. It helps businesses know the laws, regulations, and tariffs in foreign countries. It also helps businesses to form joint ventures.
US Customs and Border Protection (CBP)	The CBP enforces laws related to importing and exporting products. It also inspects all packages coming from foreign countries.
US Environmental Protection Agency (EPA)	The EPA oversees the laws for potentially hazardous imports and exports to ensure safety. Pesticides, fuels, and lead-based paints, especially on items for small children, are just a few of the products it regulates.
US Small Business Administration (SBA)	The SBA provides small businesses with the information needed to safely import and/or export products.
United States Embassies	The United States embassies in foreign countries help US entrepreneurs understand and follow local laws and customs.

Goodheart-Willcox Publisher

Figure 4-5. There are many governmental agencies available to support entrepreneurs in their global business efforts.

Copyright Goodheart-Willcox Co., Inc.

You Do the Math   Connections

Mathematics is an educational discipline that is extensively used in many other educational disciplines. Science, business, economics, accounting, engineering, and many other areas feature mathematics as an integral part of the discipline. For example, marketers must use math to forecast sales, engineers must use math to calculate loads, and economists must use math to calculate the gross domestic product.

Solve the following problems.

1. A scientist must convert the volume of liquid in a flask from cubic centimeters to cubic inches. One cubic centimeter is equal to 0.06 cubic inches, and the flask contains 28.6 cubic centimeters of liquid. How many cubic inches of liquid are in the flask?

2. A marketing manager must calculate the response rate for the latest e-mail marketing campaign. Over the course of the campaign, the marketing department sent 9,500 e-mails. The company received 1,022 responses from the promotional e-mail. What percentage of e-mails generated responses?

Section 4.2   Review

Check Your Understanding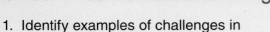

1. Identify examples of challenges in conducting business globally.

2. Name the five strategies for taking a business global.

3. Explain the advantages of establishing a joint venture in another country.

4. How are tariffs used as trade barriers?

5. Describe the role of administrative law.

Build Your Vocabulary

As you progress through this text, develop a personal glossary of key terms. This will help you build your vocabulary and prepare you for a career. Write a definition for each of the following terms and add them to your personal glossary.

exchange rate   joint venture (JV)
logistics   trade barriers
exporting   tariff
importing   administrative law
supply chain   regulation
licensing

Copyright Goodheart-Willcox Co., Inc.

Chapter Summary

Section 4.1 Local Opportunities

- There are many community resources available for entrepreneurs operating a local business.
- Small businesses benefit local economies in many ways, such as by patronizing other local businesses, providing jobs, and keeping money in the community.

Section 4.2 Go Global

- Global entrepreneurship provides many unique opportunities, as well as challenges.
- Starting your own business, exporting, importing, licensing, and joint ventures are the main strategies for entering the global market.
- It is very important to be aware of trade barriers, tariffs, and other government regulations of the countries with which you do business.

Online Activities

Complete the following activities to help you learn, practice, and expand your knowledge and skills.

Posttest. Now that you have finished the chapter, see what you learned by taking the chapter posttest.

Key Terms. Practice vocabulary for this chapter using the e-flash cards, matching activity, and vocabulary game until you are able to recognize their meanings.

Review Your Knowledge

1. Describe the ripple effect of one small business closing in a local economy.
2. Explain how the Better Business Bureau (BBB) helps businesses.
3. Identify some of the resources that the SBA provides to small businesses.
4. Explain how communication can be a challenge in global business.
5. Which governmental agencies assist small businesses with labor laws?
6. What is the role of export management companies?
7. How can an entrepreneur make a profit by licensing a product or trademark in another country?

8. What is one common reason that countries create trade barriers?
9. What is *NAFTA*?
10. Identify examples of administrative agencies of government that fall under administrative law.

Apply Your Knowledge

1. Conduct an Internet search on small businesses. What are the criteria used to classify a business as a small business?
2. Take a look around your community. What organizations actively help entrepreneurs with their businesses?
3. Visit the website for your state. Describe the information that is available for entrepreneurs.
4. Will you plan to start your business in your local community? As an entrepreneur, how will you contribute to your community?
5. Visit the website of the Small Business Administration (SBA). What information did you find that will help you start your business?
6. You have identified the business that you would like to start one day. If you had the capital to do so, to which country would you take your business?
7. Describe the culture, legal documentation, and other information that you would need to start your business in another country.
8. Research a conversion program on the Internet that converts measurement, weight, clothing sizes, etc.
9. If you take your business global, you will need either a visa or a passport. Research the country you may want to do business in and the required documents needed in that country.
10. What types of competition would you face in your chosen country if you started a business there?
11. Research and describe living conditions in your chosen country.

Copyright Goodheart-Willcox Co., Inc.

Teamwork

Go to the *Entrepreneurship* companion website and download the sample business plan for RetroAttire. This plan was written for a company in the United States. Working with your team, create a strategy for taking this business global. Select a country and think about how to take the T-shirt business into that country. As you develop the business plan throughout this text, keep in mind your strategy for taking the business global and update the business plan as needed.

Internet Research

Currency Exchange Rates. When doing business outside of the United States, it is vital to know the value of the US dollar in the local region. Search the Internet for an online *currency converter*. Select five countries and list the current value of the US dollar in each country. In which countries is the US dollar worth more than $1.00? In which countries is it worth less?

Communication Skills

College and Career Readiness

Listening. Practice active listening skills while listening to a broadcast business report on the radio, television, or podcast. Pick a single story about international business and create a report in which you analyze the following aspects of the business story: the speaker's audience, point of view, reasoning, stance, word choice, tone, points of emphasis, and organization.

Speaking. Research the features of some of the currencies used around the world. Compile information about the aspects of each type of currency that help to prevent counterfeiting, the denominations that are made available, the materials used in making the currency, the features of the currency that help to identify the country it represents, and any other interesting information you find. Use this information, along with what you already know about the features of US currency, to create a *world currency*. Using various elements (visual displays, written handouts, technological displays), present your currency to the class. Explain why you chose the features you did.

Copyright Goodheart-Willcox Co., Inc.

CTSOs

International Business Plan. Global business plan may be a competitive entrepreneurship event for your organization. This may be an individual or team event. There may be two parts to this event: the written business plan and the oral presentation of the plan.

The event calls for the development of a written proposal to start a new business in an international setting. Students are given an opportunity to present an idea for a business. A proposal will include how the business will be created, marketed, and financed. Students who participate are required to write a business plan and submit it either before the competition or on arrival at the event. Written events can be lengthy and take a lot of time to prepare. Therefore, it is important to start early.

The rules for this event are similar to other business plan presentations. However, preparing a global or international business plan requires research on doing business outside of the United States.

To prepare for the global business event, do the following.

1. Read the guidelines provided by your organization. Make certain you ask any questions about points you do not understand. It is important you follow each specific item that is outlined in the competition rules.

2. Select a business and country for the business. Do your research early. Research may take days or weeks, and you do not want to rush the process.

3. Study chapter 2 and chapter 3.

4. Practice writing an international plan by completing the teamwork activity in this chapter.

5. Study the Global Entrepreneurs features in each chapter of this text.

6. Review the Putting the Puzzle Together activities at the end of each chapter. A business plan template and a complete business plan sample are available on the student companion website at www.g-wlearning.com.

7. Visit your CTSO's website and create a checklist of the guidelines that must be followed. After you write your first draft, review the checklist and make sure you have addressed all the requirements. You will be penalized on your score if a direction is not followed exactly.

8. Ask a teacher to review your final proposal and give you feedback.

Copyright Goodheart-Willcox Co., Inc.

Building Your Business Plan—Putting the Puzzle Together

Local and Global Opportunities

Research the local and global business opportunities in your industry to help define your new business. You may also uncover new ideas about how to grow the business. There are many financial and tax incentives for entrepreneurs willing to export locally produced products. The government has rules and regulations that must be followed for both local and global ventures. Knowing where to go for information and help with the special areas of your business is vital to its success.

Goals

- Research the local opportunities available for your business.
- Research the global opportunities available for your business.
- Create business plan notes.

Directions

Access the *Entrepreneurship* companion website at www.g-wlearning.com ➜. Download each data file for the following activities. A complete sample business plan is available on the companion website to use as a reference. The name of the file is BusPlan_Sample.RetroAttire.docx.

Preparation

Activity 4-1. Local Opportunities Interview. Business opportunities are in your own backyard. Investigate the available opportunities. Start by interviewing local entrepreneurs. Ask them questions about how they made their business decisions. What advice can they give to new entrepreneurs in that field?

Activity 4-2. Global Opportunities Interview. There are many business opportunities beyond your local community. Identify local businesses that work with foreign companies or have expanded into another country. Ask the owners questions about how they made those decisions. What advice can they give to new entrepreneurs in that field?

Activity 4-3. Business Plan Notes. Create notes about the business you are interested in starting. Conduct some preliminary research about local and global opportunities. Keep your notes and resources here.

Business Plan—Business Description

In this chapter, you learned about the many local and global opportunities for starting and growing your business. These opportunities will affect both the type of business you open and its location.

1. Open your saved business plan document.

2. Locate the Business Description section of the plan. Locate the subsection called Business Location and begin writing it based on your research. Use the questions and suggestions listed in the sections to help you generate ideas. Delete the instructions and questions when you are finished writing each section.

3. Review the subsection you started earlier, called Business Overview. Depending on the local or global opportunities for your business, update this subsection of the business plan.

4. Make sure to proofread your documents and correct any errors in keyboarding, spelling, and grammar.

5. Save the document.

5 Market Research

Many of the best ideas started with identifying a market need. The inspiration for Miche Bag Company started when Michelle Romero spilled something on her favorite handbag. Frustrated that she might have to get rid of it, Romero wished that she could just replace the outside of the bag. An idea was instantly born. Using glue and scrap materials, Romero took apart her stained handbag and created a prototype that had a changeable cover. She showed the prototype to her friend Annette Cavaness and she loved it. Cavaness used her experience as an accessories buyer to help Romero develop a business plan and start Miche Bag Company. Miche Bag Company has since expanded and added accessories and other items to the line of changeable-covers product.

"I never perfected an invention that I did not think about in terms of the service it might give others....I find out what the world needs, then I proceed to invent."

—Thomas Edison, Inventor

College and Career Readiness

Reading Prep. Before reading this chapter, look at the chapter title. What does this title tell you about what you will be learning? Compare and contrast the information to be presented with information you already know about the subject matter from sources such as videos and online media..

Sections

5.1 Target Market

5.2 Do the Research

5.3 Research the Competition

Picture Yourself Here
Juliette Brindak

Juliette Brindak is the cofounder and CEO of Miss O & Friends®, a social networking website for 8- to 16-year-old girls. The site has message boards, games, and quizzes for girls only. The site also allows girls to create their own profile pages, enter contests with cool prizes, and socialize in a 100% COPPA compliant environment. In addition to entertainment, the goal of the website is to help girls build confidence and self-esteem. It has been rated one of the top three girls-only websites.

Juliette first conceived of Miss O & Friends® at age 10. She launched the website when she was 15. By the time she was 19, the company was worth over $15 million.

In 2011, the company launched a companion site for moms, called Moms with Girls^SM, where they can connect with other moms with daughters, and read articles and blogs on a variety of topics.

While running Miss O & Friends®, Juliette earned her bachelor of arts in anthropology from Washington University in St. Louis. Miss O & Friends® is based in Connecticut, the state in which Juliette grew up.

Photo © Juliette Brindak

Check Your Entrepreneurship IQ

Before you begin the chapter, see what you already know about entrepreneurship by taking the chapter pretest. The pretest is available at www.g-wlearning.com

Target Market

Objectives

After completing this section, you will be able to:

- **Discuss** the importance of target markets.
- **Explain** the different ways to segment a market.
- **Describe** how businesses use a customer profile.

ssential
Question

How do businesses benefit by identifying their target market?

Key Terms

business to consumer (B2C)
business to business (B2B)
target market
market segmentation
market segment
mass market
geographic segmentation

demographics
demographic segmentation
census
psychographic segmentation
behavioral segmentation
usage rate
buying status
customer profile

Critical Thinking

It is important for a business to identify who is most likely to buy their goods or services. Make a list of the critical factors you think businesses must consider to identify their potential customers.

Identify the Target Market

Depending on the type of business, customers may be individual consumers or other businesses. **Business to consumer (B2C)** companies sell primarily to consumers. **Business to business (B2B)** companies sell to other businesses. Some companies have both consumers and businesses as their customers.

Businesses are successful when they sell enough products to earn a profit. In order to sell goods or services, customers must want to buy them. This happens when the products satisfy enough customer *needs* or *wants*. A **target market** is the specific group of customers at which a company aims its goods and services. This group also includes those people most likely to buy the products. A target market includes customers that share similar characteristics and needs. A target market will have:

- specific wants and needs that the company can meet;
- people with the money to buy the goods or services;

Copyright Goodheart-Willcox Co., Inc.

- people willing to buy the product; and

- enough potential customers to make the business worthwhile.

As you begin the business plan, it is necessary to identify the customers most likely to buy from your business.

Most businesses will have more than one target market. So, how do you identify them? For example, if you were selling women's purses, the larger market would be women. However, would all the women in the world want to buy your products? Probably not. It would not be reasonable to think that all women will want to buy your purses. You want to know which group of women will find your purses' styles and pricing appealing.

This process is the start of identifying a target market. The description of your target market will be included in the market evaluation section of the business plan.

Market Segmentation

Market segmentation is the process of dividing a large market into smaller groups. A **market segment** is a smaller group of people, families, businesses, or organizations with common characteristics or needs. The **mass market** is the entire large market of potential customers with no segmentation.

One of the main purposes of market segmentation is to help a business determine its target market. Marketers have created four variables to help segment larger markets. A *variable* is something to which a changing value can be assigned. The variables for market segmentation are geographic, demographic, psychographic, and behavioral, as shown in Figure 5-1. Segmenting the market by these variables helps to identify needs and wants and to analyze demand in the market.

Geographic Segmentation

Geographic segmentation involves dividing a market based on where customers live. It also includes how far they will travel to do business. Customers can be geographically segmented by any number of variables.

Region

A region could be a country, state, or even a neighborhood. People in certain regions prefer specific products. For example, many Southerners like iced tea. If you are selling tea, you may segment one target market as *people in the South who like tea.*

Population Density

Customers may be grouped according to the population density of where they live. These geographic segments are urban, suburban,

Copyright Goodheart-Willcox Co., Inc.

Figure 5-1. Market segmentation can be based on different variables.

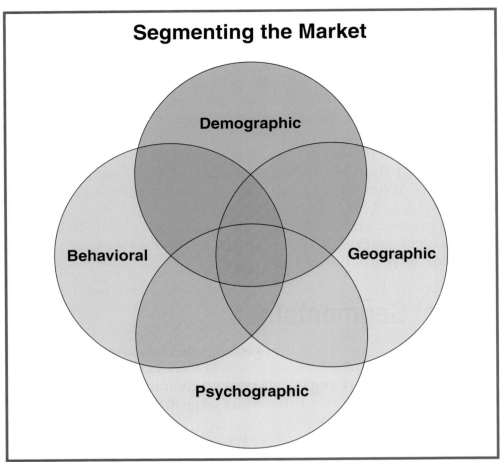

Segmenting the Market

Demographic

Behavioral

Geographic

Psychographic

Goodheart-Willcox Publisher

FYI

There are two types of urban areas: a *metropolitan* or *metro* area and a *micropolitan* or *micro* area. According to the federal government, a metro area is a core urban area of 50,000 or more in population. A micro area has at least 10,000, but less than 50,000 in population.

and rural. If a product appeals to people working on a ranch, the target market may be rural. If a product appeals to people who live in larger cities, the target market is urban.

Climate

Climate is another way to geographically segment customers. People in tropical climates will need very different products than those who live in mountainous regions. For example, a business selling snow-removal equipment needs to target customers who live in areas that get snow each winter.

Demographic Segmentation

Demographics are the qualities, such as age, gender, and income, of a specific group of people. **Demographic segmentation** is dividing the market by customers' personal statistics. Every ten years, the United States takes a **census**, or count of the people living in the country. Some of the data collected are age, gender, income, ethnicity, education level, occupation, marital status, and family size. The census information can help businesses learn the demographics of their target markets. It is important for businesses to determine which demographic segments are vital to the success of their businesses.

Age

Customers can be grouped by age. Different age groups often have different product preferences. For example, if you were born in the late 1990s or first part of the 21st century, you are part of *Generation Z,* sometimes referred to as the *iGeneration.* This age group has high interest in electronic products and information. Figure 5-2 shows a listing of the different generations.

Gender

Customers are often grouped by gender. There are goods and services preferred by men, women, or both. For example, spa services tend to be more popular with women, while more men buy hand tools. However, if a company is selling hand tools, it does not mean it will ignore women as potential customers. In fact, there may be a market for hand tools targeted to women.

Income

Customers may be segmented by income level. People with higher incomes tend to have more disposable income with which to buy higher-priced items. Those people who are not as affluent may choose to purchase less-expensive options for some products.

Ethnicity

Customers can be targeted by ethnic group or culture. People from different cultures have certain foods, clothing, and other items they prefer. If selling products that appeal to an ethnic group, target customers may be recent immigrants, first or second generation Americans, or located in another country.

Generations	
Generation name	**Born between years (approximate)**
Greatest Generation	1901–1925
Silent Generation	1926–1945
Baby Boomer Generation	1946–1964
Generation X	1965–1983
Generation Y	1984–1995
Generation Z	1996–2010

Goodheart-Willcox Publisher

Figure 5-2. People in different generations tend to have some similar characteristics, wants, and needs.

Copyright Goodheart-Willcox Co., Inc.

Education Level

Education level is another way to segment a market. A person with a high school education may have very different wants or needs than someone with a bachelor degree. Somebody with a bachelor degree may have very different wants or needs than someone with a doctorate degree.

Occupation

People in different jobs often have different wants and needs. The terms white collar and blue collar are common. *White collar* refers generally to a job in which a person is not required to wear work clothes or protective gear. *Blue collar* refers generally to a job in which a person must wear work clothes or protective gear. A person's job may affect his or her buying behavior.

Marital Status

Marital status categories are usually married, single, widowed, divorced, or separated. A person's marital status can influence

Monkey Business Images/Shutterstock.com

Demographic information, such as marital status and family size, can help define the target market.

Copyright Goodheart-Willcox Co., Inc.

purchases, such as houses, vacations, and food. A single person, for example, may purchase a smaller house and travel more often than a married couple.

Family Size

Family size is a common market segment because it affects many buying choices. For example, a family of five may choose to purchase a minivan. However, a single person might buy a sports car.

Psychographic Segmentation

Psychographics are data about people's preferences or choices. **Psychographic segmentation** is dividing the market by lifestyle choices. Psychographic variables include customers' activities, interests, attitudes, and values.

Activities

Customers can be categorized by their participation in sports and organizations. People who are members of the same sport or organization tend to have similar buying patterns. For example, physically active customers may be more likely to purchase healthier foods, such as vegetables and fruits.

Interests

Customers may be grouped by their interests. For example, those wanting to protect the environment are more likely to purchase so-called green products. People interested in science may travel to see science museums and aquariums.

Attitude

An *attitude* is how a person feels about something. Believe it or not, customers can be segmented by their attitudes. For example, customers who want fashionable clothing may shop at certain name brand stores. Customers who want to save money may be more likely to shop at discount stores.

Values

Values are what a person believes in. For example, customers valuing safety are more likely to buy a car with a good crash-test rating. Customers who value the environment may choose a hybrid or electric car.

Entrepreneur Ethics

Entrepreneurs have a responsibility to use technology in an ethical manner. Using software downloaded from the Internet without a license is unethical and illegal. It is important to set an example for employees and obtain licenses for any technology used in the business.

Behavioral Segmentation

Behavioral segmentation is dividing the market by the relationships between customers and the good or service. Behavioral variables include benefits sought, usage rate, buying status, brand loyalty, and special occasions.

Benefits Sought

Different customers often choose the same products, but for entirely different reasons. One customer may want a computer that is a great gaming platform. A second customer may want a computer that is a great sound system to play music. A third customer may only want to use a computer for checking e-mail. All of these customers are buying a computer, but each is seeking a different benefit from the product.

Usage Rate

The **usage rate** is how often a customer buys or uses a good or service. Usage rates are classified as heavy, moderate, light, and nonuser. A heavy usage rate means the person is buying the product very often. A light usage rate means the person is not buying the product very often. A moderate usage rate falls somewhere between heavy and light. A nonuser usage rate means the person never buys the product.

Buying Status

Buying status describes when a customer will buy a product. The most common are potential, first time, occasional, and regular. A potential customer is one who has not purchased the product, but is considering it. A first-time customer is one who has purchased the product for the first time. An occasional customer is one who has purchased the product more than once, but only infrequently. A regular customer is one who purchases the product on a frequent or predictable basis.

Brand Loyalty

Brand loyalty describes how dedicated a customer is to a business or its products. It is wise to target loyal customers because in general the 80/20 rule holds true. The *80/20 rule* is a basic guideline that states 80 percent of a business' sales come from 20 percent of its loyal customers.

Copyright Goodheart-Willcox Co., Inc.

Special Occasions

Customers can be segmented by purchases they make related to an event. Holidays and events such as sporting events, concerts, and festivals can change buying behavior. A person may be willing to buy a $50 concert T-shirt, but would never be willing to pay that much for a T-shirt at a retail store. The event, the concert, drove the buying decision for that person.

Customer Profile

A **customer profile** is the detailed description of target market customers based on demographic, geographic, psychographic, and behavioral information. The customer profile reflects those people in the business' target market. The more a company knows about its customers, the better the company can meet their needs. Keep in mind that customer profiles may change or expand on a regular basis.

Usage rates and buying status both refer to the likelihood someone will purchase your product.

Monkey Business Images/Shutterstock.com

Copyright Goodheart-Willcox Co., Inc.

The customer profile also helps determine promotion strategies. By knowing who is most interested in the company's products, promotional dollars can be used wisely. Instead of wasting money by trying to reach everyone, the good or service can be promoted only to those in the target market. A typical customer profile is shown in Figure 5-3.

Spending on pet products differs by age groups. The core pet market, according to the American Pet Association, consists of two groups. The first is empty nesters whose children no longer live at home. The second is families with children ages 5–15. These families are categorized as *pet enthusiasts.* The pet enthusiast family with children ages 5–15 customer profile follows.

Customer Profile
PetSets

Demographic
Age: 35–49
Marital Status: married
Have children under age 18: 38%
Average number of children: 2
Children's ages: 5–15
Education: some college
Household income: $50,000–$94,999
Pet ownership: own at least one dog

Psychographic
Considers pet to be a family member
Pet enthusiast
Travels a minimum of four times per year
Adults work outside of the home
Active Internet user—on average at
     least once per day

Geographic
Lives in a five-mile radius of McKinney, TX

Behavioral
Spends average of $1,000 per year on pet
Heavy user of pet products
Loyal to certain brands

Monkey Business Images/Shutterstock.com; Goodheart-Willcox Publisher

Figure 5-3. The customer profile will be in the target market section of the business plan.

Copyright Goodheart-Willcox Co., Inc.

Section 5.1   Review

Check Your Understanding ⤴

1. List some of the characteristics of a target market.
2. Identify the variables for market segmentation.
3. What are the geographic segments that relate to population density?
4. Name three psychographic segmentation variables.
5. Describe how a business uses a customer profile.

Build Your Vocabulary ⤴

As you progress through this text, develop a personal glossary of key terms. This will help you build your vocabulary and prepare you for a career. Write a definition for each of the following terms and add them to your personal glossary.

business to consumer (B2C)
business to business (B2B)
target market
market segmentation
market segment
mass market
geographic segmentation
demographics
demographic segmentation
census
psychographic segmentation
behavioral segmentation
usage rate
buying status
customer profile

SECTION 5.2 Do the Research

Essential Question

How does market research affect business decisions?

Objectives

After completing this section, you will be able to:

- **Explain** the importance of conducting market research.
- **Discuss** the use of a marketing information system.
- **Describe** the research process.

Key Terms

market research
marketing information system
database
secondary data
primary data
sample size
qualitative data

quantitative data
hypothesis
research plan
data analysis
data mining
statistical analysis

Critical Thinking

As you begin researching, you will segment the larger market by geographic, demographic, psychographic, and behavioral characteristics. List the factors that are most important when deciding which customers to target.

Market Research

Now that you have an idea for a business, it is time to explore if that idea can succeed. Will customers want what you have to sell? What is the best location for the business? What pricing structure will maximize profits? All of these questions can be answered through research. This research is the basis of the feasibility study that is discussed in an earlier chapter.

Market research is the gathering and analyzing of information about a business. Market research helps to:

- identify potential markets;

- define primary customers;

- identify growth opportunities; and

- learn about the competition.

Copyright Goodheart-Willcox Co., Inc.

Research helps identify industry trends, which influence what your customers will demand. Reading trade magazines, monitoring social media, and staying current with other news sources will help you discover what trends are popular for your chosen business. *Trend-spotting* will help you identify opportunities.

Research can also help you find the best location and product mix to start the business off right. Without market research to provide solid information on which to base decisions, a business is just guessing.

Is market research always right? The answer is simply, *no.* There are limitations to marketing research. Limitations may include budget restrictions, reliability of data, bias of researchers, and time constraints. Budget restrictions and time constraints may limit the type of marketing research that can be performed. Researchers may unknowingly influence the responses of subjects through the wording of questions or their tone of voice. Because of the limitations, marketing research is often only one component considered when making business decisions.

The results of any research are only as good as the research itself. If market research is done incorrectly, the results are faulty. The data collected will not help draw good conclusions or make solid business recommendations. Market research may be unreliable for a number of reasons. There are many examples of companies that have incorrectly conducted research. Perhaps the problem was stated incorrectly or the wrong questions were asked to the wrong group of people. They may have used data that were too old or not right for the company. Make sure to follow the proper research process and your results should be reliable.

SBA Tips

From the SBA website, small business owners can access various economic reports and data to help track the economy and its impact on their businesses. There are a number of reports produced by governmental agencies. Included among these reports are *Economic Indicators*, the *Beige Book*, and the *Economic Report of the President.* www.sba.gov

Marketing Information System

A **marketing information system** consists of the processes involved in collecting, analyzing, and reporting marketing research information, usually through technology. For example, some stores use information taken from customer credit card purchases to better tailor their marketing efforts. Some marketing information systems are complex, while others are simple. All marketing information systems, however, help businesses with *customer relationship management (CRM),* or developing stronger relationships with their customers.

In order to conduct a *market analysis*, data is needed. *Data* are the pieces of information gained through research. There are two types of data—secondary and primary. A **database** is a collection of data that is organized. Most businesses create a database of their customers. They may also have databases for potential customers gained from research on their target markets. Databases are an important part of any marketing information system.

Copyright Goodheart-Willcox Co., Inc.

Secondary Data

Secondary data are information that already exists. Someone has collected the data for other reasons and anyone can use it. For example, the US Census Bureau makes its census data available to the public. This secondary information is available on its website at www.census.gov. Census data can help to find a certain area's demographics and the types of industries there. Review the estimated population changes in Figure 5-4. How might these data affect your decision about where to open a business?

Secondary data are usually inexpensive and easy to find. In some cases, secondary data are free, such as the census data. Many researchers and entrepreneurs review secondary data first. If the information already exists, why go to the time and expense of collecting your own data? It is important to make sure that any secondary data you collect are timely, relevant, and accurate. If secondary data are more than five years old, they may not be useful. Also, when using secondary data, you are not in control of how the data were collected. Basing decisions on improperly collected data can result in poor decisions.

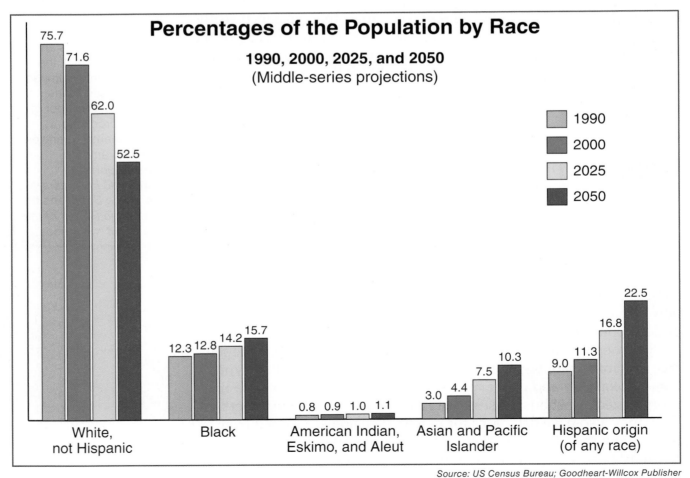

Source: US Census Bureau; Goodheart-Willcox Publisher

Figure 5-4. Census data can be used to identify population trends and shifts.

Copyright Goodheart-Willcox Co., Inc.

You can find secondary data in many places and in many formats. Secondary data are available through the Internet, databases, trade journals, and chambers of commerce. Make sure the data are from expert, reliable sources. Governmental, research-company, academic, and industry-association sources often provide reliable data. Open-source websites that allow many authors may publish inaccurate data.

Governmental Sources

Local, state, and federal governments are great places for free secondary data. Local governments can provide information about taxes, commercial development, schools, and the local demographics. State governments often provide resources for small-business owners and entrepreneurs. The federal government has a number of agencies and databases providing data on everything from population shifts to housing values. Some of these government agencies are shown in Figure 5-5. Export data are also available through the federal government.

Research-Company Sources

Reports are available from companies whose business is conducting research. Many of these companies either charge for the research data on a by-report basis or require a membership fee to access the data. Most companies also publish some of their research data on their websites. This information is not as detailed as the reports that can be purchased, but is often free. Two of the larger, well-known research companies are Dun & Bradstreet and A.C. Nielsen.

Federal Governmental Agencies	
Agency	**Information**
FedWorld	FedWorld is a program of the US Department of Commerce that assists in locating information disseminated by the federal government. It is managed by the National Technical Information Service (NTIS).
US Bureau of Economic Analysis (BEA)	The BEA provides the most current and accurate economic data related to the US economy.
US Bureau of Labor Statistics (BLS)	The BLS measures, collects, and analyzes labor market activity, working conditions, and price changes in the US economy.
US Census Bureau	The Census Bureau shares data about the US economy, businesses, and general population.
US Federal Reserve	Economists at the Federal Reserve Board provide statistics and data on a broad range of economics and finance topics.
USA.gov	USA.gov is a public portal to government information and services. It is administered by a division of the US General Services Administration's Office of Citizen Services and Innovative Technologies.

Goodheart-Willcox Publisher

Figure 5-5. Secondary research gathered from governmental sources is generally reliable.

Copyright Goodheart-Willcox Co., Inc.

Academic Sources

Universities, community colleges, and local libraries can be great resources for secondary data. Libraries house business directories, magazines, and other free resources. You can get help finding databases, governmental reports, and research conducted by the school. Most universities also have small-business organizations on campus that can provide secondary data.

Industry-Association Sources

Industry associations are great resources for entrepreneurs. *Trade publications,* or trade journals, are magazines and newsletters focusing on a specific industry. *Trade associations* have members from a specific industry. Examples of trade associations include the National Retailers Association and the American Translators Association. Both trade publications and trade associations often publish data related to the industries they serve. Industry and trade associations identify and predict trends in the marketplace. Your local chamber of commerce can also provide local demographic data and help you network with potential customers and suppliers.

Primary Data

Primary data are pieces of information collected by you or your organization. This type of data is more costly and time consuming to gather than secondary data. However, it can be much more focused and you have control over how the data are collected.

To collect primary data, the researcher must go to current or potential customers to get the desired information. The most common types of primary research are interviews, surveys, diaries, experiments, and observation. Then the researcher analyzes the raw data to make conclusions. The method used to analyze the data is very important because different methods may lead to different conclusions and business recommendations.

Primary research must be properly conducted for the data to be accurate. For example, researchers may talk to people who are not in the targeted market segment or the sample size may not be large enough. The **sample size** is the number of people in the group from which the data are collected. Statistics prove that responses from a smaller group of people also reflect those of the larger population. However, the sample size must be large enough for the results to be valid for the larger population. Data collected from a too-small sample size cannot provide valid conclusions.

Primary data can be qualitative or quantitative. **Qualitative data** are data that provide insight into what people think about a topic. **Quantitative data** are the facts and figures from which conclusions can be drawn. The information in Figure 5-6 illustrates the differences.

Copyright Goodheart-Willcox Co., Inc.

| Differences Between Qualitative and Quantitative Data ||
Senior Class Qualitative Data	Senior Class Quantitative Data
Community minded	467 members participate in community activities
Lots of school spirit	55% of males and 45% of females attend school functions
Value learning	73% are college-bound; 14% are work-bound; 13% are military-bound

Goodheart-Willcox Publisher

Figure 5-6. Both qualitative and quantitative data are useful for different reasons.

Interviews

An *interview* is a formal meeting between a researcher and an individual to obtain specific information. The researcher asks questions to learn a person's opinions about and reactions to a good, service, or idea. Interviews can take place on the phone, in person, or through web conferences. Interviews are a good way to collect qualitative data.

When interviews are conducted with a group of people, it is called a *focus group.* Focus groups usually consist of six to nine people brought together to discuss a specific topic. The participants are often paid for their time. Focus groups have a moderator who asks questions and keeps the discussion focused. Focus groups are often recorded on video and may also be watched in real time by other researchers. Focus groups are useful for gaining information about products based on interactions between participants.

Surveys

A *survey* is an organized study where participants are asked the same questions. Surveys can be conducted in person, by mail, by phone, or through the Internet. Surveys are a good way to obtain quantitative data.

Surveys can be short and simple or highly structured and request detailed responses. The success of a survey depends on a number of factors. The best surveys ask the right questions, are sent to an appropriate sample size, and get enough responses. The rate of return of surveys will vary depending on the target market segment, but can be only 10 percent or less. The sample size must reflect this in order to receive enough responses that the data can be used to make valid decisions.

The questions on a survey must not be biased or lead respondents to an answer. Questions written as such can lead to inaccurate results. Also, the order of the questions may affect the responses. It is important that the questions be properly written and the order of the questions be considered to obtain accurate data.

Copyright Goodheart-Willcox Co., Inc.

Diaries

A *diary* is a written collection of a person's thoughts, activities, or plans. It can provide a lot of information about the person. You may have been asked to keep a research diary or know someone who has a diary now. Generally, when somebody is asked to keep a diary for research purposes, he or she is asked to record actions or opinions over a specific time period. Diaries are a good way to get information that may not be given in a personal interview. It is easier for some people to write about their thoughts than express them verbally. Diaries can be very valuable research tools. They are not useful in all situations, though. Also, analyzing that much information can be expensive and time consuming.

Some of the most well-known research diaries are those used by A.C. Nielsen to determine television ratings. These diaries are given to a large sample size of households representing various demographics. Household members record the TV programs they watched during a certain period of time. This information is used by networks to keep or cancel programs based on the ratings determined by Nielsen. It is also used to set advertising costs based on how many people are watching different programs.

Experiments

The experiment method of research is much like experiments in your science classes. A situation is created and the results are analyzed. For example, have you ever wondered why children's cereals are always on the lower shelves at the grocery store? Researchers experimented with placing children's cereals on different shelves to determine which placement led to the most sales. The lower shelves were more visible to the children and they chose more cereals from them.

Taste tests are another form of experimental research. Marketers invite consumers to taste several products and rate them. If the marketers want feedback on competitors' products, they may conduct a *blind taste test.* This is when the products are not identified. The information from blind taste tests show true customer preferences based purely on taste and not on brands. This type of taste test is useful when developing new products and in sales efforts.

Observation

Researchers can also learn information by observation. One popular use for the observation method is counting traffic at given times on specific roads. This information can help local businesses plan for their peak hours of operation. In a retail store, different buying behaviors can be recorded for later viewing. This information may lead managers to change where their products are placed.

Copyright Goodheart-Willcox Co., Inc.

Research Process

Research is a key to the success of any business, especially for new businesses. Research helps reduce the risk of opening a business or creating a new product by providing data that can be used to determine what the market wants. Research can be very quick, easy, and inexpensive—or it can take time and be very expensive.

Many entrepreneurs conduct research in an *informal* way. They have a great idea and start asking questions. The answers may help with product design, choosing the right business, or finding a new use for a current product. Informal research can be as simple as watching shoppers at the mall or listening to people talk. The goal is to accurately record what is learned. These notes can help generate ideas for goods or services based on unmet needs.

Research can also be *formal*. A survey may be distributed or a focus group held to test a new product. The type of research used depends on the questions that need to be answered, as shown in Figure 5-7. The formal research process is very similar to the scientific method and includes eight basic steps:

1. Define the problem.
2. Conduct background research.
3. State a hypothesis.
4. Develop a research plan.
5. Collect the data.
6. Analyze the data.
7. Draw conclusions.
8. Make recommendations.

Figure 5-7. Answer these questions before starting your research.

Preresearch Questions

- *Why should I conduct research?* It is important to know the answer to this question. When starting a business, conducting research can help you avoid costly mistakes and save time.

- *What research is needed?* Is your research going to help you determine what type of business to start? Or is it about the product(s) you plan to sell?

- *Is the research worth doing?* As an entrepreneur, determine if the research is worth the cost and the time. Is the problem big enough to warrant research?

- *How should the research be designed?* Is there enough secondary data available, or will you need to collect primary data? If you need to collect primary data, which method is best?

- *How will I use the research?* The raw data you gather from research must be analyzed or it will not help you. What will you do with the information you learn? Any conclusions will form the basis of an action plan.

Goodheart-Willcox Publisher

Define the Problem

The first step in market research starts with defining the problem or situation. If there were no problems or unanswered questions, research would be unnecessary. For this entrepreneurship class, the problem is identifying the type of business you want to create. One of the main reasons to do market research is to ensure that money is spent wisely by starting a profitable venture. In order to define the problem as clearly as possible, answer questions such as:

- Where should I locate the business?

- What goods or services should I sell?

- What are the demographic characteristics of customers who will want to purchase my products?

There are many more questions to answer as your research continues.

Conduct Background Research

Learn more about the problem you identified in step 1. In this class, the problem, or challenge, is to create a new business. A logical place to start is finding other entrepreneurs who have solved similar problems. Personal interviews with people who started a business like yours are helpful. You can also conduct Internet research to find out all you can about the owners and their businesses. Find out how the business was financed, how the location was selected, and which promotions worked well. Find out anything that could help in understanding the challenge and move the business forward.

Green Entrepreneurs

Cleaning Electronic Equipment

A variety of electronic equipment, such as computers, cell phones, and other tools are necessary to enable a business to run efficiently. Care must be taken to keep equipment clean and maintained on a regular basis. Avoid chemical cleaners when removing the smudge marks from an LCD or TV screen or a computer monitor. Chemical cleaners may ruin some equipment finishes, and some are bad for the environment. Look for environmentally friendly cleaners that will not harm equipment to protect your investment as well as the environment.

Copyright Goodheart-Willcox Co., Inc.

State a Hypothesis

A **hypothesis** is a statement that can be tested and proved either true or false. Research is conducted to either confirm a hypothesis or disprove it. Create a hypothesis to test your business idea to make sure it is worth pursuing. For example, if you want to sell red T-shirts, the hypothesis may be: "Customers buy red T-shirts because the color red makes them feel happy." It is a good idea to test this idea to know if it is true before starting a business.

Develop a Research Plan

A **research plan** includes the specific steps to take for testing your hypothesis. Will you use secondary research, conduct primary research, or both? If you will use secondary research, the type of data and where it can be found must be identified. If primary research is needed, the collection method will need to be determined. An estimate of the cost should also be worked up before starting the research.

Data analysis will lead to conclusions about your potential customers.

Goodluz/Shutterstock.com

Copyright Goodheart-Willcox Co., Inc.

Focus on Finance

File Backups

Owning a business means that you will have many important documents and papers that must be protected from theft or fire. Any documents on your computer should be regularly backed up on an external hard drive, disk, or jump drive. Store the backups outside of your business in a safe place. Consider renting a safe deposit box at your bank to store backups of your documents. You may also consider buying space through an Internet provider to back up your files on a vendor's system. Failure to protect your records could be a costly mistake.

Collect the Data

As an entrepreneur, you may collect many types of data. It may be data about new opportunities, potential customers, trends, competition, and pricing, to name just a few. Depending on the information needed, you may collect primary or secondary data.

Analyze the Data

Raw data, by itself, is useless unless something is done with it. Analyzing the data helps draw conclusions about the hypothesis and to make sound business decisions. **Data analysis** involves studying raw data to find patterns and organizing the data into graphs and charts. You may choose to do this manually or through a software program. New data may also be compared to the data from previous studies. Remember, a market can be segmented in many different ways.

The amount of data collected in step 5 may be overwhelming. **Data mining** is the practice of searching through large amounts of computerized data to find useful patterns or trends. **Statistical analysis** is a mathematical technique for analyzing the collected data. All data must be analyzed and then interpreted to help make decisions about the business.

Draw Conclusions

The research has been conducted and the data analyzed. Based on the analysis, conclusions can be made. If "Customers buy red T-shirts because the color red makes them happy" was your hypothesis, did the data confirm or disprove it? If your research was not conclusive, start the process over with a different hypothesis.

FYI

Businesses may also use *web mining* as a market research tool. This is a process of using data mining on websites to find user viewing patterns. Knowing what a customer is viewing on a website helps a business to customize the information shown to each customer. However, some people look at web mining as invasion of privacy.

Copyright Goodheart-Willcox Co., Inc.

If the data confirmed the hypothesis, you may decide to move forward with producing or selling red T-shirts. However, there may be more research required. For example, is it important to customers to be happy? If not, then basing a decision to sell red T-shirts based on the data supporting the hypothesis may not be a good decision.

Make Recommendations

Based on research findings, you have reached a conclusion about starting a business. This information should be recorded in the marketing evaluation section of the business plan. Now you are ready to make recommendations in the business plan.

Section 5.2 | Review

Check Your Understanding ↗

1. What does market research help to accomplish?
2. Identify sources of secondary data. Why do many researchers and entrepreneurs use secondary data first?
3. Name three sources of primary data.
4. Explain the difference between qualitative and quantitative data.
5. List the steps in the formal research process.

Build Your Vocabulary ↗

As you progress through this text, develop a personal glossary of key terms. This will help you build your vocabulary and prepare you for a career. Write a definition for each of the following terms and add them to your personal glossary.

market research
marketing information system
database
secondary data
primary data
sample size
qualitative data
quantitative data
hypothesis
research plan
data analysis
data mining
statistical analysis

Copyright Goodheart-Willcox Co., Inc.

Research the Competition

Essential Question

How does a business analyze its competition?

Objectives

After completing this section, you will be able to:

- **Differentiate** between direct and indirect competition.
- **Explain** how to create a competitive analysis.
- **Describe** the components of a SWOT analysis.

Key Terms

direct competitors
indirect competitors
competitive advantage
unique selling proposition (USP)

price competition
nonprice competition
SWOT analysis

Critical Thinking

Identify the direct and indirect competitors for your new business. Explain your competitive advantage over each one.

Identify the Competition

Competition is the heart of a *market economy*. Individuals are free to create businesses and compete for customers. As an entrepreneur, you will have competitors and also be a competitor. It is just as important to research your competitors and how they operate as it is to research your target markets. Resources to research your competition include industry and association publications, Internet search results, and even word of mouth from customers and suppliers. According to the research process, the first step is to define the problem, which is identifying all competitors. These will include both direct competitors and indirect competitors.

Direct competitors are companies that sell goods or services identical or very similar to the ones you sell. For example, if you provide car maintenance and repair services, there are other companies providing the same services. The businesses directly compete.

Indirect competitors offer different, but similar, goods or services that could also meet customer needs. The products sold by indirect competitors could actually substitute for your products. For example, if your business sells fruit smoothies, an indirect competitor may be a store selling frozen yogurt. The businesses compete, but not directly.

FYI

Market research can provide valuable insight to help you reduce business risks, spot current and upcoming problems in the current market, as well as identify sales opportunities.

Copyright Goodheart-Willcox Co., Inc.

Create a Competitive Analysis

In order to sell a product, a competitive advantage over similar businesses is necessary. A **competitive advantage** is giving customers greater value, better products, or something not offered by the competition. The competitive advantage is the answer to the question: "Why would customers want to buy from this business instead of from a competitor?"

One marketing strategy to increase business is to use the business' unique selling proposition in all promotions and sales efforts. A **unique selling proposition (USP)** is a statement that lists a business' or product's special features or benefits that highlight its competitive advantage. It explains why customers should purchase goods or services from your company rather than from the competition. An example of a USP might be, "XYZ Company's lawn services are guaranteed to be the lowest in the area—or your money back." A USP may be based on price as well as nonprice factors.

Price competition occurs when price is the main reason for customers to buy from one business over another. For example, many gas stations compete through their pricing. Some customers buy on price alone. However, others think it is not worth driving around to find the lowest price.

Features and benefits are what set a product apart in nonprice competition.

Robert Kneschke/Shutterstock.com

Copyright Goodheart-Willcox Co., Inc.

Nonprice competition is based on the features and benefits of a good or service, not the price. *Features* are facts about a good or service, but *benefits* are the reasons it will make customers' lives better. For example, "our shampoo with conditioner makes your hair shiny and manageable in half the time." The feature is that the shampoo has a conditioner. The benefit is getting shiny, manageable hair in half the normal time. The customer immediately understands why he or she should use the product. Other nonprice features may include extended hours, free shipping, packaging, or customized ordering. The benefits of these services are that they make the consumers' lives easier and save their time.

Social Entrepreneurs

Peter Samuelson

Peter Samuelson is a television and film producer who is a long-time social entrepreneur. In 1982, he and his cousin, actress Emma Samms, created Starlight Children's Foundation to help grant wishes to seriously ill children. Then in 2005, while riding his bicycle on his regular trip from his Southern California home to the beach, he counted about sixty homeless people. Over the next three weeks, he began interviewing homeless people, including a woman who slept in a refrigerator box. Samuelson realized he had a refrigerator and she had a refrigerator box. He envisioned a collapsible mobile cart covered by a weather-resistant tarp that could provide shelter and dignity for homeless people. Samuelson sponsored a contest at an art school to create the design and worked with a shopping cart fabricator to manufacture it. In 2007, the creation known as EDAR, which stands for *everyone deserves a roof,* became a reality.

 # You Do the Math   Connections

The margin of error is an allowance permitted to account for changes in circumstances or miscalculations. Margin of error is commonly seen in surveys used in market research, but may also be applied to calculations to allow for rounding errors. For example, a political survey may compare the percentage of voters favoring one candidate over another. These surveys, called polls, almost always state a margin of error, such as ±3 percent. In this case, the margin of error means the stated percentages may be 3 percent too high or too low.

Solve the following problems.

1. A business calculates its weekly expenses as $12,054 with a margin of error of ±2.5 percent. What is the *maximum* the weekly expenses should be?

2. A market survey finds that 45.6 percent of American households will purchase a new smart TV in the next year. The survey has a margin of error of ±8 percent. When estimating how many smart TVs will be sold, what is the *lowest* percentage of households that can be assumed to make this purchase within the next year?

Copyright Goodheart-Willcox Co., Inc.

It is important to analyze competing companies and determine how to best compete with each one. As information is gathered about the competitors, keep it on a spreadsheet to easily see how they compare to your business. This will also help to decide how to market the business based on your USP. First, list the important features and benefits. These will include both price and nonprice factors. Next, list each direct competitor and describe their features or benefits in each category. This is the *competitive analysis* and is included in the competition section of the business plan. Figure 5-8 shows a partial competitive analysis for the company RetroAttire.

Create a SWOT Analysis

After analyzing the competition, it is time to conduct a SWOT analysis of your company and its products. A **SWOT analysis** helps a company decide its *strengths, weaknesses, opportunities,* and *threats.* This helps to decide if a business is competitive and ready for the marketplace.

- **Strengths**—internal factors that give your company a competitive advantage

- **Weaknesses**—internal factors that place your company at a disadvantage relative to competitors

- **Opportunities**—external factors that provide chances for your company to increase profits

- **Threats**—external factors that threaten your company's growth or ability to make profits

Competitive Analysis				
Variables	**RetroAttire**	**Costello**	**80s Tees**	**Back in Time**
price	$18–$30 with daily specials	$14–$20	$16–$20	$23–$30
material	100 percent cotton	50/50 blend	100 percent cotton	50/50 blend
sizes	Adult S–XXL	Adult S–XXL	Youth S–Adult XXL	Adult S–XXXXL
design	All unique, offered nowhere else	Common	Common	Common, with some unique designs
customizable	Yes	No	No	No
shipping	$0	$4–$6	$5.00 flat fee	$2.99

Goodheart-Willcox Publisher

Figure 5-8. Choose the relevant variables in your business, and then choose your top competitors to analyze.

Copyright Goodheart-Willcox Co., Inc.

A SWOT analysis should become the basis for a plan of action. Why create one if you will not take the necessary actions to take advantage of your strengths and opportunities? A SWOT analysis will also help you determine how to minimize external threats and shore up any weaknesses. An example of a SWOT analysis for the company RetroAttire is shown in Figure 5-9.

RetroAttire SWOT Analysis			
Strengths	**Weaknesses**	**Opportunities**	**Threats**
Unique retro iron-on and custom designs	Products are slightly more expensive than large retailers because they are customized	Build a brick-and-mortar store in two years	Fierce price competition from lower-end online businesses
Involved in supporting local charities and other causes	Local presence only	Focus on brand awareness, including creating a private label	Recession impacting customer to choose price over quality
Advisory board representing local sports teams, high schools, colleges	Lacking promotional plan	Find new markets including local businesses and other organizations	Continued growth of online retail clothing stores
Competitive pricing; ships within 24 hours	Current inventory limited	Expand product line and customization options	

Goodheart-Willcox Publisher

Figure 5-9. An example of a SWOT analysis.

Section 5.3　Review

Check Your Understanding 🔗

1. Explain and give an example of indirect competition.
2. What information is included in a competitive analysis?
3. What is a unique selling proposition (USP)? On what two factors might it be based?
4. What is the difference between a product's features and its benefits?
5. Explain the components of a SWOT analysis.

Build Your Vocabulary 🔗

As you progress through this text, develop a personal glossary of key terms. This will help you build your vocabulary and prepare you for a career. Write a definition for each of the following terms and add them to your personal glossary.

　direct competitors
　indirect competitors
　competitive advantage
　unique selling proposition (USP)
　price competition
　nonprice competition
　SWOT analysis

Copyright Goodheart-Willcox Co., Inc.

Chapter Summary

Section 5.1 Target Market

- Identifying a target market, along with its needs and wants, is the first step to determine who is most likely to become a customer.
- Four variables that help with market segmentation are geographic, demographic, psychographic, and behavioral variables.
- A customer profile, which is a description of the people in a business' target market, will help with promotion strategies.

Section 5.2 Do the Research

- Market research helps determine primary customers, identify growth opportunities, and learn about the competition.
- A marketing information system is created through the analysis of primary and secondary data. Primary data is collected by you and can be more focused than secondary data. Secondary data is information that already exists and can be used by anyone.
- Conducting formal research is an eight-step process. It begins with defining the problem and ends with making recommendations based on research findings.

Section 5.3 Research the Competition

- Identifying the competition includes both direct and indirect competitors. Direct competitors sell identical or similar products, while the products of indirect competitors may be suitable substitutes.
- Competitive advantage explains why customers would buy a product from one business over another. By analyzing the competition, a business can determine how to market itself and its product.
- A SWOT analysis determines the business' strengths, weaknesses, opportunities, and threats.

Online Activities

Complete the following activities to help you learn, practice, and expand your knowledge and skills.

Posttest. Now that you have finished the chapter, see what you learned by taking the chapter posttest.

Key Terms. Practice vocabulary for this chapter using the e-flash cards, matching activity, and vocabulary game until you are able to recognize their meanings.

Copyright Goodheart-Willcox Co., Inc.

Review Your Knowledge

1. What is the difference between a mass market and market segmentation?
2. Discuss the process of market segmentation.
3. What is the difference between geographic segmentation and demographic segmentation?
4. Explain a customer profile and why it is important.
5. Is market research always correct? Explain the relationship between the quality of market research and its outcome.
6. Discuss each of the steps involved in market research.
7. What is the difference between primary data and secondary data?
8. Explain the difference between direct and indirect competitors.
9. Explain the difference between price competition and nonprice competition.
10. What does a SWOT analysis accomplish? Why is it important?

Apply Your Knowledge

1. In earlier chapters, you identified the good or service you are creating in your business plan. Which demographic factors will you use to identify your target market?
2. Which geographic, psychographic, and behavioral factors will you use to identify your target market?
3. Identify the benefits of marketing research for your business. How can market research be used to identify potential markets and analyze demand for your product?
4. How can market research be used to identify and predict trends in the marketplace for your potential business? Why is trend-spotting important for you to understand as a business owner?
5. Who will your customer be for your new business? Write what you think would be an accurate customer profile for your product.

Copyright Goodheart-Willcox Co., Inc.

6. As you do research for your company, you will follow the research process. Write a hypothesis statement for your business that you will use in your research.

7. One way to collect data is to use a survey tool for your customers to give feedback. Develop a survey that you might use for your business to find out what types of products your customers need or want. The results of this market research can be used to analyze demand.

8. List three businesses that could be direct competitors to your company.

9. Make a list of the nonprice competitive factors for your product.

10. Select a local entrepreneur in your community. Based on what you know about the company and what is available on their website, create a SWOT analysis.

Teamwork

Working with your team, identify an entrepreneurial business in your community. Create a target customer profile for that customer's business. Use each of the four marketing segment variables. Share your profile with your class.

Internet Research

Limitations of Research. The results of market research are only as good as the research itself. Conduct an Internet search for *limitations of market research*. Read several articles on the topic. Based on the information you have read, create a checklist of criteria you can use in future market research projects. Write a brief summary of how the items in your checklist will improve your market research process.

Collecting Market Information. There are many ways that technology can be used to collect market information on the industry, customers, and competition. For example, e-mail, social media, and apps are used for both marketing campaigns and to gather market information. Use the Internet to research how technology can be used to gather information about your industry, customers, and competition. Summarize your findings and include specific examples.

Communication Skills

College and Career Readiness

Reading. Locate different business plans and read them to note the similarities. Identify sections of the business plans that are unique and creative. After reading, be prepared to present your findings to your class.

Writing. Write a two- to three-page report on why businesses fail. Explain how you will make sure your business does not experience the same problems.

CTSOs

Case Study Presentation. A case study presentation may be part of a Career and Technical Student Organization (CTSO) competitive event. There may be two parts to this event: the objective test and a performance portion of the case.

The activity may be an entrepreneur decision-making scenario from which your team will provide a solution. You will be presented with a case situation in which issues must be addressed that entrepreneurs face in business. The presentation will be interactive with the judges.

To prepare for this event, complete the following activities.

1. Read the guidelines provided by your CTSO. Make certain that you ask any questions about points you do not understand. It is important you follow each specific item that is outlined in the competition rules.

2. Conduct an Internet search for "entrepreneur case studies." Your team should select a case that seems appropriate to use as a practice activity. Look for a case that is no more than a page long. Read the case and discuss it with your team members. What are the important points of the case?

3. Make notes on index cards about important points to remember. Team members should exchange note cards so that each evaluates the other person's notes. Use these notes to study. You may also be able to use these notes during the event.

4. Complete the team activities at the end of each chapter in this text. This will help members learn how to interact with each other and participate effectively.

5. Assign each team member a role for the presentation. Practice performing as a team. Each team member should introduce himself or herself, review the case, make suggestions for the case, and conclude with a summary.

6. Ask your teacher to play the role of competition judge as your team reviews the case. After the presentation is complete, ask for feedback from your teacher. You may consider also having a student audience to listen and give feedback.

Copyright Goodheart-Willcox Co., Inc.

Building Your Business Plan—Putting the Puzzle Together

Research the Market

Market research will help to target your customer, identify opportunities for business growth, and learn about the competition. It will help to identify potential new markets, forecast sales, and make promotional decisions. Following the research process correctly provides more reliable results to help you make better business decisions.

Goals

- Identify your target market(s).
- Conduct primary and secondary research to segment your market.
- Create a competitive analysis for your business.
- Create business plan notes.

Directions

Access the *Entrepreneurship* companion website at www.g-wlearning.com ➡. Download each data file for the following activities. A complete sample business plan is available on the companion website to use as a reference. The name of the file is BusPlan_Sample.RetroAttire.docx.

Preparation

It is time to determine who your target market is. Your research may lead you to rethink the business model or the goods and services you plan to offer. Most entrepreneurs revise their business idea many times before presenting a business plan to a loan officer or potential investors.

Activity 5-1. Target Market. Based on the products you plan to offer, describe your target market. Who do you think will be the people or businesses most likely to buy from your business?

Activity 5-2. Market Research. To conduct a market analysis, gather secondary or primary research about your industry, potential business, or products. Use your market research to identify potential markets and analyze demand. Then, segment the market based on your data and create a customer profile.

Activity 5-3. Competitive Analysis. Determine your direct competitors and research their offerings. Create a competitive analysis for your business to help you identify its competitive advantage.

Activity 5-4. SWOT Analysis. Create a SWOT analysis to identify your business' strengths, weaknesses, opportunities, and threats.

Activity 5-5. Business Plan Notes. Create notes about the market research that you conducted. Record your primary and secondary resources.

Business Plan—Market Evaluation

In this chapter, you learned about the importance of research to the success of any business. The results of your research will affect your business decisions. Use your research data to describe your target market and analyze your competitors.

1. Open your saved business plan document.
2. Locate the Market Evaluation section of the plan. Begin writing the following subsections: Industry Conditions, Target Market, and Competition.
3. Make a note in each of these sections for any additional documents that will be included in the Appendices. Use the questions and suggestions listed in the sections to help you generate ideas. Delete the instructions and questions when you are finished recording your responses in each section. Make sure to proofread your document and correct any errors in keyboarding, spelling, and grammar.
4. Save your document.

6 Business Ownership

What do Jacob's Pharmacy and one of the world's best-known corporations have in common? In 1886, a pharmacist from Georgia, Dr. John Pemberton, created a syrup and took a gallon of it to Jacob's Pharmacy in Atlanta where it was mixed with soda water. The drink was said to be "delicious and refreshing." Pemberton formed a partnership with Frank Robinson, who created the name Coca-Cola and designed the famous script logo. That partnership eventually turned into a corporation, The Coca-Cola Company. Many small businesses start out as one type of business ownership and change to another. Like Dr. Pemberton, you have done your own research and know the product you want to sell. What type of legal ownership do you want: proprietorship, partnership, or corporation?

"There will come a time when big opportunities are presented to you, and you've got to be in a position to take advantage of them."

—Sam Walton, founder of Wal-Mart Stores, Inc.

College and Career Readiness

Reading Prep. In preparation for reading the chapter, read a newspaper or magazine article on the Great Recession and small businesses. As you read, keep in mind the author's main points and conclusions.

Sections

6.1 Start Your Business

6.2 Types of Business Ownership

Picture Yourself Here
David Graff

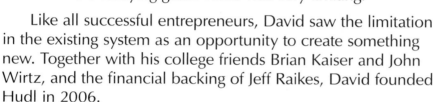

David Graff worked as a student assistant in the sports information department while earning his master's degree from the University of Nebraska-Lincoln (UNL). While at UNL, he realized the way coaches were studying game video was very limiting.

Like all successful entrepreneurs, David saw the limitation in the existing system as an opportunity to create something new. Together with his college friends Brian Kaiser and John Wirtz, and the financial backing of Jeff Raikes, David founded Hudl in 2006.

Hudl is an Internet-based system allowing coaches to upload and analyze their game video on the Internet and share that video out to their athletes. Users can then make annotations on the video in the form of text, audio commentary, or telestrator-style drawings.

Hudl can be used by coaches and players in 20 different sports. In addition, the system is used by teams from the youth level to the NFL. In 2010, David and his Hudl cofounders were listed in *Inc.* magazine's 30 Under 30 young entrepreneurs issue.

Photo © Kyle Murphy, HUDL VP User Experience

Check Your Entrepreneurship IQ

Before you begin the chapter, see what you already know about entrepreneurship by taking the chapter pretest. The pretest is available at
www.g-wlearning.com

Start Your Business

Essential Question

What are some start-up strategies an entrepreneur can use when starting a new business?

Objectives

After completing this section, you will be able to:

- **Describe** strategies and considerations for starting a new business.
- **Identify** advantages and disadvantages of purchasing a franchise.
- **Summarize** advantages and disadvantages of purchasing an existing business.
- **Discuss** the pros and cons of entering into a family business.

Key Terms

Federal Trade Commission (FTC)
International Franchise Association (IFA)
franchise disclosure document
royalty payment
capital

Critical Thinking

There are several ways for entrepreneurs to start their own businesses. Think about your new business. What would be the best way for you to start your business? Why?

Start-Up Strategies

Your business plan is starting to take shape. You have decided on the good or service you will offer and whether your company is a service, retail, or manufacturing business. The next step in the planning process is to consider a start-up strategy. Will you start a new business, purchase a franchise, buy an existing business, or join a family business?

Each start-up strategy has its pros and cons, and you will need to carefully evaluate the options. This is an important business decision and is included in the operations section of the business plan. Consider seeking legal counsel or other professional advice to help guide you in making a decision.

If you are buying or joining an existing business, take the following steps.

- Do your research.

- Establish the value of the business.

Copyright Goodheart-Willcox Co., Inc.

- Review the laws.

- Get help from the professionals.

Once you sign on the dotted line, there is no turning back. Ask questions before taking the final leap.

Review past sales records, talk with customers, and talk with current employees. Investigate the owner or parent company to learn as much as you can about the business.

Hire a professional to appraise the value of the business if it already exists. It is important to know what the business is worth before you agree to a purchase price.

There are many rules and regulations that business owners must follow. Check with local, state, and national agencies to understand all laws applying to the business and industry.

If you buy a business or franchise, or even enter a family business, you should seek legal help to finalize ownership. The attorney you hire will make sure all agreements protect your interests. An accountant can help make sure all of the finances are in order.

Start a New Business

One way to become an entrepreneur is to start a business from the ground up with a new idea. Starting a new business from the ground up can be more challenging than buying a franchise, buying an existing business, or joining a family business. You must establish your new product in the marketplace and carefully plan finances to support the new business venture.

Advantages of New Businesses

Starting a new business from the ground up could mean that your product is new and unique in the market. You may own the copyright or trademark, which can translate into profits. As the owner, you can set the guidelines by which the company operates and make decisions on your own. There are no ongoing fees as with a franchise business and no expectations that come with an existing business.

Disadvantages of New Businesses

Starting a new company from the ground up means there is no history or experience from which to draw. Many business decisions will be based on trial and error. All responsibilities related to the business and operations lie solely with the owner.

Copyright Goodheart-Willcox Co., Inc.

Franchises

A *franchise* is a legal agreement granting the right to sell a company's goods or services in a particular geographic area. Finding the right franchise opportunity requires research. Take advantage of the many resources available to help identify franchises that may fit your business needs. Investigate the franchisor and its record of performance and operation. Ask for the company's tax records and information about the management. Contact existing franchisees and ask if their experience with the franchisor has been satisfactory.

Learn about the support and training provided to franchisees. The franchisor should provide competitive and marketing information and list the sources for the information. Use an attorney to review the agreement and any other important information before making a commitment.

All businesses are monitored by the **Federal Trade Commission (FTC)**, which is the federal governmental department dedicated to consumer protection. The **International Franchise Association (IFA)** is the organization that regulates the franchising industry.

Buying a Franchise

The process of buying a franchise begins with completing a franchise application. The franchisor will run a credit check, confirm your bank account balances, and verify other information provided on the application. After the application is approved, you will receive a franchise disclosure document. The **franchise disclosure document** is a legal document that includes detailed information that a franchisee must know before purchasing a franchise. The law requires that prospective buyers receive this document 14 days before signing an agreement. In 2008, this document replaced the *uniform franchise offering circular*.

Before purchasing a franchise, seek legal help to understand state, local, and national laws governing franchises. The FTC's Franchise Rule Compliance Guide provides information on these laws. Numerous resources are also available from the IFA, SBA, US Department of Commerce, and other organizations to help make a decision.

Advantages of Franchises

Franchises are available in every business sector—from those providing services to those selling food or products. There are many advantages to buying a franchise rather than starting a new company and creating your own brand. The following sections discuss only a few advantages of purchasing a franchise. When researching franchises, you may find other appealing advantages.

FYI

One of the earliest examples of a franchise was the Singer sewing machine in the 1850s. After inventing his machine, Isaac Singer wanted to distribute his sewing machines across the country. In order to do that, he sold licenses to individuals in other parts of the country giving them the right to sell Singer sewing machines.

Copyright Goodheart-Willcox Co., Inc.

wavebreakmedia/Shutterstock.com

Franchise businesses exist in several industries, from health clubs to restaurants.

Established Company

When purchasing a franchise, you are buying the rights to an established image and brand. Customers will come to your business because of the name recognition. Hopefully, the franchise has a positive reputation in your community; this is something you should research.

Training

The franchisor will provide training so you will run the business according to their rules. This can include customer service, management, and employee training. You will learn how to run the business from people who have experience in the organization.

Financial Advice

Many small business owners are challenged with securing financing and maintaining financial records. Most franchises have programs to coach franchisees on how to obtain financing and manage the financial aspects of their businesses.

Copyright Goodheart-Willcox Co., Inc.

Lower Failure Rate

If the franchise is a secure business, the chances for success increase. You will need to research the franchise to ensure it is secure before entering into an agreement. With the support of the parent company, a franchise should be able to maintain a profitable business. Your success as a franchisee is in the franchisor's best interests.

Disadvantages of Franchises

While owning a franchise has its advantages, also be aware of the disadvantages. Franchises are expensive and have strict rules of operation. Depending on the opportunity, a franchise may be an unwise choice.

High Start-Up Costs

Many franchisors demand a large initial franchise fee for the right to sell their brand. It is not unusual for a total initial investment to run between $500,000 and $1,000,000. In addition, many franchisees are usually charged a *grand opening* fee to promote the new business.

TK Kurikawa/Shutterstock.com

Some franchises are expensive to start, but come with the support of a large company.

Copyright Goodheart-Willcox Co., Inc.

Though a franchisee must pay advertising fees, national ad campaigns will benefit the business.

Northfoto/Shutterstock.com

Royalty Payments

A **royalty payment** is the fee that franchisees must continually pay the franchisor to keep operating the franchise. These fees may be due monthly or quarterly. Many franchisors calculate royalty payments based on a percentage of total revenue or store size. The royalty payment may also be a fixed sum and expected even if the franchise is not earning income. If you end the franchise agreement early, you may still owe the remaining royalty payments through the end of the agreement. This is another important reason to fully understand a franchise agreement before signing.

Franchisor's Rules and Regulations

Franchisors have strict rules and regulations to protect their brands. You may not agree with these rules, but you are bound to follow them after signing the franchise agreement.

If buying a business or a franchise, it is important to perform your due diligence before committing to the purchase. *Due diligence* is the careful, thorough evaluation of a potential investment. This may include reviewing the business' financial statements, its intellectual property, market potential, or environmental issues, among other things.

Copyright Goodheart-Willcox Co., Inc.

Limited Goods or Services

Selling goods or services of a well-known brand can help the business get off to a great start. However, you can only sell what the franchisor dictates. This limit may not fit in with your plans for the business.

Advertising Fees

Franchisees may be required to pay into a national advertising fund. However, franchisees usually have no say in how the fees are used. Part of the advertising fees helps buy national advertising that benefits your business. The franchisor may also use the advertising fees to attract new franchise owners, which does not benefit your business at all.

Existing Businesses

In some cases, purchasing an existing business can be less risky than starting a new business. Much depends on the financial state of the business and how well it was managed by the owners. If you are considering purchasing an existing business, perform the necessary research to determine if it is a sound investment.

Advantages of Buying an Existing Business

Buying an existing business may help you earn profits faster than other start-up options. Existing businesses have a history of sales, an established customer base, and employees and processes in place. It should also already have a business plan. You may need to adjust the plan to meet your goals, but a company history is valuable when setting new goals. There are many advantages to buying an existing business.

Focus on Finance

Charitable Contributions

A *charitable contribution* is a donation of money or other asset to a nonprofit organization. Charitable contributions to registered nonprofit organizations are tax deductible and decrease the amount of taxes owed on a tax return. However, if donating money for an activity, read the details. There are occasions when only a percentage of the donation is tax deductible. Receipts to prove the donation are required by the IRS to claim a donation as a tax deduction. When making a donation, research the organization to make sure it is reputable and qualifies as a nonprofit organization. Making charitable contributions as an individual or company is good business.

Copyright Goodheart-Willcox Co., Inc.

Profits

Taking over an operation that is already generating a profit is a great way to start. Existing brand recognition and experienced employees can contribute to continued profits. In addition, you have purchased the business' goodwill, which is a valuable asset.

Location

Buying a business may mean continuing to operate in its current location. This saves time and money in trying to lease or purchase a place to run your business. You may eventually change locations, but the initial task of finding a storefront is eliminated.

Financing

It may be easier to secure financing when buying an existing business. Banks feel safer lending to a business with an established financial history and a positive track record. This may make the process of obtaining financing easier and faster.

Patents or Copyrights

Depending on the business, you may also be acquiring valuable legal rights, such as patents or copyrights. These legal rights give you exclusive ownership of the product or process. This can be a marketable advantage. Owning such rights may help the business be profitable today and in the future.

Disadvantages of Buying an Existing Business

There can be disadvantages to buying an existing business. Do your research to find out as much about the business as possible. If buying an existing business is an interesting option, investigate any potential disadvantages before making a commitment. Some disadvantages are discussed in the next sections.

Purchase Price

It may be more expensive to purchase an existing business than to start a new one. Prosperous businesses are worth more than businesses that are struggling. Businesses that are struggling may cost less, but be sure to find out why the business is struggling before buying it. You may be able to correct the problem, but the problem may not be fixable. Seek professional help to accurately estimate the business' value before negotiating the price.

SBA Tips

The SBA's Office of Advocacy was created by Congress in 1976. One of the office's missions includes conducting economic research on issues that concern small businesses. The office publishes data on characteristics of small firms and their contributions to the economy. www.sba.gov

Copyright Goodheart-Willcox Co., Inc.

Obsolete Inventory, Equipment, or Processes

When buying a business, you are also buying its problems. This can include products that are too old to sell, equipment that is inefficient or in need of repair, and processes that are not up to current industry standards. Additionally, when you buy a business, the employees come with it along with any workforce issues associated with them. Carefully analyze the business to recognize any issues that may cause problems. Make sure the issues can be resolved before buying the business.

Reluctant Partners

When buying a business, you may actually be buying out one of the partners in the business. The other partners may remain in the business. This may lead to conflict between them and you. Determine if you can work with any remaining partners before making a decision to move forward with the purchase.

Family Businesses

What do Mars, SC Johnson and Son, Kohler, and Enterprise Rent-A-Car have in common? According to *Forbes* magazine, they are some of the largest family-owned companies in the United States. When you think of a family-owned business, you may envision the small family businesses in your local community. That is how most family businesses begin, and some grow into very large companies.

Advantages of a Family Business

Does a member of your family own a business? It could be your parents, a sibling, or even an aunt or uncle. Have you considered joining that business? There are similar advantages to joining a family business as to buying an existing business. However, family businesses may be even more attractive. There are many advantages to a family business, and those listed in the next sections are just a few. If you decide to join an already-established family business, you may find many more reasons to do so.

Success

Family members are generally committed to both the short- and long-term success of the family business. The support of the family helps the business enjoy the good times and get through the not-so-good times.

Entrepreneur Ethics

Employers who hire children to work in their business must follow the US Department of Labor rules. Employers are not exempt from the labor laws when hiring their own children to work in their businesses. It is unethical, and sometimes illegal, to violate the number of hours per day that a child may legally work even if he or she is a family member.

Copyright Goodheart-Willcox Co., Inc.

mangostock/Shutterstock.com

Joining a family-owned business may have personal and financial benefits.

Capital Investment

Capital is the money and other assets owned by a business or person. By joining an existing family business, the initial *capital investment* has already been made. However, if you join the company, you may be asked to make an investment in the business.

Flexibility

The family is likely to work as a very close team. The family team may allow flexibility in hours and days worked. When you are away from the business, other members of the family team can fill in for you.

Disadvantages of a Family Business

Working with and reporting to family members can have its disadvantages. There can be disagreements within the family. In some cases, not every family member shares the same work ethic. Also, there can be conflicting interests between family members, just as between business partners.

Copyright Goodheart-Willcox Co., Inc.

Family Member Disagreements

When working with your family, you may not always have an equal vote in some situations. There may be one family member who makes the final decisions about the business. Personal disagreements between family members can cause relationship problems and have a negative impact on the business.

Family Member Responsibilities

Sometimes a family member who joins the business does not have the right skill set to be successful. If a family member is not performing at an acceptable level, it may be difficult to either correct the behavior or fire him or her. While that person may end up leaving the business, he or she will never leave the family. This can put stress on the family and cause resentment.

Conflicting Interests

The interests of some family members may be in direct conflict with others. For example, one family member may want to expand the business, while another refuses. It can be difficult to get family members to compromise so business can move forward.

There are several types of business ownership—the choice is up to you.

michaeljung/Shutterstock.com

Copyright Goodheart-Willcox Co., Inc.

Section 6.1   Review

Check Your Understanding ⤷

1. What steps should an entrepreneur take if buying or joining an existing business?
2. What are the advantages of buying a franchise?
3. List the advantages of buying an existing business.
4. Identify the advantages of buying a family business.
5. What are some of the disadvantages of a family business?

Build Your Vocabulary ⤷

As you progress through this text, develop a personal glossary of key terms. This will help you build your vocabulary and prepare you for a career. Write a definition for each of the following terms and add them to your personal glossary.

Federal Trade Commission (FTC)
International Franchise Association (IFA)
franchise disclosure document
royalty payment
capital

Copyright Goodheart-Willcox Co., Inc.

Types of Business Ownership

Essential Question

What should entrepreneurs consider when choosing a form of business ownership?

Objectives

After completing this section, you will be able to:

- **Describe** how to create a sole proprietorship.
- **Discuss** the advantages and disadvantages of partnerships.
- **Summarize** the different types of corporations.
- **Give examples** of two alternative forms of business ownership.

Key Terms

sole proprietor
DBA license
liability
partnership
limited partnership (LP)
silent partner
corporation
contract
charter

stock
stockholders
private corporation
public corporation
C corporation
subchapter S corporation
nonprofit corporation
corporate formalities

Critical Thinking

Research the different forms of business ownership. Create a list of advantages and disadvantages for each. Does this exercise help you make a decision on the type of ownership to choose?

Sole Proprietorship

A **sole proprietor** is the person who owns the business and is personally responsible for its debts. A sole proprietorship is the simplest form of business to start and own. The business is not a separate legal entity from its owner. For legal and tax situations, it is considered just an extension of the owner. According to the US Census Bureau, over 70 percent of all businesses in the United States are sole proprietorships.

Establishing a Sole Proprietorship

Many sole proprietors start their businesses with very little money. If you run a business from home, you may only need letterhead, a website, and business cards to get started. There are both advantages and disadvantages of being a sole proprietor, as shown in Figure 6-1.

Copyright Goodheart-Willcox Co., Inc.

Advantages and Disadvantages of Sole Proprietorship	
Advantages	**Disadvantages**
Complete control of business	Unlimited liability
Keep 100 percent of the profits	Assume 100 percent of the losses
Easy to create	Sole responsibility
Possible tax benefits	May need other professional expertise

Goodheart-Willcox Publisher

Figure 6-1. Consider the pros and cons of a sole proprietorship form of business ownership.

Many counties and states require sole proprietors to apply for a DBA. A **DBA license**, or a *doing business as* license, is needed to officially register a business. In some states, it is known as a *fictitious name registration*. This is necessary if you are conducting business in a name other than your own. For example, Janis Ruiz may own the business, but its name is JR Salon. A small registration fee is usually required. The bank may also require that you have a DBA license to open an account in the name of the business.

Some types of businesses also require a specific license or permit for you to become licensed. If you are opening a restaurant, for example, the business needs a restaurant license. Or, if you want to become a hair stylist, you must pass the state exam to personally earn a cosmetology license. Since there is no legal separation between you and the business, obtaining the license is your responsibility.

If hiring employees, you must have an *employer identification number (EIN)* for income tax purposes. This is true for all types of business ownership, not only for sole proprietors. An EIN is obtained from the IRS.

Advantages of Sole Proprietorship

If you decide to open as a sole proprietorship, you will be the only owner of the company. That sounds great because you make all of the decisions and keep all of the profits. There are many advantages to being your own boss.

- decision making; you alone decide how to run the business, its hours of operation, and which products to offer

- profits; as the sole business owner, you do not have to share your profits

- easy to start; sole proprietorships are easy to establish once you have your business idea

- tax benefits; the business profits are taxed at your personal tax rate, which is often less than other forms of ownership

Copyright Goodheart-Willcox Co., Inc.

Disadvantages of Sole Proprietorship

Operating as a sole proprietorship has its drawbacks. As a sole proprietor, you must raise all of the money to start the business. You personally bear all of the risk involved in the business. It also helps to have expertise in many areas to make sound business decisions.

Start-Up Capital

As a sole proprietor, it can be challenging to raise enough money to start a business. You may have to use your own savings or borrow from a financial institution. Raising funds on your own can be difficult.

Unlimited Liability

Liability means legal responsibility. As a sole proprietor, you have *unlimited liability* in the business, meaning you alone are responsible for all risks. If you are sued and lose, you alone must pay the damages. If you do not have enough assets to cover all of the damages, your business could be seized, and your personal assets may be at risk.

Limited Expertise

If you cannot afford to hire professionals, you will need to become an expert in all areas of your business. For example, you may be a good marketer, but unable to balance the books as well as an accountant. Or, you may be good at accounting, but not enjoy the sales aspects of business.

Partnership

As the old saying goes, sometimes "two heads are better than one." A **partnership** is the relationship between two or more people who join to create a business. Each person contributes money, property, labor, or skill and expects to share in the business' profits and losses. The business is not a separate legal entity from its owners. The owners are called *partners,* and ownership does not have to be equal. Partnerships are common in law, architecture, and accounting firms, but they can be found in any industry.

There are two types of partnerships. The most common is a *general partnership,* where all partners have unlimited liability. This means the partners' personal assets, including their savings, investments, and homes, can be used to pay off the business' debts.

The second type is a **limited partnership (LP)**, where there is one managing partner and at least one limited partner. Limited partners have *limited liability,* meaning they cannot lose more than the amount originally invested by each person. Therefore, they are not personally liable for the business' debts.

FYI

The federal government created the Small Business Jobs Act in 2010. It was specifically designed to promote entrepreneurship through increased funding and tax breaks.

Copyright Goodheart-Willcox Co., Inc.

However, in a limited partnership, the limited partners must remain silent partners in the business. A **silent partner** is one who invests money, but is not involved in the business' daily operations or management. If a silent partner becomes involved in operations or decision making, the limited partnership turns into a general partnership.

Establishing a Partnership

If you are going to form a partnership, have a lawyer who is experienced in partnerships draw up the partnership agreement. The *partnership agreement* details how much each partner will invest, each partner's responsibilities, and how profits are to be shared. All partners must agree to the terms of the agreement because it is a legal document.

What happens if one partner wants out of the business at some point? The partnership agreement should contain an exit strategy. As in other forms of businesses, there are advantages and disadvantages to partnerships, as shown in Figure 6-2.

Advantages of Partnership

The rewards of working with partners can be great. Shared workload and the ability to bounce ideas off others can contribute to the success of the company. There are other advantages of a partnership as discussed in the next sections.

Joint Strengths

Each partner brings individual strengths to the business. One partner might be great at the financial side, including handling the accounting and investments. Another partner might be a great marketer and salesperson.

Advantages and Disadvantages of Partnership	
Advantages	**Disadvantages**
Individual strengths	Personality conflicts
Shared risk; limited liability for limited partners	Unlimited liability for general partners
Ease of setup	Share profits and losses
More financial resources	Obtaining loans more difficult
Tax benefits	Bound by the agreement

Figure 6-2. Consider the pros and cons of a partnership form of business ownership.

Goodheart-Willcox Publisher

Copyright Goodheart-Willcox Co., Inc.

Green Entrepreneurs

Company Cars

Many businesses use company cars. When purchasing a car for business purposes, consider buying an environmentally friendly one. Hybrid and electric cars are two popular models offered by many car manufacturers. These models have new engine technology that leaves a smaller carbon footprint. Hybrid vehicles use less gasoline because they get substantially higher miles per gallon. Electric-powered vehicles reduce polluting emissions because they are only powered by electricity. There are also very small gasoline-powered cars on the market that get excellent gas mileage. Search the Internet or contact a local car dealer to learn more about which vehicles are available that will help protect the environment.

Shared Risk

Risks can be split between partners in any way that is agreed to by the partners. Initial investments, profits, losses, and even management responsibilities can be divided to lessen the burdens of running a business.

Easy Setup

In some cases, a partnership can allow a business to be created with a minimum amount of cost and paperwork. In this regard, a partnership can be similar to a sole proprietorship.

More Financial Resources

By having partners, there may be more money to invest in the business. Additionally, when applying for financing, the credit history of all partners may have a positive impact. However, a new partnership could also have a negative impact on financing, as discussed later.

Tax Benefits

Because partnerships are *not* legal entities, the partners claim the business' profits on their personal tax returns. This is similar to the tax benefits of a sole proprietorship.

Disadvantages of Partnership

There are some disadvantages each partner should understand before creating an agreement. The specific disadvantages vary, depending on the type of partnership.

Copyright Goodheart-Willcox Co., Inc.

Unlimited Liability

General partnerships have unlimited liability. This means that all partners are responsible for any decision made by another partner. For example, your partner decides to order a million gadgets. If they do not sell, the partners are all still obligated to pay for those gadgets.

Partners' Personalities

Just as friends and spouses can have disagreements, partners can as well. Many partnerships end because the partners cannot agree on how to run the business or about financial issues.

In a partnership, two or more people join together to create a business.

sematadesign/Shutterstock.com

Copyright Goodheart-Willcox Co., Inc.

Profit Sharing

All profits must still be divided as outlined in the partnership agreement. Even if one person does all the work, the partners are still bound to share profits as outlined.

Financing Issues

Banks and other financial institutions can be cautious when lending to a partnership—especially one without a proven track record. They can be concerned that the partnership will not last and the loan would not be repaid.

Corporation

A **corporation** is defined by the US Supreme Court as "an artificial being, invisible, intangible, and existing only in contemplation of the law." A corporation is considered to be a legal entity. This means it can buy property, earn money, manufacture and distribute products, pay taxes, sue or be sued, and enter into contracts. A **contract** is a legally binding agreement. In effect, the law views corporations as people, but with limited rights and privileges. Corporations are responsible for nearly 90 percent of all sales in the United States.

Establishing a Corporation

There are a number of reasons an entrepreneur may want to incorporate. A corporation's owners are not personally liable for the business risks because the corporation is the entity. Some investors prefer to fund new businesses that are incorporated because of this legal protection. However, corporations are more difficult and costly to set up.

Entrepreneurs who want to form a corporation must file a charter in the state where it wants to incorporate. A **charter** is the legal document describing the purpose, place of business, and other details of the corporation. It may also be called *articles of incorporation*. The filing fees are higher than forming sole proprietorships or partnerships.

Home state corporation is when a business incorporates in the state where it is physically located. However, businesses may also incorporate in a state without a physical location. Some corporations choose this option for financial and other business reasons. Corporations that operate in one state but incorporate in another, must also register to do business in the state in which they are physically located.

A corporation must submit a unique name that does not infringe on any copyrights. Corporations must have a board of directors who make policy and financial decisions for the corporation. They must

Copyright Goodheart-Willcox Co., Inc.

write the corporate bylaws and hold an initial organizational meeting as well as annual meetings.

The corporation must also issue shares of stock to its owners. The people who own the stock, sometimes called *shares,* own a portion of the company and are called stockholders. They receive one or more certificates stating the number of shares that they own.

Private corporations do not sell company stock publically to investors on stock exchanges. All company stock is held privately by one or more people. Private corporations are not required to release information about their sales or profits. By contrast, public corporations sell their stock on stock exchanges to any investor who wants to buy it. Publically traded companies must release all financial information related to the company.

Types of Corporations

There are important differences between the various types of corporations. All corporations are legal entities. The main difference is how they are taxed. Depending on the form chosen, there are advantages and disadvantages of incorporation, as shown in Figure 6-3.

Global Entrepreneurs

Nancy Mercolino

Nancy Mercolino is the founder and president of Ceilings Plus. The company produces innovative ceiling systems, light coves, wall panels, and column covers. It is based in Los Angeles, California, and sells all around the world. Mercolino started the company in 1987 by merging two smaller construction suppliers. The company has 160 employees. Ceilings Plus has annual sales of around $30 million. About 55 percent of the company's sales come from Europe and the Middle East.

Mercolino was able to grow Ceilings Plus by first establishing relationships with US architects and engineers. This got the products established. From there, Mercolino looked to start selling internationally. To expand into the global market, she hired an international sales director who is based in Germany. However, taking the company global was not as simple as hiring an international sales director. Mercolino had to learn about international markets and the details of exporting.

Ceilings Plus has few American competitors. Most of the competition is from European companies. The reputation of a "made in USA brand" is an advantage for the company. "Being an American-made product is a definite selling point," states Mercolino. "If our bid comes in even close to the target range, we're preferred."

Copyright Goodheart-Willcox Co., Inc.

Figure 6-3. Consider the pros and cons of incorporation as a form of business ownership.

Advantages and Disadvantages of Corporations	
Advantages	**Disadvantages**
• Perpetual life • Investors raise capital • Credibility • Limited liability for owners	• Double taxation • Cost of entry • Corporate formalities

Goodheart-Willcox Publisher

C Corporation

The most common type of corporation is a C corporation. A **C corporation** is a corporation that pays taxes on profits and provides personal liability protection for its owners. Anyone can form a C corporation. Companies that sell their stock on stock exchanges must be C corporations.

Subchapter S Corporation

A **subchapter S corporation** is a corporation that provides limited liability to its owners and is taxed like a partnership. A subchapter S corporation is intended for small businesses with fewer than 100 stockholders. Individual owners pay taxes on their own earnings, but not on earnings of the corporation. This provides small business owners with both the protection of limited liability and substantial savings on taxes. For entrepreneurs looking for an alternative to a C corporation, a subchapter S corporation may be a good solution.

Nonprofit Corporation

A **nonprofit corporation** is a company set up to accomplish a specific mission rather than generate a profit. Nonprofits are heavily regulated by the federal government and must meet specific guidelines, but they do not pay taxes. Income from sales and fund-raising are used to support the organization and its cause. Nonprofits include charitable organizations and education and religious institutions.

Advantages of a Corporation

The individual corporate shareholders are not personally responsible for the business. Because of that limited liability advantage, many small business owners choose to incorporate. In addition to limited liability, consider the following advantages:

- perpetual life; if a shareholder sells stock, the company continues to exist because it is a separate legal entity

- investors; corporations can raise money by selling stock to investors

- credibility; the *Inc.* at the end of a company's name adds credibility for many potential customers

Copyright Goodheart-Willcox Co., Inc.

Disadvantages of a Corporation

Depending on the form, disadvantages of corporations can include the following:

- double taxation; C corporations pay taxes on the corporation's profits *and* stockholders pay taxes on their individual earnings

- cost of entry is high; cost of registration and legal fees must be considered

- corporate formalities

  Corporate formalities are the records and procedures that corporations are required by law to complete. The requirements fall under three categories: corporate records, annual reporting, and meetings. The required formalities vary by state. They can include filing articles of incorporation, creating bylaws, issuing stock to owners, forming a board of directors, and paying fees. If you fail to meet any of the formalities, your business may lose the limited liability protection of being a corporation.

Alternative Forms of Ownership

There are two alternative forms of ownership that resemble both a partnership and a corporation: *limited liability company (LLC)* and *limited liability partnership (LLP)*. Both of these forms limit the personal liability of the owners and can provide tax benefits. Many small business owners wanting the benefits of a corporation cannot afford to incorporate or do not want the restrictions. One solution to this situation is to create an LLC or LLP.

 You Do the Math   Statistical Reasoning

There are three measures of the center of a data set. The *mode* is the value that occurs most frequently in the data set. The *median* is the middle number in a data set. To find the median, the numbers must be listed in numerical order. The *mean* is the average of all values in the data set. Mean is calculated by adding all values and dividing that sum by the total number of values.

Solve the following problems.

1. A recent survey of gasoline prices for a region reported these prices per gallon: $3.49, $3.67, $3.52, $3.58, and $3.56. What is the mean price per gallon?

2. A business ships telephone headsets all across the country. The various shipping costs it charged last week are: $0.99, $1.05, $0.75, $1.07, $0.99, $1.05, and $1.05. What is the mode shipping charge?

Copyright Goodheart-Willcox Co., Inc.

LLCs and LLPs are similar in that profits are reported on personal tax returns. There is limited liability, less paperwork, and owners can share the profits however they choose. In addition, there is no limit to how many stockholders can be a part of the business. The differences between them, however, can be confusing.

The owners of an LLC are called members. LLCs can choose any organizational structure the members agree to. One disadvantage of the LLC is that it has a limited life—the business ends on the retirement or death of one member. It also ends if a member decides to leave the business. LLCs are more expensive to form than sole proprietorships and partnerships and are subject to more state and federal regulations.

The owners of an LLP are called partners. The LLP has a similar business structure to a limited partnership (LP), but has no managing partner. All of the partners have limited personal liability. Professionals often prefer LLPs to partnerships, corporations, or LLCs because no partner wants to be liable for another's mistakes.

One drawback is that LLPs and LLCs are not permitted in all states. Some states limit LLCs or LLPs to specific types of businesses. For example, one reason large law and accounting firms are LLPs is that they can be an LLP in every state. Not every state allows them to operate as an LLC, though. Each state allowing LLPs determines the amount of limited liability for the partners, which can make it less desirable. Most states require LLPs to carry liability insurance and register with the state.

Section 6.2 | Review

Check Your Understanding

1. What are some of the rewards of establishing a sole proprietorship?

2. What does unlimited liability mean to an entrepreneur?

3. List the different kinds of partnerships available to entrepreneurs.

4. Describe some of the advantages of forming a business as a corporation.

5. Explain the difference between a limited liability company (LLC) and a limited liability partnership (LLP).

Build Your Vocabulary

As you progress through this text, develop a personal glossary of key terms. This will help you build your vocabulary and prepare you for a career. Write a definition for each of the following terms and add them to your personal glossary.

sole proprietor
DBA license
liability
partnership
limited partnership (LP)
silent partner
corporation
contract
charter
stock
stockholders
private corporation
public corporation
C corporation
subchapter S corporation
nonprofit corporation
corporate formalities

Chapter Summary

Section 6.1 Start Your Business

- The four different start-up strategies are starting a new business, franchising, buying an existing business, and getting involved in a family business.
- Franchising gives a business owner the rights to an established brand.
- Be sure to research any existing business you consider purchasing.
- Joining a family business has unique challenges and advantages.
- When deciding which strategy to use, research each option and seek professional advice.

Section 6.2 Types of Business Ownership

- A sole proprietorship is a simple option, but its owner is personally liable for the business.
- The three kinds of partnerships are general partnerships, limited partnerships, and silent partnerships.
- Corporations can take the form of C corporations, subchapter S corporations, or nonprofit corporations, depending on the size and purpose of the business.
- Other forms of ownership include limited liability partnerships (LLP) and limited liability companies (LLC).

Online Activities

Complete the following activities to help you learn, practice, and expand your knowledge and skills.

Posttest. Now that you have finished the chapter, see what you learned by taking the chapter posttest.

Key Terms. Practice vocabulary for this chapter using the e-flash cards, matching activity, and vocabulary game until you are able to recognize their meanings.

Review Your Knowledge

1. Which organization regulates the franchise industry?
2. List three disadvantages of buying a franchise.
3. Identify some of the disadvantages of buying an existing business.
4. What are the advantages of joining a family business?
5. Describe the three types of ownership.

Copyright Goodheart-Willcox Co., Inc.

6. Why is unlimited liability important as a sole proprietor?

7. If you want to join forces with another person and create a partnership, what legal action should you take? Explain why.

8. What is the difference between a general partnership and a limited partnership?

9. Explain the difference between private and public corporations.

10. What are corporate formalities? Explain the consequences of not meeting corporate formalities.

Apply Your Knowledge

1. You are ready to start your new business. You have an idea for the good or service. Is it possible to buy a franchise for this type of business? Research the Internet to find an evaluation checklist that you can use when considering the purchase of a franchise. Use the words "franchise checklist" to conduct your search. Read several sources, and then create your own checklist.

2. Visit the Federal Trade Commission website. Do a search for a franchise disclosure document (FDD). What did you learn from this information?

3. Franchises are one way to become an entrepreneur. Visit local franchises in your community. Ask for brochures or advertisements about becoming a franchise owner. Are any of these franchises opportunities that you would consider? Why or why not?

4. Research a family business in your community. Interview one of the family members. Ask the person to describe the experience of being part of a family business. What did you learn from this interview?

5. Make a list of ten businesses in your community that are organized as sole proprietorships. List the industry and any other information you can find about the owner. What did you learn about proprietorship from this activity? Would these businesses compete with you?

6. Make a list of ten businesses in your community that are organized as partnerships. List the industry, the number of partners, and any other information you can find. What did you learn about partnerships from this activity? Would these businesses compete with you?

7. Assume that your business will be a partnership. Research partnership agreements. Select one that you think would work for you and a potential partner. Give the reasons you selected that particular agreement.

8. Which type of legal ownership are you planning for your new business? Write several paragraphs to describe the type of ownership your business will have and why. Will it be a proprietorship? partnership? corporation?

9. Consider the start-up strategies available for your business, including starting a business from the ground up, purchasing a franchise, taking over or expanding an existing business, or joining a family business. Create a chart with each start-up strategy as a column heading. Under each, evaluate the issues that you think you would encounter for each option.

10. Write a description of your business. Next, explain why you are starting from scratch, buying a franchise, joining a family business, or buying an established business. Give your rationale for the decision.

 # Teamwork

This chapter discusses different ways to start a business and different types of legal ownership. Working with your team, agree on one way to be an entrepreneur. Is it to buy a franchise, buy an existing business, join a family business, or create a business from scratch? Create a presentation and convince your class that your decision is the winning decision. Your presentation should include the issues and obstacles involved in starting the new business and your team's solutions and strategies.

Internet Research

Forms of Business Ownership. Using the Internet, research proprietorships, partnerships, and corporations as forms of business ownership. Look at each of the options from both legal and financial perspectives. Write a paragraph about which one you think may be best for your new business and explain why.

Communication Skills

College and Career Readiness

Speaking. Participate in a collaborative classroom discussion about the pros and cons of joining a family business. Ask questions to participants that connect your ideas to the relevant evidence that has been presented.

Listening. Do an Internet search on speeches made by entrepreneurs. Select one speech of your choice and listen to it in its entirety. Present your findings and supporting evidence of the line of reasoning, organization, development, and style the speaker used to prepare his or her information. Identify the target market and the purpose of the speech.

Copyright Goodheart-Willcox Co., Inc.

CTSOs

Franchise Business Plan. Writing a business plan for a franchise is a competitive entrepreneurship event that may be offered by your Career and Technical Student Organization (CTSO). This may be an individual only event. There may be two parts to this event: the written business plan and the oral presentation of the plan.

The event calls for the development of a written proposal to start a new business by purchasing a franchise. Students are given an opportunity to present an idea for a business and how the business will be created, marketed, and financed. Students who participate are required to write a business plan and submit it either before the competition or on arrival at the event. Written events can be lengthy and take a lot of time to prepare. Therefore, it is important to start early.

The rules for this event are similar to other business plan presentations. However, writing this plan will require research on buying a franchise.

To prepare for writing a business plan for franchising, complete the following activities.

1. Read the guidelines provided by your organization. There will be specific directions given as to the parts of the business plan and how each should be presented. In addition, all final format guidelines will be given, including how to organize and submit. Make certain that you ask any questions about points that you do not understand.

2. Select a franchise that interests you. Do your research early. Research may take days or weeks, and you do not want to rush the process.

3. Study chapter 2 to learn about franchising.

4. Review the Putting the Puzzle Together activities at the end of each chapter. A business plan template and a complete business plan sample are available on the student companion website at www.g-wlearning.com.

5. Visit your CTSO's website and create a checklist of the guidelines you must follow. Ask yourself: Does this event still interest me? Can I do what is necessary to be successful at the event? If you answered "yes," move forward with the writing process.

6. Set a deadline for yourself so that you write at a comfortable pace.

7. After you write your first draft, ask a teacher or someone who owns a franchise in your community to review it and give you feedback.

8. Once you have the final version of your business plan, review the checklist you prepared again. Make sure you have addressed all the requirements. You will be penalized on your score if a direction is not followed exactly.

Copyright Goodheart-Willcox Co., Inc.

Building Your Business Plan—Putting the Puzzle Together

Business Ownership

Now that you have decided on the type of business you want to own, you will make other decisions about the business. As you learned in this chapter, there are different options for starting a business. You may open a new business, buy a franchise, purchase a business that is in operation, or join a family business. You also have many choices about ownership structure.

Goals

- Assess franchise opportunities in your industry.
- Analyze other business start-up options.
- Complete a DBA.
- Create business plan notes.

Directions

Access the *Entrepreneurship* companion website at www.g-wlearning.com . Download each data file for the following activities. A complete sample business plan is available on the companion website to use as a reference. The name of the file is BusPlan_Sample.RetroAttire.docx.

Preparation

Activity 6-1. Franchise Assessment. Research the various franchises that are available for entrepreneurs in your industry to purchase. Identify the franchise, its pros and cons, the costs of buying into the franchise, and any other requirements of the franchisor.

Activity 6-2. Business Options. In addition to considering franchises, analyze starting a new business, purchasing an existing business, or joining a family business. Review your options.

Activity 6-3. DBA. You most likely will need to file a DBA to register your business. Practice completing the sample DBA form. Include the finished document in the appendices of your business plan.

Activity 6-4. Business Plan Notes. Create notes about the type of business ownerships available to you. Keep your notes about the type of business and form of ownership.

Business Plan—Operations

In this chapter, you determined the best option for starting your business and how you want to structure the ownership. Now you will complete the part of the business plan about how you plan to structure the business and explain your decision.

1. Open your business plan document.

2. Locate the Operations section of the plan. Complete the subsection, Organizational Structure. Use the suggestions and questions listed to help you generate ideas. Delete the questions and instructions when you are finished recording your responses in each section. Make sure to proofread your document and correct any errors in keyboarding, spelling, and grammar.

3. Save your document.

©Creatas

Unit 3
Building the Business

Your Business Plan— Putting the Puzzle Together

The business plan puzzle is taking shape and you are starting to see some results from your hard work. Each section of the business plan relates to another important part of the planning process for entrepreneurs. Where is the best place to open your business, and what will the facility look like? What legal issues might directly affect your business? Will you need financial help to open the business? In this unit, you will:

Identify a location for your business.
Research legal issues that affect businesses.
Determine different methods for financing a business.

Unit Overview

There are many things to consider and decide at this stage in creating a new business. The chapters in this unit will help you focus on some of the basic steps of planning that are necessary before your business opens its doors.

In this unit, you will learn the importance of site selection and physical layout for your company. To have an effective business, appropriate space for employees, customers, and vendors is crucial. You will also learn about business and consumer laws and how they influence your day-to-day business operations. The unit concludes with suggestions and ideas on how to finance your business.

Chapters

7 Site Selection
8 Legal Issues
9 Business Funding

Entrepreneurs and the Economy

According to the Kauffman Foundation, businesses that opened after 1980—when entrepreneurship was exploding—contribute one-third of the country's current GDP. The *gross domestic product (GDP)* measures the value of all goods and services produced inside a nation's borders. It is one of the primary indicators of a country's economic strength and stability.

GDP is different than *gross national product (GNP),* which measures the value of the nation's goods and services, even those produced outside the borders. The Bureau of Economic Analysis (BEA) in the US Department of Commerce calculates GDP quarterly to evaluate economic trends.

GDP figures are adjusted by season and expressed as an annual rate of growth or decline. For example, the BEA reported that GDP "increased at an annual rate of 2.2 percent in the first quarter of 2012 over the fourth quarter of 2011." Most economists agree that a GDP growth rate of between 2 and 4 percent is healthy. During the banking crisis of 2008, GDP was negative.

Another economic indicator important to entrepreneurs is the *consumer price index (CPI).* The CPI measures the average change in prices for goods and services purchased by households. The Bureau of Labor Statistics (BLS) surveys the prices of a cross section of 80,000 goods and services to create the monthly index. Prices always change, but it is better if overall prices only rise slightly over time to keep the economy stable.

The overall rise in prices is called *inflation.* If inflation is high, the economy may be headed for trouble. Consumer purchasing power becomes limited during periods of high inflation because prices rise faster than income levels. All businesses suffer during

alphaspirit/Shutterstock.com

inflation, but small businesses tend to feel the effects of inflation the most. In general, the costs of obtaining their goods and services go up and their sales go down.

Inflation also affects GDP because the higher prices make the GDP and the economy look better than they really are. When GDP numbers are corrected for inflation, it is called *real GDP.* Make sure to use the real GDP figures when assessing economic indicators.

While studying, look for the activity icon for:

- Chapter pretests and posttests
- Key terms activities
- Section reviews
- Building Your Business Plan activities

G-WLEARNING.com

CHAPTER

7 Site Selection

Lee Rhodes, 2011 Entrepreneur of the Year and owner of glassybaby, learned a valuable lesson about the importance of location. Her company produces hand-blown glass votive holders in over 400 colors. Glassybaby first opened in Seattle, Washington, and now has three additional Washington locations. More recently, she opened a store in New York City's West Village that struggled. Rhodes now knows that a location with a studio where people can watch the glassblowing process is crucial to the store's success. Also, most New Yorkers travel on foot and, since the glass candleholders are heavy, there may be reluctance to purchase the product and carry it around the city. Online sales in the city are strong, so she hopes to find a better store location.

"The entrepreneur builds an enterprise; the technician builds a job."

—Michael Gerber, entrepreneur, instructor, and author of
Awakening the Entrepreneur Within

**College
and Career
Readiness**

Reading Prep. Before reading this chapter, look at the chapter title. What does this title tell you about what you will be learning? Compare and contrast the information to be presented with information you already know about the subject matter from sources such as videos and online media.

Sections

7.1 Choose the Location

7.2 Choose the Layout

Picture Yourself Here
Misa Chien

The food truck is one of today's most interesting dining trends. Food trucks are like restaurants on wheels. In 2009, 23-year-old Misa Chien and her friend Jennifer Green started the Nom Nom Truck, which serves Vietnamese-inspired dishes to people in Los Angeles and San Francisco. The two met at the University of California, Los Angeles. When they first started out, Misa drove the truck for a few months. This hands-on experience with the day-to-day goings-on of her company helps her be a better leader. Misa has no problem leading her team of 15 employees.

Misa, Jennifer, and the Nom Nom Truck were featured on a Food Network reality show called the Great Food Truck Race. Although Team Nom Nom did not win, the show brought greater attention to the venture as well as to Misa and Jennifer. Misa and Jennifer describe the core value of their company as the "triangle of happiness." If the customer is happy, the employees are happy, and so are Misa and Jennifer.

Photo © Misa Chien

Check Your Entrepreneurship IQ

Before you begin the chapter, see what you already know about entrepreneurship by taking the chapter pretest. The pretest is available at www.g-wlearning.com

Choose the Location

What factors must an entrepreneur consider when evaluating potential business locations?

Objectives

After completing this section, you will be able to:
- **List** the factors to consider when locating a business.
- **Describe** physical structures for a business.

Key Terms

trade area
economic indicators
brick-and-mortar business
e-business
e-commerce
hybrid business

Critical Thinking

Zoning laws are created by local governments to guide businesses on where they can and cannot be located. Give your opinion as to why zoning laws are or are not important to a community.

Analyze the Community

A **trade area** is the area from which a business expects to draw most of its customers. There are many factors that determine the trade area for a business. Depending on the size and type of the business, some trade areas will be better than others.

You may decide that the business environment in a particular state or community is best for your business. A city or state may offer incentives to open a business in a certain location. Or, your business might need to be close to a supplier or a distribution center. There are many reasons that will determine the location of your business.

Economic Indicators

Both a country's economy and a community's economy impact a business. If either economy is troubled, people will not have money to buy goods or services. It is important to choose a location where the economy is healthy and people are employed.

Copyright Goodheart-Willcox Co., Inc.

The Economics and Statistics Administration is a division of the US Department of Commerce. It publishes monthly and quarterly economic indicators. **Economic indicators** are statistics about the economy indicating how it is performing. These can include the gross domestic product (GDP), consumption expenditures, unemployment rate, inflation rate, new home sales, and stock prices. Some of a community's economic indicators may help you decide if it will be a prosperous place to locate your business.

State and Local Incentives

Capital and labor are mobile, making it easy for businesses to relocate. States and municipalities with an eye toward economic growth may offer financial incentives to attract new businesses. Tax incentives are typical. Communities may offer other incentives, such as inexpensive land and employee-training programs, to attract new businesses.

Some states offer incentives based on the type of business. For example, 45 states offer various tax breaks to movie and entertainment companies that film in those states. These companies can boost a state's economy through the money spent filming TV programs, movies, or documentaries there.

Lower taxes generally help businesses grow. Lower taxes may mean that a business will have more money to invest in new technologies, hiring employees, and expansion. The *Tax Foundation* is a nonprofit organization that has researched both consumer and

A business can only be located on property that is zoned for its type of industry, such as an industrial or commercial zone.

John Kasawa/Shutterstock.com

Copyright Goodheart-Willcox Co., Inc.

corporate tax policies since 1937. It publishes the annual State Business Tax Climate Index to help businesses identify states with favorable tax policies.

Zoning Laws

Local governments create zoning laws and regulations that define how property in specific geographic zones can be used. Zoning seeks to protect public health, safety, and welfare. Zoning regulates land use and controls building types, sizes, and heights. Common property zones are residential, commercial, industrial, agricultural, and recreational. Most zoning restrictions are the same across a city, township, or county. Research your local zoning laws by contacting the zoning board or planning office.

Residential zoning prohibits high-traffic activities in residential neighborhoods. In some cases, zoning restrictions may exist for different types of business within residential areas. This may include the nature of the business, number of employees, hours of operation, and noise and delivery issues. Commercial and industrial zones are usually limited to those forms of business.

Employees

As an entrepreneur, you may need to hire employees. Local employment agencies can answer questions about a community's labor pool. It is preferable to hire people living near your business. If you are creating a specialized business, however, make sure the local population has the skills to meet your needs. For example, a technology start-up requires a different type of employee than does a factory.

Supply Chain

It is important to consider access to the supply chain, from the suppliers to the customers, when locating a business. Consider how your business will receive shipments of materials or products and how customers will receive the goods.

Do the products need certain shipping conditions, such as refrigeration or careful handling? If your business plan requires shipping, it may be more cost effective to locate near a major transportation hub.

If the business manufactures products, materials must be brought to the facility to create the products. Being close to the suppliers or to a shipping center saves on transportation costs.

Entrepreneur Ethics

A bribe is an exchange of something of value for special consideration when doing business. Bribes are unethical as well as illegal in the United States. In some foreign countries, however, bribes are considered legal. Regardless of where a company is located, however, US business owners should not accept a bribe from an individual, government, or business entity. Also, US business owners and their employees should never offer bribes.

Copyright Goodheart-Willcox Co., Inc.

Competition

Spend time in the proposed location to assess all potential competitors. You can see customer buying patterns by knowing the sizes, locations, and number of stores nearby. Locating in a trade area close to competitors encourages customers to comparison shop. However, be sure your competitive advantage is strong when locating close to the competition.

Determine the Physical Structure

After researching and deciding on your business' location, it is time to select a physical facility. Depending on the type of goods or services you offer, there will be several options. The structure may be brick and mortar, an e-business, home based, or a hybrid.

Brick and Mortar

A **brick-and-mortar business** is a company with a physical store or facility for at least a portion of its operation. Examples are grocery stores, manufacturing plants, and doctors' offices. A brick-and-mortar business is not limited to a physical space, however. It may also offer products online.

Having a physical location where customers come in, speak with employees, and examine products can be an advantage. Some services, such as a hair salon or photography studio, require a physical location for customers to visit. However, for other services, such as carpet cleaning or plumbing, customers may never see the physical location of the business.

FYI

Between 1.8 percent and 3.0 percent of yearly retail sales are lost due to inventory shrinkage. Of that amount, 45 percent is employee theft, customer shoplifting is 33 percent, store error is 15 percent, and vendor fraud is 7 percent.

Downtown

Some cities have a thriving downtown area that attracts numerous shoppers. A downtown location may be ideal for some business types, such as flower shops or food-service carts. Parking may not be free in a downtown area, but many cities have low-cost public transportation choices to bring customers downtown.

Shopping Centers

There are many types of shopping centers. Some are *traditional malls* with anchor stores and many other retailers drawing a variety of customers. Traditional malls are usually under one roof, making it convenient for shoppers to visit stores in any weather conditions. *Town centers* are open-air malls with many retailers. They are arranged more like an older center of town with walkways and landscaping. *Strip malls* are smaller open-air shopping centers where the stores are arranged in a row with a sidewalk in front. Shopping centers have free parking.

A physical location allows customers to directly interact with the business.

Mark Winfrey/Shutterstock.com

Office Buildings or Office Parks

Some retail businesses, especially restaurants, may choose to locate in a large office building with many employees. Another choice is to locate near an *office park,* which is an area with commercial zoning for many office buildings. Workers in an office building or from a group of buildings offer a steady stream of potential customers. Some office buildings have fee-based parking, but most office parks offer free parking.

E-Business

Electronic business, called **e-business**, is any business process conducted through electronic networks using the Internet. **E-commerce** is the term for the buying and selling of goods or services through the Internet. E-commerce is one of the many types of e-business activities. *E-tailing* is conducting retail sales, in particular, through the Internet. Some e-tailers also have a brick-and-mortar facility, while others only offer products for sale on the Internet.

If the products do not require customers to visit a location, a business can be located anywhere. For example, a photo-development company can conduct business from any location in the country through e-mail and physical mail. Customers e-mail their image files

Copyright Goodheart-Willcox Co., Inc.

to the business. The files are turned into physical photos, and the photos are delivered to the customers via physical mail.

For most e-commerce businesses, as well as mail-order businesses, space is necessary for storage and order fulfillment. However, these businesses do not need physical spaces to personally serve customers. This may mean overhead costs are lower than for brick-and-mortar businesses.

Home Based

Like e-businesses, home-based businesses may have lower overhead costs than brick-and-mortar businesses. Working from home allows business owners many other advantages, too. They can schedule their own hours, take advantage of tax benefits, and enjoy more family time. They may also avoid stressful commutes or office environments and achieve personal fulfillment and independence. However, a home-based business requires more focus. It is easy to become distracted by daily events happening in the home.

Hybrid

The term *hybrid* means a combination of two or more different elements to achieve a certain goal. A **hybrid business** is the blend of two or more location types. Typically, it describes an e-business with a brick-and-mortar warehouse or factory. It may also describe brick-and-mortar or home-based companies selling products through websites. Or, it can be a home-based entrepreneur who conducts administrative tasks at home, but needs a physical manufacturing space.

A home-based business allows for more time with family.

Hurst Photo/Shutterstock.com

Social Entrepreneurs

Blake Mycoskie

Blake Mycoskie is an entrepreneur from Texas. In 2006, Mycoskie was traveling in Argentina where he observed children with no shoes. For these children, going barefoot creates a health hazard. Many develop a disease called mossy foot, which eventually causes blockage in the lymphatic system and results in a condition called elephantiasis. Also, without their feet covered, these impoverished children are unable to go to school. Mycoskie was inspired to create a company that gives away one pair of shoes to a child in need for every pair that is sold. He founded TOMS Shoes in California. By giving away shoes, TOMS Shoes is improving the health and lives of impoverished children. The shoes are made from recycled materials, so they are also environmentally friendly. TOMS Shoes is a for-profit company that operates the nonprofit company Friends of TOMS. Friends of TOMS runs the One for One program that donates shoes.

Section 7.1 Review

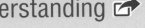

Check Your Understanding

1. When selecting a site for a business, what factors should you consider?
2. What kinds of restrictions might exist for businesses within residential areas?
3. Explain what *brick and mortar* means.
4. What is the difference between e-commerce and e-tailing?
5. What are the different types of shopping centers?

Build Your Vocabulary

As you progress through this text, develop a personal glossary of key terms. This will help you build your vocabulary and prepare you for a career. Write a definition for each of the following terms and add them to your personal glossary.

trade area
economic indicators
brick-and-mortar business
e-business
e-commerce
hybrid business

Choose the Layout

Essential Question

How does the type of business impact the layout of the business space?

Objectives

After completing this section, you will be able to:

- **Describe** financial options for obtaining a space for a business.
- **Discuss** potential layout considerations for various types of businesses.

Key Terms

lease
lessor
lessee
tenant improvement
aesthetics
visual merchandising

layout
floor plan
productivity
division of labor
specialization
law of diminishing returns

Critical Thinking

Most businesses attempt to make their physical spaces look appealing to their customers. Why is an attractive physical space important to sales? Explain the philosophy behind knowing what appeals to different types of customers.

Obtain the Space

If the business requires a brick-and-mortar facility, it is necessary to lease, build, or buy a building or space in a building. After deciding whether to lease, buy, or build a facility, evaluate the available options.

The first step in choosing a physical location is to set goals for the building. What will it be used for, and how many people must it hold? Does it need a parking lot or will it house special equipment? Every business will have different facility goals. For example, retail businesses, such as grocery stores, have different building needs than do service or manufacturing businesses.

Lease

A **lease** is a legal contract to use property owned by another person or company for a specific amount of time. Businesses may lease land, a building, an office, or even equipment.

Compared to building or buying, leasing space lowers the initial business start-up costs and involves a lower risk commitment.

Copyright Goodheart-Willcox Co., Inc.

Compare different buildings' rental prices and lease terms to find those within your business plan's budget.

The owner of a rental property is called the **lessor**. The **lessee** is the person paying to rent the property. The *lease terms* describe the rental details, such as the time period, payment schedule, and maintenance. Rent for commercial space is often priced by the square foot. For example, an 800-square-foot space leasing at $15 per square foot per year has a yearly rent of $12,000, or $1,000 per month.

Often, a rented building or space needs to be remodeled to fit the business' specific needs. **Tenant improvement** is the cost to remodel existing interior space for a new business. As an incentive to sign the lease, some lessors pay for some or all of the tenant improvement costs. It is a good idea to evaluate the potential tenant improvement costs and know who will pay for them before signing a lease.

Buy or Build

Buying an existing building generally requires additional financing, which may put a financial strain on a new business. If you

Consider your business' building needs when making location decisions.

Monkey Business Images/Shutterstock.com

Copyright Goodheart-Willcox Co., Inc.

Green Entrepreneurs

Nontoxic Paint

Business owners who have brick-and-mortar establishments may need to paint the walls in their place of business. When given the choice, look for green wall cover products that are safe for the environment. Minimize your carbon footprint by using wall paint with no- or low-zero volatile organic compounds (VOCs) that contribute to indoor pollution. Also, look for nontoxic paints that do not contain glycol.

decide to buy, thoroughly evaluate the building's exterior and interior. Make sure the site offers enough space for customer interactions, offices, storage, equipment, and restrooms. Also, consider whether you expect the business to expand in the future.

Evaluate the Exterior

A professional contractor, building inspector, or appraiser can help evaluate the soundness of a building. The entrance should be easy for customers to access and the site should have enough parking. It is important that customers can see the business sign from the traffic area, such as from the road while driving by. Your community may have signage restrictions.

Also, consider that the aesthetics of a building make an impression on customers. **Aesthetics** are the ideas or opinions about beauty. The building or site may need improvements to make it more appealing. Research the costs and possible restrictions for building improvements, such as new paint, new windows, or landscaping.

Evaluate the Interior

The interior of a business should combine form and function. Consider the space requirements. Define the purpose of the facility. Will it be used to sell products, perform services, or manufacture products? Calculate how much space is needed for customer areas, waiting areas, storage, and offices. Make sure the building has restroom facilities that meet regulations.

Check that the appliances, lights, outlets, heating and cooling equipment, and water sources are adequate. There should be enough space and power for equipment or machines. Make sure the visible items are attractive and can be maintained. Routine maintenance and cleaning should be manageable. Check that Internet access is available.

Build a New Facility

Building a new facility is usually the most expensive option and also usually requires additional financing. It also involves a more

SBA Tips

The SBA provides energy-efficiency guides specifically designed for small businesses. All business facilities need heating, cooling, and other electrical services for owners to remain in business. By using the guides' energy-savings tips, small business owners can save money by reducing energy usage in their buildings.

Copyright Goodheart-Willcox Co., Inc.

complex set of financial and legal issues. These include finding and buying suitable land and hiring an architect and contractor to design and construct the building.

Create the Layout

Visual merchandising is the process of creating floor plans and displays to attract customer attention and encourage purchases. When designing the layout, or the physical arrangement, of the business, there are many things to consider. The building type and location, customer access, equipment, and types of goods or services will determine the layout.

A floor plan is a scale drawing showing how an overall space will be divided. Depending on the business type, it shows exactly where merchandise displays, storage, customer services, production, or other areas are located. A carefully designed floor plan ensures efficient use of space and creates a positive customer experience.

There are a number of ways to create a floor plan for a business. There are inexpensive software programs that make designing a layout fairly easy. Many Internet sites can also give direction and information on layout design. As a new business owner, the best idea may be to start with graph paper and sketch a rough layout. However, if money is available, it might be wise to hire a professional interior designer. Each business type will have a different layout. Seek the help of an expert in the type of business you are opening.

An attractive layout will leave a good impression on customers.

Karkas/Shutterstock.com

Copyright Goodheart-Willcox Co., Inc.

Retail Business

A retail business layout typically requires three types of space: *selling space, storage space,* and *customer space.* The layout and interior design must appeal to customers and allow them to circulate freely through the space. The interior design, including colors, lighting, flooring, signage, or artwork should reflect the target market. For example, if girls under age 15 are the target market, choose décor that group prefers. Consider the following when creating a retail floor plan:

Sometimes a floor plan may also be referred to as the *layout* of the business.

- product

- sales per square foot

- shoplifting

- space

- aisle width

- traffic flow

The type of products offered is the first thing to consider when creating the layout for a retail business. Do the products require sales demonstrations and much customer assistance?

A retail layout should maximize the sales for each square foot of the selling space. Use the following formula to determine the sales per square foot:

$$\frac{\text{total net sales}}{\text{the total square feet of selling space}} = \text{sales per square foot}$$

Do not include storage space or any other area where products are not displayed in the calculation. A higher figure for sales per square foot means a better use of selling space. To increase sales per square foot, remove space between displays, extend shelf height, or add extra kiosks.

Preventing shoplifting is a major consideration in store layout. Choose a layout that places products so they can be easily seen by the staff. If the products are always in sight, it is harder for people in the store to engage in theft.

Customers need enough space between counters or racks not to feel crowded. They also need space to interact with each other and the salespeople. The layout should reflect these needs for space.

Leave an average of three feet for aisle width. Keep the aisles free of clutter. Customers will remain in the store longer if their shopping experience is comfortable.

One of the most important goals of a store layout is promoting good traffic flow. Did you know that 90 percent of people turn right when entering a store? Set the displays and products so customers easily move through the store and see all of the merchandise. There are five general retail layouts that direct traffic flow. These are the straight, diagonal, angular, loop, and free-flow floor plans.

Straight Floor Plan

A straight floor plan has long, straight lines, such as those in supermarkets. This provides structure directing customers through aisles with little help. The straight, or grid, floor plan is illustrated in Figure 7-1. Counters and fixtures are placed in long rows and at right angles throughout the store.

Advantages of the straight floor plan are low cost and ease of cleaning. Additionally, customers are familiar with the layout and can serve themselves. Straight floor plans are also easy to monitor for security purposes. Disadvantages include that the layout can be boring, does not encourage browsing, and leaves little room for creativity.

Diagonal Floor Plan

The diagonal floor plan is just what it says—counters and shelves are placed at diagonals, as shown in Figure 7-2. This layout is, like a straight floor plan, good for a self-service store. The diagonal floor plan can be more visually appealing than a straight floor plan. Another advantage is improved traffic flow. A disadvantage is that without the correct fixtures, it can be boring and unappealing to customers.

Angular Floor Plan

An angular floor plan places products in lines and circles to create visual interest and an upscale feel. The angular layout, as shown in Figure 7-3, is used most often by smaller, high-end boutiques. Advantages

Figure 7-1. Straight Floor Plan

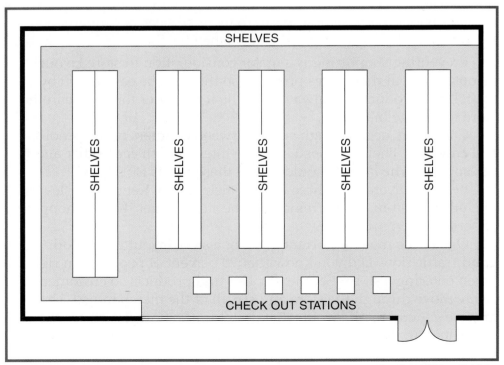

Goodheart-Willcox Publisher

Copyright Goodheart-Willcox Co., Inc.

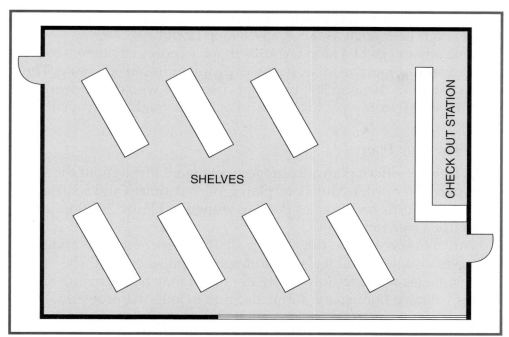

Figure 7-2. Diagonal Floor Plan

Goodheart-Willcox Publisher

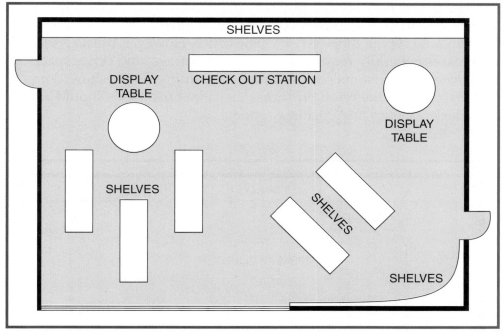

Figure 7-3. Angular Floor Plan

Goodheart-Willcox Publisher

of the angular layout include excellent traffic flow and more display options. Disadvantages are the higher cost and limited use. The angles and curves make the angular layout more expensive to design and build.

Loop Floor Plan

A loop floor plan organizes merchandise according to function and pulls customers through the store. Aisles start at the store entrance and loop around the store in a circle or rectangle, as shown in

Copyright Goodheart-Willcox Co., Inc.

Figure 7-4. Eventually, customers return to the entrance. Department stores and others, such as IKEA, use a loop layout.

One advantage of a loop layout is that it exposes customers to a wide variety of merchandise. It also encourages impulse buying. The disadvantage of the loop layout is that customers who do not want to shop the entire store may turn around or cut through departments.

Free-Flow Floor Plan

A free-flow floor plan encourages movement throughout the store in no particular order. This floor plan groups counters and fixtures in different patterns on the sales floor, as shown in Figure 7-5. Specialty stores use a free-flow layout.

Advantages of a free-flow layout are that it encourages wandering and adds visual appeal. It also encourages impulse buying. The disadvantages of a free-flow layout are that it may be confusing and wastes valuable floor space. It can also add to loitering problems.

Service Business

The layout for a service business depends largely on the type of service provided. A children's day care will have different space needs than an auto repair shop or real estate office. However, most service businesses generally require some display, storage, and office spaces. Most also need customer spaces, such as waiting rooms, showrooms, and restrooms. Like retail businesses, service businesses should also consider aesthetics and customer appeal.

Figure 7-4. Loop Floor Plan

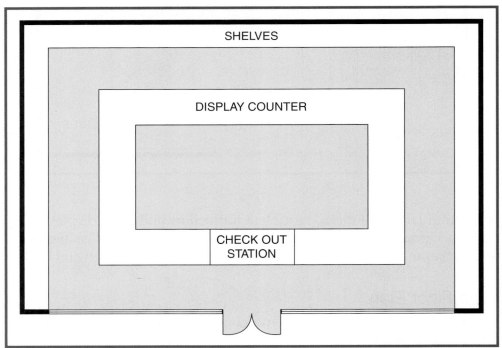

SHELVES

DISPLAY COUNTER

CHECK OUT STATION

Goodheart-Willcox Publisher

Copyright Goodheart-Willcox Co., Inc.

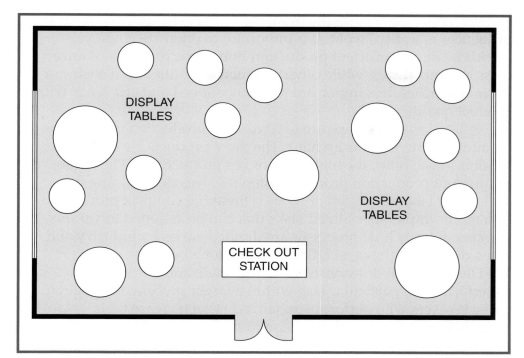

Figure 7-5. Free-Flow Floor Plan

Goodheart-Willcox Publisher

Manufacturing Business

All businesses need to maximize efficiency and promote safe working conditions. However, manufacturers require very different physical layouts than other business types. Workers are often using large or potentially dangerous equipment and may be handling raw materials.

The first step in designing a layout for a manufacturing business is to define the production needs and processes. The business may extract raw materials from natural sources, transform raw materials into usable products, or assemble products from components. Each type of manufacturing procedure requires a specific layout. There are several important considerations when determining a layout.

Focus on Finance

Business Expenses

Essential technology to conduct business may include a cell phone, Internet access, and cable television. These services can generate hefty monthly bills. Consider using a service provider that offers all three services in a bundle, or discounted, price when purchased together. Some providers offer small businesses upgraded services for a special price. Many providers extend special offers to entrepreneurs as an incentive to do business with them.

Copyright Goodheart-Willcox Co., Inc.

Production workflow is the sequence of the assembly, and it greatly influences a facility layout. It is important to organize employees' workflow into an efficient production line. Some products require mass assembly lines, while other products are built one at a time or in small batches. It is important to balance speed and efficiency with product quality.

Productivity is a measure of a worker's production in a specific amount of time, such as an hour. The more products a worker produces each hour, the higher his or her productivity. The sequence of different production processes often involves determining the division of labor. **Division of labor** is breaking complex processes into more simple, specialized tasks that can be assigned to various workers. Exactly how processes are divided varies by industry and helps determine the most efficient layout for a business.

Division of labor leads to worker specialization. **Specialization** is performing a particular task within a larger process on a regular basis. Workers who perform specialized tasks increase their efficiency and accuracy due to repetition. Specialization leads to increased productivity and potential profits for a company, as well as opportunity for business growth.

However, there is a point at which the level of productivity gained through specialization levels off or begins to decrease. This change is an example of diminishing returns. The **law of diminishing returns** is an economic concept explaining that at a certain point, the benefits generated from investing more revenue or effort decrease and no longer justify the continued investment. In the production process, diminishing returns can apply to the number of workers that are employed and increased division of labor. At some point, putting more effort into creating a product may not necessarily generate more revenue. As a business owner, it is important to know when you have reached the point of diminishing returns so you can direct efforts to keep the company moving forward. Flat or declining rates of production will most likely be a good indicator.

How materials enter the facility, move through production, and finally leave as end products are also very important layout considerations. The most common ways that materials flow in manufacturing are in a straight line, a U-shape, or an S-shape. Figure 7-6 shows an example of material flow in a straight-line manufacturing environment. Choose a layout that provides ease of receiving and shipping as well as accommodating the flow of materials.

It is also important to evaluate how the manufacturing process might affect the environment. This includes plans for waste-product disposal and controlling noise or air pollution. It is necessary for manufacturing business owners to learn and follow the state and local environmental laws related to their businesses. Use a layout that minimizes any potential harm. Being a socially responsible entrepreneur can avoid costly, time-consuming legal issues.

Copyright Goodheart-Willcox Co., Inc.

Figure 7-6. In straight-line manufacturing, materials and processes move along a straight line through the facility.

dotshock/Shutterstock.com

There are three common types of manufacturing layouts from which to choose. These are product-based, process-based, and project-based floor plans.

Product-Based Layout

A *product-based layout* places machines and equipment along the route materials move through the assembly process. This would be in a straight line, a U-shape, or an S-shape. The product begins assembly at one end and ends with the finished product at another end in an uninterrupted flow. One example of a product-based floor plan is an auto assembly line. Henry Ford may have not invented the car or the assembly line, but he made both popular. Ford made his assembly lines more efficient so automobiles could be assembled faster and cheaper. Because of this breakthrough, many more people could afford a car.

 # You Do the Math   Geometric Reasoning

The area of a two-dimensional shape considers measurements of its perimeter. The area of a rectangle, for example, is calculated by multiplying the length of two sides that meet at a right angle. The area of a circle is calculated by multiplying the constant pi (3.14) by the radius of the circle squared. To calculate the volume of a cylinder, multiply its height by the area of its base.

Solve the following problems.

1. The area of a parking lot must be calculated in order to estimate the cost of repaving it. The parking lot measures 75 feet by 125 feet. What is the area of the parking lot?

2. Enough plywood must be purchased to cover the floor in a space that is 12 feet by 25 feet. One sheet of plywood is 4 feet by 8 feet. How many sheets of plywood must be purchased?

Copyright Goodheart-Willcox Co., Inc.

Process-Based Layout

A *process-based layout* places the equipment and workers that are grouped by division of labor to maximize efficiency. The materials are brought to each specialized group or team for a different part of the process. For example, in a factory that makes fittings for sprinkler systems, the process begins by feeding steel bars into machines. The machines turn the bars into fittings. The fittings then move to another group for washing and cleaning. From that team, fittings go to the sorting department to be separated by type and placed in bins. Next, the products move to the inspection department. After inspection, the products end at the shipping department to fulfill customer orders.

Project-Based Layout

A *project-based layout* places a product that is too large or bulky to move in a fixed location. The different employees and machines must move to the product being assembled at its location. For example, factories that build large aircraft use project-based layouts.

Wholesale Business

Wholesale facilities may vary, but often include space for inventory storage. Wholesalers are generally located in warehouses close to their customers. These are most often single story buildings with some office space and possibly showrooms. The layout must make storing and delivering inventory efficient. It should also protect products from damage.

The floor plan for a wholesale business is traditionally a straight-line layout. This layout makes it easier to access products for shipping on a daily basis. Wholesale stores have high ceilings, wide aisles, a straight-line layout, and extra products at higher levels. An example of the layout of a wholesale store is shown in Figure 7-7.

E-Commerce

E-commerce businesses operating strictly through the Internet still need some physical space. An office or workspace in your home or a small rented office space is necessary for administrative work. If you sell physical goods, some type of warehousing, shipping, and storage space are also necessary. Choose the layout that best meets the functions of the space you need.

Home-Based Business

The layout for a home-based business depends on whether clients or customers will enter your home. If customers will visit your home, create a waiting area or showroom in addition to your workspace.

Copyright Goodheart-Willcox Co., Inc.

Figure 7-7. The layout of a wholesale business is spacious.

Dmitry Kalinovsky/Shutterstock.com

The layout should make it easy for customers to wait comfortably, view products, or access the necessary rooms. When possible, provide a separate entrance and parking area. It may be necessary to rent a storage area outside your home if you do not have enough space.

Section 7.2   Review

Check Your Understanding ⬀

1. Why might you want to lease rather than buy a building for your business?
2. When setting up a retail store, what criteria should you consider?
3. What are the different types of floor plans for a retail business?
4. What is production workflow? Why is it important?
5. What are the three main types of manufacturing layouts?

Build Your Vocabulary ⬀

As you progress through this text, develop a personal glossary of key terms. This will help you build your vocabulary and prepare you for a career. Write a definition for each of the following terms and add them to your personal glossary.

lease	layout
lessor	floor plan
lessee	productivity
tenant improvement	division of labor
aesthetics	specialization
visual merchandising	law of diminishing returns

Copyright Goodheart-Willcox Co., Inc.

Chapter Summary

Section 7.1 Choose the Location

- Consider the economic characteristics of a community when deciding where to locate your business.
- A business' physical structure, be it a brick-and-mortar store or e-business, is determined by the needs of the business and its customers.

Section 7.2 Choose the Layout

- The three ways to obtain space for a new business are by leasing a space, buying a space, or building a space.
- The layout of a business is important because it facilitates the business' operations, such as serving customers or shipping orders.

Online Activities

Complete the following activities to help you learn, practice, and expand your knowledge and skills.

Posttest. Now that you have finished the chapter, see what you learned by taking the chapter posttest.

Key Terms. Practice vocabulary for this chapter using the e-flash cards, matching activity, and vocabulary game until you are able to recognize their meanings.

Review Your Knowledge

1. Why should you consider the current economy in the community when choosing a location?
2. Name three of the common types of zoning laws.
3. Discuss the importance of the supply chain and how it influences your business.
4. Name the four structures a business may have.
5. If you decide to have a physical location for your business, what are the three options for obtaining space?
6. Explain the importance of a floor plan for a business.
7. Name the two floor plans that encourage impulse buying.
8. Explain the space needs of a service business.
9. How do product-based, process-based, and project-based floor plans differ?
10. Describe a traditional floor plan for a wholesale business and how it benefits this type of business.

Copyright Goodheart-Willcox Co., Inc.

Apply Your Knowledge

1. Analyze the local economy where you have decided to locate your business. What did you find out? Is your choice of locations a wise one as far as the economy is concerned?

2. Take a look at the competition in the area where you would like to locate your business. Make a list of all of the companies that will be direct and indirect competitors.

3. Explain how the supply chain will influence your business.

4. Describe the ideal type of structure for your business. Will it be a brick-and-mortar, Internet, home-based, or a hybrid model?

5. List the needs that the structure of your business will require. Consider factors such as appropriate amount of space, parking, lighting, etc. Write down as many factors as you can think of.

6. Compare and contrast the opportunities of leasing, buying, or building for your business.

7. Estimate how much it will cost to rent a space each month. If you have a home office, take into consideration how much space you would be using and what the rent and other costs are for that space. If you think you will be renting commercial or industrial space, find out what the cost would be per month.

8. Research various types of software that can be used to create a floor plan. Make a list of several that appeal to you. Next to each, write the cost of the software and its features and benefits.

9. You have chosen your business and now it is time to create a floor plan. Using the Internet, find sample floor plans that will guide you to creating your own. Even if your business will operate out of your home, create a plan for your home office.

10. What are the environmental zoning laws in your community that would influence your business? List and explain how each will affect you.

Teamwork

Working with your team, research state and local incentives that are in place for encouraging businesses to establish a company in the area. These incentives may be tax abatement, workforce development dollars, and a variety of other opportunities for new businesses. Present your findings to the class.

Internet Research

Specialization and Division of Labor. Specialization and division of labor can impact the success of a business. Use the Internet to research *specialization* and *division of labor*. With the information you find, analyze

Copyright Goodheart-Willcox Co., Inc.

the impact of specialization on productivity. Then, analyze the impact of division of labor on productivity. What did you learn from this exercise?

Law of Diminishing Returns. Using the Internet, research the economic concept of law of diminishing returns. Explain the impact of the law of diminishing returns on productivity. How does it influence the revenue and profits of a business?

College and Career Readiness

Communication Skills

Reading. Read a magazine, newspaper, or online article about the impact of technology on small businesses in today's economy. Determine the central ideas of the article and review the conclusions made by the author. Provide an accurate summary of your reading, making sure to incorporate the *who, what, when,* and *how* of this situation.

Writing. Conduct research on how much money small businesses lost in the last year due to identity theft. Write an informative report consisting of several paragraphs to describe your findings of the implications for the business.

CTSOs

Performance. Some competitive events for Career and Technical Student Organizations (CTSOs) have a performance portion. The activity could potentially be an entrepreneur decision-making scenario for which your team will provide a solution. To prepare for the performance portion of a presentation, complete the following activities.

1. Read the guidelines provided by your organization. Make certain that you ask any questions about points you do not understand. It is important you follow each specific item that is outlined in the competition rules.

2. Locate on your CTSO's website a rubric or scoring sheet for the event.

3. Confirm the use of visual aids that may be used in the presentation and amount of set-up time permitted.

4. Review the rules to confirm if questions will be asked or if the team will need to defend a case or business plan.

5. Make notes on index cards about important points to remember. Use these notes to study. You may also be able to use these notes during the event.

6. Practice the presentation. Each team member should introduce himself or herself, review the topic that is being presented, defend the topic being presented, and conclude with a summary.

7. After the presentation is complete, ask for feedback from your teacher. You may consider also having a student audience listen and give feedback.

Copyright Goodheart-Willcox Co., Inc.

Building Your Business Plan—Putting the Puzzle Together

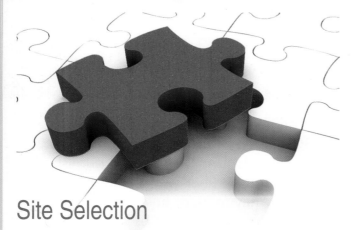

Site Selection

Location, location, location. This is a phrase entrepreneurs have heard for years. Does it really matter where your business is located? If you plan to open a business where you meet clients, the location is critical. Even if you are operating an e-business or do not meet with clients, your site is still important. There are a number of considerations for selecting both your trade area and the best site for your business.

Goals

- Research the economic indicators for your trade area.
- Determine potential locations for your business.
- Compare the costs associated with each potential location.
- Create the layout of your business.
- Create business plan notes.

Directions

Access the *Entrepreneurship* companion website at www.g-wlearning.com ↗. Download each data file for the following activities. A complete sample business plan is available on the companion website to use as a reference. The name of the file is BusPlan_Sample.RetroAttire. docx.

Preparation

Activity 7-1. Trade Area. Determine five economic indicators important to your business. Find the most recent statistics for those indicators for the country and for your trade area. This information will help you decide on a location.

Activity 7-2. Site Selection. Research locations you think would be appropriate for your business and how each could be acquired.

Activity 7-3. Site Costs. After identifying potential sites for your business, research the associated costs for those locations.

Activity 7-4. Layout. Now that you have chosen a possible business location, create the layout that makes best use of the space.

Activity 7-5. Business Plan Notes. Create notes for what you learned about your trade area and the site you selected. Also, make any notes you need about the layout of the business.

Business Plan—Business Description and Market Evaluation

In this chapter, you learned about the impact of the economy on local businesses. You decided the best place to locate your business based on sound research. You also learned about different business types and how that affects the physical layout of a building. This information will help you work on the following sections of the business plan.

1. Open your saved business plan document.

2. Locate the Business Description section of the plan. You will now complete the last subsection called Business Location.

3. Locate the Market Evaluation section of the plan. Complete the following subsections: Economic Conditions and Trade Area Analysis.

4. Use the suggestions and questions listed to help you generate ideas. Delete the instructions and questions when you are finished recording your responses. Make sure to proofread your document and correct any errors in keyboarding, spelling, and grammar.

5. Save your document.

8
Legal Issues

Adora Svitak was an entrepreneur before her twelfth birthday. She has been featured on ABC's *Good Morning America* and has been a speaker at hundreds of schools. Svitak wrote and published two books that can be purchased through her website and from other retailers. Even though Svitak may think of herself as a writer first, she is also the owner of a business. She must be aware of legal issues related to her business. Under US copyright law, her work was automatically copyrighted as soon as it was in tangible form. Copyright provides legal protection for her work. However, there are other legal aspects she must consider. She sells her books, so she must follow sales tax laws in the states where she sells her books.

"Nothing can substitute for the advice of an attorney, licensed in the state where you are doing business, reviewing your specific agreement or situation."

—Laura Plimpton, lawyer and author of *Business Contracts: Turn Any Business Contract to Your Advantage*

College and Career Readiness

Reading Prep. Before reading this chapter, preview the illustrations. As you read the chapter, cite specific textual evidence to support the information in the illustrations.

Sections

8.1 Protect Your Business

8.2 Know the Laws

Picture Yourself Here
Darnell Henderson

After graduating from the Florida College of Natural Health, Darnell Henderson created a plan to open a spa that promotes men's wellness. He identified what he saw as an unmet need—men's skin care. Darnell had personal assets and seed money to start the business, but needed additional help. The Florida Regional Minority Business Council saw the potential of Darnell's idea and helped him find additional funding and business development resources to open the spa.

In 2004, Darnell opened H.I.M., which stands for Healthy Image Men. The spa offered facials, massages, and haircuts. In addition, it sold an all-natural line of men's grooming products that Darnell developed. Later that year, Hurricanes Charley and Jean forced the spa to close. However, people continued to order Darnell's products online, so he changed his focus from the spa to grooming products. That is when H.I.M-istry was born. H.I.M-istry is a line of men's grooming products for men of all skin types and ethnic backgrounds.

Darnell was named one of *Black Enterprise* magazine's "10 Young Entrepreneurs to Watch out For." As CEO of H.I.M-istry Skincare, Inc., Darnell now focuses his business on professionally developed skin products for men.

Photo © Darnell Henderson, CEO, Founder of H.I.M-istry Grooming

Check Your Entrepreneurship IQ

Before you begin the chapter, see what you already know about entrepreneurship by taking the chapter pretest. The pretest is available at www.g-wlearning.com

SECTION 8.1 | Protect Your Business

Essential Question

How can a business protect its products and interests?

Objectives

After completing this section, you will be able to:

- **Describe** contracts and what makes them binding agreements.
- **Discuss** the nature of torts and the need for protecting a business from lawsuits.
- **Explain** the importance of protecting intellectual property.

Key Terms

agent
agency law
retainer
offer
mutual acceptance
consideration
capacity
breach of contract

tort
intellectual property
infringement
intellectual property laws
patent
trademark
copyright

Critical Thinking

Starting a business requires a variety of legal documents and contracts. Based on the type of your business, list which legal documents and contracts you think will be necessary. Next to the name of each document or contract, explain its purpose and why it will be needed.

Contracts

As a business owner, you will need many types of *contracts,* which are legally binding agreements between two or more parties. In legal terms, *binding* is another word for enforceable. *Party* refers to a person or a group entering into an agreement. The core of most contracts is a set of mutual promises. Contracts do not have to be in writing, although it is better if they are. Carefully read the entire contract and be sure you understand the terms before signing.

When a business owner contracts with another party to work on his or her behalf, that party is working as the entrepreneur's **agent.** **Agency law** deals with the relationships between an owner, also called the *principal,* and his or her agent. These relationships are called *agency relationships.* For example, if you contracted with a manufacturer to fabricate a product, the manufacturer is working on your behalf to make sure the product is made according to your requirements.

FYI

Contract law specifies what constitutes a legally binding, or enforceable, agreement.

Copyright Goodheart-Willcox Co., Inc.

Stephen Coburn/Shutterstock.com

It is easier to protect yourself with a written contract, rather than an oral one.

In addition, if you hire an outside firm to sell your product, that firm is working as your agent. On the other hand, if your company is contracted to create something for someone else, your company is the agent for that party.

Legal Advice

Seek legal advice before creating or signing any contract. Some contracts may have hidden or unintentional clauses or wording. An improperly worded contract may cost one or all of the parties money. In a worst-case scenario, the business owner may lose the business. All contracts are different, and liability depends on the ownership structure of the business.

The money invested for a lawyer to review a contract can be worth the cost. Businesses may hire lawyers on an as-needed basis to save money. Lawyers may also be hired on retainer, though, if their services are needed over a period of time. A **retainer** is the fee paid to a lawyer or other professional in advance for the services. Often, retainers are paid monthly based on the amount of work expected to be done.

Contract Conditions

A contract is created under the conditions, as illustrated in Figure 8-1. An **offer** is a proposal to provide a service or good. Offers may be oral or written. For example, if a seller offers a car for $5,000 to a buyer, an offer has been made. If the buyer agrees to purchase the car for $5,000, the offer is mutually acceptable. Both parties must agree to the offer's terms for **mutual acceptance**. However, if the seller pressures the potential buyer through force, or threat of force, the contract is not legally executed.

Copyright Goodheart-Willcox Co., Inc.

Figure 8-1. The conditions of a contract must be met for the contract to be legal.

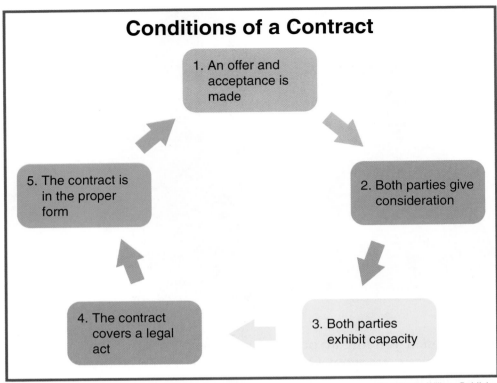

Conditions of a Contract

1. An offer and acceptance is made

2. Both parties give consideration

3. Both parties exhibit capacity

4. The contract covers a legal act

5. The contract is in the proper form

Goodheart-Willcox Publisher

In legal terms, **consideration** means something of value. Using the same example, the seller provides the car and the buyer provides $5,000. The car and the money are the consideration in the contract.

Capacity means that a person is legally able to enter into a binding agreement. *Legally binding* means that the agreement or contract is enforceable by law. In most cases, a person under the age of 18 may not be held to a contract. A person under the influence of legal or illegal substances cannot legally enter into a contract due to impaired judgment. Neither can a person of unsound mind, meaning one who has been legally declared incompetent.

Contracts involving any criminal acts are not binding. For example, a contract to buy stolen goods is not binding because selling stolen goods is a crime.

Focus on Finance

Quarterly Business Taxes

As a small business, owners generally pay state and federal taxes on a quarterly basis. Your accountant will help you estimate the amount of taxes due on each quarter's earnings. These taxes must be paid on time or the business could be subject to late payment fees or fines. It is recommended to seek advice from your tax professional for help with paying quarterly taxes for your business.

Copyright Goodheart-Willcox Co., Inc.

Contracts are necessary for transactions that cannot be completed within one year, as well as for real estate. Written contracts should be issued when selling goods or services worth more than $500. Verbal contracts can be made for goods worth less than $500. A verbal contract is also binding for transactions that can be completed within one year. It is safer to put *all* contracts in writing, though.

Even when a contract is mutually accepted, things can still go wrong. One or both parties may choose not to fulfill the contract's terms, which is a **breach of contract**. If a breach of contract occurs, either party may take legal action.

Types of Contracts

There are a variety of contracts that will be needed for the operation of the business. Some common examples of contracts include

- sales contract;

- service contract; and

- lease.

Businesses that buy and sell goods should use sales contracts. Depending on the type of business, a sales contract may be issued to the customer before goods change hands. A *sales contract* lists the items purchased, prices, and payment terms. A signature may be required to show the customer is in agreement with the terms of sale. A *service contract* is a type of sales contract for service providers. It specifies the services to be performed, timing, cost, and payment schedule. For informal sales, a sales contract may be issued in the form of a *sales receipt* when the goods are sold.

If a business needs a rented space, a lease is issued. A lease is a contract to rent. The lease terms may include what the building may be used for, the length of time, and the amount of rent.

Torts

It is important for all business owners to protect their businesses from torts. A **tort** is a civil wrong, as opposed to a criminal wrong. There are many types of torts. Some involve damage due to a business owner's negligence. For example, perhaps a business owner fails to shovel snow one day. If a shopper slips and breaks an arm on that sidewalk, a tort has occurred. The shopper could bring a civil lawsuit against that owner. Business owners who lose a civil lawsuit usually must pay money to make up for the damage.

Businesses face the risk of civil lawsuits. They can help protect their companies by carrying insurance in the event of a civil lawsuit. Insurance does not cover intentional injury to another person, but will cover most torts. However, a breach of contract is *not* considered a tort.

SBA Tips

It makes good business sense to know how to handle legal issues that affect a business. Not all legal matters require a lawyer, but understanding the issues helps considerably. Sometimes the best way for an entrepreneur to protect his or her interests is to know where to go for assistance. The SBA website provides a number of resources to help small businesses with legal issues.
www.sba.gov

Copyright Goodheart-Willcox Co., Inc.

Intellectual Property

Some entrepreneurs offer or create a special product or service to generate revenue. For example, your business may sell a product with a unique recipe or formula. All of the information surrounding this recipe must be protected from the competition. This information is the intellectual property of the business. **Intellectual property** is something that comes from a person's mind, such as an idea, invention, or process. In business, these ideas are considered proprietary information and must be protected from theft. Any use of intellectual property without permission is called **infringement**. Infringement may have legal consequences for your business.

Intellectual property laws protect a person's or company's inventions, artistic works, and other intellectual property. Certain intellectual property laws protect a business' unique phrases, symbols, and designs. Ownership of all intellectual property is implied.

There are three ways to register the different forms of intellectual property, as shown in Figure 8-2. It may be wise to use the services of an attorney who specializes in intellectual property law when registering intellectual property.

Patents

A **patent** gives the person or company the right to be the sole producer of a product for a defined period of time. Patents protect an invention that is functional or mechanical. The invention must be considered useful and inoffensive and it must be operational. This means that an idea may not be patented. A process can be patented under certain conditions. The process must be related to a particular machine or transform a substance or item into a different state or thing.

The inventor must file a patent application with the US Patent and Trademark Office. Once granted, a patent protects the inventor's intellectual property for between 14 and 20 years from the filing date.

FYI

Small businesses produce over 13 times more patents per employee than do large firms. Patents from small businesses are also twice as likely to be successful than patents from large firms.

Figure 8-2. Intellectual property laws protect ideas.

Intellectual Property Laws	
Form of Protection	**Intellectual Property**
Patent	Gives inventor the sole right to produce and sell an invention for a specific time.
Trademark	Protects phrases, names, symbols, or any unique method of identifying a company or its product.
Copyright	Protects books, magazine articles, music, paintings, or other work of authorship for the life of the creator plus 70 years.

Goodheart-Willcox Publisher

Copyright Goodheart-Willcox Co., Inc.

The patent office issues patents in three categories:

- *Utility patent* is granted for new machines, processes, or products that will be manufactured; may also be granted for improvements to existing utility patents.

- *Design patent* is granted for ornamental design for a product that will be manufactured.

- *Plant patent* is granted for different plant varieties created.

Trademarks

A **trademark** protects taglines, slogans, names, symbols, or any unique method to identify a product or company. A *service mark* is similar to a trademark, but it identifies a service rather than a product. Trademarks and service marks do not protect a work or product. They protect the way in which the product is described. The term trademark is often used to refer to both trademarks and service marks.

There are two reasons to register a trademark with the US Patent and Trademark Office. First, the trademark is then in the public, which discourages anyone else from using it. Also, a registered trademark makes it easy to prove infringement. Trademarks never expire. *Graphic marks* are also called symbols. Some can be used without being formally registered, as shown in Figure 8-3.

Copyrights

A **copyright** protects music, writings, paintings, and other original works of authorship. Copyright is automatically assigned as soon as the work is in tangible form. An idea cannot be copyrighted, but as soon as the idea is written down, the written work is copyrighted. The copyright lists the author or creator and the year the work was published. Copyrights are valid for the life of the author plus 70 years.

The © symbol or the statement "copyright by" indicates copyrighted material. Lack of the symbol or statement does *not* mean the work is not copyrighted. A copyright can be registered with the US Copyright Office, which is part of the Library of Congress. However, all legal protection of a copyright is provided whether or not the copyright is registered.

FYI

The United States and 164 other countries, or about 85 percent of the countries in the world, follow the Berne Convention international treaty when creating copyright laws.

Correct Usage of Trademark Symbols	
™	Trademark, not registered
SM	Service mark, not registered
®	Registered trademark

Goodheart-Willcox Publisher

Figure 8-3. Graphic marks are symbols that indicate legal protection of intellectual property.

Copyright Goodheart-Willcox Co., Inc.

Green Entrepreneurs

Green Equipment

When buying equipment for the business, look for the Energy Star label. The EPA and the Department of Energy created the Energy Star program to rate products. The Energy Star label ensures the product meets a certain level of energy efficiency. By looking for this label, business owners, and consumers, can be confident that the product meets environmental standards. When in doubt, check the website for the US Environmental Protection Agency for information.

Section 8.1 Review

Check Your Understanding ➦

1. Describe the meaning of agency relationships.
2. List the factors that make a contract a binding agreement.
3. Name three common contracts used in business.
4. How can entrepreneurs protect their businesses against civil lawsuits?
5. What are intellectual property laws?

Build Your Vocabulary ➦

As you progress through this text, develop a personal glossary of key terms. This will help you build your vocabulary and prepare you for a career. Write a definition for each of the following terms and add them to your personal glossary.

agent
agency law
retainer
offer
mutual acceptance
consideration
capacity
breach of contract

tort
intellectual property
infringement
intellectual
   property laws
patent
trademark
copyright

Copyright Goodheart-Willcox Co., Inc.

SECTION 8.2 Know the Laws

Essential Question

How is the US government involved in business activities?

Objectives

After completing this section, you will be able to:
- **Explain** the nature of business laws.
- **List** four important types of workplace laws.
- **Discuss** the importance of consumer protection laws.

Key Terms

business laws
labor relations laws
health and safety laws
compensation and benefits laws
equal-employment opportunity laws

workplace discrimination
sexual harassment
consumer protection laws
recall

Critical Thinking

Schools work hard to discourage discrimination of any kind. Discrimination can occur in any environment including the workplace. Make a list of the ways you will ensure that discrimination does not happen in your business.

Business Laws

It seems like there are many laws, regulations, and agencies that regulate different business practices and collect taxes. In general, **business laws** promote fair business practices and protect the best interests of employers, employees, consumers, and the government. Some laws protect customers, while others protect employees and the environment. Still others make sure that businesses compete fairly with each other. Government agencies, including the SBA, can provide additional information about different business laws.

Small business owners are subject to laws and regulations, as are other businesses. Regulations are rules that have the force of law and are issued by an agency of government. Business laws and regulations are commonly referred to as *regulatory requirements*. Some of the regulatory requirements include:

- privacy laws to keep personal information safe from theft;

- online-business laws covering the areas of privacy, security, intellectual property, and taxes;

Copyright Goodheart-Willcox Co., Inc.

- advertising laws that regulate truth in advertising and product labeling; and
- finance laws covering bankruptcy and financial reporting.

There are many legal issues a business owner may face that can impact the business. Issues such as disgruntled employees and accusations of discrimination are common complaints that can cause lawsuits. Employees and business owners mishandling confidential information or violating copyrights and patents can also result in litigation. Legal issues can potentially hurt the reputation and finances of a business.

Fair Business Practices

The Federal Trade Commission Act established the Federal Trade Commission (FTC) in 1914. The purpose of the FTC is to encourage free enterprise and prevent monopolies. A *monopoly* is a business with complete control of the entire supply of goods or services in a market. Most monopolies can have a negative effect on both consumers and other businesses. They limit competition and keep prices high. The FTC also regulates every area involving consumer protection. Some of the oldest business laws still in existence are shown in Figure 8-4.

Tax Laws

Businesses are legally obligated to follow each state's sales tax law, including products sold online that ship to the state. Businesses must obtain a *sales tax identification number* from the state's Department of Revenue to collect sales tax for the state. In this case, the retailers are acting as agents for the state and are bound by law to collect and forward the correct taxes.

Businesses with employees must obtain an employee identification number (EIN) to track federal income taxes withheld from employees' salaries or wages. The Internal Revenue Service issues EINs to businesses and requires these numbers for filing tax returns.

FYI

Protect yourself and your business by making sure the company is recognized as a legal business. Check the SBA website to learn the steps to take for registering a business.

Business Laws	
Sherman Antitrust Act (1890)	Designed to prohibit monopolies and protect consumers against price-fixing. *Price-fixing* occurs when a group of businesses agree to set prices at a certain level, usually higher than normal.
Robinson-Patman Act (1936)	Protects businesses and consumers against price discrimination. *Price discrimination* is the practice of charging different groups or individuals different prices for the same goods or services.
National Environmental Policy Act (1970)	Established national policies and goals for water, air, and soil quality; noise levels; and toxic substances.

Goodheart-Willcox Publisher

Figure 8-4. There are many laws in place that set guidelines for businesses.

Copyright Goodheart-Willcox Co., Inc.

Environmental Law

Environmental law is the body of US laws, regulations, and international treaties that address the impact of human activity on the environment. Environmental laws and regulations apply to every type of business in every industry. The United States enforces laws that regulate:

- toxic chemicals released by industrial businesses
- importing and exporting materials that pose a risk to the environment
- use of pesticides
- management of natural resources
- quality of drinking water

Businesses must make responsible decisions about their actions that relate to the environment. Examples of environmental laws are shown in Figure 8-5. The Environmental Protection Agency (EPA) is a governmental agency that enforces federal laws regarding human health and the environment. The EPA offers information and resources for individuals, businesses, and communities about environmental protection.

Legal Procedure

The US legal system interprets and enforces laws and regulations, including those that apply to businesses. The role of the legal process is to resolve disputes between people, businesses, and even those that involve agencies of the government. Legal procedure is the steps and methods involved in the legal process. This includes:

- informing parties of legal action
- holding hearings
- conducting trials
- presenting evidence
- making motions
- determining facts

Environmental Protection Laws	
Clean Air Act (1970)	Establishes the allowable air pollutant levels emitted by US businesses
Clean Water Act (1972)	Establishes the allowable water pollutant levels emitted by US businesses
Noise Control Act (1972)	Protects the public from excessive noise created by business operations
Energy Policy Act (2005)	Provides tax incentives for companies that use energy-efficient methods in the operation of their business

Goodheart-Willcox Publisher

Figure 8-5. Environmental laws and regulations apply differently to businesses within different industries.

Copyright Goodheart-Willcox Co., Inc.

A standard legal procedure is intended to ensure the fair handling of every legal action. This applies to both civil and criminal proceedings. If your business should become involved in a legal action, become familiar with legal procedure. Understand the steps that need to be taken, the order in which events will occur, and any time constraints that will be enforced. Having this information will help your issue move more smoothly through the legal process.

Workplace Laws

The US Department of Labor (DOL) enforces over 180 federal laws that apply to the workplace. These specific laws and regulations provide guidelines for employers and protect employees. Workplace laws and regulations can be grouped into four areas. These include labor relations, compensation and benefits, health and safety, and equal-employment opportunity, as shown in Figure 8-6.

Labor Relations Laws

Labor relations laws give employees the right to organize and collectively bargain with their employers. *Collective bargaining* is negotiating the terms of employment between an employer and a group of workers. For entrepreneurs with employees, it is important to become educated about current labor relations laws. These laws directly impact businesses. Figure 8-7 shows some important labor relations laws.

Health and Safety Laws

Health and safety laws are laws that establish regulations to eliminate illness and injury in the workplace. The most prominent of these laws is the *Occupational Safety and Health Act (OSHA)*. The Occupational Safety and Health Act of 1970 was created to assure safe and healthful working conditions. Occupational health and safety (OHS) focuses on the safety, health, and welfare of employees. OSHA sets and enforces workplace safety standards. The agency also assists and encourages workplace health and safety by providing research, information, education, and training for employers and workers.

Laws that Protect Employees	
Labor relations laws	Protect employees and their civil rights
Health and safety laws	Focus on safe working conditions for all employees
Compensation and benefits laws	Ensure fair and equal wages and benefits for employees
Equal-employment opportunity laws	Ensure all employees are given equal opportunities in the workplace

Goodheart-Willcox Publisher

Figure 8-6. US law protects employees' rights.

Copyright Goodheart-Willcox Co., Inc.

Labor Management Legislation		
Law	Year	Description
Norris-LaGuardia Act	1932	Supported organized labor and the formation of unions
National Labor Relations Act (Wagner Act)	1935	Established protection for the right of workers to organize and bargain collectively with their employers
Fair Labor Standards Act	1938	Established standards for minimum wage, overtime pay, child labor, and recordkeeping
Labor Management Reporting and Disclosure Act (Landrum-Griffen Act)	1959	Protected union membership rights of workers from unfair practices by unions

Goodheart-Willcox Publisher

Figure 8-7. Some laws regulate relationships between employers and employees.

Global Entrepreneurs

Garrett Gee, Ben Turley, and Kirk Ouimet

Garrett Gee, Ben Turley, and Kirk Ouimet were college friends at BYU in 2010. They created the business Scan in January, 2011. Scan creates computer applications to bridge from the real world to the digital world. Within a year of its founding, Scan's app had been downloaded more than 10 million times and was in use in over 75 countries around the world.

Gee, Turley, and Ouimet have faced many of the same challenges as have all entrepreneurs. Before the official founding of the company, their application for start-up money from Boom Startup had been denied. But, Scan received $1.7 million in February, 2011 from Google Ventures, Menlo Talent Fund, and others. Companies including Kroeger's, People Water, and Barneys New York—even some NBA teams and Lady Gaga—have used Scan's product.

In accordance with OSHA, employers must maintain a work environment that is safe for employees and visitors. Workplace safety standards include practices such as safety precautions, protective equipment, and confined spaces for dangerous production tasks. The number and type of regulations vary depending on the industry, but all businesses must provide work areas that are free from danger. Workplace safety is discussed further in chapter 14.

Health regulations include protecting employees from chemicals, toxins, and allergens that could be dangerous to health. Regulations may also require that medical attendants be on-site in the event of accidents. As with safety requirements, health regulations vary by industry.

Government-established *worker welfare regulations* are rules that ensure a basic level of worker safety, compensation, and consideration by employers. Employees must be provided with adequate restroom facilities, sanitary conditions, and other conditions that contribute to the well-being of workers.

Copyright Goodheart-Willcox Co., Inc.

Compensation and Benefits Laws

Compensation and benefits laws cover fair wages and benefits for all employees. Compensation laws address many topics; numerous laws and regulations fall under this category. Figure 8-8 explains some of the compensation laws that businesses must follow.

Equal-Employment Opportunity Laws

Equal-employment opportunity laws ensure that all workers are given an equal opportunity for employment. A large number of labor relations laws reduce discrimination in the workplace. **Workplace discrimination** occurs when a person is denied a job based on age, race, sex, religion, or nationality. Discrimination also includes denying a promotion, job assignment, equal pay, or unjustly firing someone based on any of these. Included are all areas of the employee-employer relationship, from posting open positions through termination or retirement.

The Equal Employment Opportunity Commission (EEOC) was created in 1972 to enforce antidiscrimination and other employment-related laws. In addition, the EEOC monitors **sexual harassment**, or unwanted sexual attention. Sexual harassment may create an adverse working environment. Figure 8-9 shows some of important equal-employment opportunity laws.

Consumer Protection Laws

Consumer protection laws keep people safe from harmful products. The *Consumer Product Safety Commission* determines if products are considered safe. If products are found unsafe by consumers, the agency has the power to recall them. A **recall** removes the unsafe product from the market. In the case of high-priced items such as cars, the recall is different. It requires the manufacturer to fix

Entrepreneur Ethics

It is unethical to share personal information about an employee or job applicant. Business owners may learn sensitive information about those who work for them or applicants seeking employment. It is unethical to share confidential information about employees and doing so may end in a lawsuit. Depending on the confidentiality of the topic, sharing the information may be considered slanderous. Always protect confidential information to promote ethical behavior in the organization.

Compensation Laws	
Social Security Act (1935)	Created a system of payments in which younger workers support retired or physically disabled former workers; the *Federal Insurance Contribution Act (FICA)* tax is the automatic payroll tax funding the Social Security program
Fair Labor Standards Act (1938)	Established the 40-hour workweek with overtime pay beyond that for hourly employees; established the minimum hourly wage; set the employment rules for children under age 16
Family Medical Leave Act (FMLA) (1993)	Allows up to 12 weeks of unpaid, job-protected leave for medical reasons; employers with more than 50 employees are required to follow this law
Health Insurance Portability and Accountability Act (HIPPA) (1996)	Guarantees employees insurance even if they have preexisting health conditions

Goodheart-Willcox Publisher

Figure 8-8. Compensation laws regulate benefits, wages, and labor standards.

Copyright Goodheart-Willcox Co., Inc.

Equal-Employment Opportunity Laws

Title VII of the Civil Rights Act–Title 7 (1964)	Employers cannot discriminate based on the race, color, religion, national origin, or gender of an individual.
Equal Pay Act (1963)	Employers cannot pay different wages to men and women if they perform equal work in the same workplace.
Age Discrimination in Employment Act–ADEA (1967)	It is illegal for employers to discriminate against people who are age 40 and older based on age.
Title I of the Americans with Disabilities Act–ADA (1990)	It is illegal for employers to discriminate against a qualified person with a disability in both the private sector and in government departments. Employers must make reasonable accommodations for known physical or mental limitations of an otherwise qualified individual.
The Genetic Information Nondiscrimination Act of 2008 (GINA)	Employers cannot discriminate against employees or applicants because of genetic information, such as information about any disease, disorder, or condition of an individual's family members.

Goodheart-Willcox Publisher

Figure 8-9. Equal-employment opportunity laws ensure that employees' civil rights are not violated.

 **You Do the Math**   Measurement Reasoning

Different systems of measurement are used throughout the world. The United States uses a system called the US Customary system that consists of feet, pounds, and degrees Fahrenheit. However, most of the world uses a variation of the metric system called the *Système International d'Unités (SI)*, or International System of Units. The SI system consists of meters, grams, and degrees Celsius. The following are some common conversions:

- To convert degrees Fahrenheit to degrees Celsius, subtract 32, multiply by 5, and divide by 9.
- One inch is equal to 25.4 millimeters.
- One pound is equal to 0.45 kilograms.

Solve the following problems.

1. If a carton ready for shipping weighs 18.7 kilograms, how many pounds does it weigh?
2. A business must ship a temperature-sensitive good to a country that uses the metric system. The product cannot be exposed to temperatures below 0 degrees Fahrenheit. A label must be placed on the package indicating this temperature in Celsius. What temperature must be written on the label?

the unsafe part of the vehicle at no cost to the owner. Some of the laws protecting consumers are shown in Figure 8-10.

As presented earlier, there are other types of law that protect consumers. For example, many state and local governments require service businesses to obtain licenses. Hair salons, restaurants, and other service businesses are regulated and must obtain a license to operate. There are also zoning laws that protect consumers' environments. Zoning laws ensure that businesses only operate in places zoned for business. It is important to become familiar with those laws that affect a small business.

Copyright Goodheart-Willcox Co., Inc.

Consumer Protection Laws	
Federal Food, Drug, and Cosmetic Act (1938)	Gives the US Food and Drug Administration the power to oversee the safety of all food, drugs, and cosmetics
Fair Packaging and Labeling Act (1966)	Requires labels to list the product, manufacturer's name and location, and net amount of contents
Child Protection Act (1966)	Removes potentially harmful toys from sale; allows the FDA to recall dangerous products
Truth-in-Lending Act (1968)	Requires disclosure of all finance charges on consumer credit agreements and in advertising for credit plans
Consumer Product Safety Act (1972, amended 1990)	Created the Consumer Product Safety Commission; protects the public against risks of injury or death from unsafe products
Fair Credit Billing Act (1986)	Protects consumers from unfair billing practices; gives consumers the right to dispute credit card billing errors
Nutrition Labeling and Education Act (1990)	Requires food labels to list the calories and amounts of fat, cholesterol, sodium, and fiber per serving
Children's Online Privacy Protection Act (2000)	Applies to the online collection of personal information from children under age 13; requires website owners to seek parental consent for collecting the information; sets rules for protecting children's online privacy and safety

Goodheart-Willcox Publisher

Figure 8-10. Harmful products are illegal under these laws.

Section 8.2 Review

Check Your Understanding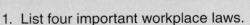

1. List four important workplace laws.
2. Give two examples of labor relations laws.
3. Explain what health and safety laws are and their importance.
4. Describe equal-employment opportunity laws and why they are important.
5. Discuss the importance of consumer protection laws.

Build Your Vocabulary

As you progress through this text, develop a personal glossary of key terms. This will help you build your vocabulary and prepare you for a career. Write a definition for each of the following terms and add them to your personal glossary.

business laws
labor relations laws
health and safety laws
compensation and benefits laws
equal-employment opportunity laws
workplace discrimination
sexual harassment
consumer protection laws
recall

Copyright Goodheart-Willcox Co., Inc.

Chapter Summary

Section 8.1 **Protect Your Business**

- A contract is an agreement between parties that is enforceable by law. Elements necessary for a valid contract include an offer, mutual acceptance, consideration, and capacity.

- Torts are noncriminal acts that result in harm. If one party believes he or she has been harmed by a tort committed by another party, a lawsuit can be filed.

- An idea, an invention, and a process are each forms of intellectual property. Infringing on intellectual property may have legal consequences.

Section 8.2 **Know the Laws**

- Business laws promote fair business practices and protect the interests of employers, employees, consumers, and the government. These laws are meant to maintain a healthy environment in which business and consumers can function.

- Labor relations laws, health and safety laws, compensation and benefit laws, and equal-employment opportunity laws provide guidelines for employers and protect employees. These laws have evolved over time and reflect how the relationship between employees and their employers has also evolved.

- Consumer protection laws are enacted to guard against harmful goods and services affecting consumers. The number and scope of consumer protection laws have greatly increased over the past 100 years.

Online Activities

Complete the following activities to help you learn, practice, and expand your knowledge and skills.

Posttest. Now that you have finished the chapter, see what you learned by taking the chapter posttest.

Key Terms. Practice vocabulary for this chapter using the e-flash cards, matching activity, and vocabulary game until you are able to recognize their meanings.

Copyright Goodheart-Willcox Co., Inc.

Review Your Knowledge

1. List the five conditions that must be met for a contract to be legally binding.
2. List three ways in which a person can lack the capacity to enter into a contract.
3. Identify examples of basic torts that a business owner should know how to protect against.
4. Explain the difference between a sales contract and service contract.
5. Describe the nature of legal procedure and the role of the legal process.
6. Explain the purpose of health and safety laws in the workplace.
7. What do compensation and benefits laws provide for employees?
8. What are consumer protection laws?
9. Discuss the nature of environmental law and the impact of these laws on the operation of a business.
10. Which consumer protection agency oversees the safety of food, drugs, and cosmetics?

Apply Your Knowledge

1. Make a list of the contracts you anticipate needing for your business. Explain why each will be important for your business.
2. As an entrepreneur, you must be knowledgeable about the legal issues and regulatory requirements that impact your business. This may require that you seek legal advice. Identify the potential legal issues and regulatory requirements that will affect your business. Make a list of questions you would ask an attorney.
3. Are you selling a good or service? Research examples and find a template for a sales contract or service contract that works for you. What details will you need to know about your business to create a contract?
4. Research the process for obtaining a copyright, trademark, or patent for your product. Print the forms for the application. See if you have enough information to start the process of completing the application.
5. Design a copyright or trademark for your new product or service. Use the Internet to get ideas for the design.
6. Use the Internet to research equal-employment opportunity laws. Write guidelines for your business making sure to follow the EEOC laws.
7. The *HIPPA Privacy Rule* established standards to protect information from being disclosed. Research the HIPPA Privacy Rule online. Create your business' policy for disclosing information.
8. Create sexual harassment guidelines for your business.

9. Use the Internet to research the Truth-in-Lending Act. What information would you need to provide customers about using credit cards in your business?

10. Contact your local government office. Ask about the laws and regulations you need to know about creating a business in your chosen area for locating your business.

 # Teamwork

Working with your team, find samples of different types of contracts. Select a contract that would be useful in your business or your teammate's business. Make a presentation to the class on how to complete the contract and the details for which to be aware.

Internet Research

Health and Safety Regulations. The Occupational Safety and Health Act of 1970 is the most prominent legislation on worker health and safety. The Occupational Safety and Health Administration provides many resources for both businesses and workers. Visit the OSHA website and research standards and regulations. Explain safety and health regulations and how OSHA enforces them.

Worker Welfare Regulations. Worker welfare, or the well-being of employees, is important for businesses of any type. Use the Internet to research worker welfare regulations. Identify several of the regulations that you find and explain how they safeguard the well-being of workers.

Communication Skills

Speaking. Using the Internet, research information on ergonomic solutions. What are some products available to entrepreneurs who need to create an ergonomic work environment? Make a presentation on your findings.

College and Career Readiness

Listening. Informative listening is the process of listening to gain specific information from the speaker. Interview a person who works in the human resources department of a company. Ask that person to explain employee attendance policies for his or her company. Make notes as the policies are described. Evaluate the speaker's point of view and reasoning. Did you listen closely enough to write accurate facts?

Copyright Goodheart-Willcox Co., Inc.

CTSOs

Team Presentations. Some competitive events for Career and Technical Student Organizations (CTSOs) have a performance portion. If it is a team event, it is important that the team making the presentation prepare to operate as a cohesive unit. To prepare for team activities, complete the following activities.

1. Read the guidelines provided by your organization. Make certain that you ask any questions about points you do not understand. It is important to follow each specific item that is outlined in the competition rules.

2. Complete the team activities at the end of each chapter in this text. This will help members learn how to interact with each other and participate effectively as a team.

3. Locate on your CTSO's website a rubric or scoring sheet for the event to see how the team will be judged.

4. Confirm the use of visual aids that may be used in the presentation and amount of set-up time permitted.

5. Review the rules to confirm if questions will be asked or if the team will need to defend a case or business plan.

6. Make notes on index cards about important points to remember. Team members should exchange note cards so that each evaluates the other person's notes. Use these notes to study. You may also be able to use these notes during the event.

7. Assign each team member a role for the presentation. Practice performing as a team. Each team member should introduce himself or herself, review the case, make suggestions for the case, and conclude with a summary.

8. Ask your teacher to play the role of competition judge as your team reviews the case. After the presentation is complete, ask for feedback from your teacher. You may also consider having a student audience to listen and give feedback.

Copyright Goodheart-Willcox Co., Inc.

Building Your Business Plan—Putting the Puzzle Together

Legal Issues

Can you imagine living without laws? You could get your driver's license at any age and drive at any speed. Everyone could do as he or she wanted. The world could easily fall into chaos. Laws are necessary to ensure the well-being of society. The same is also true for laws that apply to businesses. As an entrepreneur, some of these laws will directly affect your business. Among other things, business laws protect businesses from fraud and protect all employees' rights in the workplace.

Goals

- Create a sales or service contract.
- Identify laws that are important to creating a new business in a local community.
- Create business plan notes about contracts and workplace laws.

Directions

Access the *Entrepreneurship* companion website at www.g-wlearning.com ⬀ . Download each data file for the following activities. A complete sample business plan is available on the companion website to use as a reference. The name of the file is BusPlan_Sample.RetroAttire.docx.

Preparation

Activity 8-1. Sales or Service Contract. One of the first documents you will need for your business is a sales or service contract. Select the appropriate contract for your business. Include this in the Appendices section of the business plan.

Activity 8-2. Business Laws. Identify the potential legal issues that will affect your business. Researching local laws and regulations is an important part of creating a business plan. Complete the activity to list specific information about laws that will be important for your business.

Activity 8-3. Business Plan Notes. Complete the information about contracts and agreements that you will need for your business. Determine which workplace laws apply to your business and what you should know or do to comply with them. Keep your notes as reference information for your business plan.

Business Plan—Operations

In this chapter, you learned about legal issues and the laws that affect different businesses. These issues impact a business' employees and how the business is operated. Use the information you learned about potential legal issues in your business to help you with the following section.

1. Open your saved business plan document.

2. Locate the Operations section of the business plan and the second subsection called Risk Management Evaluation. Begin writing this subsection by listing the legal issues your business may face. This may include the contracts your business requires and the laws with which you must comply. Use the suggestions and questions listed in the template to help you generate ideas. Delete the instructions and questions when you are finished writing the part of the section pertaining to legal issues. Make sure to proofread your document and correct any errors in keyboarding, spelling, and grammar.

3. Save your document.

9 Business Funding

As consumers, friends Neil Blumenthal, David Gilboa, Andrew Hunt, and Jeffrey Raider were frustrated by the high cost of designer eyeglasses, which can cost as much as $500 a pair. These friends knew glasses are often marked up two to three times. They decided to start their own business, Warby Parker, to sell designer-style prescription glasses for under $100. For each pair the company sells, it helps a person in need to buy one pair of glasses. In order to fund the business idea, the group turned to some famous angel investors, including the former CEO of Tommy Hilfiger, Ashton Kutcher, and Lady Gaga manager Troy Carter. Most recently, a venture capital firm helped Warby Parker raise $12 million from Tiger Global, Menlo Talent Fund, and existing investors.

"Any time is a good time to start a company"

—Ron Conway, angel investor and cofounder of SV Angel

College and Career Readiness

Reading Prep. Before reading this chapter, locate an article or posting on the Internet about the projected availability of funds for start-up companies over the next year. What specific claims does the author make in this regard? Is the outlook positive or negative? What evidence does the author cite to support his or her point?

Sections

9.1 Options for Funding

9.2 Apply for Financing

Picture Yourself Here
Ooshma Garg

When you move out on your own, one thing you might miss is your family's home cooking. If you are lucky enough to live in California near the Bay Area Peninsula or San Francisco, you can call Gobble. Gobble connects customers with chefs who will create a home-cooked meal just for them.

Ooshma Garg, Gobble's founder, was inspired to start her business while working on her first company, a job-search website she created during her junior year at Stanford University. As a student and entrepreneur, she did not have much time for healthy eating. Her parents suggested she search for home-cooked meals using online classified ads. This experience gave her the idea to create Gobble. With Gobble, you can have food delivered, or you can pick it up at one of their two locations. The food is fresh, healthy, and creative.

Ooshma saw a need and filled it by creating her own company. The next time you come across a problem, step back for a minute and see if that problem is really an opportunity to start your own business.

Photo © Ooshma Garg

Check Your Entrepreneurship IQ

Before you begin the chapter, see what you already know about entrepreneurship by taking the chapter pretest. The pretest is available at www.g-wlearning.com

SECTION 9.1 | Options for Funding

?Essential Question

What options for funding are available to entrepreneurs?

Objectives

After completing this section, you will be able to:

- **Explain** how entrepreneurs can practice the art of bootstrapping.
- **Differentiate** between the ways to fund a start-up.
- **List** examples of start-up costs and ongoing operating expenses.

Key Terms

bootstrapping
start-up capital
equity
equity financing
angel investor
venture capitalist
debt financing
collateral
operating capital

line of credit
peer-to-peer lending
trade credit
start-up costs
inventory
fixed expenses
variable expenses
break-even point

Critical Thinking

Financing a business is a big step in anyone's career. What challenges might you face when looking for ways to finance your new business?

Art of Bootstrapping

Your first business venture may have been during a summer when you were much younger. Remember that lemonade stand, pet-care service, golf-ball stand, or babysitting service? You may have borrowed supplies from home, found lost balls at a nearby golf course, or simply printed some flyers advertising your services. If only all new businesses were that simple to start. Some businesses may be simple to start, but most are not.

That first business venture may have been pure profit because someone else provided the materials or initial funding. The next business venture may not be that easy. Before asking for outside financial assistance, it may be a good idea to look around and see what resources you already have. Most entrepreneurs practice the art of **bootstrapping**, or cutting all unnecessary expenses and operating on as little cash as possible.

Copyright Goodheart-Willcox Co., Inc.

Bootstrapping is a sound business practice and can reduce the amount of money that would otherwise need to be borrowed. In your personal life, you may have used bootstrapping practices without realizing it. Perhaps you reduced extra spending to save for a vacation, buy a car, or get a new phone. There are many ways for entrepreneurs to engage in bootstrapping when starting a business, as shown in Figure 9-1.

FYI

Worldwide, over 99 percent of all new businesses are self funded.

Have No Employees

Hiring employees is a major expense for a business. Many entrepreneurs do not hire employees when the business is first started. If help is needed in the business, temporary employees can be hired through an agency. Contracted services, such as an attorney, can also be hired. By delaying hiring permanent employees, the business can be established and begin generating revenue.

Barter

Bartering is the exchange of goods or services for other goods or services. No money changes hands. Nearly $10 billion in business-to-business bartering is conducted each year, and it is on the rise. For example, an accountant wants to open his or her own accounting firm. A friend of the accountant just opened an advertising agency. The accountant may provide accounting services in exchange for advertising services. No money was exchanged, but both entrepreneurs provided a service needed for their new businesses.

Use Free Resources

There are many professional resources and services available at no cost to business owners. SCORE, the SBA, and state websites offer advice and other resources at no charge. Social media can also be a free resource to use as a marketing tool.

Bootstrapping	
• Have no employees	• Use personal assets
• Barter	• Negotiate
• Use free resources	• Monitor expenditures

Goodheart-Willcox Publisher

Figure 9-1. Bootstrapping will reduce business expenses.

Use Personal Assets

Many entrepreneurs start home-based businesses to save on start-up and operating costs. They use their own equipment, such as a computer, fax, and printer. If additional equipment is needed, leasing instead of buying will help to save the up-front costs.

Negotiate

You may be surprised that many vendors are willing to offer better terms than what they advertise. Many vendors began as small business owners and are willing to help new entrepreneurs. They may not negotiate on price, but might be willing to negotiate terms. Instead of a payment due in 30 days, ask if the vendor will give you a 45- or 60-day payment window.

Monitor Expenses Closely

While a nice dinner out or lunch on the run sounds like a good idea, the cost can quickly add up. Plan to eat your meals at home or pack them. Cut back on utilities, reduce your phone or subscription TV plan, or postpone a vacation. Continue driving that old car or walk or bike as much as possible. There are many more ways to conserve cash.

Start-Up Capital

Every entrepreneur needs cash to start the business and keep it running. Start-up capital is the cash used to start the business. Few people have enough cash on hand to completely fund a business. So, they must look for other sources of start-up capital. Two common sources of financing are equity financing and debt financing.

Equity Financing

Equity is the amount of ownership a person has in a business. Entrepreneurs who start a business only using their own funds have 100 percent equity in that business. This is called self funding.

Equity financing is raising money for a business in exchange for a percentage of the ownership. For example, buying stock is really purchasing a percentage of ownership in that company. Many entrepreneurs use a combination of self funding and equity financing. There are several types of equity financing, as shown in Figure 9-2.

Personal Savings

Many entrepreneurs use their own money as equity capital. This can include money from savings accounts, selling stock, cash in a retirement fund, or using other personal resources.

Copyright Goodheart-Willcox Co., Inc.

Equity Financing Options

- **Personal savings**
- **Family and friends**
- **Partnership**
- **Angel investors**
- **Venture capitalists**

Dean Drobot/Shutterstock.com; Goodheart-Willcox Publisher

Figure 9-2. Asking family or friends to invest in your business is just one way to get equity financing.

Family and Friends

It is very common for entrepreneurs to ask people they know to help fund a business. Before inviting family and friends to invest in your company, think about what could happen to the relationships should something go wrong with the business. There may be other investment alternatives that better suit your situation.

Partnership

Another option for raising equity capital is to take on partners in the business. Partners can contribute to the start-up funding and share in responsibility and operations of the business. Like other equity options, a formal partnership agreement is necessary. The different types of business partnerships were discussed in chapter 6.

Angel Investors

Angel investors, or *angels*, are private investors who want to fund promising start-up businesses. An angel investor often has relevant business experience that will help the company. He or she is interested in adding value as well as making a return on the investment. Angels are a good source of funding for new businesses as they will often take on more risk than a bank. They tend to invest amounts of money up to $1 million.

Some angel investors with specific industry experience want to actively participate in the business to protect their investment. They may charge a monthly management fee. Other angels do not choose active participation in the operation. However, they are part owners in the company and expect a good return on the money invested.

Sometimes, a number of angel investors will organize into an *angel group* to pool their resources.

Venture Capitalists

Venture capitalists, or *VCs*, are professional investors or investing groups looking to fund new start-ups or expansions of existing companies. *Venture capital* is the money invested in businesses by venture capitalists. VCs manage large investment funds and are always looking for suitable investment opportunities. They are willing to invest more money than angels in riskier start-ups to earn a high rate of return on the investment. Most venture capitalists require 25 percent or more equity in the company.

Venture capitalists tend to prefer investing in start-ups run by experienced entrepreneurs with a history of rapid growth in previous start-ups. Most VCs invest a minimum of $3–$5 million. They often fund new or expanding high-tech or other successful companies. Less than 1 percent of all businesses are funded by VCs.

Unlike angel investors, venture capitalists rarely have personal experience in the industries in which they invest. Many, however, do have general management experience and want to remain involved in the business to protect the investment. Like some angel investors, there are also some VCs who leave the daily business operations to the experts.

Debt Financing

Debt financing is borrowing money for business purposes. Debt financing can help to start or expand a business. It may also help a company remain in business through an economic downturn. One advantage of debt financing over investors and partners is that the entrepreneur remains the business owner. One disadvantage is that, just like credit card debt, the loan must be repaid plus the interest. For those with poor credit, the interest rates can be higher. There are many ways to obtain debt financing, as shown in Figure 9-3.

Debt financing requires an application process, which is covered later in this chapter. Typically, a formal application form along with financial statements are required. Like with other types of loans, it is important for the applicant to have a good credit rating. Some larger loans require collateral. **Collateral** is an asset pledged that will be claimed by the lender if the loan is not repaid. Loans that require collateral are known as *secured loans*. Examples of collateral include a home, vehicle, or individual retirement account (IRA).

Loans that do not require collateral, like credit card transactions, are known as *unsecured loans*. For bank loans less than $100,000, collateral may not be required and might be based primarily on credit history.

Copyright Goodheart-Willcox Co., Inc.

Debt Financing Options

- Banks and credit unions
- Peer-to-peer or social lending
- Trade credit
- SBA-assisted loans
- Retirement accounts
- Family and friends

Monkey Business Images/Shutterstock.com; Goodheart-Willcox Publisher

Figure 9-3. Debt financing does not give ownership to the lender.

Banks and Credit Unions

The traditional way to obtain a loan is through a bank or credit union. At one time, banks were the best resource for obtaining start-up and operating capital for entrepreneurs. **Operating capital** is the money needed to support day-to-day business operations. However, due to the banking crisis of the early 21st century, tougher loan criteria have been established. This has made it more difficult to get a loan than in the years before the crisis.

After a business is established and has a good credit history, a bank or credit union may extend a line of credit. A **line of credit** is a specific dollar amount that a business can draw against as needed. The business accesses money from the line of credit and pays it back on a regular basis, usually monthly. Lines of credit often help companies with cash-flow problems at certain times of the year or through economic downturns. For example, a ski resort might use a line of credit to pay employees during an unusually warm winter.

Banks and credit unions might also extend credit to an established company through an overdraft agreement. An *overdraft agreement* allows a business to write checks for more than what is in the checking account. The institution pays the check through a line of credit and charges the company a fee for the overdraft protection.

Peer-to-Peer or Social Lending

Peer-to-peer lending is borrowing money from investors via a website. It is also known as *social lending* and is gaining in popularity for loans under $25,000. Applicants create and post a loan listing that explains the purpose of the loan and the amount needed. Potential investors review the loan listings and choose to fund loans that meet

Entrepreneur Ethics

When applying for funding, it is important that an entrepreneur is truthful in the loan application and business plan. Making up information to gain trust of financial authorities is unethical and could cost a future opportunity for the business. Applicants should always tell the truth about their skills, experience, and financial status. Present information in a positive light, but honestly. Financial institutions will usually discover any untruths, which would cost the entrepreneur that loan.

Copyright Goodheart-Willcox Co., Inc.

their criteria. Like banks and credit unions, the loans go through an approval process. Good credit scores ensure better interest rates.

So why is peer-to-peer lending different from a traditional loan? In this process, there is no lending institution. It is more like borrowing money from family or friends, except in most cases, the borrowers and lenders do not know each other. The advantages of peer-to-peer loans are potentially lower interest rates and short repayment time frames. The disadvantages are up-front fees, personal information is on a public site, and low loan amounts.

Trade Credit

Trade credit is when one business grants a line of credit to another business for the purchase of goods and services. The line of credit is most often 30 or 60 days. This means that it is possible to make an interest-free purchase for 30 or 60 days. Payment is due in full at the end of the time period. The real benefit of trade credit is that you are getting products interest free for 30 or 60 days. Trade credit is most often used by established businesses. While most new businesses may have difficulty getting trade credit initially, it never hurts to ask.

SBA-Assisted Loans

The SBA works with banks to provide small business loans, but does not directly lend money. Instead, the SBA operates its Small Loan Advantage program. Under this program, the SBA guarantees 85 percent of a bank loan up to $150,000. For loans greater than $150,000, the SBA guarantees 75 percent of the loan amount. To qualify, a business owner must personally guarantee the loan by showing sufficient cash available for repayment. There are a number of different types of SBA-assisted lending programs for small business funding including:

- Small Business Investment Company (SBIC) program;

- microloans;

- 7(a) loans; and

- Certified Development Company (CDC)/504 loan program.

Companies in the SBIC program focus on funding for socially or economically disadvantaged businesses. Functioning as a type of venture capitalist, companies in the SBIC program are privately managed investment firms licensed by the SBA. A company in the SBIC program offers financial assistance through equity funding, loans, and management consulting to small businesses. A minority enterprise small business investment company (MESBIC) is a private institution that invests only in minority-owned businesses. *Minority-owned* means that at least one minority owner owns 51 percent or more of a company.

There are over 300 SBICs in the United States that can loan money to a small business. The SBA defines small businesses by industry: fewer than 500 employees for most manufacturing concerns; 100 employees for wholesalers; and less than $7 million in revenue for retailers. SBICs define small businesses using different standards.

Copyright Goodheart-Willcox Co., Inc.

Social Entrepreneurs

Matt Golden

Matt Golden was an energy consultant who helped homeowners and businesses develop solar power systems. Golden realized he could offer so much more to homeowners by making their homes and lives more sustainable. In the United States, 30 percent of all electricity is consumed by homes, and 21.5 percent of the total greenhouse gas emissions is due to home-energy consumption. The Department of Energy estimates that 40 percent of energy used in homes is wasted because of inefficiency, however.

In 2004, Golden's desire to help homeowners waste less energy led to cofounding Recurve, a company providing home-energy modeling and services. Each month, Recurve helps 30 to 40 homeowners by adding insulation, sealing cracks, and other tasks to improve energy efficiency. It also provides tablet-based, energy-auditing software to the building industry. Recurve's services help homeowners reduce their energy costs, which also reduces their carbon footprints by lowering greenhouse gas emissions.

Microloans are provided to nonprofits through 170 US nonprofit lenders. The lenders receive money from the SBA to provide short-term loans up to $50,000 for nonprofits. The average loan amount is $13,000, and interest rates are comparable to banks and credit unions. Microloans may be used for working capital, purchase of inventory or supplies, furniture or fixtures, or machines or equipment. They cannot be used to pay existing debts or purchase real estate. Microloans must be paid off within six years.

The *7(a) loan program* provides financial help to businesses with special needs. For example, funds are available for loans to businesses that export to foreign countries or operate in rural areas. 7(a) loans are designed for small business owners with poor credit or no collateral. 7(a) loans can help entrepreneurs who would not be able to obtain conventional loans due to their credit ratings or business type.

A *Certified Development Company (CDC)* is a nonprofit corporation that stimulates economic growth in a community through small business lending. CDCs make long-term, fixed-rate 504 loans that may only be used to purchase land, buildings, equipment, and machinery. These loans may also be used to build new or renovate existing facilities. The applicant may finance up to 90 percent of the project.

Retirement Accounts

Many people do not realize they can borrow from their IRAs or 401(k)s. Money can be borrowed from an IRA interest free for 60 days,

Copyright Goodheart-Willcox Co., Inc.

which might be helpful to get through a short-term cash flow problem. Some 401(k) plans permit borrowing for any reason, but most allow loans only for specifically defined reasons outlined in the plan. A person may borrow up to $50,000 from savings in a 401(k), but must pay interest along with the repayment of the loan.

Caution should be used when borrowing from retirement accounts. There are very strict IRS laws about how loans can be used and repaid. There may also be tax consequences for borrowing from an IRA.

Family and Friends

An entrepreneur may get a loan from a relative or friend to help fund the business. This would be the only case where a loan application is unnecessary. One advantage to getting a loan from someone you know very well is the possibility of negotiating a lower interest rate. A family member or friend may also give you a better repayment schedule than a bank or credit union might. Some people may think that a formal loan agreement is not necessary for loans from relatives. However, this is not true. It is important to sign a formal agreement with *any* lender so there are no misunderstandings and there is legal protection for both sides.

Start-Up Costs

Financial plans are a summary of where a business is financially at the present time and the future expectations of the business. Financial plans are a part of the business plan and are necessary to persuade parties or financial institutions to invest in or lend money to a start-up business.

An important step in creating a financial plan is to analyze start-up costs. **Start-up costs** are the initial expenses necessary to open the doors of a business. Some expenses will be one-time costs, such as furniture, equipment, filing a DBA license, utility deposits, and the initial inventory. Other start-up costs, such as rent, are reoccurring operating expenses. Typical one-time start-up costs are similar to those in Figure 9-4. There are start-up cost calculators on the Internet to help estimate these costs.

These costs also include the inventory of product that the business will sell. **Inventory** is the assortment or selection of items that a

Figure 9-4. Think of ways you can save money on one-time start-up costs.

One-Time Start-Up Costs	
• Rent deposit	• DBA license
• Tenant improvements	• Utility deposits
• Furniture	• Initial inventory
• Computer, printer, and other office equipment	

Goodheart-Willcox Publisher

Copyright Goodheart-Willcox Co., Inc.

business has on hand to sell to customers at a particular point in time. It is also known as *goods on hand* or *inventory on hand*.

While identifying the exact start-up costs for a business, determine whether each expense is essential. If an expense is essential, is there a way to lower the cost of obtaining it? For example, if your current computer and printer will suffice, do not include new ones as equipment in the start-up budget.

Operating Expenses

The ongoing *operating expenses* keep a company in business. Operating expenses are classified as fixed and variable expenses. Fixed expenses are expenses that remain the same every month. They include salaries, mortgage payments, and insurance. Variable expenses are expenses that can change on a monthly basis. They include the cost of advertising and utilities, as shown in Figure 9-5.

Over one-third of small business owners underestimate their operating expenses, according to Hiscox USA research. The same survey shows that 20 percent of small business owners underestimated their start-up costs. For many business owners, underestimating start-up costs and operating expenses can mean the end of the venture.

Planning for Success

Outline your plan for success in the business plan. Be honest and as accurate as possible when projecting the start-up costs. It is in the best interest of those helping to fund the business for you to succeed. It is important to have enough start-up capital to remain in business for at least a year without making a profit.

Follow the *rule of two:* expect everything to cost twice as much and take twice as long as you think it will. The exception is when projecting sales. Cut the revenue projections in half. It is better to be pleasantly surprised by higher-than-expected sales than to scramble for additional funding when sales are lower than expected. Consider the following when making projections to include in the business plan.

| Monthly Operating Expenses ||
Fixed Expenses	Variable Expenses
• Insurance	• Advertising
• Mortgage	• Fees
• Phone	• Office supplies
• Rent	• Utilities
• Salary	• Miscellaneous

Goodheart-Willcox Publisher

Figure 9-5. Be realistic when estimating ongoing operating expenses.

Project Start-Up and Operating Expenses

The challenge: Projecting exactly what the business can afford before incurring expenses.

The solution: Do some homework. Review financial reports from publicly traded companies in your industry to learn their types of operating expenses. Ask area business owners who are not direct competitors about their typical operating expenses. Do not forget to include estimated taxes and initial inventory. Use a start-up cost calculator on the Internet to help estimate start-up costs. A SCORE mentor may also be able to help set realistic amounts for start-up and operating expenses. Consider working with an accounting professional to help guide you through this process.

Budget for Owner Capital Withdrawal

The challenge: Withdraw capital for yourself.

The solution: Business owners do not receive a salary from their business. Salaries are compensation paid to employees, not the owner. However, an owner may withdraw cash or assets from the business for personal use. It is very common for owners to make a withdrawal, called a *drawing*, from the business. Build in an amount for personal withdrawals starting somewhere between 9 and 12 months after the business opens.

Price Products Correctly

The challenge: Accurate pricing of products is crucial to business success.

The solution: Before pricing products, do research and seek professional advice to help determine acceptable pricing. Pricing must be competitive and allow the business to make a profit. *Profit margin* is the amount by which product sales exceed the cost to the business of producing them. It is often shown as a percentage. Each industry has acceptable profit margin guidelines for pricing purposes. Some businesses calculate the cost of creating the product and then double that amount to set the price. Other businesses add a percentage of desired profit to the cost of creating the product. Your industry and the competition will dictate what is acceptable.

Forecast Sales Accurately

The challenge: Accurate sales forecasts are necessary to predict revenue and profits.

The solution: Having a great product does not mean that people will immediately beat down your door to purchase it. Follow the *rule of two* by cutting your best sales estimate in half. It is better to underestimate potential revenue than to overestimate it and come up short on revenue. This is especially critical when applying for a loan. Bankers and investors want realistic sales forecasts. Use a sales-forecasting worksheet for your projections. You can find samples at the SCORE or SBA websites.

Copyright Goodheart-Willcox Co., Inc.

Calculate the Break-Even Point

The challenge: It is only after the break-even point is reached that profits are earned. The **break-even point** is the amount of revenue a business must generate in order to equal its expenses.

The solution: Do not assume that by selling more products, profits will increase. This may happen over time, but initially variable expenses may also increase and actually reduce the profit margin. Many entrepreneurs do not know their break-even point and end up running out of cash before making a profit.

First, estimate total costs by adding the fixed and variable expenses. Then project sales for a year. Plot the sales and expenses on a graph, as shown in Figure 9-6. The break-even point is where the two lines intersect. After finding the break-even point, assume it will take more sales than you project to reach that point.

After reaching the break-even point, evaluate the marginal benefit and cost to producing various quantities of additional products. *Marginal benefit* measures the potential gains of producing more products that sell because the profit margin is higher. *Marginal cost* measures the potential losses from producing more products that might not sell. While the products may cost less to make, there is also the risk they will not sell and will decrease profits.

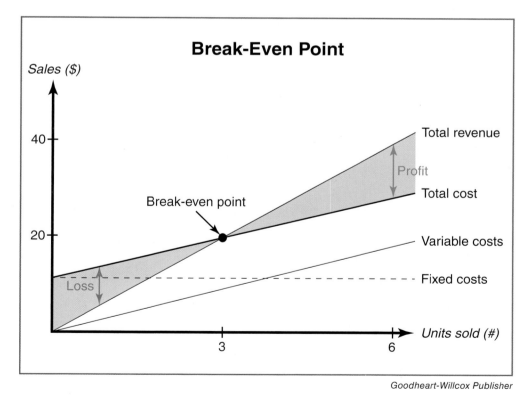

Goodheart-Willcox Publisher

Figure 9-6. A business will not earn a profit until the break-even point is reached.

Copyright Goodheart-Willcox Co., Inc.

Section 9.1   Review

Check Your Understanding ⇮

1. List five common bootstrapping practices.
2. Why do some entrepreneurs use bootstrapping?
3. What is a risk of equity financing?
4. Give examples of financial institutions where you can obtain debt financing.
5. List some of the typical start-up costs new owners encounter.

Build Your Vocabulary ⇮

As you progress through this text, develop a personal glossary of key terms. This will help you build your vocabulary and prepare you for a career. Write a definition for each of the following terms and add them to your personal glossary.

bootstrapping
start-up capital
equity
equity financing
angel investor
venture capitalist
debt financing
collateral
operating capital

line of credit
peer-to-peer lending
trade credit
start-up costs
inventory
fixed expenses
variable expenses
break-even point

Copyright Goodheart-Willcox Co., Inc.

SECTION 9.2 | Apply for Financing

Essential Question

How do lenders evaluate businesses for financing?

Objectives

After completing this section, you will be able to:

- **Explain** the business loan application process.
- **Describe** three pro forma statements that accompany a business loan application.

Key Terms

cosigner
pro forma cash flow statement
pro forma income statement
pro forma balance sheet
assets
fixed assets
liquid assets

accounts receivable
illiquid assets
liabilities
short-term liabilities
accounts payable
long-term liabilities
owner's equity

Critical Thinking

When applying for a loan, lenders want information about your personal finances as well as your business projections. Make a list of items you think a financial institution will want from entrepreneurs seeking a loan.

Business Loan Application Process

Applying for and obtaining a business loan is a complex process. A bank or credit union may be more likely to lend to existing customers with other accounts. However, there is no guarantee you will be granted a loan. It may be necessary to apply for a loan multiple times until you are successful.

When applying for debt or equity financing, applicants are asked to provide documentation proving they are good credit risks. That documentation may be the deciding factor in getting a business off the ground.

What You Need

All lenders have a loan application that must be completed. The application will ask for many details, so it is important to take your time and complete it fully and accurately. Education, experience, past jobs, current debt, and the business projections all help the lender evaluate your application.

Copyright Goodheart-Willcox Co., Inc.

Most lenders require many of the same things when applying for a loan. These are typical items required for any small business loan application:

- résumés

- personal financial statement

- business plan

- income tax returns

- bank statements

- possible collateral

It is important to provide résumés for all owners. Most lenders require that the applicants have some management or business experience, especially for start-up loans. Owners' résumés should reflect this. Many loan programs require owners with more than a 20 percent ownership in a business to submit signed personal financial statements. This is true for sole proprietorships, partnerships, and corporations.

All business loan programs require a sound business plan be submitted with the loan application. The financial plans section of the business plan includes details about raising capital and future plans for the business. It also contains the pro forma income, cash flow, and balance sheet financial statements. These are discussed later. In addition, the following items may be requested, which are included in the business plan appendices:

- DBA, licenses, and registrations required to conduct business

- Articles of Incorporation or partnership agreement

- copies of supplier contracts

- franchise agreement

- commercial leases

Focus on Finance

Asset Depreciation

As a business owner, you will most likely have to purchase business assets, such as computers, furniture, and other equipment. Business assets *depreciate,* or lose value, each year. Tax laws allow business owners to use yearly depreciation values as a tax-deductible expense. This depreciation expense decreases net profit on which taxes are paid, which lowers the taxes paid. It helps to keep accurate records and the receipts for your business assets. Your accountant will need this information when filing quarterly tax returns.

Copyright Goodheart-Willcox Co., Inc.

Most loan programs require applicants to submit personal and, if possible, business income tax returns for the previous three years. Many loan programs also require one year of personal and business bank statements.

Collateral requirements vary greatly, often by the requested loan amount and degree of risk. It is a good idea to prepare a document describing the cost and value of any collateral used to secure a loan.

How Lenders Evaluate Applicants

Lenders making personal loans evaluate applicants on character, capacity, and capital, which are known as the *three Cs of credit*. However, when applying for a business loan, the criteria are somewhat different. This criteria is known as the *five Cs of banking*. The five Cs of banking include character, cash flow, capital, collateral, and conditions.

Character

All lenders run a credit report to learn an applicant's history of creating and paying debt. The report will come from a credit bureau that tracks individuals and their debt. Each consumer is rated according to the types of debt they have, on-time payments, and how

Stephen Coburn/Shutterstock.com

The business plan must be included in a loan application.

Copyright Goodheart-Willcox Co., Inc.

quickly debt is repaid. The higher a credit score, the better the rating. Credit scores play a part in the ability to get a loan.

Cash Flow

Lenders want to know that a business can generate enough cash flow to repay the loan on time. Sometimes, lenders ask for a cosigner on the loan. A **cosigner** is a person who signs a loan with the applicant and takes on equal responsibility for repaying it. The cosigner usually has a better established financial history than the primary applicant.

Capital

Lenders look for businesses that have sufficient cash to operate. Money to operate the business is capital, which is the difference between assets and liabilities.

Collateral

If the loan is large enough, lenders require collateral to secure it. Collateral comes in many forms and is valued by lenders in different ways. For example, an entrepreneur may use the equity in his or her house as collateral for a loan.

Conditions

Lenders assess the economic conditions of the business' industry, the potential for the business to grow, and the form of ownership. They also consider the business location, competition, and applicant's insurance coverage. Given the conditions they find, the lender defines the terms under which a loan would be given. These terms may be as simple as the owner buying insurance for the business, or they may be more complex.

SBA Tips

Work smarter, not harder. The SBA helps entrepreneurs identify ways to finance a business as well as help develop pro forma financial statements. They offer online courses, podcasts, and videos as resources when seeking information about business funding.
www.sba.gov

Pro Forma Financial Statements

Each component of the loan application process is important. One of the major parts is the financial statements that support the business plan. A financial plan generally includes three financial statements: cash flow statement, income statement, and balance sheet. *Pro forma financial statements* are financial statements based on the best estimate of the business' future revenue and expenses. *Revenue* is the earnings that a business receives for the goods and services it sells. Revenue is categorized as operating revenue or non-operating revenue. *Operating revenue* is generated from the business operations and is usually classified as sales. *Non-operating revenue* is generated from sources other than business operations, such as interest on savings accounts. *Expenses* are the costs involved in operating a business. Operating expenses are the expenses generated while running a business,

Copyright Goodheart-Willcox Co., Inc.

such as advertising and employee salaries. The pro forma cash flow statement, pro forma income statement, and pro forma balance sheet will be completed as part of the application. They are also included in the Appendices of the business plan.

Sales forecasting is a complicated part of the business plan and is necessary to complete pro forma financial statements. The goal of the sales forecast is to not only project revenue, but to make sure the business has enough product to sell. There are multiple methods used to forecast sales. Sales forecasting should be done in dollars as well as number of units that are projected to be sold. Sales forecasts are usually done for monthly, quarterly, and yearly time periods.

Pro Forma Cash Flow Statement

A **pro forma cash flow statement** reports the anticipated flow of cash into and out of the business. *Cash flow* is the movement of money in and out of a business. Without cash flowing into a business, expenses cannot be paid. Employees will not receive their paychecks, inventory will not be purchased, and dividends will not be issued to investors. An example of a service business' projected cash flow is shown in Figure 9-7.

To prepare a pro forma cash flow statement, project the amount of sales, or cash in, expected for the first twelve months. Next, project the expenses, or cash out, for the same time period. If you project receiving more cash from sales than is spent on expenses, the cash

FYI

According to the *Global Entrepreneurship Monitor*, from 2008 to 2010, the main reasons new entrepreneurs failed were they ran out of money due to low sales or they could not obtain the financing necessary to continue operating.

Sophia's Web Design Co.
Pro Forma Cash Flow Statement
Year Ended December, 20--

	Jan.	Feb.	Mar.	Apr.	May	June	July	Aug.	Sept.	Oct.	Nov.	Dec.
Cash Receipts	$2,000	$3,500	$4,000	$4,200	$5,600	$8,200	$8,500	$8,600	$9,000	$9,100	$9,200	$9,600
Cash Disbursements												
Advertising Expense	200	200	200	200	200	300	200	200	200	200	200	200
Rent Expense	400	400	400	400	400	400	400	400	400	400	400	400
Insurance Expense	50	50	50	50	50	50	50	50	50	50	50	50
Supplies Expense	100	100	50	50	50	75	25	25	200	25	25	25
Utilities Expense	150	150	150	150	150	150	150	150	150	150	150	150
Total Disbursements	900	900	850	850	850	975	825	825	1,000	825	825	825
Net Cash Flow	$1,100	$2,600	$3,150	$3,350	$4,750	$7,225	$7,675	$7,775	$8,000	$8,275	$8,375	$8,775

Goodheart-Willcox Publisher

Figure 9-7. Use a pro forma cash flow statement to predict the best and worst outcomes.

Copyright Goodheart-Willcox Co., Inc.

flow is positive. If you project spending more than the amount of cash taken in, the cash flow is negative. It is a good idea to project several levels of sales to understand the best- and worst-case scenarios.

Cash flow statements can be used as the basis for budgeting. A *budget* is a spending plan for a fixed period of time. A *cash budget* is an estimate of cash forecasted to be received and spent over time. Budgets help a business ensure there is enough money to cover expenses. Budgets also help monitor the business in handling its money wisely and making a profit.

Pro Forma Income Statement

A **pro forma income statement** projects the financial progress of the business. The pro forma income statement is also known as a *pro forma profit and loss statement (P & L)*. A lender or investor may require a forecast for one year or multiple years. The two main sections of an income statement are revenue and expenses. An example of a pro forma income statement for a three-year period is shown in Figure 9-8.

Pro Forma Balance Sheet

The **pro forma balance sheet** reports a business' assets, liabilities, and owner's equity. The pro forma balance sheet provides a snapshot of a business' financial position. The pro forma balance sheet in Figure 9-9 shows the financial position of the business when this entrepreneur applied for a loan.

Assets are the property or items of value owned by a business. Cash and equipment are examples of the assets of a business. Assets may be fixed, liquid, or illiquid. **Fixed assets** are the items of value

Figure 9-8. The pro forma income statement is used to project income over a period of time.

Sophia's Web Design Co.

Pro Forma Income Statement

Year Ended December, 20--

	Year 1	Year 2	Year 3
Revenue			
Sales	$76,500	$81,500	$92,000
Expenses			
Advertising Expense	15,000	16,000	18,000
Rent Expense	48,000	48,000	48,000
Insurance Expense	600	700	800
Supplies Expense	750	900	1,200
Utilities Expense	1,800	2,000	2,100
Total Expenses	66,150	66,150	70,100
Net Income	$10,350	$15,350	$21,900

Goodheart-Willcox Publisher

Copyright Goodheart-Willcox Co., Inc.

Sophia's Web Design Co.
Pro Forma Balance Sheet
Year Ended December, 20--

Assets

Cash	$5,000	
Accounts Receivable	9,600	
Equipment	32,000	
Total Assets		46,600

Liabilities

Accounts Payable	$12,000	
Notes Payable	10,000	
Total Liabilities		22,000

Owner's Equity

Sophia Nguyen, Capital	24,600
Total Liabilities and Owner's Equity	$46,600

Figure 9-9. The pro forma balance sheet shows assets, liabilities, and equity.

Goodheart-Willcox Publisher

that may take time to sell. A building or heavy equipment is a fixed asset. **Liquid assets** are items easily turned into cash. Cash is the most liquid asset for a business. A checking account and accounts receivables are also considered liquid assets. **Accounts receivable** is money owed to a business by customers for goods or services delivered. **Illiquid assets** are items that cannot be sold quickly without suffering a loss. Examples of illiquid items are stocks or artwork that may not have buyers willing to pay top value when the owner wants to sell.

 You Do the Math   Functions

Both businesses and individuals invest money and take out loans. Compound interest is exponential. This means that previously earned interest itself earns interest in the future. This can be thought of as interest on interest. The future value of a balance with compound interest is calculated by multiplying the present value by one plus the annual interest rate taken to the power of the number of terms.

$$FV = PV \times (1 + r)^n$$

In this equation, *FV* is the future value, *PV* is the present value, *r* is the annual interest rate, and *n* is the period of time over which interest is compounded.

Solve the following problems.

1. $10,000 has been placed in a certificate of deposit (CD) that earns 3.78 percent interest per year. The term of the CD is three years. At the end of the term, what will be the total amount of money in the CD?

2. A business owner has taken out a small business loan for $25,000 over a term of five years. The interest rate is 2.9 percent annually. How much interest will have been paid at the end of the loan?

Copyright Goodheart-Willcox Co., Inc.

Liabilities are the business' debts, or what it owes to others. Liabilities may be short term or long term. **Short-term liabilities** are those expected to be paid within the current year. This includes salaries and accounts payable. **Accounts payable** is the money a business owes to suppliers for goods or services received. **Long-term liabilities** are debts that extend beyond the current year. Long-term liabilities can include repayment of a bank loan and rent.

The difference between a business' assets and its liabilities is called **owner's equity.** Owner's equity is also known as the owner's *net worth.* This information on a balance sheet is expressed as the *accounting equation:*

assets = liabilities + owner's equity (net worth)

A lender may also ask for owners' personal financial statements showing assets and liabilities unrelated to the business. Personal financial status will be reviewed along with the financial status of the business.

Green Entrepreneurs

Investor Presentations

When entrepreneurs are seeking funding, they are often asked to make presentations to their potential investors. These presentations usually include financial documents and other information that investors require to review funding requests. However, the environmental cost of the paper and the ink can be quite high to print many copies of the business plan and other documents. Consider only handing out the important information needed for the presentation. Explain that you follow green business practices and will e-mail pdfs of the complete documentation to everyone present.

Section 9.2 | Review

Check Your Understanding ⤷

1. How do banks use the five Cs of banking to evaluate business loan applicants?

2. What purpose do pro forma statements serve?

3. Name three pro forma statements required in the loan application process.

4. Define liquid assets and illiquid assets. Explain the difference between these types of assets.

5. What are liabilities? Identify examples of short-term liabilities and long-term liabilities.

Build Your Vocabulary ⤷

As you progress through this text, develop a personal glossary of key terms. This will help you build your vocabulary and prepare you for a career. Write a definition for each of the following terms and add them to your personal glossary.

cosigner
pro forma cash flow
   statement
pro forma income
   statement
pro forma balance
   sheet
assets
fixed assets

liquid assets
accounts
   receivable
illiquid assets
liabilities
short-term liabilities
accounts payable
long-term liabilities
owner's equity

Chapter Summary

Section 9.1 Options for Funding

- Most entrepreneurs cut all unnecessary expenses and operate on as little cash as possible before looking to others to fund their ventures. This practice is known as bootstrapping.
- Ways to fund a start-up include self funding, equity financing, and debt financing.
- Start-up costs include one-time costs and recurring operating expenses, both fixed and variable.

Section 9.2 Apply for Financing

- As part of the process of obtaining a business loan, the applicant must provide a lot of documentation to help determine whether the business is creditworthy.
- A pro forma balance sheet, income statement, and cash flow statements are required as part of the business loan application process.

Online Activities

Complete the following activities to help you learn, practice, and expand your knowledge and skills.

Posttest. Now that you have finished the chapter, see what you learned by taking the chapter posttest.

Key Terms. Practice vocabulary for this chapter using the e-flash cards, matching activity, and vocabulary game until you are able to recognize their meanings.

Review Your Knowledge

1. What percentage of equity does a self-funding entrepreneur have in his or her business?
2. Why are angel investors a particularly good source of funding for a new business?
3. Explain the difference between fixed expenses and variable expenses.
4. Describe the loan application process.
5. What are the five Cs of banking?
6. Why does the bank require an applicant to produce pro forma financial statements?

Copyright Goodheart-Willcox Co., Inc.

7. Analyze the pro forma cash flow statement shown in Figure 9-7. What does it report? Discuss the importance of budgeting and cash flow for a business.

8. Analyze the pro forma profit and loss statement shown in Figure 9-8. What does it report?

9. Evaluate the pro forma balance sheet in Figure 9-9. What does the pro forma balance sheet report? Why is the accounting equation necessary for this financial statement?

10. State the *accounting equation.*

Apply Your Knowledge

1. Create a chart for ways to bootstrap your business. For each method suggested in Figure 9-1, write a description for how you would apply this to your business. For example, for personal assets, write down each personal asset you are willing to use for your business.

2. Create a chart for equity financing options for your business. For each method suggested in Figure 9-2, write a description for how you would apply this to your business. For example, for personal savings, write down each account you have and the amount of money you are willing to use for your business.

3. Create a chart for debt financing options for your business. For each debt financing method suggested in Figure 9-3, write a description of how you would apply this to your business. For example, for banks and credit unions, list potential places you would contact for a loan.

4. Research "applying for a small business loan" and report your findings. Did your research uncover any challenges that you did not anticipate?

5. When you are ready to apply for a loan, you will have to complete an application. Research small business loan applications on the Internet. Select an application form and complete it. How long did it take you to complete the form? What did you learn from this exercise?

6. When you apply for a loan, you will have to show collateral. Make a list of items you could use as collateral for a loan.

7. Research the loan application process for one equity financing option and for one debt financing option. Report what you learned.

8. You will have many start-up costs and financial requirements for your business. Research the start-up costs and other financial requirements for your type of business. Record your findings and use this information to determine the financial plan.

9. Find a start-up cost calculator on the Internet and calculate the start-up costs for your business. Were the costs affordable?

10. Create a personal balance sheet of your assets, liabilities, and owner's equity. What is the formula used to calculate owner's equity?

Copyright Goodheart-Willcox Co., Inc.

Teamwork

Working with your team, create flash cards for each of the following terms: assets, cash, accounts receivable, fixed assets, liquid assets, illiquid assets, inventory goods on hand, and accounts payable. Write the term on the front of each card. On the back of each card, define the term and give a brief explanation of its importance to the finances of a business. The team leader should use the flash cards as a study tool to help the group prepare for your next test.

Internet Research

Business Revenues. Conduct an Internet search for the terms "operating revenue" and "non-operating revenue." Read explanations and information from several of the sources you find. List examples of each revenue type. Evaluate how each type of revenue would apply to your business.

Business Expenses. Conduct an Internet search for expenses related to the type of business you plan to open. List and categorize all of the expenses your research identifies. Were there any expenses you had not planned for or considered?

Communication Skills

College and Career Readiness

Reading. Read a magazine, newspaper, or online article about a current ethical or unethical situation that has occurred involving an entrepreneur. Determine the central ideas and conclusions of the article. Provide an accurate summary of your reading, making sure to incorporate the *who, what, when,* and *how* of this ethical or unethical situation.

Writing. Research the history of borrowing money. Where did the concept of loans originate? Write an informative report, consisting of several paragraphs to describe your findings.

Copyright Goodheart-Willcox Co., Inc.

CTSOs

Business Financial Plan. Creating a business financial plan is a competitive entrepreneurship event that may be offered by your Career and Technical Student Organization (CTSO). This may be an individual or team event. There may be two parts to this event: the written plan and the oral presentation of the plan.

The event calls for the development of a written business plan that will likely be prejudged before the competition. Written events can be lengthy and take a lot of time to prepare. Therefore, it is important to start early.

The rules for this event are similar to other business plan presentations. However, writing this plan will require research on the means of financing a business and the institutions and individuals that provide such financing.

To prepare for writing a financial plan, complete the following activities.

1. Read the guidelines provided by your organization. There will be specific directions given as to the parts of the business plan and how each should be presented. In addition, all final format guidelines will be given including how to organize and submit. Make certain that you ask any questions about points that you do not understand.

2. Read the topic that is assigned for research by your CTSO. Do your research early. Research may take days or weeks, and you do not want to rush the process.

3. Study this chapter to learn about financial plans.

4. Visit your CTSO's website and create a checklist of the guidelines you must follow. Ask yourself: Does this event still interest me? Can I do what is necessary to be successful at the event? If you answered "yes," move forward with the writing process.

6. Set a deadline for yourself so that you write at a comfortable pace.

7. After you write your first draft, ask a teacher to review it and give you feedback.

8. Once you have the final version of your finance plan, review the checklist you prepared again. Make sure you have addressed all the requirements. You will be penalized on your score if a direction is not followed exactly.

9. Practice presenting the presentation.

Building Your Business Plan—Putting the Puzzle Together

Finance the Business

One reason to write a business plan is to obtain start-up financing. For many entrepreneurs, funding is one of the most difficult steps to take when starting a business. There are many ways to secure funding for your business, however. If at first someone tells you *no,* do not give up. Ask someone else.

Goals

- Identify sources of capital.
- Identify the start-up costs.
- Create a pro forma balance sheet to reflect your business on opening day.
- Complete pro forma cash flow statement for the first year of operation.
- Complete pro forma income statement for the first three years of operation.
- Practice completing a sample loan application.
- Create business plan notes.

Directions

Access the *Entrepreneurship* companion website at www.g-wlearning.com. Download each data file for the following activities. A complete sample business plan is available on the companion website to use as a reference. The name of the file is BusPlan_Sample.RetroAttire. docx.

Preparation—Funding

Activity 9-1. Sources of Funding.
Activity 9-2. Start-Up Costs.
Activity 9-3. Pro Forma Balance Sheet.
Activity 9-4. Pro Forma Cash Flow Statement.
Activity 9-5. Pro Forma Income Statement.
Activity 9-6. Loan Application.
Activity 9-7. Business Plan Notes.

Business Plan—Financial Plans

Lenders and investors will ask for projections showing how your business will make enough money to remain profitable. They want to know you can make loan payments or repay investors with interest. They also expect to see plans for growth for one year, two years, and three years. You may be asked to project even further into the future. Lenders and investors are looking for businesses that will make money over the long term. You will also outline plans for risks such as a changing economy or the death of an owner.

1. Open your saved business plan document.

2. Locate the Financial Plans section. Complete the opening narrative. Use the suggestions and questions listed to help generate ideas. Delete the instructions and questions when you are finished recording your responses in each section. Make sure to proofread your document and correct any errors in keyboarding, spelling, and grammar.

3. List all of the financial documents you have completed and include them in the Appendices.

4. Continue to update the Bibliography section to reflect your sources of information and any templates you used.

5. Save the document.

©Creatas

Unit 4
Examining the Four Ps of Marketing

Your Business Plan—Putting the Puzzle Together

The next key pieces in the business plan puzzle are the four Ps of marketing—product, price, place, and promotion. How will you know if the business is offering the products customers want at the right prices? Are the products easy to buy? Do you offer delivery? What is the best medium to use for reaching the target market? In this unit, you will:

Determine the product, price, and place for the business.

Select the best strategies to promote the business and sell its products.

Propose an initial marketing strategy.

Unit Overview

For a business to be successful, customers first need to know about the business and want to do business there. This makes marketing decisions some of the most important ones for business owners. Marketing is more than just starting a business and hoping customers will find it.

The chapters in this unit focus on the many different parts of the marketing process. They cover product mix, pricing strategies, and getting the product in the hands of the end users. You will also learn about various ways to promote the business as well as about the selling process itself. The unit ends with information on how to create a marketing plan.

Chapters

10 Product, Price, and Place

11 Promotion and Selling

12 Marketing Plan

Entrepreneurs and the Economy

Entrepreneurs who know their target markets well also understand the differences between selling products to consumers versus businesses. In addition, knowing the categories of goods helps a business choose the best marketing strategies for its product type.

The three basic categories of consumer goods are convenience goods, shopping goods, and specialty goods. *Convenience goods* are bought with little effort for immediate use and include most grocery items and gasoline. The target market for convenience goods is broad and may only be limited by location.

Shopping goods are purchased after comparing price, quality, and style. They are purchased less often than convenience goods, and include more expensive items such as appliances and furniture. The target market for specialty goods is narrower and defined by demographics and buying characteristics.

Specialty goods are unique items that consumers are willing to spend considerable time, effort, and money to buy. Examples include a unique sports car or rare antiques. Specialty goods have the smallest target markets because purchases are based on personal preference, brand name, or special features.

Business products are a bit more complex and fall into one of five different categories.

- *Raw materials* become part of a product, such as wood, plastic pellets, or metal.
- *Process materials* are used in making a product, but are not identifiable, such as food preservatives or industrial glue.
- *Component parts* are assembled and become a part of a finished product, such as computer chips, tires, or switches.
- *Major equipment* is large tools and machines used for production, such as furnaces, cranes, or bulldozers.

alphaspirit/Shutterstock.com

- *Accessory equipment* is standard business equipment, such as computers, calculators, or hand tools.

The target markets for business products will be diverse and are defined primarily by function. For example, if you make and sell bulldozers, find companies that need them and narrow your sales and marketing efforts to that group.

While studying, look for the activity icon for:

- Chapter pretests and posttests
- Key terms activities
- Section reviews
- Building Your Business Plan activities

G-W LEARNING.com

10 Product, Price, and Place

Entrepreneurs Candice Cabe and Nadine Lubkowitz had a great idea for a product: women's shoes with interchangeable heels. This would allow women to purchase a single pair of shoes that could be used as anything from low heels to high heels. The idea led Cabe and Lubkowitz to found the company Day2Night Convertible Heels. The problem they faced was taking their product idea from conception to reality. In June 2011, they were able to partner with a Massachusetts prototype company, hire some summer engineering interns, and begin the development of a prototype heel that would be removable and still strong enough to last. The first model of shoes comes with five different-height snap-on heels. The company established an initial sale price of $149 per pair.

"I think it's very important that whatever you're trying to make, sell, or teach has to be basically good. A bad product and you know what? You won't be here in ten years."

—Martha Stewart, founder of
Martha Stewart Living Omnimedia

College and Career Readiness

Reading Prep. Scan this chapter and look for information presented as fact. As you read this chapter, try to determine which topics are fact and which ones are the author's opinion. After reading the chapter, research the topics and verify which are facts and which are opinions.

Sections

10.1 Product

10.2 Price

10.3 Place

Picture Yourself Here
Brian Taylor

While studying at the University of Michigan, Brian Taylor frequently made popcorn seasoned with a variety of spices. Friends loved it and would always ask for his special spice blends. Brian knew he was onto something. During his last two years of school, he put together a team of flavor experts to come up with a variety of seasonings to use on popcorn.

After graduating from college in 2000, Brian started Kernel Season's in Illinois. He first worked alone selling the seasonings at one Chicago movie theater. Soon the business expanded.

Today, his popcorn seasonings are found in movie theaters and grocery stores nationwide. The flavors range from butter, salt, and kettle corn to jalapeño, apple cinnamon, and barbeque. As the president and founder of Kernel Season's, Brian focuses on developing new products, sales, and marketing.

Photo © Kernel Season's, Brian Taylor

Check Your Entrepreneurship IQ

Before you begin the chapter, see what you already know about entrepreneurship by taking the chapter pretest. The pretest is available at www.g-wlearning.com

SECTION 10.1 | Product

What is a product?

Objectives

After completing this section, you will be able to:

- **Define** product as it applies to the four Ps of marketing.
- **Describe** common elements of product.
- **Describe** potential product strategies that may be used by an entrepreneur.

Key Terms

product mix	product positioning
product line	brand
features	branding
warranty	logo
guarantee	tagline
packaging	prototype
product planning	product life cycle

Critical Thinking

Deciding the appropriate sizes, materials, and potential environmental issues for your products' packaging requires time and money. Based on the products your business may offer, which factors will most influence the packaging you select? If you are providing a service, think about creative ways to package your marketing materials.

What Is Product?

A *product* is anything that can be bought and sold. It is also one of the *four Ps of marketing*—product, price, place, and promotion. The product can be goods, service, or an idea. Goods are tangible. They physically exist and can be touched. A service or an idea is intangible. It is not physical and cannot be touched. Products are grouped by those sold mainly to consumers and those sold mainly to businesses. Some goods and services are used by both groups.

A **product mix** is all of the goods and services that a business sells. Usually the product mix involves goods and services that relate to each other in some way. Small businesses may only sell a limited number of goods, while large corporations can offer thousands of different goods. For example, the product mix for a local stationery store may include invitations, specialty paper, greeting cards, and pens. Some businesses offer only one type of goods or service, such as carpet cleaning.

Copyright Goodheart-Willcox Co., Inc.

Products are generally organized into product lines. A **product line** is the group of closely related products within the product mix. For example, a shoe store may sell several different lines of shoes, such as athletic, dress, and casual shoes. A *product item* is the specific model, color, or size of products in a line. For example, the shoe store's product items include the different styles, colors, and sizes of shoes. Perhaps the store has five identical, size-nine brown shoes. They are not considered different items, but the quantity (five) of one item (size-nine brown shoes). The *product width* is the number of product lines a company offers. *Product depth* is the number of product items in a product line.

Product management is a function of marketing that determines the product mix a business should offer to meet customers' needs. Activities can include developing a new good or service or improving an existing one. Other decisions must be made about which brands, quantities, colors, sizes, features, and options to offer. Effective product management contributes to both customer satisfaction and business profits.

Product Elements

All products have certain elements that may be changed to meet customer needs. These elements can be organized into three categories:

- features
- usage
- protection

Understanding these elements can enable a business to more effectively achieve customer satisfaction.

These three product items are in one product line of men's shirts.

Dmitry Kalinovsky/Shutterstock.com

Copyright Goodheart-Willcox Co., Inc.

Features

Features are facts about a good or service. For example, a feature of a tablet computer is the size of its display screen. A service feature for the tablet may be available technical support or data services. Sometimes, optional features can be added to a product by customer request. For example, options on an automobile might include a sunroof and leather seats. Options allow consumers to customize products to their specific needs and wants.

Extended product features apply after the sale of a good or service. Examples of these are product warranties and guarantees. A **warranty** is a written document that states the quality of a product with a promise to correct certain problems that might occur. The warranty promises that the manufacturer will replace or repair faulty items. A **guarantee** is a promise that a product has a certain quality or will perform in a specific way. A guarantee is similar to a warranty, but is not a written document.

Usage

Usage means the way something is used. Product usage includes the available instructions, installation, and technical support.

- *Instructions* are steps that must be carried out in a specific order to successfully complete a task.

- *Installation* is the act or process of putting an item in a certain place and getting it ready for use. Installation is a service offered with many large or complex products.

- *Technical support* includes the people and resources available to help customers with usage problems.

Protection

Protection is a broad category that includes safety inspections, packaging, warranties, and maintenance and repair services. The various forms of protection may be intended to protect the product, the user, or both.

Green Entrepreneurs

Company Uniforms

If your employees or you will be wearing a company uniform, consider purchasing clothing that is made from recycled materials. Some manufacturers are using recycled clothing to produce new clothing. Other manufacturers are reusing over 1 million water bottles a year to produce a recycled fabric used in clothing. Look for the green recycling symbol or ask your supplier to show you clothing produced from recycled materials.

Copyright Goodheart-Willcox Co., Inc.

Most manufacturers work diligently to verify product safety through quality control checks during the manufacturing process. In addition, certain laws establish safety standards for some products. The safety features of products may influence consumer buying decisions.

Packaging protects products until customers are ready to use them. The packaging contains information about the product, such as contents, nutritional information, and weight. Some packaging contains safety precautions and directions to prevent injury to the user.

Complex machinery, vehicles, and other equipment often require regular maintenance to remain in safe, working order. The availability and cost of maintenance and repair services can affect consumer buying decisions and overall satisfaction.

Product Strategies

Product strategy is all of the decisions made about a given product. The first decision a business must make is to select which products it will offer. The next step is to begin product planning. **Product planning** is the process of deciding which product elements to include that will appeal to the target market. Detailed product planning helps marketers make product decisions to distinguish their products from others.

There are many decisions to be made about the products a business will offer. The first decisions are related to selecting the appropriate products and setting the scope of the product plan. The *scope* is the guideline of how many strategies to include as part of the plan. Focusing on one or two strategies can be more effective than five or six strategies.

Decisions must be made through all of the processes involved in getting products to the end users. Product strategies help with **product positioning**, which is distinguishing your products from competing products. The right strategies will help you meet customer needs and beat the competition.

There are a number of product-positioning strategies. These include branding, packaging and labeling, and developing new products when necessary. In addition, it is a good idea to frequently review current products and determine where they are in the product life cycle. This helps ensure that the needs and wants of customers are being met.

Branding

A **brand** is a name, term, or design that sets a product or business apart from its competitors. What do Kleenex®, Crock-Pot®, and Google have in common? They are all established, registered products with powerful brands. In fact, these brands are so strong that those names are used instead of the product categories. For example, most people ask for a Kleenex®, not a facial tissue.

Copyright Goodheart-Willcox Co., Inc.

Social media can give an entrepreneur insight into the needs and wants of potential customers.

Dragon Images/Shutterstock.com

FYI

Increased brand loyalty usually means increased sales. For this reason, strong brands are worth millions of dollars to the companies that own them. Companies spend a lot of money ensuring their brand-name products are protected and the names are not used elsewhere.

Branding a product is using its personality, image, and history to position it favorably in the minds of consumers. One goal of branding is to equate the brand name with quality. In some cases, the brand is the name of the company, such as IBM or Intel®. Well-developed and well-promoted brands build *brand loyalty.*

The tangible elements of a brand are its name, tagline or slogan, and logo. A **logo** is a graphic symbol closely associated with a brand. It may also be called a *brand mark.* A logo may or may not include the brand name. Along with a logo, businesses often create a catchy or memorable tagline to strengthen the brand. A **tagline,** or *slogan,* is a phrase or sentence that summarizes some essential part of the product. For example, almost everyone knows the Nike tagline *Just Do It* and the *You're in Good Hands with Allstate* slogan.

Packaging and Labeling

Another important strategy for product positioning of goods is the choice of packaging. Attractive and colorful packaging draws attention to the products and can become part of the brand. Packaging and labels should be consistent with the desired brand image. Packaging and labels are sometimes the first places consumers see information about a product's features, benefits, and performance.

Customers are very perceptive about the wrappers on the outside of their favorite products. Many businesses make a conscious effort to choose containers that are easily recycled or are made with recycled materials. For these businesses, one of the primary packaging concerns is to select *green materials,* or ones that do not harm the environment.

Copyright Goodheart-Willcox Co., Inc.

Depending on the product, packaging can influence its safety and quality. Breakable items need more packaging than sturdy items. This can increase the cost of the product. Weight and size of the package may affect the expense of shipping or storing.

Some products are subject to labeling laws, which require listing contents and the country of origin. These laws especially affect foods and clothing. It is necessary to research the legal requirements for labeling products. When selling products globally, laws related to the product may differ from laws in the United States.

New Product Development

The business is going well and you think it is time to add a new product. Sounds good, but do not jump too soon. Make sure it is the right time to add a new product. Research is necessary to make sure a new product or service is the best business decision. Confirm that the business can financially support a new product and that the product will generate sales.

Product life cycle is discussed later in this chapter. After a product completes its life cycle, a new product or service may be needed to replace lost revenue. Develop ideas for new products or how to improve old ones. Generating ideas and brainstorming are discussed in chapter 2. Many of the same steps used to create new business ideas will be repeated when creating a new product.

Generate Ideas

Brainstorming is a good way to start generating ideas for new products. Observe, think creatively, and bounce ideas off others. What new product or product improvement makes sense for the business?

Conduct Research

Conduct primary and secondary research to learn whether the product will meet customer needs and wants. Talk to people in the industry, research trends, read articles, and gather information. Pay attention to social media discussions and what are the current trends.

Investigate a Concept

Talk to the target market. Send surveys or hold focus groups to discover how to meet the needs of the market. If the first new product idea does not test well, develop another one.

Analyze the Finances

Research the cost to bring a new product to market or to revise a current product. Are funds available to create and market the product? Look at the market research to see if the product will generate enough sales to cover costs and make the desired profit.

Copyright Goodheart-Willcox Co., Inc.

Design the Product

After proving the new product meets the needs of the market and can be sold at a profit, it is time to design the product. This is the stage where the idea is converted into reality. During the design phase, details of how to produce the product are planned. Product branding is also part of the design phase. Usually numerous designs are completed and evaluated.

Build a Prototype

A **prototype** is a working model for a new product for testing purposes. Large companies may create several prototypes for a single idea. But, creating prototypes can be expensive. To save money, an entrepreneur may choose to create a prototype of only one of the designs. Once the prototype is approved, the product can go into full production.

Market the Product

Many businesses spend a lot of money to introduce new products. It is important to decide which marketing strategies will best reach the target market. The marketing strategies and the budget for marketing should be determined before the product is created.

Product Review

As the business matures, the market will change and product offerings will need to be adjusted for the business to remain competitive. Businesses constantly need to review product offerings to determine if the product mix is still correct for the market.

Another way to remain competitive is to repurpose a current product. To *repurpose* a product is to use it for something different than its original function. A good example is Arm & Hammer baking soda. By positioning the product as a cleaning agent as well as a baking ingredient, the company got new life out of an old product.

A **product life cycle** consists of the stages a product goes through from the beginning to the end. Certain products, such as computers or cell phones, can have a short life cycle due to rapidly changing technology. The four stages of the product life cycle are introduction, growth, maturity, and decline, as illustrated in Figure 10-1. When a product enters the decline stage, it may be necessary to stop making or selling the product.

Introduction Stage

The *introduction stage* is the time when a new product is first brought to the market. At this stage, often very few people know about the product. The costs to create a new product tend to be higher. Also, sales are low in this stage. Therefore, a product may be the least profitable in this stage of the life cycle.

Copyright Goodheart-Willcox Co., Inc.

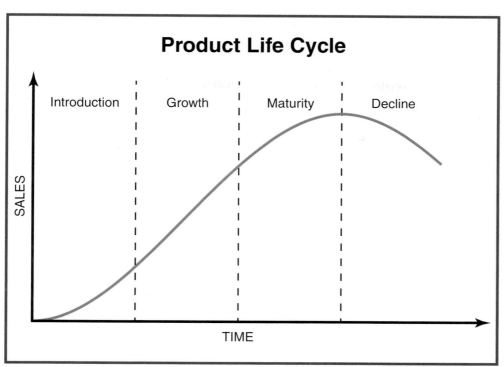

Figure 10-1. The four stages of the product life cycle.

Goodheart-Willcox Publisher

Growth Stage

The *growth stage* is defined as the period during which sales of the product increase rapidly. To keep the product sales high, new models of the product may be introduced. Modifications may also be made to the product to keep customers interested or meet new needs.

Maturity Stage

The *maturity stage* occurs when product sales are no longer increasing quickly, but they are not decreasing quickly. Maturity can happen when the market becomes saturated with a product or a newer, better product is introduced to fill the need. During the maturity stage, competition for customers is very intense. At this stage, it may also be important to look for new ways that customers might use a product or identify new markets for the product to avoid losing revenue.

Decline Stage

Mature products eventually enter the decline stage. During the *decline stage,* sales decrease. If sales rapidly decline, it may be time to stop producing the product. In some cases, sales may decline so much that the best decision is to stop selling the product.

Copyright Goodheart-Willcox Co., Inc.

Section 10.1 | Review

Check Your Understanding ➦

1. What is the product mix?
2. Explain the importance of product management. How does it contribute to the success of a business?
3. Identify extended product features that may become part of the product mix strategy. How do extended product features meet customer needs?
4. List three product-positioning strategies.
5. List the four stages of the product cycle.

Build Your Vocabulary ➦

As you progress through this text, develop a personal glossary of key terms. This will help you build your vocabulary and prepare you for a career. Write a definition for each of the following terms and add them to your personal glossary.

product mix	product positioning
product line	brand
features	branding
warranty	logo
guarantee	tagline
packaging	prototype
product planning	product life cycle

Copyright Goodheart-Willcox Co., Inc.

SECTION 10.2 Price

Essential Question

What decisions must businesses make about product pricing?

Objectives

After completing this section, you will be able to:

- **Define** price as it applies to the four Ps of marketing.
- **Describe** factors that impact pricing decisions.
- **Explain** the importance of establishing pricing objectives.
- **Describe** the different pricing strategies.
- **Give** examples of different pricing techniques.
- **Identify** technology that can be used to set prices.

Key Terms 📱

value
list price
selling price
manufacturer's suggested retail price
   (MSRP)
pricing objectives
profit margin
market share
return on sales (ROS)

return on investment (ROI)
pricing strategies
cost-based pricing
markup
keystone pricing
demand-based pricing
competition-based pricing
psychological pricing

Critical Thinking

To be competitive, you may offer discounts or different pricing options for customers. Research the companies that will compete with your business. What pricing models do they use?

What Is Price?

Price is the amount of money requested or exchanged for a product. It is also one of the *four Ps of marketing*. Correctly pricing goods and services is a challenge for every business. There are three important parts to determining a correct price. The price:

- must cover the costs of producing and selling the product;
- should provide the desired level of profit for the business; and
- must be what customers are willing to pay for the product.

Some customers base purchases on product price alone.

Value is another important factor in pricing. **Value** is the relative worth of something to a person. Some business owners use price to establish and communicate the value of a product in the customer's

FYI

A small business may be able to charge higher prices because of excellent, personalized service to its customers. That service is the business' value proposition or unique selling proposition.

mind. Customers may be willing to pay more if they believe in the value of the product or service. A product's *value proposition* or *unique selling proposition* explains the value of the product over others that are similar.

Creating a pricing policy is an important task for a business owner. A *pricing policy* is how a business sets its wholesale and retail prices based on product cost, demand for a product, perceived value, and competition in the market. Accurately establishing product prices plays an important role in the success of a business and its profitability.

List Price

Most businesses have several tiers, or levels, of pricing. The **list price** is the established price printed in a catalog or on a price tag. The list price does not include any *discounts,* or price reductions. List price is sometimes referred to as *full price.*

Selling Price

The **selling price** is the price a customer actually pays for the product after discounts and coupons. It may also be called the *market price.* Discounts are shown as a percentage, such as *40 percent off,* or as a dollar figure, such as *$20 off.* For example, an item you want to purchase has a list price of $100. It also has an advertised 40 percent discount. After applying the discount, the selling price is $60.

A MSRP reduces price competition among similar products.

iStock.com/Yuri

Copyright Goodheart-Willcox Co., Inc.

Manufacturer's Suggested Retail Price

Some retailers use the **manufacturer's suggested retail price (MSRP)**, which is the list price recommended by a manufacturer. The MSRP is only a suggested price. Retailers are not usually required to use it. However, some high-end manufacturers require retailers to use the MSRP. Often, these manufacturers produce well-known brands and do not want price competition among the retailers offering the products. For example, distributors of video games are usually required to use the MSRP so smaller stores can compete with larger stores. Large stores can buy in large quantities to reduce per-unit cost. If the large stores were not required to use the MSRP, they could set a price below what the smaller stores pay to purchase the same games. By requiring products to be sold at the MSRP, the brand name and price is preserved.

Pricing Factors

All businesses have factors that impact their pricing decisions. Expenses, competition, regulation compliance, a product's life cycle, and supply and demand may affect prices. Each business will need to take into consideration some or all of these factors. Pricing policies take into consideration expenses, competition, and governmental regulations.

Expenses

All goods and services have certain expenses related to creating them and getting them to the end users. Expenses such as employee wages, shipping, utilities, rent, and other operating expenses affect pricing. There are two basic types of expenses: fixed and variable.

Fixed expenses do not change and are not affected by the number of products that are produced or sold. Fixed expenses include rent, salaries, and loan payments. Whether 100 or 1,000 items are sold in a month, fixed expenses remain the same.

Variable expenses change based on activity of the business. Variable expenses include advertising, packaging, and shipping. The cost of extending credit, which is discussed in a later chapter, may also be included. Figure 10-2 shows examples of fixed and variable expenses.

Competition

Competitors are going to pay attention to your prices. You need to also pay attention to their prices as well. Will you charge a higher price, a lower price, or match the price of competitors? As discussed in chapter 5, *price competition* is pricing a product lower than the competition to encourage customers to buy your product. *Nonprice competition* is positioning a product as more valuable to the customer because of service, appearance, or other factors unrelated to its price.

Copyright Goodheart-Willcox Co., Inc.

Figure 10-2. Fixed
expenses do not change,
while variable expenses
change often.

Types of Expenses	
Fixed Expenses	**Variable Expenses**
Equipment rental	Advertising and promotion
Insurance	Bonuses
Interest	Credit card payment
Licenses	Hourly wages
Loan payments	Office supplies
Mortgage	Packaging
Rent	Sales commissions
Salaries	Shipping and handling
Service payments (cell phone, Internet, subscription TV)	Utilities

Goodheart-Willcox Publisher

Governmental Regulations

There are many state and federal laws that regulate pricing to prevent monopolies and to promote fair competition. As discussed earlier, both businesses and consumers are affected by unfair pricing practices. Some unfair pricing practices include:

- *bait and switch;* it is illegal to advertise one product with the intent of persuading a customer to buy a more expensive item;

- *price-fixing;* it is illegal for a group of businesses to agree to keep their prices in the same range;

- *price ceilings;* laws may prohibit setting prices too high;

- *price floors;* laws may prohibit setting prices too low;

- *price discrimination;* it is illegal to sell the same product to different customers at different prices based on personal characteristics;

- *deceptive pricing;* pricing products in a way to intentionally mislead a customer is illegal; and

- *predatory pricing;* it is illegal to set very low prices to remove competition, such as foreign companies that price their products below the same domestic ones to drive the domestic companies out of business.

Product Life Cycle

The stage of a product in its life cycle influences pricing. In the introduction stage of many products, the prices are often higher. Higher prices may reflect the lack of competition and could help the business recover some development costs.

When competitors enter the market during the growth stage, however, they may set lower prices to attract new customers. Products

Copyright Goodheart-Willcox Co., Inc.

Anatoly Tiplyashin/Shutterstock.com

Nonprice competition relies on a product's value and qualities.

can become less expensive to produce during the growth phase, which would also help to lower the prices.

During the maturity and decline phases of a product, prices are often lowered even further to stimulate sales. Businesses hope to recoup declining revenues by selling more items at lower prices.

Supply and Demand

The supply of available product and the demand for the product sometimes determine its price. If everyone wants a product, demand is high. When there are not enough products to meet demand, the supply is low. High demand and low supply mean the business can charge more for the product because customers are likely willing to pay more for it.

If only a few people want a product, demand is low. If there are more products than there are people who want them, supply is high. In this situation, the price for the product must be lower to encourage customers to buy it. Pricing affects supply and demand as shown in Figure 10-3.

A market is *elastic* when a small change in price produces a relatively large change in the amount of the items demanded. A market is *inelastic* when the price of a product has no effect on the demand for it.

Pricing Objectives

Pricing objectives are the goals defined in the business and marketing plans for the overall pricing policies of the company.

Copyright Goodheart-Willcox Co., Inc.

Figure 10-3. The effects of pricing on supply and demand.

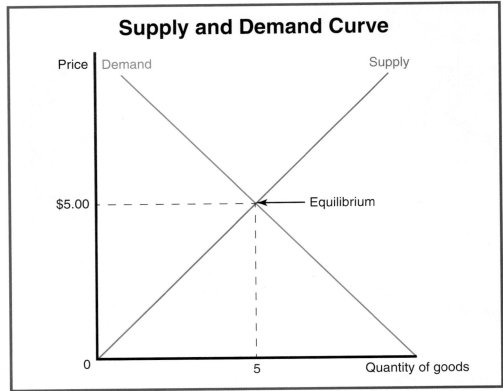

Goodheart-Willcox Publisher

Businesses set pricing objectives based on the pricing policies and short- and long-term financial goals for the company. The mission statement may also impact pricing objectives. For example, if the mission statement says the business is a price leader, that in part determines pricing objectives. Pricing objectives include maximizing sales, maximizing profits, increasing market share, maximizing return on sales, improving return on investment, and creating an image.

Keep in mind that pricing objectives are moving targets and will be regularly revised. The price of a product must be at a level that encourages customers to purchase the product. It must also be at a level that generates enough profit for the business.

Maximize Sales

Maximizing sales is a pricing objective based on selling a large quantity of products at lower profit margins. A **profit margin** is the amount by which revenue from sales exceeds the costs of making the product and selling it. For example, if a product costs $10 to make and sell and it is priced at $15, the profit margin is $5.

Another way to maximize sales is to offer volume pricing. *Volume pricing* is when the list price is lowered based on the amount purchased. In volume pricing, the price decreases as the volume purchased increases. For example, the list price may be $25 each for quantities of 100 or less, $20 each for quantities of 101 to 500, and $15 each for quantities over 500.

Copyright Goodheart-Willcox Co., Inc.

Maximize Profits

Maximizing profit per sale is a pricing objective that revolves around fewer sales, but with increased profit margins. A business charges the highest price a customer will pay before deciding that the price exceeds the value. The high-end jewelry industry is an example of where maximizing profit per sale is used as a pricing objective.

Increase Market Share

Market share is the percentage of the total sales in a given market that one business conducts. All of the competing businesses account for 100 percent of the market. Market share is determined by dividing one company's total revenue by the total revenue of the market. For example, four advertising agencies in a town have combined revenue of $4 million. If one of the agency's revenue is $2 million, that agency has a 50 percent market share. The goal of increasing market share is to gain additional customers, which often means taking customers from competitors. It can also mean attracting new customers into the market.

Maximize Return on Sales

Return on sales (ROS) is a measure of a company's profitability and is equal to the net income divided by total sales. ROS reflects how well a company has controlled costs. For example, if a business has a net income of $10,000 from sales of $20,000, the ROS is 50 percent.

$$\frac{\text{net income}}{\text{total sales}} = \text{ROS}$$

$$\frac{\$10,000}{\$20,000} = 50 \text{ percent}$$

Improve Return on Investment

Return on investment (ROI) is a common measure of profitability for a business. It is based on the amount earned from the investment in the business. One way of determining ROI is to divide net profit by total assets. For example, if a business has a net profit of $50,000 and assets of $150,000, the ROI is 33 percent.

$$\frac{\text{net profit}}{\text{total assets}} = \text{ROI}$$

$$\frac{\$50,000}{\$150,000} = 33 \text{ percent}$$

Copyright Goodheart-Willcox Co., Inc.

SBA Tips

Looking for small business counseling and training close to home? The SBA provides small business counseling and training through a variety of programs and resource partners across the country. Resources are available both locally and online.
www.sba.gov

Create an Image

Pricing may influence how customers perceive the business or the product. The image of a business or product is how a customer perceives it. High prices tend to create an image of high-end products. Low prices tend to create an image of discount products. Be sure the image set by the pricing matches the image outlined in the business plan.

Pricing Strategies

Pricing strategies are business decisions about pricing and how prices are set to make a profit. To stay in business, all companies, except for nonprofits, must generate a profit. A *pricing structure* is a consistent plan for pricing product that achieves the goals of the company. It influences how a customer perceives your product and business.

There are many ways to set prices, but they all start with knowing a product's break-even point. The *break-even point* is where sales equal expenses. It is often expressed as the number of items needed to sell in order to recover expenses. After the break-even point is reached, the business starts to make a profit. To determine how many units of a product must be sold to meet the expenses, complete a break-even analysis. A simple break-even analysis is:

$$\frac{\text{cost} \times \text{number of units}}{\text{selling price}} = \text{break-even point}$$

For example, a business sells tablet computers and recently ordered 100 units of a new model. Each tablet computer costs $140 to produce. The pricing strategy is to sell the tablets for $250 each. How many tablets would need to be sold to reach the break-even point? Complete the break-even analysis:

$$\frac{\text{cost} \times \text{number of units}}{\text{selling price}} = \text{break-even point}$$

$$\frac{\$140 \times 100}{\$250} = \text{break-even point}$$

$$56 \text{ tablets} = \text{break-even point}$$

Cost-Based Pricing

Cost-based pricing uses the cost of the product to set the product's selling price. The first step is to accurately determine the actual cost to the business of the item. If it is a service, consider using the hourly cost of the employee's time. If it is a good, use the actual cost to produce the item. If you are selling an idea, base the cost on the number of hours spent developing the idea plus your time.

Copyright Goodheart-Willcox Co., Inc.

Next, add the **markup**, which is the desired amount of profit added, to determine the final price. It is important to accurately estimate the profit needed based on product costs. The following equation expresses cost-based pricing.

cost + markup = selling price

In the previous example, the cost for computer tablets is $140 each. Suppose based on the other costs associated with buying and selling these tablets, you must make $156 in profit on each tablet. This form of markup is called *dollar markup* because it is expressed as a dollar amount, not a percentage. What would be the selling price?

cost + dollar markup = selling price

$140 + $156 = selling price

$296 = selling price

Some businesses prefer to use a *percentage markup* to determine selling prices. They establish a percent of profit necessary for each item and add that amount to the cost to determine the selling price. For example, your business model may state that you must make a 40 percent profit on all sales. Using a 40-percent-markup scenario, the $140 tablet computer would have to be priced at $196.

(cost × markup percent) + cost = selling price

($140 × 40 percent) + $140 =

$56 + $140 =

$196 =

Some businesses use keystone pricing. **Keystone pricing** is doubling the total cost of a product to determine its selling price. For example, under keystone pricing, the $140 tablet would be priced at $280 ($140 × 2). Most businesses use a percentage markup rather than a dollar markup to determine the selling price.

Focus on Finance

Rule of 72

If you plan to open a business, it is never too early to start getting your personal finances in order. Set a monthly savings goal and stick to it. Another tool is the *Rule of 72*. The Rule of 72 is a simple way to determine how long it will take you to double your money. Simply divide 72 by the interest rate you will earn. For example, perhaps you will need $10,000 to open your business. You have $5,000 now. How long would it take to double your $5,000 if you invest it at a 4 percent interest rate? The answer would be 13 years (72 ÷ 4 = 13).

Copyright Goodheart-Willcox Co., Inc.

Entrepreneur Ethics

Integrity is defined as the honesty of a person's actions. Integrity and ethics go together in both personal and professional lives. As a leader, the entrepreneur establishes the reputation of the business in the community. An entrepreneur who displays integrity creates a positive culture for employees, customers, and the community.

Demand-Based Pricing

Demand-based pricing is a pricing method based on what customers are willing to pay. It is also called *value-based pricing* and reflects the customer's perceptions of a product's value. Demand-based pricing is most effective when the product is unique or there is a high demand for it.

For example, a small business is the only one nearby selling new bracelets popular with middle school students. The students could order the bracelets online for $7 plus shipping and handling, but they would not arrive for weeks. Because they are in high demand, the small business can charge $12 for the bracelets and make a higher profit.

Competition-Based Pricing

Competition-based pricing is a pricing method based primarily on what the competitors charge. The business makes a decision to price above, below, or at the competitor's prices. To effectively use a competition-based pricing strategy, monitor the competitor's prices often and make necessary adjustments. Competition-based pricing does not take into account the cost of producing the product, however, and may not provide enough or any profit.

Pricing Techniques

The last step in pricing products is to select the techniques that work best for the product or service. There are multiple pricing techniques. Two common ones are psychological pricing and discount pricing.

Psychological Pricing

Psychological pricing is a pricing technique used by retailers to influence buying decisions. It relies on the nature of human psychology to make prices appear more attractive to consumers. There are six main types of psychological pricing:

- prestige pricing
- odd pricing
- even pricing
- buy one, get one
- bundling
- price lining

Copyright Goodheart-Willcox Co., Inc.

Prestige pricing conveys a high-end image to the customer.

1000 Words/Shutterstock.com

Prestige Pricing

Prestige pricing is setting prices high to convey quality and status. Customers see a higher price and think the product is better than lower-priced competing products. High-end fashion designers and car manufacturers often use prestige pricing.

Odd Pricing

Odd pricing sets the sale price so it ends in an odd number, most often 5 or 9. The psychology behind this technique is that $9.95 sounds less than $10.00, even though it is only a five-cent difference. Odd pricing conveys value.

Even Pricing

Even pricing sets the sale price so it ends in an even number, most often 0. Prices might be set at $40, $100, or $14,000. Customers see the even number and think the product is better than one priced for value. Even pricing conveys quality.

Copyright Goodheart-Willcox Co., Inc.

Buy One, Get One

The buy one, get one (BOGO) technique gives customers a free or reduced-price item when another is purchased at full price. Depending on the promotion, the items may be the same or similar. Some stores have buy two, get one promotions and other similar offers. The BOGO technique conveys savings and value.

Bundling

Bundling combines two or more products for one price. Bundling can reduce the overall price when compared to buying the items separately. For example, a clothing store might bundle a $10 hat and a $20 T-shirt for a single price of $25. This bundled price saves the customer $5, and the store has sold two items instead of one. Bundling conveys savings and value.

Price Lining

Price lining is setting different levels of prices for similar products. This is done to differentiate between the quality and features of the products. Retailers sometimes use the terms *good, better, best* to describe their products and prices. *Good* conveys value, *best* conveys quality, and *better* conveys a balance between the two.

Discount Pricing

In retail businesses (B2C), when items are discounted from the list prices, they are *on sale.* Companies that sell products to other businesses (B2B) also use discount pricing techniques. The five most popular forms of discount pricing are:

- cash discount;
- promotional discount;
- quantity discount;
- seasonal discount; and
- trade discount.

Cash Discount

A cash discount is usually a percentage removed from the total invoice amount. It is offered to encourage a customer to pay a bill early. A cash discount often shows up in a format similar to 2/10, net 30. The *2* reflects the percentage off the invoice total. The *10* indicates the number of days the customer has to pay the bill to receive the discount. The *30* stands for the number of days the customer has to pay the bill without receiving a penalty. This discount would be read, "2 percent off if paid within 10 days, otherwise the entire bill is due in 30 days." Cash discounts encourage customers to pay bills early, which helps the business' cash flow.

Copyright Goodheart-Willcox Co., Inc.

Promotional Discount

Promotional discounts are offered for a limited time to entice customers to buy during that period. After the promotional period is over, the price goes back to the regular price. For example, a Fourth of July sale may offer 20 percent off an item, but on July 5th, the item is full price.

Quantity Discount

A quantity discount offers a reduced per-item price for larger numbers of an item purchased. Many companies offer quantity discounts as an incentive for buying more product. The more the customer buys, the more money he or she saves on each item. For example, if a customer buys 48 sweatshirts, the price may be $22 per shirt. If the customer buys 96 shirts, however, the price may be $18 per shirt.

Seasonal Discount

Seasonal discounts are special prices to encourage customers to buy at off-peak times of the year. For example, swimsuits may be on sale in February because summer is when most swimsuits are purchased at full price. Seasonal discounts can also apply to off-peak days or hours. A restaurant might offer Monday-night specials since Mondays are slow for the restaurant business.

Global Entrepreneurs

Mark Zuckerberg

In the early 2000s, Mark Zuckerberg was at Harvard University studying computer science and psychology and already had the knowledge to create a website. Little did he know then that in a few years the website he was to create would be the foundation of the multibillion dollar, international corporation Facebook. Facebook was launched on February 4, 2004. Initially, it was only open to Harvard students. In March 2004, Facebook expanded to other Ivy League schools, including Columbia, Yale, Stanford, and NYU. In October 2005, Facebook went global. It expanded to the United Kingdom, Puerto Rico, and Mexico first, followed by other countries.

Facebook earns revenue primarily by selling advertisements that are placed on Facebook pages. Over one-third of Facebook's revenue comes from international sources, and international revenue has been increasing every year. Since its launch in 2004, Facebook has become an essential tool in the world of international advertising.

Trade Discount

A trade discount is the amount a vendor reduces the MSRP for businesses. This is a standard B2B procedure. Manufacturers give trade discounts to the stores so they can in turn resell the items at the full MSRP. This takes into account the fact that retailers must mark up product prices to make a profit.

Prices

After considering pricing factors, pricing objectives, pricing strategies, and pricing techniques, you are ready to set a price for the product or service. Review the mission statement and goals for the business to make sure the price is in line with what the business is trying to do. To streamline the process, many businesses use *web-based pricing software* or other pricing technology. Automating the process using technology makes it efficient and saves time in monitoring pricing.

Remember that pricing strategies may change as a business grows. Take into account that most businesses cannot sell every product at the list price. Some products may be put on sale, some on permanent clearance, and some donated to a charity.

Section 10.2 Review

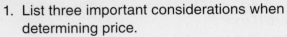

Check Your Understanding ⤴

1. List three important considerations when determining price.
2. Give three examples of unfair and illegal pricing practices.
3. Describe the importance of supply and demand in pricing your product.
4. What are two commonly used pricing techniques?
5. List the five most popular forms of discount pricing.

Build Your Vocabulary ⤴

As you progress through this text, develop a personal glossary of key terms. This will help you build your vocabulary and prepare you for a career. Write a definition for each of the following terms and add them to your personal glossary.

value
list price
selling price
manufacturer's
   suggested retail
   price (MSRP)
pricing objectives
profit margin
market share
return on sales
   (ROS)

return on
   investment (ROI)
pricing strategies
cost-based pricing
markup
keystone pricing
demand-based
   pricing
competition-based
   pricing
psychological
   pricing

SECTION 10.3 **Place**

?Essential **Q**uestion

How does place affect the availability and cost of products?

Objectives

After completing this section, you will be able to:

- **Define** place as it applies to the four Ps of marketing.
- **Discuss** the importance of managing a business' supply chain.
- **Explain** the channels of distribution.
- **List** factors that impact place strategies.

Key Terms 📇

place
supply chain management
intermediaries
inventory
channel of distribution
direct channel

indirect channel
transportation
bulk-breaking
freight forwarder
utility

Critical Thinking

Are you going to be a manufacturer, wholesaler, or retailer? Think about the supply chain that will apply to your business. Sketch the supply chain in proper order.

What Is Place?

Place is a part of the *four Ps of marketing*. In marketing, **place** refers to the activities involved in getting a good or service to the end users. Place is also known as *distribution*. Physical distribution activities include order processing, warehousing or storage, material handling, and transportation. The objective of place is to deliver exactly what the end user wants. This must happen at the right time, in the right place, and at the right price.

Supply Chain

As discussed earlier, a *supply chain* is the businesses, people, and activities involved in turning raw materials into products and delivering them to end users. The supply chain for some businesses can be very short. For other businesses, it can be rather lengthy.

FYI

Proper distribution is crucial to the success of any business. It can influence customer goodwill, the ability to sell products, and the company's profitability. It may even be a determining factor in whether or not a business remains open.

One part of a supply chain consists of businesses that supply the raw materials, component parts, and other supplies to manufacturers for production. Another part of the supply chain is the businesses involved in logistics. *Logistics* is physically moving products from the manufacturers to distributors, retailers, or end users. The final part of the supply chain is selling the product or service to the end users, either consumers, businesses, or both.

Supply chain management is coordinating the events happening throughout the supply chain. Effective supply chain management results in the following benefits:

- streamlined inventories
- lower operating costs
- timely product availability
- increased customer satisfaction

The people or businesses between the manufacturers or producers and the end users are called **intermediaries.** There are several types of intermediaries, including wholesalers, retailers, and agents. Figure 10-4 outlines characteristics of intermediaries.

Figure 10-4. Each type of intermediary meets a different set of needs.

Intermediaries	
Type	**Characteristics**
Wholesaler	• Breaks down bulk packages into smaller quantities for resale • Buys from manufacturers or producers and resells to retailers • Takes ownership of the products • Provides storage facilities • Often takes on some marketing responsibilities (i.e., provide marketing support in the form of shelf signs, flyers, or advertising) • Extends credit to retailers • Provides sales information and training
Retailer	• Has personal relationships with end users • Takes on most of the marketing responsibilities • Often extends consumer credit • Sets the final selling price to end users
Agent (broker)	• Does not take ownership of products • Connects buyers and sellers • Takes a commission, which is a percentage of the sale of the product • Is useful for international trade and for services
Internet	• Helps niche products reach a large audience • Is convenient for making purchases • Uses e-commerce technology for payments • May eliminate some other intermediaries because producers can use it to reach end users directly and inexpensively

Goodheart-Willcox Publisher

Copyright Goodheart-Willcox Co., Inc.

Wholesalers, or distributors, purchase large amounts of goods directly from manufacturers. Once goods are purchased, they are put into inventory until it is time for distribution. **Inventory** is the assortment or selection of items that a business has on hand at a particular point in time. Inventory is costly, so it must be effectively managed and protected against theft or damage. *Inventory control* is the activities and processes involved in managing the products in inventory and related costs. Some of the activities related to inventory control are:

- physically storing goods in warehouses with a system to identify their placement

- keeping count of each item in the warehouse

- maintaining a record of the dollar value of each item in inventory

- monitoring items as they come in to and out of inventory

Inventory control is discussed in chapter 15.

Wholesalers store goods and resell them in smaller amounts to various retailers. A *retailer* buys products either from wholesalers or directly from manufacturers and resells them to consumers. The Internet is also considered an intermediary between the businesses creating or reselling products and the end users.

Agents, also known as *brokers,* are different from wholesalers because they do not take possession of the product. Instead, they bring buyers and sellers together. The agent may be hired by the buyer or the seller. For example, realtors are agents. They may represent either the buyer or seller of a home. Realtors never take possession of the home, though. They bring together the person selling a house and the person who wants to buy it. The goal of an agent is to create a favorable exchange for both buyer and seller. Agents can be used anywhere in the distribution channel. They are especially useful in facilitating international trade.

Channel of Distribution

The **channel of distribution** is the path that goods take through the supply chain. Think about the pencil you are using right now. How did it get from its original manufacturer to you? It may have been manufactured, sold to a wholesaler, sold to a retailer, and then purchased by you. Or, you may have bought it from the wholesaler's website. The path the pencil took to reach you is the channel of distribution.

Distribution is not free. There are many costs associated with getting products to the end users. These distribution costs increase the prices charged for goods or services. Therefore, it is important to find efficient ways to distribute products that keep costs under control.

Copyright Goodheart-Willcox Co., Inc.

Even though there are additional costs involved, distribution services are important to a business. The investment a company makes in efficient physical distribution can add value to goods, services, and intellectual property, which can keep customers happy and returning. Many distribution factors, such as good customer services, accurate order processing, and safe handling of product, contribute to creating positive business reputations and company value. Customers are usually willing to pay for efficient delivery and expect to:

- receive goods as promised and in perfect condition

- receive services, such as carpet cleaning and appliance repair, at the date and time requested

- be able to download digital or intellectual product immediately, when paid for, in a quick and efficient manner to any personal device they may own

Types of Distribution Channels

There are two distribution channels a product can take: direct or indirect. Figure 10-5 shows the two different types of distribution channels.

A **direct channel** is when goods or services go directly from the manufacturer to the end user. For example, a child care business provides services directly to the parent or guardian of the child. Most service businesses use direct channels of distribution.

Figure 10-5. Channels of distribution depend on the good or service that is delivered.

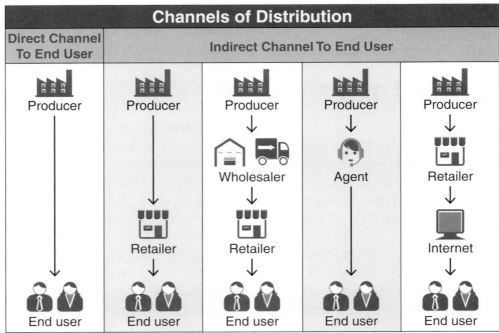

Vinko93/Shutterstock.com; Goodheart-Willcox Publisher

Copyright Goodheart-Willcox Co., Inc.

An **indirect channel** uses intermediaries to get the product from the manufacture to the end users. For example, a bicycle may go from the producer, to a wholesaler, and the retailer before reaching the end user.

Transportation Options

Transportation is the physical movement of products through the channel of distribution. If the channel of distribution includes moving products from one place to another, there are a number of transportation options. The six main types of transportation are truck, train, plane, ship, pipeline, and digital, as shown in Figure 10-6.

Transportation Modes for Distribution		
Transportation Mode	**Advantages**	**Disadvantages**
Road	• Can deliver door to door • Flexible schedules • Can be modified for specific cargo (i.e., refrigerator trucks)	• Weather delays • Traffic delays • Maintenance problems
Rail	• Send large quantities over long distances • Inexpensive • Can carry trucks closer to the destination • Can be modified for cargo (flatbed railcars for intermodal containers)	• Slower method of transportation • Minimal destination flexibility • Needs a second mode of transportation to get to final destination
Air	• Fastest mode of transportation • Less chance of damage to items • Can save on warehousing as products arrive as needed	• Most expensive • Weather delays • Maintenance problems • Needs a second mode of transportation to get to final destination
Water	• Send large quantities over long distances • Can be modified for cargo (i.e., tankers for oil) • Inexpensive	• Slowest method • No destination flexibility • Needs a second mode of transportation to get to final destination
Pipeline	• Not subject to weather delays • Fewer maintenance issues • Low operating costs	• Can only carry products that flow (i.e., gasoline) • Expensive to build • Leaks linked to environmental damage • Needs a second mode of transportation to get to final destination
Digital	• Low to no operating cost • Easy access • Very fast delivery	• Only for electronic goods or services

Goodheart-Willcox Publisher; Source: US Census Statistical Abstract

Figure 10-6. Each transportation method has its drawbacks.

Copyright Goodheart-Willcox Co., Inc.

Place Strategies

The first and most important strategy related to place is determining the exact channel of distribution. For example, products that must get to end users quickly need a direct channel or a short indirect channel. Milk is an example of a product that must reach the end user quickly. Durable products with no expiration date can have a longer channel of distribution.

The strategy for place should provide timely delivery for the lowest cost. Transportation, storage, and utility costs are factors to consider when determining the strategy for place.

Transportation Costs

FYI

A *freight forwarder* is a company that organizes shipments. It is not a shipper or carrier, rather it specializes in the logistics of supply-chain management and assists companies in contracting carriers.

Each type of transportation has different costs, efficiencies, and time constraints. For example, when shipping large quantities of durable products, it may be okay to choose a less expensive, slower mode of transportation. However, when shipping perishable goods, a more expensive, faster mode of transportation may be necessary.

Some place strategies involve product handling activities, which affect transportation costs. Activities associated with product handling include bulk-breaking and freight forwarding. Breaking bulk is one product handling activity that can be included in place strategies. **Bulk-breaking** is the process of separating a large quantity of goods into smaller quantities for resale. Intermediaries buy goods in bulk and then break the bulk quantity into smaller lots of goods to resell. For example, it is easier and cheaper to ship a pallet of copy paper rather than 40 individual cartons separately. The office supply store buys copy paper by the pallet and then sells cartons or individual reams to customers.

Transportation costs can be managed using the services of freight forwarders. A **freight forwarder** is a company that organizes shipments. Shipments from various companies are combined into one sizeable shipment. The freight forwarder hires a transportation company to move the shipments from various companies as one large shipment. By putting smaller shipments together, companies save money in the shipment of their goods.

Storage Costs

Storage is also critical to the strategy for place. Products need protection from weather, theft, and damage. Retail and manufacturing businesses need areas to store physical inventory. This may increase distribution costs, which will affect the final product pricing. If a business does not have enough storage space in the facility, it will need to rent, lease, or build space.

Copyright Goodheart-Willcox Co., Inc.

 # You Do the Math   Algebraic Reasoning

The order of operations is a set of rules stating which operations in an equation are performed first. The order of operations is often stated using the acronym PEMDAS. PEMDAS stands for parentheses, exponents, multiplication and division, and addition and subtraction. This means anything inside parentheses is computed first. Exponents are computed next. Then, any multiplication and division operations are computed. Finally, any addition and subtraction operations are computed to find the answer to the problem. The equation is solved from left to right by applying PEMDAS.

Find the solution to these equations.

1. $8 - (4 \cdot 3) + 2^3 \div 2 =$
2. $11^2 + (45 \times 2) =$

Large companies, such as Neiman-Marcus and Ford, have their own storage facilities. Smaller companies often either lease a storage facility or use wholesalers to store products until they are needed. Some warehouse facilities provide delivery to the end user. By using this type of warehousing service, a business can reduce inventory-storage costs and losses due to damage or theft. Managing inventory is discussed in chapter 15.

Utility Costs

Utility is the attribute that makes a product capable of satisfying a need or want. There are four types of utility that add perceived value—place, time, possession, and form. All of these utilities are associated with the distribution of goods or services from the creators to the end users. Based on the specific good or service, some utility costs will be necessary and directly affect place strategies; others will not apply.

Place Utility

Place utility means placing products where they are needed and are useful. For example, if you sell sunscreen lotion, it makes sense to have it available at the beach where people who need it can buy it.

Time Utility

Time utility is getting a product delivered to the end user when it is needed. Timing is everything. If the product is late, the business could lose a customer and goodwill is damaged.

Copyright Goodheart-Willcox Co., Inc.

Possession Utility

Possession utility is the satisfaction that a customer receives from owning a good or receiving a needed service. An example of possession utility is owning a car you have wanted for a long time.

Form Utility

Form utility increases the desirability of a product by physically changing it. For example, changing a laundry detergent from powdered to liquid form may mean it works better in some washing machines.

Section 10.3 Review

Check Your Understanding ↪

1. What is a supply chain?
2. List three types of intermediaries.
3. What are the two types of distribution channels?
4. Define effective channels of distribution strategies, including the activities associated with transportation, product handling, and storage. List the six main types of transportation.
5. What are the four types of utility?

Build Your Vocabulary ↪

As you progress through this text, develop a personal glossary of key terms. This will help you build your vocabulary and prepare you for a career. Write a definition for each of the following terms and add them to your personal glossary.

place	direct channel
supply chain management	indirect channel
	transportation
intermediaries	bulk-breaking
inventory	freight forwarder
channel of distribution	utility

Chapter Summary

Section 10.1 **Product**

- Product, together with place, price, and promotion, make up the four Ps of marketing. A product can be a good, service, or idea.
- All products have certain elements that may be changed to meet customer needs. These include product features, extended product features, usage, and protection. Effectively using product elements can help a business achieve greater customer satisfaction.
- Using the appropriate product strategy will help the business out-sell the competition and meet a consumer need. Product strategies include branding, packaging and labeling, and developing new products.

Section 10.2 **Price**

- Price is one of the four Ps of marketing. A product's price will have a significant effect on whether or when a company will make a profit.
- Pricing decisions are determined by a number of factors. Included among these are expenses, competition, laws and regulations, product life cycle, as well as supply and demand.
- Price objectives are driven by the short- and long-term goals of the company. Finding the right price requires finding the right balance between an amount at which customers will buy and one that generates enough profit for the business.
- Pricing strategy is based on a company's pricing objectives. Pricing can be cost-based, demand-based, or competition-based.
- Pricing techniques include psychology pricing and discount pricing. Psychology pricing is most often applied to retail prices, the price at which something is sold to a consumer. Discount pricing is used in both B2B transactions as well as B2C transactions.
- Many businesses use web-based pricing software or other pricing technology when determining prices. Using technology makes the process more efficient.

Section 10.3 **Place**

- Place is one of the four Ps of marketing. Place is the means by which customers will receive the products.
- Efficient management of a supply chain is important to a business' success. Effective supply chain management streamlines inventories, lowers operating costs, ensures timely product availability, and increases customer satisfaction.
- The paths that goods take through the supply chain are channels of distribution. There are both direct and indirect channels of distribution. Choosing which channel to use is first based on the type of good being sold.

Copyright Goodheart-Willcox Co., Inc.

- Transportation, storage, and utility costs are factors that impact place strategy. A place strategy is determining how to get products to customers in a timely manner at the lowest cost.

Online Activities

Complete the following activities to help you learn, practice, and expand your knowledge and skills.

➡ **Posttest.** Now that you have finished the chapter, see what you learned by taking the chapter posttest.

➡ **Key Terms.** Practice vocabulary for this chapter using the e-flash cards, matching activity, and vocabulary game until you are able to recognize their meanings.

Review Your Knowledge

1. Describe a product line.
2. Why is branding important for a business? What are elements of a brand?
3. Describe the process of developing a new product.
4. What is the difference between the list price and the selling price?
5. Explain the difference between fixed expenses and variable expenses.
6. Why does product life cycle affect pricing?
7. List and describe some of the guidelines that can be used to set pricing objectives.
8. Pricing factors, objectives, and strategies are components of a pricing policy. Compare and contrast each component. How are they similar, different, and where do they overlap?
9. Describe supply chain management. What are the benefits of effective supply chain management?
10. What are some of the place decisions an entrepreneur must make? Explain how distribution can add value to goods, services, and intellectual property.

Apply Your Knowledge

1. You have selected the good or service that you want to create. Describe the product mix. How many product lines will you have? What is the product line, product item, and product width?
2. As part of product mix strategies, create the brand that you might use for your product. If appropriate, create branding elements, such as a logo or slogan.

Copyright Goodheart-Willcox Co., Inc.

3. Create product mix strategies that include extended product features for your good or service. Describe how you will address features, usage, and protection for your product.

4. Explain the nature of product planning for a new business. Part of product planning is to set the scope of what is to be accomplished in order to keep focus on the important elements of a project. Explain the scope of product planning and its importance.

5. Identify and analyze each of the six pricing objectives discussed in this chapter. Explain how these will apply to your business. Which do you think will work better for your business?

6. Research cost-based pricing, demand-based pricing, and competition-based pricing for the industry that you have selected. Which method do you think would work better for your product based on what you have learned that others in your industry have used?

7. Determine the break-even point of a product where 200 units are produced for a cost of $500 each and a selling price of $1,000. What pricing strategy is being used?

8. Describe the supply chain that will apply to your business. How many intermediaries do you think you will require?

9. Based on what you have learned in this chapter and research on your industry, what do you think is a reasonable price for your product?

10. The formula for calculating markup is **cost + markup = selling price**. If the cost of your product is $120 and you want to make 10 percent profit, what is the markup? What is the selling price? You have a good customer that wants a cash discount on your selling price because he buys in large quantities. He wants to buy 100 items with a 2 percent discount off your selling price. What would his total discount be?

Teamwork

Working with your team, select a product with which you are familiar that has gone through its life cycle and is no longer in the marketplace. Create a flow chart that illustrates the life cycle of the product. For each stage, explain what the producer experienced. What did you learn from this activity?

Internet Research

Pricing Structures. Conduct an Internet search for business pricing structures and guides that apply to goods, services, and ideas. Create a chart with three columns: Goods, Services, and Ideas. List the considerations for developing a pricing structure that apply to each category. Highlight the considerations that are unique to each category to communicate the differences among the pricing structures.

Copyright Goodheart-Willcox Co., Inc.

College
and Career
Readiness

Communication Skills

Speaking. Using the Internet, research information on *unique selling proposition (USP).* Present your findings to the class using visuals to convey examples to your audience.

Listening. Listening combines hearing with evaluating. While your teacher is presenting a lesson, take notes and evaluate his or her point of view about the material that is being presented. What did you learn about listening?

CTSOs

Community Service Project. Many competitive events for Career and Technical Student Organizations (CTSOs) student competitions offer events that include a community service project. This project is usually carried out by the entire CTSO chapter and will take several months to complete. There will be two parts of the event—written and oral. The chapter will designate several members to represent the team at the competitive event.

To prepare for this event, complete the following activities.

1. Read the guidelines provided by your organization. Make certain that you ask any questions about points you do not understand. It is important you follow each specific item that is outlined in the competition rules.

2. Contact the association immediately at the end of the state conference to prepare for next year's event.

3. As a team, select a theme for your chapter's community service project.

4. Decide which roles are needed for the team. There may be one person who is the captain, one person who is the secretary, and any other roles that will be necessary to create the plan. Ask your instructor for guidance in assigning roles to team members.

5. Study chapter 3.

6. Identify your target audience, which may include business, school, and community groups.

7. Brainstorm with members of your chapters. List the benefits and opportunities of supporting a community service project.

8. This project will probably span the school year. During regular chapter meetings, create a draft of the report based on direction from the CTSO. Write and refine drafts until the final report is finished.

Copyright Goodheart-Willcox Co., Inc.

Building Your Business Plan—Putting the Puzzle Together

Product, Price, and Place

Three of the four Ps of marketing—product, price, and place—were discussed in this chapter. Research plays an important role in making the product, price, and place decisions. The first step is to offer the products your target market wants and needs. The second step is to price your goods or services competitively, yet still make a profit to remain in business. The third step is to manage your business' supply chain so the products get to the customers when and where they are needed. Product, price, and place strategies will be closely examined by potential funders.

Goals

- Identify the features and benefits of your business' goods or services.
- Choose a pricing strategy.
- Describe the business' supply chain and best channel of distribution.
- Create business plan notes.

Directions

Access the *Entrepreneurship* companion website at www.g-wlearning.com 📲. Download each data file for the following activities. A complete sample business plan is available on the companion website to use as a reference. The name of the file is BusPlan_Sample.RetroAttire.docx.

Preparation

Activity 10-1. Product. Describe the goods or services your business will offer. Discuss the features and benefits for each and write your unique selling proposition (USP).

Activity 10-2. Price. Choose one of your business' goods or services and research all the fixed and variable costs that may affect its final pricing. Develop and recommend a pricing structure for your entrepreneurial venture.

Activity 10-3. Place. Describe the supply chain and channel of distribution for your business' goods or services. Identify activities within channel of distribution strategies that impact inventory control.

Activity 10-4. Business Plan Notes. Create notes about the research you did when determining the strategies for your business' product, price, and place.

Business Plan—Business Description and Operations

Now it is time to finalize the goods or services you plan to offer. You will also determine how to price your products and deliver them to the end users. In this activity, you will start to write the Goods or Services subsection of the Business Description section and the Marketing Strategies subsection of the Operations section.

1. Open your saved business plan document.

2. Locate the Business Description section of the plan. Begin writing the Goods or Services subsection.

3. Locate the Operations section of the plan. Begin writing the Marketing Strategies subsection of your plan. At this point, you will address the Product, Price, and Place portions of this subsection.

4. Use the suggestions and questions listed to help you generate ideas. Delete the instructions and questions when you are finished recording your responses. Make sure to proofread your document and correct any errors in keyboarding, spelling, and grammar.

5. Save your document.

CHAPTER

11 Promotions and Selling

Adam Nelson's young son woke up the family at 5:00 a.m. every day because he did not know when it was time to get out of bed. A natural entrepreneur, Nelson worked to develop a night-light, the Good Nite Lite, that would tell children when it was time to sleep and to wake up. Unfortunately, retailers were not interested. Nelson refused to take *no* for an answer, however, and found alternative ways to promote and sell his night-light. He hired a public relations firm that worked with *Parents* magazine, which published an article on the product. After that publicity, orders poured into his website. Currently, about 90 percent of sales are from Internet sales and 10 percent from retail store sales.

> "Marketing is not a battle of products; it's a battle of perceptions."

—Al Ries and Jack Trout,
marketing consultants and authors

College and Career Readiness

Reading Prep. Before reading this chapter, look at the quote on the opening page. How does this quote relate to what is being presented in the content?

Sections

11.1 Promotions

11.2 Personal Selling

Picture Yourself Here
Shayna Turk

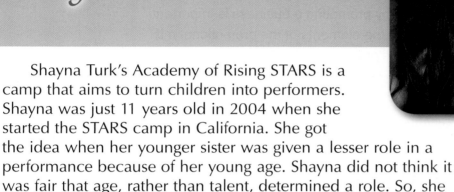

Shayna Turk's Academy of Rising STARS is a camp that aims to turn children into performers. Shayna was just 11 years old in 2004 when she started the STARS camp in California. She got the idea when her younger sister was given a lesser role in a performance because of her young age. Shayna did not think it was fair that age, rather than talent, determined a role. So, she started her own camp to teach choreography, singing, and acting as well as confidence to young performers.

STARS first camp performance was *You're a Good Man, Charlie Brown* starring Shayna's sister and twelve of her friends. They performed on a stage in their grandparents' back room. The camp grew and now has over 30 young actors. In 2010, the National Federation of Independent Business Young Entrepreneur Foundation and Visa, Inc., named Shayna the Young Entrepreneur of the Year.

Shayna is also involved with the Music for the Heart Foundation. The foundation provides funds for children with congenital heart defects to access the specialized care they need. All of the proceeds from STARS performances benefit the foundation. Entrepreneurship can be about more than making a name or making money—it can make a difference in people's lives.

Photo © Mary Ann Haplin Photography

Check Your Entrepreneurship IQ

Before you begin the chapter, see what you already know about entrepreneurship by taking the chapter pretest. The pretest is available at www.g-wlearning.com

Promotions

Objectives

After completing this section, you will be able to:
- **State** why promoting a business is important.
- **Explain** the elements of the promotional mix.
- **Describe** promotional strategies.

Essential Question

What are some elements of effective promotion campaigns?

Key Terms

institutional promotion
product promotion
metrics
promotional mix
circulation
electronic promotion
quick response (QR) code

uniform resource locator (URL)
search engine optimization (SEO)
mobile app
publicity
press release
press kit
press conference

Critical Thinking

Commercials on television do not have the same number of viewers they once had. Make a list of the reasons you think that viewership of commercials has decreased over the last ten years.

Promoting the Business and Its Products

Promotion is all of the communication techniques sellers use to inform or motivate people to buy their products. It is one of the four Ps of marketing. Promotion of goods or services is an important part of an overall marketing plan.

Institutional promotion is promoting a company, rather than a specific product. Promoting a company's brand or image makes consumers aware of the company. An example of an institutional promotion is shown in Figure 11-1. This business is advertising how it helps the local environment. The promotion is designed to increase awareness and create goodwill, which hopefully will also increase sales.

Product promotion is promoting specific goods or services offered by the business. Figure 11-2 shows a product promotion for the same business illustrated in Figure 11-1. Most promotional campaigns are product promotions.

Copyright Goodheart-Willcox Co., Inc.

Institutional Promotion

Judy's Flowers

Judy's Flowers supports the
Campaign for a Cleaner Tampa.

Visit our website at
www.JudysFlowersTampa.com

nata_danilenko/Shutterstock.com; Goodheart-Willcox Publisher

Figure 11-1. An institutional promotion promotes the entire business.

Product Promotion

Judy's Flowers

Find unique floral arrangements for
your special occasions at Judy's Flowers.

Visit our website at
www.JudysFlowersTampa.com

nata_danilenko/Shutterstock.com; Goodheart-Willcox Publisher

Figure 11-2. A product promotion promotes a specific good or service.

Promotion activities can be expensive. Regardless of the cost, every dollar spent on promotions should provide a return on the investment. How the success of a promotion is measured depends on the goal of the promotion. The goal of promotions may be to bring in more sales dollars overall, increase sales of a particular product, increase brand awareness, or appeal to a new target market. Most businesses use a set of metrics when budgeting for promotions. **Metrics** are standards of measurement that provide ways to measure the effectiveness of a promotion. Examples of this measurement may be keeping count of website hits after the promotion goes live or calculating how many sales came directly from the promotion over a specific amount of time. Metrics help the business determine their *market penetration*, which involves increasing sales in the existing target market.

Copyright Goodheart-Willcox Co., Inc.

Some of the most common marketing metrics include the following:

- *New-customer metrics* measure market share, cost of acquiring new customers, customer awareness levels, and brand awareness.

- *Customer-retention metrics* measure customer retention and loss rates, brand loyalty, return visits, and the likelihood customers will refer a brand.

- *Product metrics* measure overall customer satisfaction, ease of learning and using a product, and first-time user satisfaction.

Businesses may classify their promotional mix using categories other than advertising, sales promotion, electronic promotion, and public relations.

Promotional Mix

There are many ways to promote a business or its goods or services. The **promotional mix** is a combination of the elements used in a promotional campaign. A promotional mix can include advertising, sales promotion, public relations, and personal selling. As shown in Figure 11-3, the pieces of the promotional mix fit together to create the overall promotional campaign.

Successful promotional campaigns mix different promotional elements to create meaningful experiences or stories for the customers.

Figure 11-3. The pieces of the promotional mix fit together to form the promotional campaign.

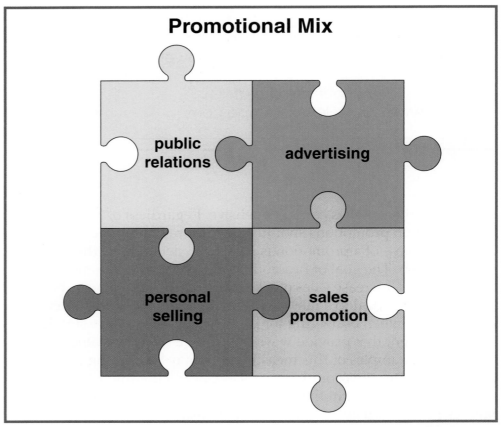

Goodheart-Willcox Publisher

All of the promotional elements are rarely used at the same time. However, today's sophisticated shopper needs to see more than just print or online ads to make a purchase.

Advertising

Advertising is any communication paid for by an identified sponsor. Traditional advertising includes print and broadcast media. However, other media may be used.

Advertising is generally the key piece of a promotional mix. An *ad* provides the features and benefits about a product, such as the price, a description, and the *wow* factors. Effective advertising uses messages tailored to the people most likely to buy the product. In other words, the *target market*.

Businesses often use advertising to presell products. *Preselling* a product is creating interest and demand before the buyer can receive the product.

All forms of advertising have two sets of costs. One set of costs pays for the creation of the advertisements. Every ad must be written, designed, and physically created for delivery to the media where it will run. The second set of costs pays for the space or time in which the ad will run. Ads are purchased to run on specific days, in specified places, or at specific times.

Print Media

Print media is one of the most effective forms of advertising. Print advertising includes ads placed in newspapers, magazines, direct mailings, directories, on outdoor signage, and in transit promotion.

The cost to place print ads in newspapers, magazines, and directories is based on circulation and ad size. **Circulation** is the number of copies distributed to subscribers and other outlets. Direct mailing costs depend on the cost of creating the mailer and the number of pieces mailed. Other print media outlets determine cost by the average number of people who will see the ad in a month.

Newspapers. Although print newspaper sales have declined, newspapers are still a viable advertising medium. Consumers often look at newspaper ads to learn about new products and current sales. There are *coupon clippers* who physically cut coupons or print them online to save money on advertised products. Coupons generally have a promotion code that designates where the coupon originally appeared, such as in a newspaper or online. Business owners can use this code to track consumer response to ads and coupons.

For a small business owner, advertising in a local newspaper can be an affordable option. Local newspapers have lower circulations than papers with national distribution. This means the cost to advertise in local papers is lower. In addition, the people reading a local paper are probably closer to your location.

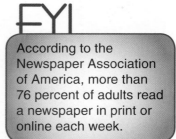

According to the Newspaper Association of America, more than 76 percent of adults read a newspaper in print or online each week.

Copyright Goodheart-Willcox Co., Inc.

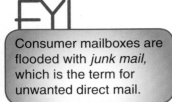

Consumer mailboxes are flooded with *junk mail*, which is the term for unwanted direct mail.

Magazines. Magazines are purchased by those in specific target markets based on demographics and psychographics. Magazines have a longer life than print newspapers because people tend to keep magazines longer than newspapers. Ads in a magazine, just like the articles, can be repeatedly seen by the reader. Advertisers tend to receive more value for the cost of a magazine ad even though the circulation may be lower than newspapers. Advertising in a national magazine can be quite expensive. However, local magazines may have lower rates.

Direct Mail. Direct mail includes catalogs, brochures, postcards, and letters sent through the postal service. Established businesses often send direct-mail offers to current customers from their own *customer database.* If a business wants to reach new potential customers, it can purchase a list of addresses in its target market from a company that sells mailing lists.

Some businesses prefer to use a *direct mail house* to manage their direct mailings. These companies can purchase the mailing list, create the pieces, and mail them for the business.

In recent years, the number of direct-mail pieces has decreased in favor of electronic campaigns. Electronic campaigns are generally less expensive than traditional direct mailings and may get to the consumer faster.

Directories. Telephone books are still in demand. These directories list names, addresses, and phone numbers in alphabetical order. Directories reach all consumer demographics. Included in most phone books are the yellow pages for business listings, advertisements, and coupons. Yellow pages advertising can be affordable for a small business owner. Phone books are used repeatedly, so the ad is seen over and over.

Leonard Zhukovsky/Shutterstock.com

Advertising on public transportation is an example of a print media transit promotion.

Outdoor Signage. Outdoor billboards are a common form of advertising that has been around since the 19th century. Small business owners can find billboards an affordable advertising method to display promotional messages 7 days a week, 24 hours a day. Other forms of outdoor advertising include skywriting, blimps, and hot air balloons.

Transit Promotion. Transit advertising can be found on the outside or inside of buses, taxis, subways, and commuter trains. Transit ads have high visibility and are generally an inexpensive way to advertise to reach an audience.

Broadcast Media

Television and radio are the two forms of broadcast media. Radio and television ads, or *commercials,* reach a large number of people daily. Even though commercials are typically 15-, 30-, or 60-second messages, they are quite expensive. It is the commercials that pay for most of the programming on television and radio stations.

Television. The most expensive form of advertising is television because it can reach the most people. Similar to other forms of advertising, television commercials are designed to appeal to specific target markets. Making commercials is often like making short movies, which is one reason they are so expensive.

Commercial time can be purchased on the national level or the local level. Large companies, such as Dell or Macy's, buy commercial time on the national level. Local television advertising is a more affordable option for small businesses and reaches only the local target market.

Consumers have increasing choices about networks and programs to watch. Before subscription television became common in the 1970s, there were only four channel choices—three network channels and public broadcasting. Subscription television changed the face of television as an advertising medium. There are hundreds of subscription channels available and the list is growing. Much of the programming on subscription television appeals to a narrow target market.

Have you ever wondered why some commercials only run during certain television programs? Much research is conducted by A.C. Nielsen to learn who is watching every program and for how long. These numbers determine the prices networks and stations charge for running commercials during different programs. Popular programs with many viewers have higher rates for commercial time. For example, the most expensive commercial time is during a Super Bowl.

Infomercials are paid product demonstrations. This programming is watched by some consumers. The cost of an infomercial may be less than other television ads since infomercials tend to run at times with low viewership. Infomercials are longer than commercials, usually 30 minutes, and can be a good way to sell a new product.

Radio. Radio is an affordable advertising option for most businesses to reach local customers. Radio advertising is generally less expensive than television.

FYI

According to the Outdoor Advertising Association of America, there are approximately 400,000 billboards in the United States. Out of that number, only 3,200 are electronic.

There are numerous radio stations. They play music or have talk programming that attracts very different target markets. Classical music and talk radio stations tend to have older listeners, while rock and pop music stations may have teen and young adult audiences.

Research tells the stations how many people in different demographics listen at various times. This research makes it easier to choose the stations and what time periods to buy for a radio ad campaign. For example, placing sporting goods commercials on a sports station is a sure way to reach potential customers.

Sales Promotion

The goal of a sales promotion is to encourage the customer to buy a product as soon as possible. These efforts may also increase sales and create a positive image for a business. Sales promotions can combine print media with more personal techniques to help a customer make an immediate purchase. Sales promotions can include coupons, rebates, promotional items, samples, loyalty programs, contests and sweepstakes, trade shows, and displays.

Coupons

A *coupon* is a printed or electronic offer giving a discount for goods or services bought before a certain date. Once the expiration date has passed, the coupon cannot be redeemed. Coupons are given to customers as an incentive to purchase a new product or to increase sales of established products.

Rebates

Companies may offer a *manufacturers rebate,* which is a return of a portion of the item's purchase price. Unlike coupons, rebates are received after a product is purchased. Rebates also have expiration dates.

To receive a rebate, the customer is required to complete a form and mail it to the manufacturer. Increasingly, rebates can be applied for online. The manufacturer then sends a check for the rebate amount to the purchaser. However, it may take months for the customer to receive a rebate.

Manufacturers offer rebates to encourage customers to make an immediate purchase of a product. By offering rebates, manufacturers can also capture customer data for future campaigns or market research.

Promotional Items

Promotional items are special items that businesses give away to remind customers about their products and business. Marketers sometimes call these *marketing premiums.* Promotional items can

Entrepreneur Ethics

It is unethical to take part in deceptive advertising or marketing practices. Entrepreneurs must comply with truth-in-advertising laws and make sure that no product message is misleading. This is not only an ethical and legal consideration, but is also considered a good business practice.

Copyright Goodheart-Willcox Co., Inc.

include inexpensive things, such as key chains, calendars, pens, and pencils. They may also be more expensive items, such as blankets, calculators, or books. Businesses include their name, address, phone number, and website on these items hoping the customer will remember the company when making the next purchase.

Samples

When introducing a new product, companies may give small product samples so customers can try the new items. Samples give customers the product experience, hopefully liking the product and then purchasing it. Product samples are given out in stores, such as food samples in markets. They may also be small, individual samples sent by direct mail, such as those sent by cosmetic companies.

Loyalty Programs

Many companies reward customers for their continued business through loyalty programs. Loyalty programs can take many forms. The most common ones revolve around giving customers a free product or service after making a certain number of purchases. For example, a juice store may give a small card that is punched every time the customer buys a smoothie. After 12 punches, the next smoothie is free.

Contests and Sweepstakes

Contests and sweepstakes are promotional tools used to encourage current and potential customers to visit a store or provide contact information. The goal for these promotional tools is to capture data for future campaigns or market research purposes. In contests, a customer must do something to win, such as submit a video of using the product. Sweepstakes are games of chance where prizes are given to randomly selected winners from the entries received.

Trade Shows

Many businesses, large and small, exhibit at industry trade shows and conventions. Businesses use trade shows to introduce new products or sell existing products to potential customers. Trade shows provide a face-to-face opportunity to talk with customers, gather sales leads, and give a promotional item or sample of a product or service. An example of a trade show is shown in Figure 11-4.

Displays

Visual merchandising is displaying merchandise in locations where the customer can clearly see the product. Displays build awareness as well as encourage potential customers to purchase. Many stores will conveniently display merchandise at the checkout counter to stimulate sales. These are called *point of purchase (POP)* displays.

Copyright Goodheart-Willcox Co., Inc.

Figure 11-4. Trade shows are opportunities to show off products and meet with customers.

pcruciatti/Shutterstock.com

Electronic Promotion

Electronic promotion is any promotional effort carried out on the Internet or other technology that uses digital information. It includes having a web presence and using web advertising, social media, e-mail campaigns, and mobile applications. Electronic promotion crosses all elements of the marketing mix: advertising, sales promotion, public relations, and personal selling.

Many consumers like electronic promotions and expect them. Marketers like electronic promotions because they are generally low in cost and can be updated quickly and efficiently. These promotions are also easy to track.

Marketers sometimes combine traditional promotion with electronic promotion. This is an *integrated marketing campaign* and has wide audience appeal. For example, a print brochure is sent to a customer describing the features and benefits of the product. The brochure includes a QR code for the customer to scan and go directly to the product's web page. **Quick response (QR) codes** are bar codes that, when scanned with a smartphone, connect the user to a website or other digital information. As shown in Figure 11-5, QR codes are an inexpensive way for businesses to make special digital offers or promote certain portions of a business.

Copyright Goodheart-Willcox Co., Inc.

Quick Response (QR) Codes

Judy's Flowers

Check our weekly specials by scanning the QR code!

Visit our website at www.JudysFlowersTampa.com

Figure 11-5. QR codes can be used to promote a business.

nata_danilenko/Shutterstock.com; Goodheart-Willcox Publisher

Web Presence

Having a web presence is more than simply creating a website and hoping people will visit it. A website should be an informational and promotional link to current customers. It also serves as an informational resource for potential customers. Prior to designing a website, decide what the site should do for the business. Some objectives might be to:

- advertise the business;

- sell products;

- capture client information;

- reach a global audience; and

- present a socially responsible image.

A web log, or *blog,* is a website on which a person, business, or organization posts updates on a regular basis in a journal format. Blogs can be a way to share information with customers or potential customers about products or the business. A business blog can be linked to the main commerce website or stand as its own website.

Search engines include sites like Google, Yahoo, and Bing, among others. Search engines sift through all websites related to the search term and provide a list of websites from which to choose. Every website and web page has a uniform resource locator. A **uniform resource locator (URL)** is the unique address of a document, web page, or website on the Internet.

How do businesses happen to be at the top of a list returned by a search engine? **Search engine optimization (SEO)** is the process of indexing a website to rank it higher on the list when a search is conducted. This process includes using special coding and typical search terms in the website text. SEO helps increase the chances of higher rankings on any Internet search engine.

Copyright Goodheart-Willcox Co., Inc.

Web Advertising

Web advertising is placing ads on websites whose typical viewers are the business' target market. Most digital advertising is inexpensive compared to traditional print and broadcast methods. A business' website is a form of advertising, but it does not have to be the only digital space in which to advertise. There are many types of web advertising available, including the following.

- Banner ads are placed at the top of a website, typically in a box, and look similar to a print ad.

- Floating ads literally float across or around the screen and disappear in seconds.

- Search-engine ads have a word limit and can be purchased directly from a search engine to ensure the website appears on the first page of results.

- Pop-up ads literally pop up when a website is clicked open; customers can typically close these on the screen or block them completely.

- Pop-under ads are similar to pop-up ads, but they appear after the web page is closed; customers can typically close these on the screen or block them completely.

- YouTube videos are an inexpensive way to advertise a company and its product.

Be aware, though, that some digital advertisements are not welcomed by all potential customers.

Most search engines have metrics such as Google AdWords for paid advertisers. Advertisers are usually charged on a per-click basis. They provide daily reports to track how many people see the ads and how many purchased because of the ad. Make sure to know the target audience and the type of digital advertising that will best reach them. It is important to measure if dollars spent on digital advertising are providing a return on investment.

Social Media

Social media is an Internet-based tool that connects people with similar interests. Social media also allows a business to share information with its customers. Businesses can take advantage of social media sites to make special offers to encourage purchases. They can also create a dialogue with people about products, suggestions, and other topics of interest.

Before launching a social media campaign, it may be necessary to research the options and seek professional assistance. Each form of social media comes with its own rules and regulations. Most sites require users to join and provide some level of personal information.

FYI

A web-design professional can be consulted when a website is created. These professionals are experts in using SEO techniques.

Professional Networking. Professional networking sites such as LinkedIn can be an effective way to promote a business. Professional networking is an especially effective tool for entrepreneurs. LinkedIn also has a job-search function and is a good way to find employees.

Social Networking. Social networking sites such as Facebook and Twitter provide opportunities for businesses to create a company page. A business can post targeted advertising, customer testimonials, and special offers to the community that *likes* its Facebook page. Twitter provides a vehicle to get instant access to customers and potential customers via 140-character posts.

Locational Networking. Locational tools such as Foursquare and Yelp appeal to customers looking for businesses in specific geographic areas. These are excellent tools for new entrepreneurs wanting to attract customers in surrounding neighborhoods by offering discounts or specials.

YouTube. YouTube is a video-sharing website. It is a good way for a business to post demonstrations of new products at no cost. It also has the ability for customers to comment and recommend goods or services.

E-mail Campaigns

E-mail can be an effective way to provide information, new product updates, or announce sales. However, if not used correctly, it can quickly create a negative image of a business. Some e-mails are seen in the same way as junk mail or unsolicited telemarketer phone calls.

Spam. Unsolicited e-mail is called *spam* and reflects poorly on any business sending it. The last thing you want to do is offend a customer. Before sending an e-mail campaign, research e-mail etiquette and the CAN-SPAM Act passed in 2004. This act is enforced by the Federal Trade Commission (FTC) and allows individuals to report companies sending spam. E-mails that violate the CAN-SPAM Act rules are subject to penalties of up to $16,000.

One way for a business to avoid being labeled a spammer is to send e-mails only to those who signed up for e-mail updates through the company's website. Also, only send e-mail to those customers who have given their permission.

E-mail Tips. In order to get the most from e-mail campaigns, consider a few simple suggestions. Most companies push their e-mails out between midnight and 6:00 a.m. hoping to catch people arriving for work or getting up to start their day. However, many people simply delete these morning e-mails because of the number they receive. Consider sending e-mails between 10:00 a.m. and 3:00 p.m. People are more likely to take the time to read and respond to e-mails when their inboxes are not overfilled.

The subject line of an e-mail is critical. E-mail etiquette suggests that your company name appear in the subject line. It is also important to know that some words will trigger e-mail–provider filters to automatically send the e-mail to the spam folder. Words like *free, act now, offer,* or *credit* will almost always be flagged by filters.

Keep the message or offer short and to the point. When a customer opens an e-mail, it should take them no more than 15–20 seconds to understand it. Avoid too many graphics or other elements that may cause the e-mail to open slowly.

FYI

The CAN-SPAM Act requires that e-mails with advertising messages provide an option to unsubscribe from future e-mails.

Mobile Applications

Mobile application software, or a **mobile app**, is developed for use by mobile devices such as smartphones or tablets. Many companies use apps to promote their websites or market individual products.

Marketing pieces can use QR codes that encourage customers to get the app by visiting the website and downloading it. Companies hope that if their apps are on a customer's phone, he or she will visit the website often. Repeat visits to the website may encourage customers to buy the product.

A second type of app that companies use is called a native app. A *native app* is an application that resides on the mobile device rather than on the website. Native apps, such as calendars, games, and maps, are created and sold to customers. The strategy for offering a native app includes creating a revenue stream as well as for promotional purposes.

Public Relations

Activities that promote goodwill between the company and the public are called *public relations (PR)*. **Publicity** is unpaid media coverage for a newsworthy business, person, or product. Publicity is important to businesses because it is viewed as a third-party endorsement since it is informational and not paid for by the business.

Public relations is classified as either proactive or reactive. *Proactive public relations* is when the company presents itself in a positive manner to build an image, but not in response to an event. Companies issue press releases and other communications to explain their contributions to the community, environment, and other socially responsible activities.

Reactive public relations is used to counteract a negative perception or public feedback related to the company. This is often due to any form of negative publicity covered in the media. Businesses need to take action to reestablish the positive image of the company. A good example of this is the efforts by BP to help clean up the Gulf of Mexico after its 2010 oil spill.

Established businesses may hire PR managers or specialists to coordinate communication with the media. Entrepreneurs, however,

Social Entrepreneurs

Eric Kaster and Sattie Clark

Husband and wife team Eric Kaster and Sattie Clark wanted to start a metalworking business. They had three goals: use resources from their local community, do not add to a landfill, and promote keeping resources local. Their business, Eleek, is located in Portland, Oregon. Founded in 2000, it manufactures lighting, sinks, and other home fixtures. Using a philosophy similar to the local-food movement, Kaster and Clark hope Eleek will inspire other manufacturers to reuse scrap materials from local communities. About 80 percent of Eleek's supplies come from within 50 miles of Portland. Additionally, by directly melting down reclaimed metal, Eleek's process eliminates the recycling steps in which scrap metal is sent to China, turned into pellets, and shipped back to the United States. It partnered with a local nonprofit organization called the Rebuilding Center, which promotes the reuse of building materials.

are usually the public relations contact until the business grows enough to hire someone to fill that role.

In general, most public relations activities are free. It takes time for the business to create the campaign, but there are few other associated costs. Some forms of PR include press releases, press kits, and press conferences.

Press Release

A **press release**, or *news release,* is a story featuring useful company information written by the company's PR contact. Press releases are sent to selected media that will reach the target market. Many industry associations will help guide this process.

Press releases announce new products, locations, businesses, and community events. They can also provide information about revenue and earnings, business partnerships, and new employees. Press releases should be written in an article format and not like an advertisement. The media will not run promotional information for free.

Press Kit

A **press kit** is a packet of information distributed to the media about a new business opening or other major business events. Press kits can include marketing materials, photos, videos, frequently asked questions (FAQ) sheets, and other important information.

Copyright Goodheart-Willcox Co., Inc.

Press Conference

A **press conference** is a meeting arranged by a business or organization in which the media is invited to attend. Press conferences are called to make major announcements that affect a large number of people. Large press conferences may be televised and covered by major print and broadcast media. Smaller press conferences may just include local media.

Promotional Strategies

Businesses with great products may fail without solid promotional strategies in place to communicate with current and potential customers. The goal is to determine the best promotional mix for the money that was invested. The methods used to reach the market should relate to the marketing plan objectives. Marketing plan objectives are discussed in chapter 12. For example, are you trying to generate awareness of a new product or attract customers from your competitors? Promotional strategies create customer demand in two ways: pushing the products to the customers for purchase and pulling the customers in to buy the products.

Push Promotional Strategy

The *push promotional strategy* involves taking the product directly to the customer. Depending on the type of business, push strategies may be different. For example, trade shows, visual merchandising displays, and sales calls are all push strategies for retailers or service businesses. A manufacturer's push strategy, however, may include offering discounts and sale promotions to push products through the supply chain to the retailers.

New businesses often use a push strategy to generate interest and be competitive in the market. A new business' first promotion may be to create a *launch,* or push, to introduce its goods or services. Once the business or product is established, this can be integrated with a pull promotional strategy.

Pull Promotional Strategy

The *pull promotional strategy* involves leading the customer to actively seek out the product. A retailer's pull strategy may be to use discounts and sales promotions to pull customers into the stores. Supply and demand is the basis of a pull strategy. If customers want a product, the retailers will stock it.

SBA Tips

The SBA has numerous free podcasts with expert insight and guidance about starting your own business. Whether you are sitting down to write your business or promotional plan, wondering about your legal obligations, or researching your financing options, you will find the information you need on the SBA website. www.sba.gov

Section 11.1 **Review**

Check Your Understanding ➭

1. List the different items in the promotional mix.
2. What is the purpose of sales promotions?
3. Explain the difference between a coupon and a rebate.
4. List several ways that electronic promotions can be executed as part of the promotional mix.
5. Name and describe two promotional strategies used to create promotional demand.

Build Your Vocabulary ➭

As you progress through this text, develop a personal glossary of key terms. This will help you build your vocabulary and prepare you for a career. Write a definition for each of the following terms and add them to your personal glossary.

institutional promotion
product promotion
metrics
promotional mix
circulation
electronic promotion
quick response (QR) code
uniform resource locator (URL)
search engine optimization (SEO)
mobile app
publicity
press release
press kit
press conference

Copyright Goodheart-Willcox Co., Inc.

Personal Selling

Essential Question

What are the steps involved in the sales process?

Objectives

After completing this section, you will be able to:

- **Explain** the concept of developing a sales force.
- **Identify** the steps of personal selling.
- **Describe** the importance of knowing the competition.

Key Terms

personal selling
sales force
sales quota
prospecting

selling process
rational buying motives
emotional buying motives
AIDA

Critical Thinking

Consider the possibility of having a sales force for your business someday. Describe the methods you would use to train your sales force to sell your products.

Developing a Sales Force

You have a great new business. Now a sales strategy is needed to actively sell the product. **Personal selling** is any direct contact between a salesperson and a customer. As a new entrepreneur, you may be the primary salesperson until the company grows enough to add a sales force. A **sales force** is a team of employees involved in personal selling for a business. The development of the sales force is important to the success of a business.

Customers appreciate face-to-face interaction when making a buying decision. While the other pieces of the promotional mix are important, personal contact is at the top of most lists of customer preferences.

Sales Goals

Before the selling process can take place, sales goals should be established. For new businesses, these goals come from the sales forecasting done when creating pro forma financial statements. For established businesses, sales forecasting is a necessary annual activity that also determines sales goals. Sales forecasting is discussed in greater detail in several other chapters.

Copyright Goodheart-Willcox Co., Inc.

Sales goals may be in the form of dollars or units. A **sales quota**, or expected sales for a certain time period, is assigned to each salesperson. Quotas are set on potential sales in a sales territory or other guidelines established by the company.

Sales goals encourage and motivate the sales team to sell product. Setting sales goals also helps a business determine how much marketing effort will be needed to achieve the sales forecast.

Prospecting

Prospecting is the process of finding potential customers. Potential customers are also known as *prospects* or *leads.* Nearly every marketing activity is designed to generate prospects. Leads can be generated from website requests, trade shows or conventions, coupons, or even a guest book at the cash register.

Cold calling is another way to prospect. *Cold calling* is the process of making contact with people who are not expecting a sales contact. Cold calls are based on customer lists, phone directories, or other sources of customer information.

Selling Process

The **selling process** is an organized method or approach to product sales. The development of an effective sales force begins with creating an effective sales process. The sales process may vary by business type, but the intent is the same. For example, some businesses visit customers to sell goods or services. Other businesses only sell to customers who come into a store or call to place orders. As shown in Figure 11-6, the selling process generally includes six steps.

Approach the Customer

Personal selling often involves face-to-face interaction with the customer. The first minutes of conversation sets the tone for the rest

Focus on Finance

Counterfeit Cash

As a business owner, you will probably be accepting cash for goods or services. Counterfeit, or fake, money can be a problem for those who accept cash. Before opening your doors for business, ask your local banker to review the steps in identifying counterfeit money with you. The banker will also be able to tell you what to do if someone tries to pay you with money not printed by the US Treasury Department.

Copyright Goodheart-Willcox Co., Inc.

Selling Process

1. Approach the customer

2. Determine customer needs

3. Present the good or service

4. Answer questions or objections about the product

5. Close the sale

6. Provide customer service after the sale

Kzenon, Monkey Business Images/Shutterstock.com; Goodheart-Willcox Publisher

Figure 11-6. The six steps of the selling process.

of the discussion. If in a retail setting, welcome customers when they come through the door. When approaching a customer in his or her place of business, introduce yourself and shake hands. Interaction with the customer should be professional and should show interest in meeting the customer's wants and needs.

Determine the Customer Needs

Customers have many different reasons or motives for buying products. **Rational buying motives** are based on reason. Some products just naturally appeal to customers' rational buying motives, such as needing a new computer for school. **Emotional buying motives** are based more on feelings than reason. Buying a music CD or the latest style of shoe may stem from emotional buying motives.

Sometimes, rational and emotional buying motives are combined. For example, a customer needs a new computer for rational reasons. However, he or she may also want the newest model with all of the upgrades for emotional reasons.

Understanding the customer means finding out about all the needs and wants as they relate to the product. Examples of rational and emotional buying motives are shown in Figure 11-7.

Copyright Goodheart-Willcox Co., Inc.

Some sales experts believe that a customer goes through four stages of a buying process before making a purchase. One model, illustrated in Figure 11-8, is **AIDA**, which stands for *attention, interest, desire,* and *action.*

Attention

Capture the customer's attention. Ask questions about what the customer is looking for in a product. Show interest in the customer.

Interest

Capture the customer's interest. The customer has to be interested in the business or product to make a purchase. Establish a friendly atmosphere so the customer feels free to ask questions. Also, take time to ask the customers questions to determine their preferences. Then give them the information they need to make a purchase decision.

Buying Motives	
Rational buying motives	**Emotional buying motives**
• Features	• Popularity
• Quality	• Acceptance
• Durability	• Romance
• Dependability	• Thrill seeking
• Price	• Adventure
• Design	• Prestige
• Safety	• Anxiety

Goodheart-Willcox Publisher

Figure 11-7. Know your target market's buying motives.

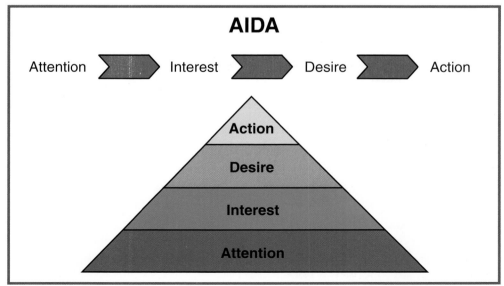

Figure 11-8. AIDA

Goodheart-Willcox Publisher

Desire

Convince the customer to want the product. Explain the features and benefits of the product and describe its *unique selling proposition.* Tell the customer how the product will make his or her life better or easier. Demonstrate the product, if possible.

Action

Persuade the customer to take action and buy the good or service. Determine if the customer has any objections to the sale so they can be addressed positively. If necessary, ask the customer for the business.

Present the Product

Customers like to experience products before committing to a purchase. Create a product demonstration when possible or put product samples in the customers' hands. For example, salespeople in car dealerships always offer test drives. They also demonstrate knowledge about the particular model a customer is thinking of buying. If the knowledge and sales expertise is missing, the customer may buy at a different dealership. This would cost the original dealership a potential sale and profit.

In a new business, the entrepreneur, who may be the primary salesperson for the business, knows the product features and benefits better than anyone. However, as the business grows, salespeople will probably be hired and will need product training. It is important that anyone selling be considered a product expert.

Sales tools are helpful in learning to be a product expert and to present a product. Brochures, websites, and other marketing pieces are helpful in making a presentation.

Answer Questions or Objections

Customers will ask questions about the products offered. They want to learn more than just *features,* or what a product does.

Green Entrepreneurs

Marketing Resources

As a business owner, it will be necessary to find phone numbers and other contact information for vendors and customers. Instead of using a print directory, consider using an online resource. Notify the company that sends print directories that the business no longer needs a print copy. However, if a print directory is needed, recycle it when the new copy is available. By recycling these directories, we can save thousands of tons of paper each year and save space in the landfills.

Copyright Goodheart-Willcox Co., Inc.

Customers want to know why they should buy it. The *benefits* are the solutions to consumer problems—or the reasons why to buy the product. How will the customers' lives be changed for the better by it? For example, one feature of a cordless drill is the number of hours it can be used on one charge. One benefit of owning the drill, however, is having the ability to make your own furniture.

A sales team of trained product experts makes selling easier. Product experts are also prepared for any objections and questions. Remember to keep the customer as the primary focus during the entire sales process.

Close the Sale

The most important step in the sales process is closing the sale. Always ask for the customer's business and aim for closing the sale during the personal selling interaction. Depending on the nature of a business, some negotiating may be necessary in price or other services. Be prepared to make decisions that will encourage the customer to buy.

Provide Customer Service After the Sale

Service after the sale is also very important to gain repeat business and to promote goodwill. During the selling process, it is a good idea to let customers know what is provided after completing the sale. If the business offers help and advice for using the product, tell the customer this. Describe the policy for returns or exchanges. Explain how the customer should contact the business if there are any issues to resolve.

FYI

Customers expect salespeople to provide good service and maintain a high standard of professional ethics. Businesses will lose customers if customers find unfair pricing or the goods or services are substandard.

 You Do the Math   Problem Solving and Reasoning

When solving word problems, you must identify the elements of the math problem and solve it. An important key to solving word problems is to make sure enough information has been provided to solve the stated problem. If some information is not provided, the problem cannot be solved.

Solve the following problems.

1. Darren orders office supplies every Monday. This week he must order 23 reams of paper, 2,000 envelopes, and 12 boxes of tape. He wants to know how much this will cost. Is there enough information to solve this problem? If not, what information is missing?

2. Lana travels for work. On Monday, she drove 48 miles. On Tuesday, she drove 37 miles. On Thursday, she drove 76 miles. She is reimbursed for gasoline at a rate of 53 cents per mile. Lana wants to determine how many miles per gallon she averaged while traveling. Is there enough information to solve this problem? If not, what information is missing?

Copyright Goodheart-Willcox Co., Inc.

After the sale, make follow-up calls and send thank-you letters. These small efforts mean a lot to customers. They encourage repeat business and good recommendations to other potential customers. Good customer service is a foundation of goodwill.

Know the Competition

In the marketing-evaluation stage of business development, the competition is identified and analyzed. Customers also probably know that a product can be purchased from any number of competitors. In order to sell a product, know its strengths and weaknesses. Be prepared to identify why the

- product is better;

- customer service is better;

- price is better; and

- customer should buy the product from you rather than the competition.

Competition can be brutal, so it is important to know everything possible about the competing businesses. Being prepared can help win business from the competition and build a solid customer base.

Section 11.2 Review

Check Your Understanding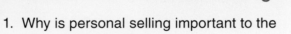

1. Why is personal selling important to the success of a business?

2. List seven emotional buying motives.

3. List seven rational buying motives.

4. What does the acronym AIDA represent?

5. Why is it important to attend to customer service even after the sale has been made?

Build Your Vocabulary

As you progress through this text, develop a personal glossary of key terms. This will help you build your vocabulary and prepare you for a career. Write a definition for each of the following terms and add them to your personal glossary.

personal selling
sales force
sales quota
prospecting
selling process

rational buying
    motives
emotional buying
    motives
AIDA

Chapter Summary

Section 11.1 **Promotions**

- Promotion is an important part of an overall marketing plan. It is one of the four Ps of marketing. The other three are product, price, and place.
- A promotional mix is putting various aspects of promotion to use in a promotional campaign.
- Promotional strategies are used to reach the market and should relate to the marketing plan objectives.

Section 11.2 **Personal Selling**

- Customers prefer to have personal contact and face-to-face interactions when making a buying decision.
- There are six steps in the personal selling process. The first step is to approach the customer. Then, present the product; answer questions or objections about the product; and close the sale. Last but not least, provide customer service after the sale.
- It is crucial for a salesperson to know everything there is to know about the products the company sells.

Online Activities

Complete the following activities to help you learn, practice, and expand your knowledge and skills.

Posttest. Now that you have finished the chapter, see what you learned by taking the chapter posttest.

Key Terms. Practice vocabulary for this chapter using the e-flash cards, matching activity, and vocabulary game until you are able to recognize their meanings.

Review Your Knowledge

1. What is the difference between institutional and product promotion?
2. Explain the purpose of advertising.
3. Discuss the differences between proactive and reactive public relations.
4. Discuss press releases, press kits, and press conferences.
5. Describe the concept of electronic promotion.

6. Development of the sales force is important for the success of a business. List and describe the steps in the selling process that an effective sales force would apply.
7. Explain the difference between rational and emotional buying motives.
8. Describe the AIDA process.
9. Why is it important to know the competition?
10. When selling to the customer, list the things about the product that a salesperson should be prepared to discuss.

Apply Your Knowledge

1. Create a features and benefits analysis for your good or service.
2. Think about how you will promote your business. Write copy for an institutional promotion and copy for a good or service promotion.
3. Research the effectiveness of direct mail for your type of business. Which piece is recommended as most effective? Design a direct mail piece for your products.
4. Research how to write a press release. Write a press release announcing the opening of your business.
5. Research marketing premium ideas for your business. Select one premium item that you would like to use. How many will you purchase? What will it cost?
6. E-mail campaigns are effective ways to communicate with customers. Research the spam laws. Make a list of acceptable practices and those that are not acceptable.
7. Sales promotions encourage customers to buy as soon as possible. Create a sales promotion for your new product, such as a contest, coupon, or rebate. Write copy for the promotion and new product launch that is appropriate for print media and a version for an e-mail campaign. Explain how you could incorporate QR codes in your promotion.
8. Research using social media for small businesses. Make a list of dos and don'ts that you will want to consider as you create your electronic promotion.
9. Research QR codes. How would you implement these in your promotions plan?
10. Create metrics that you will use for your marketing campaign. Describe how you will use these to evaluate market penetration, effectiveness on sales activities, and overall effectiveness of the campaign.

Copyright Goodheart-Willcox Co., Inc.

Teamwork

Each team member has been planning his or her business throughout this text. Have one team member volunteer to use his or her business in a sales presentation. Work together to create a slide show or product demonstration to sell the product and present to your class. Use your imagination. Create a brochure, promotional item, or any other item that will help you make this sales presentation. Observe, evaluate, and critique the other class members' sales presentations.

Internet Research

Personal Selling. As a new entrepreneur, you may be the only salesperson when your business is first organized. Use the Internet to research the topic of *personal selling*. Make notes on how you can use these strategies in your new business.

Sales Force Development. A sales force is an important asset for a business. Use the Internet to research the function, hiring, and training of a sales team. Summarize your findings. Next, make recommendations on how you would develop a sales force for your company.

Communication Skills

College and Career Readiness

Reading. Read a magazine, newspaper, or online article about a sales promotion for a small business that caused negative customer reaction. Determine the central ideas of the article and review the conclusions made by the author.

Writing. Conduct research on effective sales strategies. Write an informative report, consisting of several paragraphs to describe your findings of the implications of positive or negative sales strategies on a business.

Copyright Goodheart-Willcox Co., Inc.

CTSOs

Extemporaneous Speaking. Extemporaneous speaking is a competitive event you might enter with your Career and Technical Student Organization (CTSO). This event allows you to display your communication skills of speaking, organizing, and making an oral presentation. At the competition, you will be given several topics from which to choose. You will also be given a time limit to create and deliver the speech. You will be evaluated on your verbal and nonverbal skills as well as the tone and projection of your voice.

To prepare for the extemporaneous speaking event, do the following.

1. Read the guidelines provided by your organization. Make certain that you ask any questions about points you do not understand. It is important you follow each specific item that is outlined in the competition rules.

2. Ask your instructor for several topics on entrepreneurship so you can practice making impromptu speeches.

3. Once you have an assigned practice topic from your instructor, jot down your ideas and points you want to cover. An important part about making this type of presentation is that you will have only a few minutes to prepare. Being able to write down your main ideas quickly will enable you to focus on what you will actually say in the presentation.

4. Practice the presentation. You should introduce yourself, review the topic that is being presented, defend the topic being presented, and conclude with a summary.

5. Ask your teacher to play the role of Competition Judge as your team reviews the case. After the presentation is complete, ask for feedback from your teacher. You may consider also having a student audience to listen and give feedback.

6. For the event, bring paper and pencils to record notes. Supplies may or may not be provided.

Copyright Goodheart-Willcox Co., Inc.

Building Your Business Plan—Putting the Puzzle Together

Promotion and Selling

No business needs promotion more than a new business. Lenders and investors want to know an entrepreneur's plans to attract customers and generate revenue. The promotional choices a small business owner makes during the first year of operation may be critical to its success. Start by researching the costs for different local media and the markets they reach.

Goals

- Research local media options for promotions.
- Determine the promotional mix for the first year.
- Define the sales process for your business.
- Create business plan notes.

Directions

Access the *Entrepreneurship* companion website at www.g-wlearning.com ➦. Download each data file for the following activities. A complete sample business plan is available on the companion website to use as a reference. The name of the file is BusPlan_Sample.RetroAttire. docx.

Preparation

Activity 11-1. Media Research. Research the media options for both advertising and public-relations services in your community. List their costs, advantages, and disadvantages.

Activity 11-2. Promotional Mix. Select elements of the promotional mix that you will use in a promotional plan for your new business.

Activity 11-3. Sales Process. Develop a visual that describes the sales process for your business.

Activity 11-4. Business Plan Notes. Create notes about the promotion and selling ideas that you will consider for your business.

Business Plan—Operations

Your business plan is now addressing the last of the four Ps of marketing—promotion. Define and explain your business' promotional strategies and personal selling efforts in detail. In this activity, you will continue writing the Marketing Strategies subsection of the Operations section.

1. Open your saved business plan document.

2. Locate the Operations section of the plan. Continue writing the Marketing Strategies subsection of your plan. At this point, you will address the Promotions portion of this subsection. Note that the budget and time line will be addressed in the next chapter.

3. Use the suggestions and questions listed to help you generate ideas. Delete the instructions and questions when you are finished recording your responses. Make sure to proofread your document and correct any errors in keyboarding, spelling, and grammar.

4. Save your document.

CHAPTER

12 Marketing Plan

At the age of 16, Houston high school student Michael Dell began selling newspaper subscriptions. After selling just a few, he realized that most of the people buying a subscription from him had either just moved to Houston or were newly married. He quickly devised a marketing plan. He would target selling to those two groups. Dell hired assistants to gather names and addresses of newlyweds and new home purchasers at the county courthouse while he targeted sales to those two markets. Dell's income from selling newspaper subscriptions earned him about $18,000. Why was he so successful at selling newspapers? Because he had a marketing plan. In 1984, at the age of 19, Dell formed a company you may know: Dell Computer Corporation.

"If you don't believe in your product, or if you're not consistent and regular in the way you promote it, the odds of succeeding go way down."

—Jay Levinson, author of *Guerilla Marketing*

College and Career Readiness

Reading Prep. Scan this chapter and look for information presented as fact. As you read this chapter, try to determine which topics are fact and which ones are the author's opinion. After reading the chapter, research the topics and verify which are facts and which are opinions.

Sections

12.1 Develop a Marketing Plan

12.2 Write a Marketing Plan

Picture Yourself Here
Omar Soliman

Omar Soliman started College Hunks Hauling Junk® when he was just 22 years old. Omar wrote the business plan in his entrepreneurship class during his senior year at the University of Miami in Coral Gables, Florida. He submitted his plan to the Leigh Rothschild Entrepreneurship Competition and won first place with a $10,000 prize.

College Hunks Hauling Junk® offers a variety of services, including junk removal, trash removal, and moving services to both homes and businesses. Located in Tampa, Florida, College Hunks Hauling Junk® employs the most college students in the nation. It even has a University of Home Services, which provides the student-employees an opportunity to become experts in a trade and learn how to run a business.

Today, College Hunks Hauling Junk® is a national company that has worked for the federal government, Fortune 500 companies, and over 70,000 homeowners. Omar's company was named one of *Entrepreneur* magazine's top new franchises. Just think, it all stemmed from an entrepreneurship class like the one you are in today.

Photo © Omar Soliman

Check Your Entrepreneurship IQ

Before you begin the chapter, see what you already know about entrepreneurship by taking the chapter pretest. The pretest is available at

www.g-wlearning.com

Develop a Marketing Plan

?Essential Question

Why is a marketing plan important?

Objectives

After completing this section, you will be able to:
- **Explain** the importance of a marketing plan.
- **Define** the marketing mix.
- **Identify** different marketing plan templates.

Key Terms

marketing
marketing plan
product strategy

price strategy
place strategy
promotion strategy

Critical Thinking

Think about the purpose of the marketing plan. What are the components you think are important for the marketing plan? Why?

What Is a Marketing Plan?

Before discussing the marketing plan, it is important to understand the term marketing. **Marketing** consists of customer-focused activities intended to generate a transaction. Marketing touches every aspect of a business' operations.

Successful marketing efforts take time, money, and advance planning. A **marketing plan** is a document describing a business' marketing objectives and the strategies and tactics to achieve them. Marketing plans are generally written a year in advance of being implemented. They can be modified, however, throughout the year to address market changes or take advantage of new opportunities.

As you write the business plan, include the initial marketing information in the Market Evaluation and Operations sections. The business plan is the original document used to help create the business. As the company gets off the ground, update the business plan each year. Or, separate documents may be created each year for investors to review as needed. One of those documents will probably be a marketing plan. The marketing plan generally answers the five questions shown in Figure 12-1.

Copyright Goodheart-Willcox Co., Inc.

Marketing Plan Questions
• What are the current economic and competitive situations affecting the business?
• What are the marketing objectives for the upcoming year?
• What are the best strategies to implement for the business to achieve its marketing objectives?
• What are the most efficient marketing tactics for each strategy?
• How will the success of the marketing plan be measured?

Goodheart-Willcox Publisher

Figure 12-1. Five questions that your marketing plan will answer.

Every company's marketing plan is unique and will change over time. The first full marketing plan will probably be developed a year or two after the business opens. One helpful way to understand a marketing plan is to view the document itself as a set of travel plans. The marketing objective is *where* you plan to travel, such as to Europe or the West Coast. The marketing strategies are *how* to get to the area, such as flying or driving. The marketing tactics are the specific *paths* taken to reach the final destination, such as highways and roads.

Marketing Mix

Decisions about the marketing mix, or the four Ps of marketing, is the foundation of a marketing plan. Those decisions provide the important framework for choosing specific marketing tactics for implementing the plan.

Product Decisions

Product strategies include the decisions about the goods or services a business offers. Product strategies can include decisions on quantities, sizes, packaging, warranties, brand names, image, and design. Describe the benefits as they relate to how the product will make the customer's life better or easier.

Price Decisions

Price strategies include business decisions about the markup, profit margin, discounts offered, or list price versus selling price. Pricing policies affect a company's image. As appropriate, discuss price points, percentage of annual sales, and each product's profit. How does the pricing compare with competitors? Decide if higher prices will mean greater quality to the customer. Determine if prices need to be lower to increase sales and generate the desired profit.

The marketing plan is a compass for keeping your business moving in the right direction as it conducts daily activities as well as long-term tasks.

Copyright Goodheart-Willcox Co., Inc.

Global Entrepreneurs

Robert Johnson

In 1980, Robert Johnson launched Black Entertainment Television. It was the first cable television network devoted solely to programming for African-Americans. It is now known as BET and is a division of Viacom.

When Johnson started BET, cable television was relatively new. Advertisers were unsure about putting money into cable programming when the broadcasting networks were still the dominant source of information and programming. Johnson also had to deal with advertisers that did not think the African-American community would be viewers of cable television.

Johnson offers this advice: "I say to young people, never doubt your decision and never be afraid to work hard. Start at the bottom and grow to the top—that is entrepreneurship. You will make sacrifices to get there. Demonstrate passion in what you do and try to convince people that you are willing to work harder for yourself than someone else."

As cable television gained popularity, more people were exposed to BET. This allowed the network to grow and expand. It now has three sister networks: BET Hip-Hop, BET Gospel, and Centric (formerly BET Jazz). The BET networks reach more than 90 million households in the United States, United Kingdom, Caribbean, sub-Saharan Africa, and Canada.

Place Decisions

Place strategies include all of the decisions about how and where the products will be sold. These involve decisions not only about a physical location, but how goods or services move through the distribution channel. Is the product offered on the Internet, internationally, locally, or through other stores? Place decisions also include transportation of product, warehousing, inventory control, and order processing. Determine how the location affects the selling process and sales efforts. Will the business hire salespeople, independent sales reps, or agents? If applicable, describe the advantages to customers of the product-delivery process. Decide if setup is also part of the delivery process.

Promotion Decisions

Promotion strategies include decisions about which advertising, sales promotions, public-relations, and personal-selling activities to pursue. These decisions ultimately lead to identifying the promotional mix. Promotion decisions also include determining who will handle specific promotions and public relations efforts. In a newly formed

Copyright Goodheart-Willcox Co., Inc.

Goodluz/Shutterstock.com

When making decisions about place, consider distribution channels to and from your business.

business, the business owner may act as the marketing manager or hire an agency to do the work.

Marketing Plan Templates

Marketing plans, like business plans, can take on many different looks. There is no right or wrong way to write a plan. Many professional business organizations provide free or low-cost templates to use when writing a marketing plan. As long as all of the important information is covered, it is the business' choice about how to present the information. Sources of templates include:

- Small Business Administration (SBA);

- universities;

- chambers of commerce;

- Service Corps of Retired Executives (SCORE);

- state websites; and

- industry groups such as entrepreneur or small business owner organizations.

Each organization treats the marketing plan a little differently. However, most marketing plan templates have the same components. The names and order of components may be different. The key to the marketing plan is that it looks professional, provides detailed information, and resembles the business plan's style.

Section 12.1 Review

Check Your Understanding 🡢

1. What is a marketing plan?
2. How frequently are marketing plans written?
3. List four types of decisions that have to be made when determining the marketing mix.
4. Decisions made regarding transportation, warehousing, inventory controls, and order processing are part of what strategy?
5. Name four sources from which an entrepreneur can get a marketing plan template.

Build Your Vocabulary 🡢

As you progress through this text, develop a personal glossary of key terms. This will help you build your vocabulary and prepare you for a career. Write a definition for each of the following terms and add them to your personal glossary.

marketing	price strategy
marketing plan	place strategy
product strategy	promotion strategy

SECTION 12.2 Write a Marketing Plan

?E ssential **Q** uestion

What basic information is included in the marketing plan for a business?

Objectives

After completing this section, you will be able to:

- **Summarize** the parts of a marketing plan.
- **Format** a marketing plan.

Key Terms

situation analysis
marketing objective
marketing strategy

marketing tactic
action plan

Critical Thinking

Think about the economic situation your new business will find itself in when it opens. Describe the economy, your business' target market, and the competition as they will affect your marketing efforts.

Marketing Plan

Every marketing plan will be different because every business and its marketing objectives are different. Businesses generally define marketing plan sections to fit the particular business type. Decide which parts are important for your business and how to best present the information. The marketing plan template you choose may help you make those decisions.

All marketing plans include the following basic information, although the terms may change. The following topics are addressed in earlier chapters.

- situation analysis: introduction, target market, competition

- marketing objectives: corporate goals, marketing goals

- marketing strategies: product, price, place, promotion

- marketing tactics: activities for every strategy

- action plan: time line, budget, metrics

Copyright Goodheart-Willcox Co., Inc.

Your marketing plan will be unique to your business.

Monkey Business Images/Shutterstock.com

Situation Analysis

A business cannot determine where to go or how to get there without knowing where it has been. The **situation analysis** is a snapshot of the environment in which a business has been operating over a given time. It begins with an introductory statement of the economic situation as it relates to marketing and sales. It then defines the target markets. The competition and company positioning are also part of the situation analysis. You might want to use the primary and secondary market research collected to start the business to complete part of the situation analysis.

Target Market

The target market part of the marketing plan records research data collected on current and potential customers:

- Define the target market by using demographic, geographic, economic, behavioral, and psychographic data.

Copyright Goodheart-Willcox Co., Inc.

- Estimate the total size of the target market; it is important to be as accurate as possible.
- Include information from marketing studies, reports, or test-marketing activities completed that describe marketing trends.
- Describe factors that may affect purchasing, such as season, price, availability, emotions, services, or tax considerations.

Competition

In the competition part of the marketing plan, list both direct and indirect competitors. Outline the product lines they offer and their market share. Describe your business' competitive advantage. Explain why your product is different or better than the competitors. Does your business offer a wider variety, better prices, better sizing than the competition?

- Include a competitive analysis.
- Discuss the unique selling proposition (USP) as well as the value proposition for the business or the products.

Marketing Objectives

Marketing objectives are the goals a business wants to achieve during a given time, usually one year, by implementing the marketing plan. Most businesses have several marketing objectives that address both corporate and marketing goals. A corporate goal may be setting yearly sales. Marketing goals include defining market share and image. *Market share* is the percentage of total sales in a market that is held by one business. Examples of marketing objectives might be:

- increase sales in 20-- by 15 percent (corporate goal); and
- increase company brand awareness and market share by 10 percent in 20-- (marketing goal).

SBA Tips

The SBA has a *Small Business Marketing Guide* that gives directions for writing a marketing plan. A marketing plan will help you achieve your goals and help make sure that you are using your money wisely.
www.sba.gov

Focus on Finance

Filing Taxes

If your business is legally classified as a sole proprietorship or a single-member limited liability company (LLC), you will file a Schedule C when doing your income taxes to report the earnings from your business. Schedule C has the details about your business including its name, address, owner, and employer ID or Social Security number. You will then record the earnings, expenses, and other accounting details of the business to calculate the net profit. The net profit is then transferred to your personal tax return form. It is recommended that you check with your tax professional for advice on completing tax returns for your business.

Copyright Goodheart-Willcox Co., Inc.

The marketing objectives should be written as SMART goals, which are discussed in chapter 1. *SMART goals* are specific, measurable, attainable, realistic, and timely. They may be short-term goals, which are achieved in less than one year. Or, they may be long-term goals, those which can be achieved in a year or more.

Marketing Strategies

In a marketing plan, the **marketing strategies** are the decisions made about product, price, place, and promotion. Marketing strategies outline the *who, what, when, where,* and *how* of the marketing process.

The marketing strategies directly support the marketing objectives. For example, some marketing strategies to achieve the marketing goal outlined above might include:

- offer one new product each year;

- provide free delivery to customers within ten miles of the store;

- price products at or below the competitor's products; and

- increase sales in the critical teen demographic by 25 percent through promotions.

Marketing Tactics

Marketing tactics consist of the specific activities to carry out the marketing strategies. Every marketing strategy will have a set of tactics designed to accomplish it. This may be the longest section of the marketing plan because it lists very specific activities. Include a one-year promotional plan for advertising, sales promotions, public relations, and personal selling.

Green Entrepreneurs

Environmentally Friendly Paper

Business owners spend a lot of time and money on marketing materials. If promotional pieces, such as brochures or loyalty cards are more effective in print form, consider using environmentally friendly supplies. Today, some paper is made from by-products of sugar cane instead of wood pulp. Sugar cane biodegrades faster than wood products and is cleaner to produce. Many office supply companies are now carrying sugar cane paper with more new green products to come. This can be a perfect paper stock alternative for your marketing collateral.

Copyright Goodheart-Willcox Co., Inc.

arek_malang/Shutterstock.com

A marketing tactic is a specific activity that will promote your business, such as holding a sale at a certain time of the year.

For example, several marketing tactics for the promotion strategy previously outlined might include:

- offer 20 percent discount coupons to students through area high school newspapers or websites;

- promote a "buy one, get one half off" Facebook promotion during the summer months; and

- purchase a 26-week advertising schedule on the local rock radio station.

Action Plan

The **action plan** includes a detailed time line, the associated budget, and the metrics to evaluate the effectiveness of any campaigns. A strong marketing plan includes an action plan to ensure the marketing efforts remain on track and funds are spent wisely and appropriately. The action plan sorts out all the details of the marketing tactics.

Time Line

The time line lists when each activity starts, where it happens or runs, the end date, and the person responsible. A time line keeps the business on track and moves the plan forward.

Entrepreneur Ethics

Social networking media is commonly used by organizations to reach current customers and attract new ones. Those who are writing a business' marketing communication must be ethical when using social media sites, such as Facebook or Twitter. While the exposure on social networking sites is great for both new and established companies, make sure the information posted is accurate and not misleading.

Copyright Goodheart-Willcox Co., Inc.

Budget

The budget includes the costs to implement the marketing and promotional activities. Some tactics may have several sets of costs, such as the costs to both produce and run radio ads.

Metrics

An action plan also includes the methods and metrics that will be used to track and evaluate marketing activities. Marketing is an

You Do the Math Statistical Reasoning

Qualitative data include things that can be observed, but not measured. Smell, taste, color, appearance, and texture are all examples of types of qualitative data. On the other hand, quantitative data include things that can be measured. Distance, weight, cost, speed, and temperature are all examples of types of quantitative data.

Solve the following problems.

1. The catalog description of a product reads as follows: attractive, blue product has a smooth finish, fits in a space 5 inches wide, and weighs 14 ounces. List the qualitative data and quantitative data in this description.

2. A business describes its customer service staff as follows: a staff of 17 pleasant and helpful representatives includes five certified technicians and two master technicians. List the qualitative data and quantitative data in this description.

The marketing plan should be well written and attractive because it may be shown to investors.

Pressmaster/Shutterstock.com

Copyright Goodheart-Willcox Co., Inc.

expensive part of operating a business. It is important to have a system in place to measure its effectiveness. Marketers look for a good *return on investment (ROI)* for the dollars spent on marketing.

Depending on the activity, the metrics used to measure success will differ. Sometimes it is easy to tie sales directly to marketing activities by using coupons or electronic product codes. Other times it may be harder to track direct sales. For instance, effectiveness may be measured for some electronic promotions by the number of website hits during a given time period. SEO tools like Google AdWords have several metrics for campaign measurement on search engine websites. Regardless of the metrics used, it is important to track all campaigns to see if they are worth repeating.

Format the Marketing Plan

At some point, the marketing plan may be presented to investors or lenders to show what drives the company's revenue. Just like the business plan, a marketing plan should be:

- well written; sentences and paragraphs must make sense and describe the marketing plans;

- grammatically correct; words selected must be appropriate and the punctuation used should be accurate;

- exciting and enthusiastic; describe ideas and plans in the most inviting way possible;

- unique; marketing is the place to showcase creativity; and

- attractive; make the marketing plan a compatible part of the business plan.

Section 12.2 Review

Check Your Understanding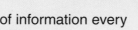

1. List five pieces of information every marketing plan should include.

2. By what categories are target markets defined?

3. What is market share?

4. What five words make up the SMART goals acronym?

5. What is the connection between a marketing strategy and marketing tactics?

Build Your Vocabulary

As you progress through this text, develop a personal glossary of key terms. This will help you build your vocabulary and prepare you for a career. Write a definition for each of the following terms and add them to your personal glossary.

situation analysis
marketing objective
marketing strategy
marketing tactic
action plan

Chapter Summary

Section 12.1 Develop a Marketing Plan

- Marketing plans play a critical role in a company's success. The marketing plan provides specific information about how marketing efforts will be carried out.
- The marketing mix is a plan for marketing a good, service, or institution. The decisions made about place, promotion, price, and product are part of the marketing mix.
- Different businesses will use different marketing plan templates. However, all the templates have similar components. Many different resources provide marketing templates they have developed free or at a low cost.

Section 12.2 Write a Marketing Plan

- Five major parts make up all marketing plans. They are situation analysis (introduction, target market, competition), marketing objectives (corporate goals, marketing goals), marketing strategies (product, price, place, promotion), marketing tactics (activities for every strategy), and an action plan (time line, budget, metrics).
- The marketing plan, just like a business plan, will be seen by those inside as well as outside of the organization. A marketing plan should be well written, grammatically correct, exciting and enthusiastic, unique, and attractive. The marketing plan should be a compatible part of the business plan.

Online Activities

Complete the following activities to help you learn, practice, and expand your knowledge and skills.

📲 **Posttest.** Now that you have finished the chapter, see what you learned by taking the chapter posttest.

📲 **Key Terms.** Practice vocabulary for this chapter using the e-flash cards, matching activity, and vocabulary game until you are able to recognize their meanings.

Review Your Knowledge

1. Which questions does a marketing plan answer for the business?
2. Explain the purpose of a marketing plan template.
3. Why is it important to create a marketing plan that is professional in its appearance?
4. What target market information should be included in the marketing plan?
5. The marketing plan should include information about your marketing mix. What is included in the marketing mix?

Copyright Goodheart-Willcox Co., Inc.

6. Describe the action plan.
7. What are metrics?
8. Decisions about the markup, profit margin, discounts offered, or list price versus selling price are part of what piece of the marketing mix?
9. What five questions should the marketing plan address?
10. What is the difference between a business plan and a marketing plan?

Apply Your Knowledge

1. For your business, answer the five essential questions that need to be addressed in your marketing plan.
2. Research various marketing templates that are available from various organizations. Select one that works for you.
3. Write objectives for your business using SMART goals.
4. Identify at least four short-term goals for your business.
5. Write three long-term goals for your business.
6. List three competitors for your business. List the strengths and weaknesses of each.
7. Research marketing action plans and calendars that show marketing events in an organization. Create an imaginary marketing calendar for your business.
8. Marketing budgets will be very important for your business. Research the average amount a business similar to yours will need to budget for marketing.
9. Research various ways that businesses similar to yours track marketing efforts. Select a system that you think will provide you solid information on the effectiveness of your marketing activities.
10. Research various ways that businesses similar to yours forecasts sales. Create an imaginary sales forecast for your business.

Teamwork

Working in teams, create a template for a marketing plan. Select a template from those you researched on the Internet. Each team member should take a section of the selected template and customize it to be more appropriate for your use. Present the template to your class. Which team created the template that was most appealing?

Internet Research

Writing a Marketing Plan. Use the Internet to research the steps involved in writing a marketing plan. Make a list of the recommendations that the research resources suggest following. Find various marketing plan templates online, and choose one for the marketing plan for your business.

Copyright Goodheart-Willcox Co., Inc.

Communication Skills

College and Career Readiness

Speaking. There are many instances when you will be required to persuade the listener. When you persuade, you convince a person to take a course of action which you propose. Prepare for a conversation with a classmate to persuade that person to approve your idea for a marketing template.

Listening. Passive listening is casually listening to someone speak. Passive listening is appropriate when you do not have to interact with the speaker. Listen to a song on the radio. After it has played, evaluate what you heard and write down the lyrics that you remember.

CTSOs

Objective Test. Some competitive events for Career and Technical Student Organizations (CTSOs) require that entrants complete an objective part of the event. This event will typically be an objective test that includes terminology and concepts related to being an entrepreneur. Participants are usually allowed one hour to complete the objective part of the event. To prepare for the concepts portion of the entrepreneur objective test, complete the following activities.

1. Read the guidelines provided by your organization. Make certain that you ask any questions about points you do not understand. It is important you follow each specific item that is outlined in the competition rules.

2. Visit the organization's website and look for entrepreneurial concepts tests that were used in previous years. Many organizations post these tests for students to use as practice for future competitions.

3. Look for the evaluation criteria or rubric for the event. This will help you determine what the judge will be looking for in your presentation.

4. Review the checkpoint questions at the end of each section of this text.

5. For additional practice, review the end-of-chapter activities.

6. Create flash cards for each vocabulary term with its definition on the other side. Ask a friend to use these cards to review with you.

7. Ask your instructor to give you practice tests for each chapter of this text. It is important that you are familiar with answering multiple choice and true/false questions. Have someone time you as you take a practice test.

Copyright Goodheart-Willcox Co., Inc.

Building Your Business Plan—Putting the Puzzle Together

Marketing Plan

A marketing plan is an important document that describes the overall marketing objectives for the business and the strategies to achieve them. As an entrepreneur, you need a marketing plan to serve as a road map to help drive sales efforts.

For your first year in business, there will probably not be a separate marketing plan. However, the initial marketing efforts will be detailed in the business plan. Lenders and investors expect to see your marketing strategies for at least the first full year in business. There may be separate budgets, promotion schedules, and other supporting documents added to the Appendices section of the business plan.

Objectives

- Identify marketing objectives, strategies, and tactics.
- Create business plan notes.

Directions

Access the *Entrepreneurship* companion website at www.g-wlearning.com ➦. Download each data file for the following activities. A complete sample business plan is available on the companion website to use as a reference. The name of the file is BusPlan_Sample.RetroAttire. docx.

Preparation

Activity 12-1. Operations Checklist. Review the checklist to make sure all parts of the Marketing Strategies section of the business plan are complete.

Activity 12-2. Business Plan Notes. Create notes about any information that you might need for a marketing plan after your business is in operation.

Business Plan—Operations

The marketing portion of the business plan is nearly complete. In this activity, you will finish the Marketing Strategies subsection of the Operations section.

1. Open your saved business plan document.

2. Locate the Operations section of the plan. Based on the information you learned in this unit, finish writing the Marketing Strategies subsection of your plan. Use the suggestions and questions listed to help you generate ideas. Delete the instructions and questions when you are finished recording your responses. Make sure to proofread your document and correct any errors in keyboarding, spelling, and grammar.

3. Save your document.

Stephen Coburn/Shutterstock.com

Unit 5
Managing the Business

Your Business Plan—Putting the Puzzle Together

The Operations section will be complete by the end of this unit and a good portion of the Financial Plans section will be addressed. What types of risk may threaten your business, and how will you manage cash flow to pay the bills? In this unit, you will:

Describe management functions.

Determine human resources policies.

Discuss how to manage purchases and inventory.

Investigate how to manage the different risks that may affect your business.

Develop accounting procedures and financial statements.

Unit Overview

There are many critical management functions and processes necessary to run a successful business. Performing the management functions of planning, organizing, staffing, leading, and controlling helps managers reach their goals and objectives. Management responsibilities include overseeing of human resources, assigning individuals to purchasing and inventory management, and planning for risks to help the business avoid disasters both physical and financial. Unit 5 shows you some of the important management tasks that can help you create a successful business.

Chapters

13 Management Functions

14 Human Resources Management

15 Purchases and Inventory Management

16 Risk Management

17 Financial Management

Entrepreneurs and the Economy

The *Federal Reserve System,* also known as the *Fed,* is the central bank for the United States. The Fed's goal is to keep the economy stable and able to grow. Its functions allow banks, businesses, and individuals to conduct business. It sets monetary policies that affect buying, selling, saving, and spending. Entrepreneurs are small business owners, and the Fed's decisions impact both the business environment and customers' ability to pay for goods and services.

For example, the Fed sets interest rates for banks that borrow from it. This is known as the *discount rate,* which is set every two weeks. The discount rate determines the interest rates that banks then charge their customers who borrow money. It also affects the interest rates businesses charge customers who buy on credit. Typically, banks add several percentage points to the discount rate, which is how they make money on loans. For example, if the discount rate is 2 percent, the *prime rate,* or the rate banks charge their best customers, may be around 6 percent.

A customer's credit history directly affects the interest rates that may be offered. Rates that are either at or close to the current prime rate are usually given to customers with excellent credit histories. These customers are considered less risky than those with poor credit histories. Those with poor credit histories will have to pay higher rates. This is one reason it is so important for entrepreneurs to maintain a good-to-excellent credit history.

Lower interest rates save on the money charged to borrow. For example, as a business owner, you may need a loan to buy a company car. If you qualify for a 4 percent

alphaspirit/Shutterstock.com

interest rate for a four-year $10,000 loan, the total cost to borrow would be $838. If, however, you could only qualify for a 5.5 percent interest rate on that loan, the total cost would be $1,163. By having better credit and receiving a lower interest rate, you pay $325 less over the life of the loan.

While studying, look for the activity icon for:

- Chapter pretests and posttests
- Key terms activities
- Section reviews
- Building Your Business Plan activities

G-W LEARNING.com

CHAPTER

13 Management Functions

In 1936, David Abt started a retail business called Abt Radio. Today, Abt Electronics in Glenview, Illinois, is a 350,000-square-foot electronics store with 200 service and delivery trucks and 1,100 employees. That growth did not just happen by accident. The success of the business can be attributed to a number of factors. One of the main reasons for its success has been its great customer service. Great customer service does not come easy. It requires recruiting the best employees and having a management structure that allows them to succeed. Part of the management plan also involves maintaining a compensation program that works to keep employees. As the company has grown and expanded, it has had to continue to hire additional employees.

"Good management consists in showing average people how to do the work of superior people."

—John D. Rockefeller, industrialist, philanthropist, and founder of Standard Oil Company

College and Career Readiness

Reading Prep. In preparation for reading this chapter, read over the terms listed for each section. What terms are already familiar to you? Which ones are not familiar at all? As you read, think about how your understanding of the meaning of a given term agrees with the text or is different.

Sections

13.1 Managers

13.2 Management Styles and Communication

Picture Yourself Here
Monique Péan

Monique Péan is known for designing sustainable fine jewelry inspired by the many places she has visited. Her work has been featured in *Vogue, Elle,* and *InStyle* magazines and has been worn by First Lady Michelle Obama.

Monique is based in New York and has a line of jewelry inspired by Alaskan native culture. She uses 100 percent recycled gold and considers her jewelry socially responsible, wearable art. Ten percent of the profits from this special collection support Alaskan native arts and culture. Monique also founded The Vanessa Péan Foundation, which provides scholarships to underprivileged students in Haiti.

Monique took fashion-design courses in New York and is a graduate of the University of Pennsylvania. Her mentor is former Tiffany & Co. CEO Michael J. Kowalski. A mentor is an advisor who has experience in the industry in which you wish to work. A mentor can be a valuable asset when starting your own business.

Photo © kevinsturman

Check Your Entrepreneurship IQ

Before you begin the chapter, see what you already know about entrepreneurship by taking the chapter pretest. The pretest is available at www.g-wlearning.com

Managers

What role does management play in the success of a business?

Objectives

After completing this section, you will be able to:

- **List** the processes and tasks involved in managing a business.
- **Describe** effective leadership.
- **Explain** how to build a team.

Key Terms

strategic planning
tactical planning
operational planning
chain of command
organizational chart
staffing
controlling

time-management skills
personal information management (PIM)
collaboration skills
critical-thinking skills
listening skills

Critical Thinking

Your business is now up and running. You need to start thinking about building a team. Make a list of the characteristics that you would use as criteria for hiring people for your business.

Business Management

Congratulations! The new business is going well and there is more work than you can handle. This may be the time to start thinking about hiring employees to help the business grow. Many entrepreneurs do everything for their new business, as shown in Figure 13-1. However, no business owner can do everything by himself or herself indefinitely.

Among the many skills an entrepreneur needs are good management and leadership skills. When an entrepreneur adds employees to the business, he or she becomes a manager. A *manager* is the person responsible for carrying out the goals of the business. One idea of a manager's role is directing people. This might not sound appealing. However, another way to think of a manager is as a mentor. A *mentor* is someone who teaches or gives help and advice to a less-experienced person or group.

Copyright Goodheart-Willcox Co., Inc.

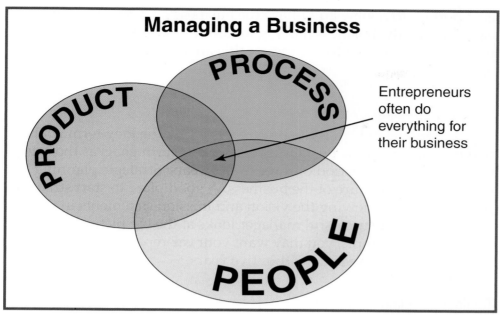

Managing a Business

PRODUCT

PROCESS

PEOPLE

Entrepreneurs often do everything for their business

Goodheart-Willcox Publisher

Figure 13-1. Most new business owners manage every area of the business.

Management is the process of controlling and making decisions about a business. This means managing all areas of the business to achieve the goals that are set. Good managers share their visions and business goals with employees. This helps employees become part of the team that turns the vision into a reality. Successful managers do not just look at one part of the business, they look at the entire management process, as illustrated in Figure 13-2.

Plan

A common saying in the business world is, "failing to plan is planning to fail." During *business planning,* managers set goals and create a roadmap for how to achieve them. The company's business plan contains its initial goals and the plans for achieving them. It

FYI

Local colleges and adult education programs offer management classes. These can help an entrepreneur learn about how to manage employees.

Management Process	
Plan	Set goals and decide how to achieve them.
Organize	Arrange tasks, people, and resources to accomplish the work.
Staff	Hire the best and the most talented people.
Lead	Motivate and direct employees through clear instructions and by communicating policies and procedures.
Control	Monitor financial and personnel performance, compare actual performance with goals, and take corrective action when needed.

Goodheart-Willcox Publisher

Figure 13-2. Managers perform many tasks during the management process.

Copyright Goodheart-Willcox Co., Inc.

is important to review and revise the business plan on a regular basis to keep the business moving forward. A successful business-planning process involves three specific areas: strategic, tactical, and operational.

Strategic Planning

Strategic planning is the process of setting the long-term goals of the company. Many businesses define long-term goals as those to be achieved over a period of three to five years. Strategic planning looks at the big picture of the business. A good place to start strategic planning is by reviewing the vision and mission statements in the business plan. A successful manager looks at the big picture of the business. For example, you may want your car-repair business to double its current revenue within five years.

Tactical Planning

Tactical planning is the process of setting the short-term goals for the company. Short-term goals are typically those set for the next 6 to 24 months. Tactical planning looks at the immediate needs of the business. Set specific sales and other goals and determine how to reach each goal. For example, the business plan for your car-repair business may include a sales goal of $100,000 by the end of the third quarter.

Operational Planning

Operational planning is the process of setting the day-to-day goals for the company. Based on the tactical plan, those goals are further refined to reflect monthly, weekly, or daily tasks. For example, your car-repair business may have an operational goal of 40 car repairs and 50 oil changes per week. Often, operational goals are assigned to certain employees and used to measure their performances.

Entrepreneur Ethics

Business owners may encounter others who categorize people using biased words and comments. Using age, gender, race, disability, ethnicity, or any other criterion based on who a person is as a way to describe others is unethical and sometimes illegal. Bias-free language should be used in all communication, whether verbal or printed, to show respect for those with whom the business comes in contact.

Focus on Finance

Sales Taxes

As an entrepreneur, you will be selling goods or services. Check with your city, state, and federal tax offices to make sure you understand sales taxes for which you will be responsible. Cities and states generally have a sales tax on all products that are sold. Business owners collect these taxes from the customer and then pay the tax to the government. Make certain that you are fully aware of all sales taxes before you open your doors for business.

Organize

To *organize* is to arrange the parts of a system so each part depends on the others. Managers organize the available people and resources to accomplish the business' goals. They assign specific job functions and titles to the employees to designate responsibility in the company. The **chain of command** is an organization's structure of decision-making responsibilities, from the highest to the lowest levels of authority. Most businesses create an organizational chart to show the chain of command in the company. An **organizational chart** is a diagram of employee positions showing how the positions interact within the chain of command. An example of an organizational chart is shown in Figure 13-3. The organizational chart is included in the business plan.

Staff

The **staffing** function is the process of hiring people and matching them to the best position for their talents. This function includes the human resources elements of hiring, training, and establishing salaries and benefits. Finding the right employees can be challenging. A business is only as good as its employees; so, staffing is critical to a business' success. The human resources functions are discussed in detail later in this text.

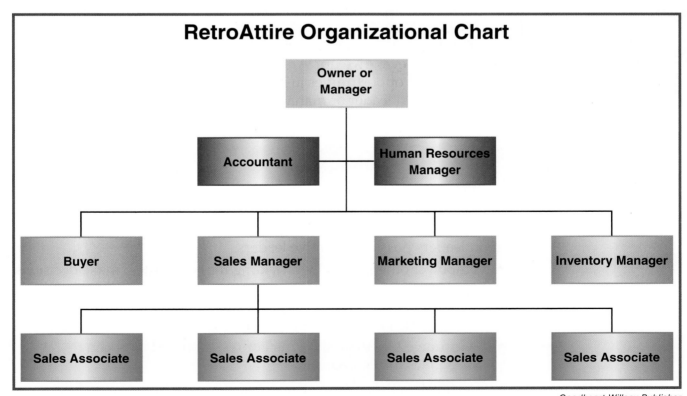

Goodheart-Willcox Publisher

Figure 13-3. Typical organizational chart format.

Lead

Successful managers lead or direct employees by giving clear, concise instructions and other necessary information. Successful managers also fully understand the assigned tasks and can train employees in correct company processes and procedures. Mentoring is a part of this management function, especially as it relates to achieving specific goals. Leadership is discussed in more detail later in this chapter.

Control

Controlling is monitoring the progress a business has made in meeting its goals at any given time and making needed corrections. Actual performance is compared to the stated goals of the business. A manager takes corrective action when needed and may adjust the planned goals and performance standards. The employee evaluation process falls under this managerial function.

Leadership

Many entrepreneurs and managers are natural leaders. Others learn their leadership skills over time. A successful business owner shows leadership by selling his or her vision for the company. Leaders motivate and inspire employees, vendors, and customers to believe in the business.

Think about entrepreneurs you know or about whom you have read. Do they ever give up? Are they excited about what they do? Are their next opportunities just around the corner? While every entrepreneurial leader or manager is different, some traits and basic skills are common to the successful ones.

Traits

Effective leaders possess positive traits, or characteristics, that make them good at working with and motivating others. The list of effective leadership traits is long, but there are some traits that most good leaders possess. Effective leaders

- empower others to act by providing the authority to make decisions;

- lead by example and model the expected behavior;

- create and support a positive corporate culture;

- encourage others by showing appreciation and providing incentives to succeed; and

- establish and manage relationships by spending time and energy with peers, suppliers, staff, and customers.

FYI

Leadership is a critical skill in business. Much information can be found on the Internet, in books, and in trade magazines related to the importance of effective leadership.

Copyright Goodheart-Willcox Co., Inc.

Successful entrepreneurs have leadership traits and skills in common.

William Perugini/Shutterstock.com

Skills

A skill is a learned ability that a person can do well. The phrase *good people skills* is often used when describing skills of leaders. This refers to good communication or *listening and speaking skills.* Good leaders are also good communicators. They have the ability to work well with others to complete tasks on time.

Good leaders and managers can quickly identify problems and make sound decisions to benefit the business. **Time-management skills** are the ability to use time wisely by setting priorities. Time management is the practice of organizing time and work assignments to increase personal efficiency. Tasks must be prioritized by determining which should be completed before others. SMART goals and detailed schedules must be created and followed to optimize results. The difference between average and excellent entrepreneurs is often how well they prioritize assignments, not how hard they work.

Personal information management (PIM) is a system that individuals use to acquire, organize, maintain, retrieve, and use information. An example of a PIM system is Microsoft Outlook. Using this software, an individual can keep a schedule, record contact information, and complete other activities that help organize personal information.

Copyright Goodheart-Willcox Co., Inc.

Interpersonal Skills

People skills are interpersonal skills—those skills you use to communicate with people around you. Effective leaders have good listening and communication skills, as well as the ability to work with people to get the job done. Some people find interpersonal skills the hardest to master. However, interpersonal skills may be the most important skills since the majority of a manager's time is spent leading and directing others.

Business Skills

In order to run a business, it is important for a leader to have basic business skills. These basic skills are the job-specific abilities needed to perform in a specialized field. Recordkeeping skills, the ability to write letters in proper business format, and knowledge about business organization are just some of the skills that are important for the entrepreneur to master.

Planning and Problem-Solving Skills

Good leaders have the ability to think analytically, to visualize the business as a whole, and understand how all of the parts of the business fit together. A manager who has planning skills has the ability to think and visualize the future as well as anticipate change. A manager also should possess problem-solving skills. These skills involve having the ability to identify a problem and then take measures to solve the situation to benefit the organization. Effective leaders know how to create a plan and engage others to follow it.

Team Building

A *team* is two or more people working together toward the same goal. All teams have a leader and at least one member. Entrepreneurs develop and lead many teams while running a business. These may include teams of employees, vendors, bankers, contractors, or other people with whom the business interacts. The support of team members is crucial for a business to be successful. Effective team members are

- cooperative and work together toward the team's goals;
- committed to the goal and vision of the company;
- good communicators who are willing to share information with the rest of the team; and
- responsible and dependable.

Team building takes time and effort. As a team grows, the member roles are expanded and redefined as needed.

Copyright Goodheart-Willcox Co., Inc.

Effective team members have good interpersonal skills. Interpersonal skills help people communicate effectively with each other. Some examples of important interpersonal skills for effective team members are as follows:

- **Collaboration skills** enable individuals to work with others to achieve a common goal. This includes sharing ideas and compromising for the greater good of the team. To *compromise* is to give up an individual idea so that the group can come to a solution.

- **Critical-thinking skills** are the ability to analyze a situation, interpret information, and make reasonable decisions.

- *Verbal skills* are the ability to communicate effectively using spoken or written words.

- *Nonverbal skills* are the ability to communicate effectively using body language, eye contact, personal space, behavior, and attitude. Nonverbal skills can send clear messages without using words.

- **Listening skills** are the ability of an individual to hear what a person says and understand what is being said.

Section 13.1 Review

Check Your Understanding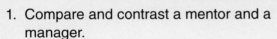

1. Compare and contrast a mentor and a manager.
2. List the five functions of the management process.
3. Compare and contrast the three areas of planning.
4. Describe the staffing function of the management process.
5. Describe the controlling function of the management process.

Build Your Vocabulary

As you progress through this text, develop a personal glossary of key terms. This will help you build your vocabulary and prepare you for a career. Write a definition for each of the following terms and add them to your personal glossary.

strategic planning
tactical planning
operational
  planning
chain of command
organizational chart
staffing
controlling
time-management
  skills

personal
  information
  management
  (PIM)
collaboration skills
critical-thinking
  skills
listening skills

Copyright Goodheart-Willcox Co., Inc.

Management Styles and Communication

Objectives

After completing this section, you will be able to:

- **Describe** the four common management styles.
- **Identify** elements that make effective managers.
- **Explain** the importance of communication in business.

?Essential **Q**uestion

How do management styles influence the way a business operates?

Key Terms

management style
situational management
democratic style
autocratic style
consulting style
laissez-faire style

empower
open-door policy
speaking
listening
writing
four Cs of communication

Critical Thinking

There is more than one way to manage and motivate other people. Some styles are more effective for different types of businesses. Which management style do you think will be most effective for you and your business? Explain why you chose this management style.

Management Styles

A **management style** is how a person leads employees or a group. In general, there are four management styles. Some managers use only one style. Others operate under situational management. **Situational management** is when a manager behaves differently according to each situation. A management style can also depend on the manager's own personality and the personalities of the employees. The four management styles are democratic, autocratic, consulting, and laissez-faire.

Democratic Style

In the **democratic style** of management, the leader allows and encourages all members of the group to participate and share ideas equally. Since all members participate, this style is often called the *participatory style.*

The democratic style draws on the knowledge and skills employees already possess. Managers using this style delegate authority and involve workers in the decision-making process. This gives the staff responsibility to complete tasks however they think is best. Involvement in the business keeps employees motivated and gives them a sense of importance. However, because many people may be involved in the decision-making process, decisions can take time.

Autocratic Style

In the **autocratic style** of management, the leader makes all decisions without input from others. An effective leader can quickly make decisions when this style is used since no other opinions are solicited. When working under an effective autocratic leader, employees usually complete tasks on time, but may feel unmotivated because they have no input. However, since the entire operation revolves around the autocratic leader, if the leader is ineffective or not present, the operation can quickly have problems.

Consulting Style

The **consulting style** of management is a combination of the democratic and autocratic styles. A manager using this style asks for opinions of the employees, which makes employees feel respected and involved. The manager makes the final decision, but only after considering input from the employees. This management style works well in many business environments. Decisions can be made quickly, but the input of employees is also valued.

Green Entrepreneurs

Batteries

Technologically aware business owners stay on top of the latest in equipment to make their jobs more efficient. However, it is important to respect the environment when using equipment that requires batteries. The batteries in cell phones and other portable devices are hazardous and will harm the environment if they are thrown in a landfill. Batteries should always be properly recycled by a reputable organization and never thrown in the regular trash. To be environmentally informed and save money, consider using rechargeable batteries. Rechargeable batteries can be used many times over and will save trips to the store to purchase disposable batteries.

Copyright Goodheart-Willcox Co., Inc.

Consulting style management incorporates opinions from employees when making decisions.

Pressmaster/Shutterstock.com

Laissez-Faire Style

A manager with a **laissez-faire style** allows employees to make their own decisions about how to complete tasks. There is little involvement from the manager in the daily operation of the group or department. The manager answers questions and provides information, but spends most of his or her time looking at the big picture of how the department or company is functioning. This management style works well for experienced staff, but may not work for new employees with little experience.

Effective Managers

Effective managers are people who make positive contributions to the business. They know how to work well with everyone, from employees and upper management to customers and vendors. Both managers and business owners must be professional and provide an example of appropriate workplace conduct. They must conform to *business etiquette*, which is the art of using good manners in a work situation. Effective managers also make the most of available resources. Managers need to use many different skills.

Your attitude also impacts your work ethic. Those with a strong work ethic place high importance on working hard, being productive, creating positive interactions, and efficiently performing assigned tasks as directed. Demonstrating a strong work ethic will contribute to your professional success and the success of your employees.

FYI

Laissez-faire, pronounced *la-zay-fare*, comes from French and means "to let do." In English, this phrase has come to mean "let people do as they will." In other words, a laissez-faire management style is a *hands-off* style of management.

Copyright Goodheart-Willcox Co., Inc.

Use Motivational Techniques

An effective manager understands what motivates people. Often, money is not what keeps people coming to work each day. Some people are more motivated by having their ideas and input respected. While there are many motivational techniques, they all revolve around some form of recognition and clear, consistent communication.

Effective managers motivate employees by listening to their feedback and respecting the input. Effective managers also use positive motivational techniques to help employees enjoy their jobs and appreciate the company. Giving a cash bonus is a motivational technique, but many motivational techniques cost no money at all.

One of the best ways to motivate is simply to show appreciation for and recognize each employee's contributions. For example, some businesses have an employee of the month award. Each month, someone is officially recognized for a job well done with his or her picture posted in a prominent place.

Setting goals that can be met also motivates employees to meet those goals. Some businesses even hold employee competitions and reward those who meet the goals. This is common in the sales area.

Delegate Work

Delegating work means giving other employees the authority to complete tasks. This is a sign of an effective manager. Delegating tasks and responsibility also helps employees learn the business faster and contribute more. The manager then has more time to focus on other aspects of growing the business.

Mentoring and coaching others by delegating work provides positive on-the-job training. The goal of every new employee should be to quickly develop the ability to train other new employees.

Effective managers, except those using the autocratic style, empower their employees. To **empower** employees means giving them the authority to make decisions.

Have an Open-Door Policy

An **open-door policy** means employees are free to talk with any manager at any time. The goal of having an open-door policy is to encourage employee feedback and mutual trust. To accomplish this, employees must know that their questions or concerns are always welcome.

Businesses with open-door policies allow both managers and employees to create a productive workplace. In addition, potential negative situations can be identified and handled before a crisis develops.

Copyright Goodheart-Willcox Co., Inc.

Delegating work helps both the employer and the employees.

holbox/Shutterstock.com

Learn from Mistakes

No person is perfect. It is inevitable that business owners and managers will make some mistakes. Good managers learn from their mistakes, though. They analyze the situation and determine what went wrong to avoid making the same mistake again.

Employees will also make mistakes. One of the most important managerial duties is to help employees to learn from their mistakes. Effective managers use the opportunity to create a *teachable moment* and guide the employee to correcting the mistake. This helps employees grow and learn how to handle different situations.

Manage Stress

Every employee and manager will experience stress at some point in their working careers. Continued stress can lead to an unproductive workplace or missed workdays. Learning how to identify and manage stress is important for managers. Stressed managers may contribute to a stressful work environment for others or even affect customer relations. Calm, focused managers can create a healthier workplace and even help any stressed employees to keep the business running smoothly. The first step is to identify what is causing stress for a person.

Stress management techniques are actions that can reduce stress. They can include things such as getting more rest or exercise, taking short breaks from stressful situations or looking at issues from a different perspective. Depending on the source of stress, sometimes just talking about issues helps to reduce stress.

Copyright Goodheart-Willcox Co., Inc.

Treat Employees Equally

In addition to complying with the equal-opportunity workplace laws, treating employees equally is part of being professional. A company's codes of ethics and conduct should address workplace respect, regardless of gender, age, race, religion, or any other criterion. Managers, in particular, should model this behavior and encourage it in others. Effective managers have no obvious favorites, nor do they treat certain employees poorly.

Employees may come from various ethnic backgrounds. As a result, they may have different cultural backgrounds or belief systems. For instance, in some cultures people do not want public praise. In that case, the employee should be privately complimented. Standards of communication are necessary to make sure all employees are treated with respect.

Business Communication Skills

Successful managers and business owners understand the importance of professional business communication. They develop the necessary skills to communicate with customers, employees, and suppliers. Speaking, listening, and writing are basic business communication skills. Different forms of communication may be required in various situations. For example, sales may take place through e-mail, while customer service takes place over the phone.

SBA Tips

The Small Loan Advantage and the Community Advantage are new SBA programs that increase the number of smaller loans going to small businesses and entrepreneurs in underserved communities. The maximum loan size under these programs is $250,000, with a large portion guaranteed by the government. These loans are available through 600 financial institutions aligned with the SBA. www.sba.gov

Social Entrepreneurs

Peter Frykman

As part of a mechanical engineering PhD course at Stanford University, Peter Frykman made a trip to Ethiopia. While there, he realized the need for better irrigation systems for small-plot farmers. The existing type of irrigation was flood irrigation in which farmers dig small trenches through their crops and flood them with water. Drip irrigation uses water more efficiently than flood irrigation and can increase crop production by 20 percent to 50 percent. However, existing drip-irrigation systems were either costly or complicated. Realizing the social impact an efficient irrigation system could have on farmers in developing countries, Frykman began working on a manufacturing process to produce a low-cost system. In 2008, he founded Driptech to manufacture the systems. Driptech is based in California with offices in Pune, India, and Beijing, China. The company's mission is to alleviate poverty by providing to small-plot farmers with irrigation solutions that are affordable and water efficient.

Copyright Goodheart-Willcox Co., Inc.

Speaking

Speaking is verbal communication with others. When speaking with others, always be polite and do not interrupt. When speaking with someone for the first time, identify yourself at the beginning of the conversation. During the conversation, wait until the other person is finished talking before answering any questions or giving input. Effective speakers always keep their purpose for speaking in mind.

Sometimes the first contact a person may have with a business is over the phone. When speaking on the phone, be pleasant with the caller even if the situation is stressful or the caller is upset. When taking phone messages, write clearly and include the correct contact information.

Some entrepreneurs must give oral presentations to make sales or gain clients. Presentation software or flipcharts can be used to create visual aids for presentations. If using visual aids, make sure they are large enough to read and use short, bulleted phrases. Effective speakers correctly and clearly pronounce their words.

It is important for presenters to know how to speak well in public. There are numerous classes that help business people learn the skills for effective public speaking. If your business revenue depends on making presentations, look into taking Toastmasters or Dale Carnegie classes.

Entrepreneurs must be confident when introducing themselves. When introducing yourself, tell the person your name and the name of your company. When the other person gives his or her name, repeat the person's name as you greet him or her. Saying a person's name after being introduced will help you remember it. When approaching someone you have met before but do not know well, introduce yourself again. This saves all parties from embarrassment if names have been forgotten. Doing this also shows your professionalism.

 You Do the Math   Algebraic Reasoning

In algebra, letters stand in place of unknown numbers. These letters are called *variables*. When a variable appears with numbers and signs for adding, subtracting, multiplying, or dividing, the expression is called a *variable expression*. For example, *x* + 5 is a variable expression.

Solve the following problems.

1. Travis sells advertising space in the local newspaper. The price for an ad is based on how many inches of vertical space it fills. The rate for ad space is $2.37 per inch. Write a variable expression to calculate the price of ad space.

2. A business orders $350 worth of office equipment from a single supplier each month. Payment for the order is made in a single payment or is sometimes divided into equal smaller payments. Write a variable expression to calculate equal payment amounts for the office equipment order.

Listening

To be an effective listener, a manager first has to understand the difference between hearing and listening. Hearing is a physical process. You hear sounds. **Listening** involves evaluating what is heard.

In business, effective listeners engage in *active listening*. They listen for specific information and identify the purpose of the speaker. Carefully listen to what the speaker is saying and use prior knowledge to evaluate it. Effective listeners show attention to the speaker and take notes as needed. When feedback to the speaker is required, effective listeners provide it.

iofoto/Shutterstock.com

Speaking, listening, and writing are three basic business communication skills.

Copyright Goodheart-Willcox Co., Inc.

Writing

Writing is communicating using visible words and characters. Follow proper business etiquette in all written business communication. The **four Cs of communication** are the qualities of clarity, conciseness, courtesy, and correctness. These standards apply to all types of written communication. Communication that contains typographical errors or poor language usage reflects negatively on both you and the business for which you work.

Use the accepted business letter format for formal letters. E-mail is a time-saver, but it is still important to be professional—even in informal communication. A few e-mail tips include the following.

- *Never* use texting language.

- Use the subject line to show an e-mail's content or purpose.

- Use correct spelling, grammar, and punctuation.

- Keep messages brief, concise, and professional.

- Use sentence case only; do not write in all capital letters.

- Use a company signature with contact information.

- Send timely responses, but do not overload a person's inbox with too many e-mails.

- Always remember e-mail is company property; it can be forwarded to anyone.

Section 13.2 Review

Check Your Understanding ↗

1. List and describe the four management styles.

2. Describe an effective manager.

3. Explain the importance of empowering employees.

4. What does it mean to learn from your mistakes?

5. Why are professional business communication skills so important for a manager or business owner to possess?

Build Your Vocabulary ↗

As you progress through this text, develop a personal glossary of key terms. This will help you build your vocabulary and prepare you for a career. Write a definition for each of the following terms and add them to your personal glossary.

management style
situational
    management
democratic style
autocratic style
consulting style
laissez-faire style

empower
open-door policy
speaking
listening
writing
four Cs of
    communication

Chapter Summary

Section 13.1 **Managers**

- Business management is the process of reaching organizational goals efficiently and effectively by utilizing people and other resources so the business may deliver goods or services. Planning, organizing, staffing, leading, and controlling are all essential business management functions.

- Effective management requires effective leadership. Leaders have a strong vision for the company, and motivate and inspire employees, vendors, and customers.

- Building a strong and effective team takes time and effort. Leaders promote strong teams by helping all members work cooperatively to realize the leader's vision.

Section 13.2 **Management Styles and Communication**

- There are four basic management styles—democratic, autocratic, consulting, and laissez-faire. The difference between the styles revolves around how a manager approaches decision making.

- Technical skills or job-specific skills, conceptual and decision-making skills, as well as people skills are essential for managers. In addition, a manager must motivate employees, delegate work, listen to the employees' ideas and concerns, learn from mistakes, and show respect and equal treatment to everyone.

- Successful managers and business owners practice a high level of professional business communication at all times. Effective communication is not just speaking. It is also listening and writing.

Online Activities

Complete the following activities to help you learn, practice, and expand your knowledge and skills.

📲 **Posttest.** Now that you have finished the chapter, see what you learned by taking the chapter posttest.

📲 **Key Terms.** Practice vocabulary for this chapter using the e-flash cards, matching activity, and vocabulary game until you are able to recognize their meanings.

Review Your Knowledge

1. What is someone who teaches or gives help and advice to a less-experienced person called?

2. Why is an organizational chart important?

Copyright Goodheart-Willcox Co., Inc.

3. What stage of the management process involves setting goals?

4. What is the difference between strategic planning and tactical planning?

5. Explain the importance of operational planning.

6. What are the four different management styles?

7. Why is it important to share the company's vision with customers and employees?

8. List some of the effective management skills necessary to be a good leader.

9. List some of the characteristics of an effective manager.

10. What motivates employees?

Apply Your Knowledge

1. As a manager, which of the five management processes would you find the hardest to perform? Which is most critical for your business?

2. An entrepreneur must demand that team members work together effectively and apply common courtesies. Create an outline of communication expectations for your team. Include the following categories: listening skills, verbal skills, and nonverbal skills. Under each category, write appropriate suggestions that explain how each should be applied. In addition, explain the importance of team collaboration and the impact on your company's success.

3. Imagine that you are in year one of your business. Will you need employees? Describe your organization.

4. Imagine that you are in year five of your business. List the positions you will have in the business and describe each.

5. List and describe the leadership skills you currently possess that will make you successful in business. Identify the leadership skills that you need to develop to improve your chances of success.

6. Suppose you are visiting the office of a potential investor for your business. When you arrive, you are instructed to go to the CEO's office. Because this is the first meeting, you will introduce yourself to the CEO. Then, you will discuss the goals of your business and explain why investing in your company is a good decision. Prepare an information presentation about your business that you would use in this situation.

7. Which leadership style best describes you? Why?

8. List and describe the management skills you currently possess that will make you successful in business.

9. Professional behavior is required in the workplace. Describe what *professionalism* means to you. How can you demonstrate professionalism by conducting yourself in a manner appropriate for your business? How can you demonstrate a positive, productive work ethic to help employees perform their assigned tasks?

Copyright Goodheart-Willcox Co., Inc.

10. As a leader and entrepreneur, how will you learn from your mistakes to improve your leadership of the company?

Teamwork

Working with a classmate, select a small businesses in your community. Call the owner, visit the website of the business, or make an in-person visit. Ask the owner to describe his or her philosophy about managing employees in the business. What management traits does he or she think are important for new managers? Compare and contrast this person's opinion to the information presented in this chapter. Present your findings to the class.

Internet Research

Personal Information Management (PIM). Using the Internet, research *personal information management (PIM) systems*. Identify a system that would work for you as an entrepreneur. Demonstrate how you can incorporate a PIM system into your daily business activities to help you prioritize tasks, follow schedules, and optimize efficiency.

Communication Skills

College and Career Readiness

Reading. Read a magazine, newspaper, or online article about the importance of leadership in the workplace. Determine the central ideas of the article and review the conclusions made by the author. Provide an accurate summary of your reading, making sure to incorporate the *who, what, when,* and *how* of this situation.

Writing. Generate ideas that relate to the importance of time-management skills. Write a script that you could use to explain to a friend how an entrepreneur can demonstrate good time-management skills. Discuss why prioritizing tasks is important. Describe how an entrepreneur can learn or improve time-management skills, such as by creating schedules and setting SMART goals to optimize efficiency.

Listening. Practice active-listening skills while your teacher presents a lesson. Focus on the message and monitor yourself for understanding. Were there any barriers to effective listening? How did you use prior experiences to help you understand what was being said? Share your ideas in a group discussion.

Copyright Goodheart-Willcox Co., Inc.

CTSOs

Promoting Entrepreneurship. Some Career and Technical Student Organizations (CTSOs) have competitive events where the chapter spends the school year developing and carrying out a marketing campaign that promotes entrepreneurship. This event provides chapters with the opportunity to demonstrate knowledge of entrepreneurial concepts while making presentations to audiences in their community. For the competition, the chapter is required to prepare a report detailing a marketing campaign and present the report to a panel of judges. To prepare for an entrepreneurship marketing campaign chapter project, complete the following activities.

1. Read the guidelines provided by your organization. Make certain that you ask any questions about points you do not understand. It is important to follow each specific item that is outlined in the competition rules.

2. Contact the association immediately at the end of the state conference to prepare for next year's event.

3. As a team, select a theme for the marketing campaign to promote entrepreneurship.

4. Decide which roles are needed for the team. There may be one person who is the captain, one person who is the secretary, and any other roles that will be necessary to create the plan. Ask your instructor for guidance in assigning roles to team members.

5. Study chapter 11 for ideas for the campaign and chapter 12 for marketing ideas.

6. Identify your target audience, which may include business, school, and community groups.

7. Brainstorm with members of your chapter. Make a list of the benefits and opportunities available through entrepreneurship that can be communicated beyond your chapter membership.

8. This project will probably span the school year. During regular chapter meetings, create a draft of the report based on direction from the CTSO. Write and refine drafts until the final report is finished.

Copyright Goodheart-Willcox Co., Inc.

Building Your Business Plan—Putting the Puzzle Together

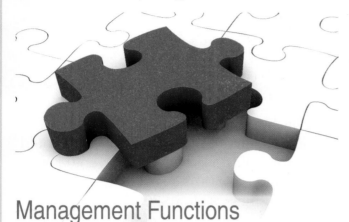

Management Functions

One of the most important roles an entrepreneur takes on is the one of manager. As the sole employee, many new entrepreneurs manage every area of the business until it grows large enough to add staff. Some people assume that managing a business and other people comes naturally. In fact, there are processes and skills related to the management function that are helpful to learn and develop. Planning, organizing, staffing, leading, and controlling are all part of the managerial process.

Goals

- Create an organizational chart for your business.
- Create business plan notes.

Directions

Access the *Entrepreneurship* companion website at www.g-wlearning.com [icon]. Download each data file for the following activities. A complete sample business plan is available on the companion website to use as a reference. The name of the file is Bus Plan_Sample.RetroAttire. docx.

Preparation

Activity 13-1. Organizational Chart. Create an organizational chart for your business. If the business will open with less than five employees, create a future organizational chart for the business when it grows larger.

Activity 13-2. Business Plan Notes. Complete the information about your leadership style and skills and traits you have that will make you a good manager. Keep your notes as reference information for your business plan.

Business Plan—Operations

In this chapter, you learned about becoming an effective manager and a leader. Now, you will work on the portions of the Operations section of the business plan that relate to management.

1. Open your saved business plan document.

2. Locate the Operations section of the business plan and the Management Team subsection. Describe your management plans for strategic, tactical, and operational planning.

3. Begin writing the Human Resources subsection as it relates to managing employees. Describe the management structure.

4. Add the organizational chart to the Appendices. Use the suggestions and questions listed in each section of the template to help you generate ideas. Delete the instructions and questions when you are finished writing each section. Make sure to proofread your document and correct any errors in keyboarding, spelling, and grammar.

5. Save your document.

14 Human Resources Management

Brian Scudamore started his business right after he graduated from high school. He saw a junk-hauling truck and thought he could do the same thing to help pay for college. What would eventually become an international corporation, 1-800-GOT-JUNK, was started in 1989. Scudamore started his business with a $700 investment and a 23-year-old pickup truck. After just one week, Scudamore hired his first employee. Lacking in human resources management experience, he simply hired a friend. While many entrepreneurs hire contract workers or outsource their needs, Scudamore believes in hiring employees. He believes investing in employees instead of contracting them shows dedication to and faith in the business. What will you do when you need to add staff to your business?

"People are definitely a company's greatest asset. It doesn't make any difference whether the product is cars or cosmetics. A company is only as good as the people it keeps."

—Mary Kay Ash, founder of Mary Kay Cosmetics

College and Career Readiness

Reading Prep. Recall all the things you know about entrepreneurship. As you read, think of how the new information presented in the text matches or challenges your prior understanding of the topic. Think of direct connections you can make between the old material and the new material.

Sections

14.1 Human Resources

14.2 Develop the Staff

Picture Yourself Here
Darryl Bordenave Jr.

In 2007, Darryl Bordenave Jr. founded Ruckage Design Company in Atlanta, Georgia. He was just 18 years old and became one of Atlanta's youngest entrepreneurs.

Darryl began designing clothing at the age of 13, sewing all his work by hand. It was not until he enrolled in college that he was introduced to the sewing machine. He explains: "While other college students were waiting for the professor to teach them about designing, I was taking it upon myself to do it for myself. I would participate in fashion shows getting the experience that I needed for the fashion industry. By getting involved in fashion events and fashion shows, I have been able to network and build up my contacts. It really helped put my face and company out there."

Like most entrepreneurs, Darryl feels there is always room for improvement. When asked about the key factors for being an entrepreneur, he replies "DREAM—or drive, resources, eagerness, ambition, and motivation." He also believes successful businesses should give back to the community. Darryl put together a national campaign called the D.R.E.A.M. Tour. The D.R.E.A.M. Tour visits different high schools and colleges to put on inspirational performances and encourage students to follow their own dreams.

Photo © James L. Young Photography Inc.

Check Your Entrepreneurship IQ

Before you begin the chapter, see what you already know about entrepreneurship by taking the chapter pretest. The pretest is available at www.g-wlearning.com

SECTION 14.1 Human Resources

Essential Question

What is the role of human resource management in the operation of a business?

Objectives

After completing this section, you will be able to:

- **Describe** the importance of human resources management in a business.
- **Explain** the management function of staffing a business.
- **Identify** the steps involved in the hiring process.
- **Discuss** various forms of employee compensation.

Key Terms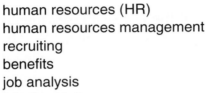

human resources (HR)
human resources management
recruiting
benefits
job analysis
job description
job posting

compensation
overtime pay
commission
bonus
profit sharing
stock option

Critical Thinking

Interview adults in your family about their employment compensation packages. Find out what they like or dislike about them. Describe the forms of compensation you may want to offer your employees after your business is established and successful.

HR

HR—you have heard the acronym many times. HR is at the core of every business. **Human resources (HR)** are the employees who work for a company. Human resources are important to the economy. As a business expands, it will probably add employees. Once the team grows, human resources become critical to the success of a business.

However, a small business owner may not be able to hire a full-time human resources manager and may instead have to assume the role. Managing employees might seem like an easy job. Just hire people who want to work and then let them do the jobs. However, finding and managing employees may be the most difficult, time-consuming, and costly part of doing business.

Human resources management is facilitating and managing employees in an organization. Human resources managers play an important, strategic role in a company. It is their goal to help

Copyright Goodheart-Willcox Co., Inc.

management meet the vision of the company by performing vital tasks such as hiring, training, payroll, and everything in between. Figure 14-1 shows some HR management tasks.

Attracting the best employees is always the number one HR goal for a manager or business owner. The perfect employee with every necessary skill does not just appear at a company's doorstep. Recruiting is the process of finding suitable people and getting them to join a company.

In addition to wages, benefits are often provided to employees. Benefits are the extras over and above regular pay given to employees by employers. Benefit offerings such as vacation time and health insurance are determined by the employer. Full-time employees usually receive benefits when they are offered. However, part-time employees typically are not offered benefits.

Benefits are additional ways businesses reward their employees for their work, although benefits are costly. These can include health, dental, vision, and life insurance; disability protection; retirement plans; paid sick and vacation days; and education reimbursement.

Staffing

Staffing is a management function, as discussed in chapter 13, and the manager plays an important role in this step. Staffing the business, or hiring employees, is a decision that should be taken seriously. The staff are the face of the business, so it is important to hire only the best and the brightest candidates. This important HR task helps a company meet its mission.

As manager, and entrepreneur, the decision to add employees should be based on the needs of the business, not its wants. Employees are expensive resources. Before adding new staff, analyze the situation

Human Resources Management	
Staffing	Finding and hiring qualified employees
Training	Planning for and providing the specialized training each employee needs
Payroll	Paying employee and contractor salaries, state and federal income taxes, and maintaining employee records
Benefits	Overseeing the benefits package, making sure practices meet legal requirements
Recordkeeping	Maintaining personnel files
Employment laws	Ensuring fair treatment of employees, including following equal opportunity, safety, and other workplace-related laws

Figure 14-1. Human resources management involves a wide variety of employee-related functions.

Goodheart-Willcox Publisher

Copyright Goodheart-Willcox Co., Inc.

to make sure it is the correct move for the business at the time. For established businesses, human resources planning includes working with the management team to set goals for a company's growth. The management team establishes the financial milestones to be met before new employees are hired.

Identify Needs

The first step in hiring or replacing employees is to analyze the needs of the business. New employees should fill a need for the business as well as relieve the manager of some responsibilities.

Does the company have the money to pay for employees? If the answer is yes, how many hours will employees be needed to work, and will they be paid a salary, wages, or commission?

Does the place of business have enough space for additional employees? If not, can the business afford to move to a larger facility?

Are there skills needed for the business that the owner does not have? What new skills does the business need?

By going through the exercise of identifying needs, an owner may discover that a full-time employee is not necessary. If the business has a seasonal cycle, a part-time or temporary employee might be enough. High school and college interns are also a good source for inexpensive short-term help. When hiring a new employee, determine the weekly hours and wages for a new position to make sure the company can afford the employee.

Create a Job Analysis

Once a company knows it needs employees, the next step is to complete a job analysis for each position. A **job analysis** identifies a new position's job requirements, employee qualifications, and how success will be evaluated. It lists the:

- tasks and duties of the position;

- methods and equipment used;

- necessary skills and experience level;

- physical limitations for the position;

- preferred level of education;

- level of management responsibility; and

- goals for the position and how they will be measured.

Established businesses may hire a human resources specialist to conduct job analyses for future positions. For new businesses, however, the owner is probably the best person to do this task for the first employees.

Copyright Goodheart-Willcox Co., Inc.

Analyze the business' needs to find out how many employees you should hire, and if they should be full time.

auremar/Shutterstock.com

Write a Job Description

The next step is to write a **job description** that defines the position and the expectations. It is based on the job analysis. The job description should be detailed. An example of a short, basic job description is shown in Figure 14-2. A job description:

- gives the title of the position and to whom it reports;

- gives a salary range or salary ranking;

- describes all of the responsibilities of the position;

- lists and describes skills, knowledge, and other specific talents required to perform the job; and

- lists education and experience required for the position.

The job description is helpful when recruiting and also to use as a guideline for employee evaluations. An attorney or human resources specialist can help to create a job description.

Job Description

Job title: Customer Service Representative
Reports to: Regional Sales Manager
Supervises: n/a
Salary rank: 8
Key responsibilities:
- Troubleshoot customer complaints
- Provide support for product inquiries
- Generate sales leads
- Maintain information in a customer relationship management (CRM) software system
- Attend training when requested

Job skills: Present product features and benefits in person, over the telephone, and via e-mail. Communicate clearly and concisely with customers to provide solutions for their needs. Comfortable with cold calling. Manage multiple customer relationships.

Computer skills: Must be proficient in a CRM program, Microsoft Office Suite, and social media.

Experience and education: Bachelor degree and one year of sales or CRM experience or equivalent of five years sales and CRM experience.

Goodheart-Willcox Publisher

Figure 14-2. Job description sample.

Create an Application

A job application is important to the hiring process for any business. Even though many applicants submit résumés, they may not be complete or not include the person's references. Have all applicants complete a standardized job application to ensure you have the necessary information. Some businesses ask applicants to complete online applications on the business' websites.

New businesses may not yet have a job application for candidates to complete. Job application forms can be purchased online or from an office supply store to customize to meet the needs of the business. Remember to follow the state and federal guidelines for job applications and seek professional legal guidance on the final form.

Recruit

Once the job description and application are created, recruiting begins. As a new business owner, recruiting may be a greater challenge than it is for established companies. Established businesses

Copyright Goodheart-Willcox Co., Inc.

> **CUSTOMER SERVICE REPRESENTATIVE**
>
> Full- and part-time schedules available. Must enjoy working with people and as part of a team.
>
> Minimum qualifications: Bachelor degree preferred with one or more years in sales or customer service. For more information and to apply online, visit www.RetroAttire.com.

Goodheart-Willcox Publisher

Figure 14-3. Classified print advertisement or copy to use in a job posting.

may offer higher salaries or more benefits. However, there are many people looking for growth opportunities who want to work for start-up businesses.

Write the **job posting**, which is the advertisement for an open position. A typical job posting is shown in Figure 14-3. There are multiple places to post open jobs or make an announcement to attract potential candidates. Most job seekers use the Internet to find open positions. It is easy and inexpensive for businesses to post jobs on many online sites. There are other ways to find qualified candidates.

Company Website

A company website is recommended for all businesses, especially new ones. This is the perfect place to post job listings for new employees. Applicants may also be directed to fill out a job application on the website.

Online Employment Sites

Numerous online sites exist for employers to advertise job openings. Employment websites like Monster, Indeed, CareerBuilder, and SimplyHired are job boards for posting open positions.

Social Media

Social media sites can be very effective in attracting potential employees as well as generating new customers. Twitter, Facebook, and YouTube are several examples of free social media tools businesses use for recruiting purposes. Some social media sites for professionals, such as LinkedIn, may have a small fee to post a listing, but are free for job seekers. Social media sites are good for networking purposes as well.

Career and College Placement Offices

Career and technical centers, colleges, and universities operate career-placement offices as a student service. The placement offices encourage any business to post job listings that will fit graduate job skills. It is a free service for both the businesses to post and students to search for open jobs.

When hiring employees, it is important to follow the laws on employee eligibility. Small business owners must make sure they verify employment eligibility and do not discriminate when hiring employees. The governmental e-verify system can be used to determine employment eligibility.

Global Entrepreneurs

James Dowd and Justin Brown

Many entrepreneurs do not create something completely new; they just look to improve an existing product or service. Native New Yorker James Dowd worked in sales at shipping company DHL. He eventually saw an opportunity not being met in shipping and started First Global Xpress (FGX) in 2001 with the help of investors. Dowd soon recruited Justin Brown, a young sales executive.

FGX is an international air-shipping company that promises overseas shipping 24 hours faster than traditional shippers and offers lower rates. The company achieves these results by operating differently from traditional shippers. Doing things differently also allows FGX to reduce the carbon footprint of the shipping process.

To keep costs down, FGX does not have its own planes. Instead, it contracts with about 115 commercial airlines to carry packages. By doing this, the company does not need to keep its own fleet of planes. It also makes use of the airlines' existing means of moving packages. Other shippers send parcels through a local hub at the point of shipping and the point of delivery. Not only does this hub-and-spoke system slow down the shipping process, FGX believes the system allows more opportunities for packages to be lost or damaged.

Job Fairs

Job fairs are a great way to actually meet potential employees. Various organizations sell booth space for employers to present information about their businesses. Job seekers go to the employers' booths for which they are interested in working. They discuss job opportunities, submit résumés, and complete applications.

Classified Ads

One of the oldest methods of recruiting is using the newspaper classified ads. Print newspapers may not be the most cost-effective tool. However, some print newspapers also are available online and may attract job seekers who are used to searching online.

Employment Agencies

Some businesses use private or governmental employment agencies to recruit for them. These services are usually costly. Therefore, they may not be an affordable option for a new business.

Copyright Goodheart-Willcox Co., Inc.

Applications and résumés outline a potential employee's qualities and skills.

Production Perig/Shutterstock.com

Hiring Process

The hiring process takes a lot of time, and time is money. An efficient hiring process is important. The person interviewing should not be distracted from keeping the company running by hiring an employee. It is also important that the person hiring understands current state and federal laws and guidelines for hiring employees.

Once the business starts receiving applications or résumés, start screening them for a potential fit. Some applicants will have the experience, education, and skills that match the job description. Others will match only part of the job description. Still others will not match at all. Use your judgment to select several top candidates and begin the interviewing process.

It is important that the interviewer not be distracted when conducting an interview. Phone or face-to-face interviews may take place outside of the business' working hours.

When interviewing candidates, there are very strict guidelines that must be followed to avoid discrimination. Interviewers may not ask questions about a person's age, marital status, race, religion, citizenship, or national origin. If certain information is needed to

Entrepreneur Ethics

Employers have employees that come and go in the business. As employees leave, their potential new employers may contact former employers to confirm the employee's job experience. It is important to maintain an ethical attitude when sharing information about former employees to new employers. Stick to the facts of employment and do not share confidential information that may jeopardize their new job opportunities.

qualify a person for a job, there are appropriate ways to word the questions, as shown in Figure 14-4.

A typical hiring process is as follows.

1. Screen the applications.

2. Set up a phone interview.

3. Set up a face-to-face interview.

4. Perform a background check on the final candidates.

5. If the open position requires specific skills, conduct an employment test to evaluate them.

6. Make the final hiring decision.

7. Call the candidate to verbally extend a job offer.

8. Inform the candidates who were not hired by sending a polite rejection letter.

Figure 14-4. Some questions may not be legally asked during an interview.

Interviewing Guidelines	
Possible Discrimination	**Legal Questions to Ask Applicants**
Age It is against the law to refuse to hire a qualified candidate based on age.	• Are you over 18? • What are your career plans?
Gender It is important that you do not make judgments about a person's abilities based on their gender.	• What can you do for our company? • Explain your previous experience working with others.
Heath and physical information Any necessary information about physical abilities to perform a job can be learned without asking personal questions.	• Will you be able to reach our display shelves, which are over five feet? • Will you be able to lift more than 40 pounds?
Marital or family status. Some employers may be worried that men and women who are planning to have children soon will leave the company. While you cannot legally ask that question, there are ways to ensure that the people you hire still plan to work even after having children.	• Did you receive a degree or work under a different name? • Will you be able to work overtime?
Citizenship It is illegal to discriminate based on citizenship status or nationality.	• Are you authorized to work in the United States?

Goodheart-Willcox Publisher

Copyright Goodheart-Willcox Co., Inc.

Review the potential candidates for fit in the company. Select the top candidates to begin the interviewing process.

The initial contact with a candidate may be a phone interview. By having a phone conversation with the person, candidates may be eliminated or selected for a face-to-face interview.

The face-to-face interview is the time to meet the candidates who have passed the phone screening. It is the opportunity to sell the business and find the right person for the job.

Confirm the previous job experience and education listed on the application or résumé. Contact the references provided and, if needed, do any type of security checks.

There are three types of employment tests. *Ability tests* monitor the physical, mental, and clerical abilities of applicants. For example, an assembly line worker may be tested to see if he or she has manual dexterity. *Performance tests* evaluate the applicant's ability to perform the job. For example, if the job is for a copywriter, a writing test may be given to assess the person's writing ability. *Personality tests* measure applicants' personality traits. Evaluating personality traits may make it easier to know how an applicant might work with customers and other employees.

Select the person that most closely fits the business' needs and corporate culture. This is the person who will be extended an offer of employment.

Do not make a job offer by e-mail. After the candidate accepts the position, put the offer in writing along with the salary, start date, and any pre-employment conditions. Drug screening is often considered part of the pre-employment process.

Sending rejected candidates a polite letter is common courtesy and leaves a positive impression with those people, which is good for business.

Compensation

Compensation includes wages or salaries, incentives, and benefits. It can also be called a *compensation package*. Wages and salaries may be calculated differently. Wages are typically paid per hour that the employee works. Under certain circumstances, hourly employees earn **overtime pay**, which is typically 1 1/2 times their hourly rate. A salary is a set amount of income established for a given period of time, such as one month or one year.

Salaried positions do not earn overtime pay. Incentives for salaried employees for working long hours or reaching set goals, or to keep top performers, may include the following.

- **Commissions** on sales are a percentage of the sale paid to the salesperson.

- **Bonuses** are cash awards given to employees who reach certain performance goals.

SBA Tips

Approximately 70 percent of all US exporters have less than 20 employees. Increasing US exports benefits the entire economy. The SBA has several very attractive lending programs to help entrepreneurs start or expand export business activities. The International Trade Loan Program and the Export Working Loan Program lend to small exporters for working capital and expansion. Many loans are guaranteed up to 90 percent by the government.
www.sba.gov

Copyright Goodheart-Willcox Co., Inc.

- Retirement plan contributions may be made, such as to a 401(k) or a pension.

- **Profit sharing** is the distribution of a percentage of the profits to employees, usually on an annual basis.

- **Stock options** are shares of company stock that employees can purchase at a discount as a form of compensation.

As a new business owner, your compensation plan may be very simple. However, as the business grows, a compensation program may need more attention. Seek professional human resources management advice when evaluating various compensation packages.

Green Entrepreneurs

Recycle Printer Cartridges

Recycling printer ink cartridges instead of buying new ones is a way to save money and help the environment. Many office-supply stores offer an ink refilling service, which is less expensive than buying new cartridges. Office-supply stores may also offer recycling programs where new cartridges are sold at reduced prices when used ones are brought in. The used cartridges are refilled and then sold to customers at much lower prices than new ones. Either way, this can save money and landfill space by recycling printer cartridges.

Copyright Goodheart-Willcox Co., Inc.

Section 14.1 Review

Check Your Understanding ⇱

1. List three challenges associated with hiring and managing employees.
2. What is the difference between a job analysis and a job description?
3. What methods can be used to recruit employees?
4. What procedures could be used in screening applicants?
5. What are the different ways to compensate employees?

Build Your Vocabulary ⇱

As you progress through this text, develop a personal glossary of key terms. This will help you build your vocabulary and prepare you for a career. Write a definition for each of the following terms and add them to your personal glossary.

human resources (HR)
human resources management
recruiting
benefits
job analysis
job description
job posting
compensation
overtime pay
commission
bonus
profit sharing
stock option

Copyright Goodheart-Willcox Co., Inc.

Develop the Staff

Objectives

After completing this section, you will be able to:

- **List** various ways to provide employee training.
- **Summarize** the relationship existing between employers and employees.
- **Describe** two types of HR manuals.

ssential
uestion

How do businesses carry out the task of developing their staff?

Key Terms

orientation
professional development
performance appraisal
promotion
ergonomics
conflict resolution

employee-complaint procedure
labor relations
policy manual
employee handbook
intranet

Critical Thinking

Research options that employers can use for employee training. Make a list of possible resources you might choose to use for training employees in your business. Next to each option, write a brief description of its pros and cons.

Training

All employees need some form of training, especially the recent hires. To have a business that runs efficiently, provide regular training on how to maintain and improve job skills. Technology changes quickly, and training is needed to keep everyone up to date. Employees may also need to be trained on how to interact well with each other, customers, and vendors.

Orientation

An **orientation** period helps new employees become familiar with the business, fellow employees, and the job duties. Employees who are welcomed into the business are likely to feel more secure as they learn about their positions. Every orientation period will be different and will include company-specific information. Some orientations last one day, while others take place over weeks.

Copyright Goodheart-Willcox Co., Inc.

Company Mission and Operations

Each employee should know the purpose of the business and what products are manufactured or sold. Take this opportunity to review the company's vision and mission statements.

Job Routine

Job procedures, performance expectations, and the method for evaluation should be explained. The employee should be told the amount of time the supervisor thinks it will take to learn how to do the job well. New employees should be introduced to their coworkers and managers.

Human Resources Rules

The details of the compensation package should be explained. Also, any rules or regulations that are specific to the business should be discussed.

Professional Development

Professional development is training on the skills and knowledge that contribute to employees' personal growth and career advancement. Some businesses pay for classes taken by employees that help them do their jobs better. Businesses have many options for offering professional development training, including the following.

- on-the-job training; a new employee observes how an experienced worker performs his or her job

- classroom instruction; employees are taught in a classroom setting, which may include role-playing and video or workbook instruction

- e-learning; educational programs, classes, or other electronic training tools may be accessed on the Internet to provide specific instruction

- job rotation; employees are rotated through different jobs to learn a full set of skills

- conferences and seminars; employees may attend professional conferences, seminars, or web-based seminars to stay up to date on the industry

- mentoring; each new employee is assigned to an experienced employee for continuous instruction and guidance while working

- coaching; employees receive instruction and feedback from a manager who coaches them in their job performance

Providing professional development training helps to build and maintain employee morale and may even attract higher-quality employees.

FYI

Creating and maintaining a daily planner can help an employee develop a systematic approach to his or her job. New employee training can include a demonstration on how to maintain a daily planner.

Copyright Goodheart-Willcox Co., Inc.

Professional development
will create a high-quality
staff and attract skilled new
applicants.

Goodluz/Shutterstock.com

Employer-Employee Relationship

Workers provide the human resource factor of production that makes business possible. The relationship between employers and their employees is more than the exchange of labor for money. Self-worth, dignity, satisfaction, and a sense of pride come from the jobs performed by your employees. There is often a social aspect to the workplace because employees want to enjoy the people in their working environments.

Employees want to feel appreciated and valued as a contributor to the business. No one wants to work for an employer who does not value the work he or she does. Provide opportunities for advancement and pay increases to keep employees motivated. Even small business owners can still reward employees for their work and help them grow professionally.

Employees have the right to expect fair treatment at work. Chapter 8 details the workplace laws that protect both employers and employees. Clean and safe facilities are also important to job satisfaction.

Listen to what your employees say about the business. They can have many creative, helpful ideas. When a conflict arises, learn

Copyright Goodheart-Willcox Co., Inc.

Focus on Finance

Investment Portfolios

An investment portfolio is the collection of assets, stocks, bonds, and other investments owned by an individual. As a business owner, consider creating a separate investment portfolio for your business as part of a financial plan.

As revenues increase, you may decide to put that extra money not necessary for daily business operations to work by making investments with it. Creating and adding to an investment portfolio is a good way to continually build wealth for the future of the company. Consult a financial planner to help you form a solid financial plan for your business.

how to quickly and reasonably resolve it to prevent poor morale or breakdown of the team.

Employee Evaluation

The evaluation process is one way to ensure employees know they are valued. Each business establishes a time period in which to evaluate employees. Employee evaluations are part of the management process of controlling.

Some organizations complete a performance appraisal after the first 30 days, every six months, or on an annual basis. A **performance appraisal** is the assessment of an employee's job performance and the progress made toward achieving set goals. Part of an appraisal is providing feedback to improve performance and assist with professional development. Most employers use a combination of objective and subjective appraisals in a performance appraisal.

Objective appraisals are based on the achievement of specific goals. They are usually easy to measure because they are often based on sales goals or completion of certain tasks. For example, one measurement may be an employee's daily sales goals. The given amount of expected daily sales is either met or not met.

Subjective appraisals are based on the individual's behaviors and behavioral traits. For example, a behavioral appraisal might include measuring attendance according to a rating scale. The scale might range from *always early to work* to *frequently late* with categories in between. Behavioral traits might include attitude, initiative, and leadership skills.

Managers may also ask employees to complete a self-appraisal. This helps employees have a sense of ownership in the business and their careers. The performance goals for the upcoming year are set in the review process. The appraisal, as well as self-appraisal, should be conducted using an appraisal form, as shown in Figure 14-5.

A new business owner will most likely need to create an appraisal form. Free templates can be found on many human resources-related websites.

Copyright Goodheart-Willcox Co., Inc.

Seek advice from a human resources specialist or attorney when creating the final appraisal form. It is important to follow state and federal laws when evaluating employee performance.

Promotion

As multiple employees are hired, it is a good policy to recognize those who perform at an outstanding level by promoting them. **Promotion** is moving an employee to a higher-level position. It is a motivating tool and also reinforces leadership. Promotions are often tied to excellent performance appraisals. They allow employees to apply individual skills and talents and become more involved in the business. Make sure the policy for promotions is applied fairly.

Termination

Nearly every business will have employees who choose to leave or are dismissed. This may be one of the least popular parts of business ownership. In every case, losing an employee should be handled with sensitivity. Some very good employees will take new positions elsewhere. Those employees will need to be replaced.

There are times when a company may have to trim staff due to economic reasons, not because of poor performance. In these cases, employees may receive a severance pay based on the length of time with the company. *Severance pay* is compensation intended to help employees while they look for another job. Employees are also owed any accumulated vacation or sick days and may be eligible to receive unemployment.

Sometimes owners must dismiss an employee for other reasons, such as poor job performance, breaking rules, or theft. A poor performance appraisal may start the process of termination. However, the employee should be given the opportunity to understand how to either improve or correct behaviors. If the employee cannot or will not meet the expectations, then the employer may legally dismiss him or her.

To prevent a *wrongful termination* lawsuit, however, document all meetings, discussions, and issues in writing. Documentation is very important when working with problem employees.

Workplace Safety

Workplace safety in the United States has continuously improved since the beginning of the 20th century. Gradually, injury, death, and illness related to working conditions have declined. This is due to a change in the type of work done today and in the safety precautions that have been put in place. Many workers now spend extended periods of time in front of computers. This can also result in injury. **Ergonomics** is the science of adapting the workstation to fit the needs of the worker and lessen the chance of injury. Figure 14-6 depicts the best way for a worker to sit at a computer workstation.

Copyright Goodheart-Willcox Co., Inc.

RetroAttire
Employee Performance Review

EMPLOYEE INFORMATION

Name	Employee ID
Job Title	Date
Department	Manager
Review Period to	

RATINGS

	1 = Poor	2 = Fair	3 = Satisfactory	4 = Good	5 = Excellent
Job Knowledge	❏	❏	❏	❏	❏
Comments					
Work Quality	❏	❏	❏	❏	❏
Comments					
Attendance/Punctuality	❏	❏	❏	❏	❏
Comments					
Initiative	❏	❏	❏	❏	❏
Comments					
Communication/Listening Skills	❏	❏	❏	❏	❏
Comments					
Dependability	❏	❏	❏	❏	❏
Comments					

Overall Rating *(average the rating numbers above)*

EVALUATION
ADDITIONAL COMMENTS

GOALS
*(as agreed upon
by employee and
manager)*

VERIFICATION OF REVIEW

By signing this form, you confirm that you have discussed this review in detail with your supervisor. Signing this form does not necessarily indicate that you agree with this evaluation.

Employee Signature	Date
Manager Signature	Date

Goodheart-Willcox Publisher

Figure 14-5. Employee performance appraisal example.

Copyright Goodheart-Willcox Co., Inc.

Workplace Accidents

Falling hazards, lifting hazards, and material-storage hazards account for most of the workplace accidents that occur in offices. Falling hazards are sources of potential injuries from slipping or falling. Falls are the most common workplace accident in an office setting. Falls can result in broken bones, head injuries, and muscle strains. Avoiding workplace falls is relatively simple:

- Close drawers completely.

- Do not stand on a chair or box to reach.

- Secure cords, rugs, and mats.

Lifting hazards are sources of potential injury from improperly lifting or carrying items. Most back injuries are caused by improper lifting. To avoid injuries resulting from lifting:

- make several small trips with items rather than one trip with an overly heavy load;

- use dollies or handcarts whenever possible;

- lift with the legs, not the back; and

- never carry an item that blocks vision.

Material-storage hazards are sources of potential injury that come from the improper storage of files, books, office equipment, or other items. A cluttered workplace is an unsafe workplace. Material stacked

Figure 14-6. Ergonomic workstations help prevent back and neck pain, eyestrain, and headaches caused by improper placement of monitors, desks, and chairs.

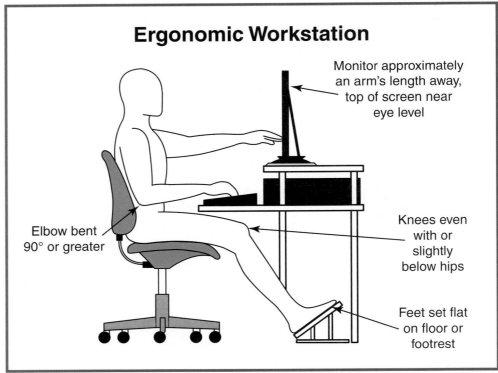

Ergonomic Workstation

Monitor approximately an arm's length away, top of screen near eye level

Elbow bent 90° or greater

Knees even with or slightly below hips

Feet set flat on floor or footrest

Goodheart-Willcox Publisher

Copyright Goodheart-Willcox Co., Inc.

too high can fall on employees. Paper and files that are stored on the floor or in the hall are a fire risk. To prevent injuries:

- do not stack boxes or papers on top of tall cabinets;

- store heavier objects on lower shelves; and

- keep aisles and hallways clear.

Maintaining a safe workplace is the joint responsibility of the employer and employee. The employer makes sure the facility and working conditions are such that accidents are unlikely to occur. The employee uses common sense and care while at the office.

Conflict Resolution

Conflict is a part of life. However, conflict in the workplace can harm a business if not resolved fairly and in a constructive manner. **Conflict resolution** is solving problems that usually arise when people or groups have different goals or needs. Every conflict is different, but there are several recommended steps for addressing most conflicts in the workplace.

- Listen first, talk second.

- Be calm, courteous, and try to diffuse anger.

- Separate the problems from the people; do not allow blaming.

- Determine the real, underlying issues; they may be totally valid.

- Make sure all parties agree to the facts.

- Explore the various solutions together; keep those who are not involved in the situation out of the discussions.

- Find a solution agreeable to all parties; if that is not possible, a mediator may be needed to make a final decision.

Employee Complaints

Create an **employee-complaint procedure**, which is a formal process for employees to share their issues with management. Put the procedure in writing and make sure all employees understand it. Complaint procedures usually follow the chain of authority. For example, the employee should first bring the problem to his or her direct manager. If that manager cannot resolve it, the complaint will go to the next management level.

Labor Relations

Labor relations is how the employer and employees behave toward each other, particularly during contract negotiations. Employees have the legal right to organize and bargain collectively with their employers. *Collective bargaining* is negotiating the terms of

The government offers tax credits to employers for hiring certain groups as well as to employers that modify their workplace to accommodate the needs of their disabled employees. Details on tax credits can be found on the IRS or SBA websites.

employment between an employer and a group of workers. This right was established in 1935 by the National Labor Relations Act (NLRA). Some industries have unions that negotiate contracts, wages, hours, and other employment terms and conditions with the businesses. The union leaders will also work with the management of a business to resolve any conflicts for its members.

HR Manuals

Most businesses have a policy manual to guide the management team as well as a handbook for employees. A **policy manual** outlines the company policies and procedures. This manual covers policies and how managers should apply them in the workplace. There are many free templates available on the Internet to help small businesses develop their own HR manuals.

The **employee handbook** translates the policies of the business into day-to-day information that the employees need to know. It may also list employee expectations, such as a dress code or lunch and break schedules. An employee handbook is a good way to provide company information for employees. Included in this handbook are topics such as compensation, benefits, rules, and other policies that management expects employees to follow, as shown in Figure 14-7.

Figure 14-7. Topics commonly covered in an employee handbook.

Employee Handbook Sections	
Employee Safety and Security	Company's commitment to safety, security procedures, anti-harassment guidelines, evacuation procedures
Compensation	Payroll practices, incentives, performance-based compensation, retirement plan options, overtime, wage or salary increases
Attendance	Time-keeping practices, vacation and sick days, lunch and breaks, hours of operation, medical leave
Benefits	Insurances offered, Social Security contribution, disability, tuition reimbursement, flextime options
Policies	Substance abuse, nondiscrimination, employee dress code, use of company property, Internet use, personnel records kept, workplace privacy, observed holidays
Procedures	Performance evaluations, employee complaints, company forms, supplies, telephone policies
Employee Communication	Staff meetings, board meetings, company newsletter, suggestion box, bulletin board information

Goodheart-Willcox Publisher

Copyright Goodheart-Willcox Co., Inc.

Rules and policies listed in an employee handbook are always subject to change. It is common practice to update an employee handbook at least once per year to reflect changes and updates. Many businesses post their employee handbooks on the company's intranet, or internal computer network. This method allows the company to easily update the manual as needed. It also greatly reduces printing costs and is a green business practice.

Keep in mind that information in a manual or handbook does *not* create a contract between the business and the employee. HR manuals are only intended guidelines for the business' daily operations. All employee handbooks should contain a disclaimer stating the handbook does not create a contract.

 You Do the Math   **Problem Solving and Reasoning**

In business and at home, you may be faced with checking the work of others. When presented with figures, it is often a good idea to check the solution for accuracy and effectiveness. For example, a business calculates the fuel economy of its delivery truck to be 19 miles per gallon. However, the fuel used on a 20-mile delivery run is four gallons. This means that either the calculation is incorrect or the reported usage is incorrect.

Solve the following problems.

1. A business sells 387 units of product for an average of $27.48 each. It reports the gross sales are $10,634.78. Is the reported sales figure correct?

2. Harris drives 687 miles in 16 hours. He uses 18.5 gallons of gasoline. He states that his car gets 47 miles to the gallon. Is he correct?

Copyright Goodheart-Willcox Co., Inc.

Section 14.2 Review

Check Your Understanding ⤏

1. List the professional development techniques employed by businesses.
2. How can an employer motivate his or her employees?
3. What is the difference between an objective and a subjective performance appraisal?
4. What factors have contributed to increased workplace safety over the past 100 years?
5. What are the steps in constructive conflict resolution managers can practice?

Build Your Vocabulary ⤏

As you progress through this text, develop a personal glossary of key terms. This will help you build your vocabulary and prepare you for a career. Write a definition for each of the following terms and add them to your personal glossary.

orientation
professional
   development
performance
   appraisal
promotion
ergonomics
conflict resolution

employee-
   complaint
   procedure
labor relations
policy manual
employee
   handbook
intranet

Copyright Goodheart-Willcox Co., Inc.

Chapter Summary

Section 14.1 **Human Resources**

- Human resources management is facilitating and managing employees in an organization. It is the goal of a human resources manager to help the company meet its vision and to perform tasks such as hiring, training, payroll, and other vital duties.

- Staffing is a function of management and needs to be taken seriously because the employees represent the business. There are several things management needs to consider before hiring anyone: indentifying business needs, considering the finances required to pay employees, and assessing the available space in which the employees will work.

- After the decision is made to hire a new employee, create a job analysis. Next, create a job description. Recruit employees based on those individuals who meet the job description. Be sure to create or purchase an application form, which will be used as a screening tool.

- Compensation is another important consideration when deciding to take on a new employee or keeping an existing one. Salary, wages, commission, and bonuses can be part of an overall compensation plan. What benefits to offer will impact the business' bottom line as well as its ability to retain good employees.

Section 14.2 **Develop the Staff**

- The first step in training new employees is through an orientation. Additional training beyond the orientation stage might include: on-the-job training, classroom instruction, e-learning, mentoring, coaching, job rotation, and conferences.

- Motivating employees is very important, especially when trying to maintain a staff of competent employees. To foster a positive relationship between the employer and employee, the employer should recognize the work employees perform; create a positive working environment by listening to what employees say; provide a safe working environment; and provide opportunities for advancement and pay.

- There are two basic types of HR manuals: the policy manual and the employee handbook. Each is designed to communicate operating procedures of an organization as well as the role of the employees within it. These manuals may be available in hard copy or online as part of the company's intranet.

Copyright Goodheart-Willcox Co., Inc.

Online Activities

Complete the following activities to help you learn, practice, and expand your knowledge and skills.

Posttest. Now that you have finished the chapter, see what you learned by taking the chapter posttest.

Key Terms. Practice vocabulary for this chapter using the e-flash cards, matching activity, and vocabulary game until you are able to recognize their meanings.

Review Your Knowledge

1. Describe the importance of human resources management.
2. What tasks does the human resources manager perform?
3. Before staffing your business, what steps should you take?
4. How do HR professionals advertise that there is an open position in a company?
5. What is the step-by-step process for hiring employees?
6. What are the three types of tests used to evaluate candidates for potential employment?
7. What should you include in the orientation training for a new employee?
8. What role does ergonomics play in preventing workplace injuries?
9. What is the difference between a policy manual and an employee manual?
10. What are the three controlling functions of management?

Apply Your Knowledge

1. You have identified your business and the goods or services you will offer. You probably will not hire employees when your business gets off the ground. However, you may want to hire employees as you grow. Using the information to identify your needs for staffing, analyze the needs of your company and when you think you would add staff.
2. Identify the first position you would want to fill in your organization. Why is this position important for you to hire first?
3. Write a job posting that you could use to recruit the first position you will be hiring in your organization. Identify the different media you will use to place the advertisement.
4. Visit the website for the US Equal Opportunity Commission. Select the tab for employers. Make notes on important issues that you need to know when hiring employees. What three issues do you think are most important as they relate to your company? Why?

Copyright Goodheart-Willcox Co., Inc.

5. Research on the Internet for job interviewing techniques. Create a list of questions you might use to interview potential candidates.

6. Select one policy that you think would be the most important in your employee manual. Write several paragraphs to describe what you would expect from your employees for that policy.

7. Describe the orientation program you would use for new employees.

8. Research a human resources topic such as hiring an employee, firing an employee, or harassment. After you have selected a topic, write a policy for that area that you think is fair and legal.

9. Would you find it difficult to discipline an employee? Why or why not?

10. List factors you would use as a guideline to promote an employee.

 # Teamwork

In this chapter, the process for hiring employees is covered. Working in teams of two, each member should create a résumé, cover letter, and a thank-you letter for an interview. One team member should be the employer and the other team member the employee. Practice interviewing techniques and rotate roles of employer and employee.

Internet Research

Job Descriptions. Using the Internet, find job descriptions for positions similar to those you might need for your business. Identify the common skills, education, and salary noted in the job postings you find. Save these examples for future reference.

Communication Skills

College and Career Readiness

Reading. Carefully consider the use of the term *human resources* in this chapter. What connotation does this term have? How does using the term *human resources* today compare with the term *personnel* that was common 25 years ago? Do you think the term readily conveys its meaning to the reader? Why or why not?

Writing. Using the Internet, research information on workplace accidents. Create a narrative that describes circumstances that led to a workplace accident. Next, create another narrative that describes how that same accident could have been avoided. Be sure to include a lot of details. Pay close attention to the sequence of events as you develop your narrative.

Copyright Goodheart-Willcox Co., Inc.

CTSOs

Role-Play and Interview Events. Some competitive entrepreneurial events for Career and Technical Student Organizations (CTSOs) require that entrants complete a role-playing activity or interview. Those who participate will be provided information about a company or situation and given time to practice. A judge or panel of judges will review the presentations or conduct the interview.

To prepare for the role-playing activity or interview event, complete the following activities.

1. Read the guidelines provided by your organization. Make certain that you ask any questions about points you do not understand. It is important to follow each specific item that is outlined in the competition rules.

2. Visit the organization's website and look for role-play and interview events that were used in previous years. Many organizations post these events for students to use as practice for future competitions. Also, look for the evaluation criteria or rubric for the event. This will help you determine what the judge will be looking for in your presentation.

3. Practice in front of a mirror. Are you comfortable speaking without reading directly from your notes?

4. Ask a friend or a teacher to listen to your presentation or conduct an interview with you.

5. Give special attention to your posture and how you present yourself.

6. Concentrate on the tone of voice. Be pleasant and loud enough to hear, but do not shout.

7. Make eye contact with the listener. Do not stare, but engage the person's attention.

8. After you have made your presentation, ask for constructive feedback.

Copyright Goodheart-Willcox Co., Inc.

Building Your Business Plan—Putting the Puzzle Together

Human Resources Management

The most important part of any business is the employees. They are the face of the business and who customers see and interact with. Trustworthy and efficient employees can help make the company a success or a failure. Attracting and managing employees is time-consuming, but necessary. It is important the employees know your rules, policies, and procedures. Treat them fairly, create a safe work environment, and encourage a positive relationship.

Goals

- Create a job description for the first employee you plan to hire.
- Create a job application for your business.
- Create business plan notes.

Directions

Access the *Entrepreneurship* companion website at www.g-wlearning.com. Download each data file for the following activities. A complete sample business plan is available on the companion website to use as a reference. The name of the file is BusPlan_Sample.RetroAttire.docx.

Preparation

Activity 14-1. Job Description. Create a job description for your first employee.

Activity 14-2. Job Application. Research job applications on the Internet to create a job application for your business.

Activity 14-3. Business Plan Notes. Create notes about human resources needs for your business. Keep your notes and research sources here.

Business Plan—Operations

In this chapter, you learned about the importance of human resources management. In this activity, you will complete the Human Resources section of the business plan. Use the information you learned about recruiting and managing your employees to help you with the following sections.

1. Open your saved business plan document.

2. Locate the Operations section of the business plan and the subsection called Human Resources. Use the suggestions and questions listed in the template to help you generate ideas. Delete the instructions and questions when you are finished writing the section. Make sure to proofread your document and correct any errors in keyboarding, spelling, and grammar.

3. Save your document.

CHAPTER

15 Purchases and Inventory Management

Inventory is what many companies sell to make money. But, inventory is also a cost to companies. This means that most companies try to manage their inventories, making sure there is enough on hand to provide customers with products—but not too much, which would tie up cash in inventory. Stephen Caroll, owner of Walking Equipment Company, knows this firsthand. He uses software and other technologies to manage his inventory and the upwards of 500 packages his company ships every day. Caroll explains that using technology allows his company to "no longer sit on inventory I don't need." Storing unneeded inventory is very expensive for most companies. Through efficient electronic inventory management, Caroll can increase the cash flow for Walking Equipment Company.

> *"I'm convinced that about half of what separates the successful entrepreneurs from the unsuccessful ones is pure perseverance."*

—Steve Jobs, cofounder of Apple Inc.

College and Career Readiness

Reading Prep. Before reading this chapter, undertake some research on the Internet on inventory control and management. Read one or two articles on the topic. As you read, consider the similarities and differences between the Internet articles and the text. Compare the different approaches the authors take to the material.

Sections

15.1 Purchases

15.2 Inventory

Rebecca Ufkes

In 1995, Rebecca Ufkes founded UEC Electronics in Charleston, South Carolina, with five employees. UEC designs and manufactures electronic products and systems that are used by the aerospace industry and the US Department of Defense. UEC developed the Ground Renewable Expeditionary Energy Network System (GREENS). This is a system for energy collection, storage, and distribution. GREENS is being used by troops in Afghanistan to power the energy needs of their frontline combat positions.

UEC Electronics grew due to Rebecca's focus and determination as well as her willingness to seek guidance when needed. She has used resources, such as the Charleston Small Business Development Center and the US Navy's Manufacturing Technical Assistance Program. UEC also participated in the Department of Defense's Mentor Protégé Program.

Rebecca earned a bachelor of science degree in mechanical engineering from Michigan Technical University and an MBA from The Citadel. She was named South Carolina's Small Business Person of the Year in 2010. Rebecca was honored at the White House as a Champion of Change, someone whose innovation helps the country meet the challenges of the 21st century.

Photo © Rebecca Ufkes

Check Your Entrepreneurship IQ

Before you begin the chapter, see what you already know about entrepreneurship by taking the chapter pretest. The pretest is available at
www.g-wlearning.com

SECTION 15.1 Purchases

How can a business manage the purchasing process?

Objectives

After completing this section, you will be able to:

- **Describe** the purchasing process.
- **Explain** the steps involved in managing the purchasing process.

Key Terms

purchasing
purchasing management
electronic data interchange (EDI)
vendor
sourcing
product specification sheet

economy of scale
purchase order (PO)
packing slip
receiving record
invoice
quality control

Critical Thinking

Before purchasing merchandise for your business, it will be necessary to research potential vendors or suppliers. The process will be similar to how you make an important personal purchase, such as a cell phone. What information will you want to know before deciding to make a purchase?

Purchasing Inventory

Purchasing is the process of buying goods and materials from other businesses. The goods and materials a business has on hand are called its *inventory*. **Purchasing management** is ordering the necessary goods and materials, receiving them into stock on arrival, and paying the vendor for the order. For a small business, an entrepreneur might handle all the aspects of purchasing. However, in larger businesses, a buyer or purchasing manager would handle these duties.

Much planning goes into purchasing inventory for a business. Retailers spend an average of 70 cents of every dollar in sales on inventory. Depending on the business, inventory may be purchased daily, weekly, monthly, or less often.

Electronic data interchange (EDI) is the standard transfer between organizations of electronic data for business transactions, such as orders, confirmations, and invoices. Most of the purchasing process takes place electronically to maximize efficiency and easily maintain purchase records.

Manage the Purchasing Process

Customer needs and wants constantly change. In order to maintain a successful business, inventory must be adjusted to meet those needs. Before the purchasing process takes place, it is necessary to study the market as well as customers' buying and behavioral habits. Determine which products are popular with the target market customers. How often do they purchase your product or service? Look for new trends coming in the next few months. Knowing the customer is one of the keys to stocking the correct merchandise. There are eight specific steps to help manage the purchasing process.

1. Identify inventory needs.

2. Identify vendors.

3. Select the vendor.

4. Negotiate the purchase.

5. Make the purchase.

6. Receive the order.

7. Pay the invoice.

8. Evaluate the vendor.

Identify Inventory Needs

The initial inventory is purchased before a business opens. The type and quality of merchandise depend on the business' goals as stated in the business plan. The ongoing sales projections help to determine the correct quantity of goods to keep in inventory for meeting customer needs. After the business is open for a period of time, it is also important to track actual sales history. Both of these activities help businesses avoid being out of stock of any items and missing sales opportunities.

However, a business needs to avoid purchasing too much new product for inventory in the event sales projections were incorrect. On the other hand, a business does not want to fail to meet customer needs by not having the latest product. It is necessary to have a reorder point for each product. This practice puts a control in place before the inventory gets too low. Inventory management is discussed in greater detail in the next section.

Identify Vendors

Vendors are companies that sell products to other businesses. Vendors are also called *suppliers*. Depending on the goods and services offered by a business, there may be many vendors from which to choose. For example, a retail business typically uses

Entrepreneur Ethics

When purchasing merchandise to resell to customers, seek vendors who are respected businesses. Avoid buying merchandise that does not come from a reliable source as it may be counterfeit or made illegally in another country. Ensure your vendors follow acceptable labor and environmental practices.

Copyright Goodheart-Willcox Co., Inc.

vendors of finished goods and services that support business operations. However, a manufacturing business must find suppliers that provide the raw materials to create a product. This is known as sourcing. **Sourcing** is finding suppliers of materials needed for the production of a product.

The quality and pricing of products from different vendors may vary greatly. Check with other business contacts in your industry for vendor recommendations. The Better Business Bureau also provides reports on vendor standings in the community.

Select the Vendor

Evaluate each possible vendor before purchasing product. In addition to price, some considerations for vendor selection include reliability, delivery time, and service. Service is an important consideration when evaluating vendors. Keep in mind your business needs and hours of operation when gathering information about vendors. Are sales representatives and customer service representatives available during the hours you may need them? What is the return policy? What is the delivery schedule? Can emergency or unscheduled deliveries be accommodated? Be sure to review all of the support services that vendors offer to their clients.

After reviewing and comparing potential vendors, choose the one that meets initial and ongoing inventory needs for the business. Have

Keeping track of sales will aid in inventory management.

iStock.com/XiXinXing

Copyright Goodheart-Willcox Co., Inc.

several vendor options for times when the first choice may not be able to fulfill an order. Developing good relationships with vendors is also important. A vendor with which you have a good relationship may be more willing to speed up an order or offer other help when needed.

Negotiate the Purchase

Negotiation involves getting a good price and payment schedule for the merchandise as well as having it delivered on time. You may get a number of quotes, or bids, from different vendors to compare their offerings. Ask the vendors for a product specification sheet that describes the merchandise selected for purchase. A **product specification sheet** provides product facts including sizes, colors, materials, and weights. When used for bidding purposes, it should also include pricing, payment terms, delivery, and other issues important to making a purchase decision. After the price and terms are negotiated, request an official bid stating the agreement for purchase.

FYI

In business, vendors are also often referred to as *suppliers*. The product specification sheet may also be called a *spec sheet*.

Quality and Value

The quality of products a business can offer ranges from high-end and expensive to low-end and inexpensive. The key to negotiating for quality is to insist on *value*, or getting the highest quality for the lowest possible price. Remember, a business must still mark up the price it paid for items to earn a profit on customer sales. The choice of product quality also depends on how much the target market is willing to pay for certain items.

It is wise for business owners to understand how quality and price affect value in their industries to negotiate the best deals. Sometimes vendors offer higher quality merchandise for very good prices to encourage a business to also buy items that are inexpensive. This is an area open for negotiation that varies by vendor.

Economies of Scale

Most vendors offer *quantity discounts,* or a reduced per-item price based on the quantity purchased, to encourage larger orders. The greater the quantity purchased, the lower the per-unit price. This practice is similar to buying household items in bulk because the price per item is lower than when buying only one. It is usually more cost effective for businesses to purchase inventory in larger quantities to obtain the lower unit prices. After markup to the list prices, the profit margin on the goods sold is greater.

Quantity discounts are based on the economy of scale. **Economy of scale** is the decrease in unit cost of a product resulting from large-scale manufacturing operations. As more of a product is made, efficiency of production increases. This, in turn, reduces the cost per piece.

Copyright Goodheart-Willcox Co., Inc.

Focus on Finance

Diminishing Marginal Utility

In economics, the law of diminishing marginal utility deals with human psychology and the satisfaction, or usefulness, of goods based on quantity. It states that there is a point at which having more of something becomes less desirable. This is also called the *threshold of demand.* For example, how many red sweaters does a person actually want or need? It depends on the person, but it seems likely that after two or three, the marginal utility would greatly decrease. This explains why consumers like variety and will purchase substitute products. It may also help a business owner when purchasing inventory to vary the styles or increase product lines.

An economy of scale can also apply to the cost of shipping and handling. For example, the per-item shipping-and-handling cost on larger orders may be less than when purchasing fewer products. Transportation costs can be spread over the total cost of all the products purchased and not just one item.

Make the Purchase

After deciding on which vendor to purchase from, the next step is completing a purchase order for the product. A **purchase order (PO)** is the form a buyer sends to the vendor to officially place an order. It lists the negotiated quantities, varieties, and prices for the products ordered. The purchase order includes the buyer's company information and details about the products, shipping, and payment, as shown in Figure 15-1. POs should be consecutively numbered so the recordkeeping system remains sequential. Copies of the PO are made for the business' records and for the vendor.

Receive the Order

Tracking purchases is an important step to make sure orders are delivered when promised. When a shipment of goods is received, it includes a **packing slip** that lists the contents of the box or container. It is important for the person receiving the shipment to immediately verify the contents by comparing them to the packing slip. The *confirmation process* ensures that everything has been received according to the PO.

Sometimes the contents will not match the packing slip, or products may have become damaged in the shipping process. In those cases, a receiving record is used to help the vendor correct an order. A **receiving record** is a form on which all merchandise received is listed

Copyright Goodheart-Willcox Co., Inc.

Judy's Flowers		**PURCHASE ORDER**			
123 Main Street Tampa, FL 33601 Phone: (813) 555-1234 Fax: (813) 555-1235					
PO #: 003725			**Date:** 03/31/20--		
Vendor Name/Address: Magnolia Floral Wholesale 9807 Second Avenue Atlanta, GA 30060 (678) 555-1236		**Vendor ID:** 24	**Customer ID:** 1068A		

SHIPPING METHOD	SHIPPING TERMS		DELIVERY DATE		
Ground	Received by 05/01/20--		05/01/20--		

Item	Job	Description	Qty	Unit Price	Line Total
013188	12	4″ by 4″ square vase	24	3.70	88.80
011088	12	4.5″ by 10″ cylinder bowl vase	60	11.25	675.00
012488	12	12″ by 5″ curved vase	48	6.15	295.20

1. Please send two copies of your invoice.
2. Enter this order in accordance with the prices, terms, delivery method, and specifications listed above.
3. Please notify us immediately if you are unable to ship as specified.
4. Send all correspondence to:
   Judy's Flowers
   E-mail: judy@judysflowerstampa.com
   Fax: (813) 555-1235

Subtotal		1,059.00
For resale? (Yes)/ No	Tax ID: 12-3456789	Sales Tax —
	Shipping	126.95
Total	Net 30 days	**$1,185.95**
Authorized by: *Judy Jackson*		Date: 3/31/20--

nata_danilenko/Shutterstock.com; Goodheart-Willcox Publisher

Figure 15-1. Make sure your business' purchase order form includes the necessary information.

as it comes into the place of business. After receiving and inspecting the shipment, the details should be recorded on a receiving record and filed for future use.

Pay the Invoice

An **invoice** is the vendor's bill requesting payment for goods shipped or services provided. After an order is shipped, the vendor sends an invoice to the buyer listing the goods purchased with the amount owed and payment terms. Before paying an invoice, make sure the costs and payment terms listed on the invoice match those on

Copyright Goodheart-Willcox Co., Inc.

the PO. Also, verify that the receiving record matches what was billed. Most vendors expect payment either on receipt or within 30 days. Sometimes vendors will offer a *cash discount* to encourage businesses to pay invoices early. Cash discounts are discussed in chapter 10.

Evaluate the Vendor

The person or department responsible for receiving shipments helps to evaluate vendors. Checking the merchandise shipped for any damages, shortages, or overages is crucial. At this point, the business is performing quality control. **Quality control** is the activity of checking goods as they are produced or received to ensure the quality meets expectations.

If a vendor continues to be reliable, provide value and consistent product quality, then the vendor can be used again. A good time to evaluate vendors is after receiving their invoices. A form similar to the one shown in Figure 15-2 can be used to monitor the track record of vendors over time. A rating scale is helpful to score the criteria.

Vendor Evaluation Form

Vendors	Date	Availability of products	Quality	Reliability	On-time delivery	Damages or discrepancies	Service	Price
Vendor #1								
Vendor #2								
Vendor #3								
Vendor #4								

Goodheart-Willcox Publisher

Figure 15-2. Rating vendors will help you evaluate which companies to do business with.

Copyright Goodheart-Willcox Co., Inc.

Section 15.1 | Review

Check Your Understanding ⤤

1. Describe what is meant by inventory.
2. List the eight steps in managing the purchasing process.
3. Why is establishing a reorder point an important part of managing inventory?
4. Explain why the cost per unit decreases as the number of items manufactured increases.
5. Why is it important to track shipped items?

Build Your Vocabulary ⤤

As you progress through this text, develop a personal glossary of key terms. This will help you build your vocabulary and prepare you for a career. Write a definition for each of the following terms and add them to your personal glossary.

purchasing
purchasing
  management
electronic data
  interchange (EDI)
vendor
sourcing
product
  specification
  sheet

economy of scale
purchase order
  (PO)
packing slip
receiving record
invoice
quality control

SECTION 15.2 Inventory

?Essential Question

How does inventory management affect business success?

Objectives

After completing this section, you will be able to:

- **Explain** inventory management.
- **Describe** two systems for inventory control.
- **Summarize** the role sales forecasting plays in planning inventory.

Key Terms

inventory management
lead time
buffer stock
stockout
physical inventory
perpetual inventory-control system
manual-tag system
unit-control system

point-of-sale (POS) software
radio frequency identification (RFID)
periodic inventory-control system
just-in-time (JIT) inventory-control
   system
80/20 inventory rule
productive inventory
turnover rate

Critical Thinking

Not having the correct inventory to meet customer demand may be one of the factors that causes a business to fail. What can you do to make sure you always have in inventory the merchandise your customers want to buy?

Inventory Management

    Every business wants to maximize its profit. One way to do this is to manage the inventory. **Inventory management** is the process of tracking product orders, keeping an adequate supply and assortment of products, and storing products in a warehouse and retail locations. In addition, inventory management includes managing the other direct costs involved with inventory. When purchasing inventory, there are many factors that need to be considered.

- lead time

- buffer stock

- carrying costs

FYI

Two ideas for saving money when purchasing products is to participate in group purchasing or to barter for products. There are trade, for-profit, and nonprofit organizations that participate in group purchasing.

Copyright Goodheart-Willcox Co., Inc.

Green Entrepreneurs

Reusable Bags

When buying office supplies or other items for the business, consider bringing along a reusable bag. Reusable bags save thousands of pounds of landfill waste every year. While there are different schools of thought on this topic, it is generally accepted that plastic bags take nearly 1,000 years to degrade. Additionally, discarded plastic bags can pose threats to wildlife and contaminate the soil. As a business owner, think about the possibilities of recyclable packaging that you might offer your customers.

Lead Time

It takes time for vendors to process an order and send it to the business. **Lead time** is the total time it takes from placing an order until it is received. Lead time could be days, months, or longer, depending on the product and vendor. The product may need to be made or assembled or the vendor may not have enough of the product in stock when the order is placed. Lead time must be taken into consideration when planning for inventory purchases.

Buffer Stock

Forecasting sales is always a challenge for business. It can be difficult to gauge how much product is needed each day or month of a selling season. To help avoid running out of inventory, stock may be maintained as a buffer or cushion. **Buffer stock** is additional stock kept above the minimum amount required to meet forecasted sales. This helps prevent the business from running out of stock.

Some businesses anticipate that some products sell more on a seasonal basis. For example, many more barbeque grills are sold in the summer than in the winter. *Anticipation stock* is the necessary extra stock of products that sell more in certain seasons.

Carrying Costs

There are costs directly related to carrying, or holding, inventory that are also part of inventory management. They include the following.

- *Capital costs* are related to borrowing cash from lenders to purchase inventory from vendors.

- *Inventory-service costs* are related to the clerical work and physical handling related directly to the inventory.

Copyright Goodheart-Willcox Co., Inc.

- *Storage costs* are for renting warehouse space or building a company-owned warehouse.

- *Inventory-risk costs* include the cost of employee or customer theft, slow-moving inventory, damaged or obsolete inventory, and non-selling merchandise that must be destroyed or donated for a tax write-off.

- *Insurance premiums and taxes* are calculated as a percentage of the inventory value.

The cost of carrying inventory is often described as a percentage of the inventory value, as shown in Figure 15-3. Businesses use this percentage to help them determine how much profit can be made on current inventory. Carrying costs can usually run between 24 percent and 48 percent of the inventory value per year.

Inventory-Control Systems

Small businesses might use an informal method of checking how much inventory is available for sale. However, it is a good idea to start

Figure 15-3. Costs of Carrying Inventory

Calculating Inventory Carrying Rate and Costs

1. Add up your annual inventory costs:
 Example:
   $1,200 = storage
   $2,300 = handling
   $2,500 = clerical
   $5,000 = obsolete, damaged, and dead products (markdowns and losses)
   $4,000 = theft
 $15,000 total inventory costs

2. Divide the inventory costs by the inventory value: Example: $15,000 ÷ $100,000 = 15%

3. Add the percentages for insurance and taxes:
   5% = insurance premiums as a percentage of inventory value
   6% = taxes as a percentage of inventory value
 11%

4. Add all of the percentages: 15% + 11% = 26%   inventory carrying rate = 26% (or .26)
5. Multiply the inventory value by the inventory carrying rate: carrying costs = $100,000 × .26 = $26,000

Goodheart-Willcox Publisher

Copyright Goodheart-Willcox Co., Inc.

a formal inventory system as soon as possible to avoid a stockout. A **stockout** is running out of stock. There are three primary types of retail inventory-control systems: perpetual, periodic, and just-in-time. Every business has different inventory needs, so choose the system that best fits the place strategies of your business plan.

No matter which inventory-control system a business uses, it is important to conduct a physical inventory once or twice a year. A **physical inventory** is an actual count of items in inventory. It is used to verify the inventory-control system's counts. If there are differences in the counts, the physical count is considered accurate. The records of the inventory-control system must be adjusted to reflect the physical count.

No inventory system is flawless because it cannot record theft, vendor returns, or damaged products.

Perpetual Inventory

A **perpetual inventory-control system** is a method of counting inventory that shows the quantity on hand at all times. The system records the receipt of goods into stock and all merchandise sales. There are two types of perpetual inventory systems—manual and computerized.

Manual Perpetual Inventory-Control System

In a *manual perpetual inventory-control system,* the inventory is calculated by physically counting and recording individual items. A person records each item that comes into inventory and each item that goes out of inventory as a sale or vendor return. This information is recorded on a spreadsheet or entered into a software program. The important part to note is that the inventory is done manually, not automatically.

One example of a manual perpetual inventory-control system is the manual-tag system that some small retailers use. A **manual-tag system** simply tracks sales by removing price tags when the products are sold. The retailer keeps the tags and uses them to deduct the sales from the inventory.

Another example of a manual perpetual inventory-control system is the **unit-control system** in which a visual determination is made when more stock is needed. This can be done by actually *eyeballing* the inventory to see if the inventory looks low. It can also be done by using bin tickets. A *bin ticket* is a tiny card placed by the product. It lists the stock number, description, minimum and maximum quantities, and cost in a code known only by store employees. A set number of bin tickets are placed with the merchandise. Each time inventory is sold, a bin ticket is removed. When the supply of bin tickets gets low, it is a visual signal to order more inventory.

In both manual-tag and unit-control systems, the reorder point is determined manually. The business must physically place POs and hope the lead time is acceptable. A manual perpetual inventory-control

Copyright Goodheart-Willcox Co., Inc.

system can work for a small company. However, it may not be the most efficient use of time and leaves a business open to human errors.

Computerized Perpetual Inventory-Control System

While manual systems have their place, most businesses use a *computerized inventory-control system,* which allows more control and information. Inventory software programs track incoming inventory and sales. The software can run sales and inventory reports to track costs, track sales by salesperson or by category, and manage sales tax by state if needed. Daily sales reports can also be generated making

A manual-tag system can work well for a small business.

MJTH/Shutterstock.com

Copyright Goodheart-Willcox Co., Inc.

it easier to balance the cash drawer. The software may also analyze profit by items sold. Some software can automatically reorder standard products.

Most retail businesses use cash registers with point-of-sale software. **Point-of-sale (POS) software** records each sale when it happens. When a product's bar code is scanned, the merchandise is immediately deducted from inventory. So, management always has a current inventory count.

POS software allows different reorder points to be entered for various products. Depending on the system, it automatically alerts an owner when it is time to order more merchandise or immediately places the order. This prevents stockouts and helps the business run efficiently. POS systems also improve pricing accuracy, which eliminates the human error factor of keying in information.

Another computerized inventory system is the radio frequency identification system. **Radio frequency identification (RFID)** is a system that uses computer chips attached to inventory items and radio frequency receivers to track inventory. You may be familiar with the computer chip that is placed under the skin of the family pet. This chip identifies the pet and its owner when scanned. This is a type of RFID system. Many businesses use RFID systems to track inventory as it moves within a building.

Periodic Inventory-Control System

A **periodic inventory-control system** involves taking a physical count of merchandise at regular periods, such as weekly or monthly. The business actually counts everything that is in inventory and compares those numbers to the reorder points. Taking physical inventories is time-consuming, so it is only done at intervals. Because the count is only completed at given times, the actual inventory is not accurate on a day-to-day basis. A periodic inventory-control system is typically used by small businesses or businesses without inventory software.

Just-in-Time (JIT) Inventory-Control System

Carrying too much inventory can reduce the profitability of a company. The **just-in-time (JIT) inventory-control system** keeps a minimal amount of production materials or sales inventory on hand at all times. JIT was developed in Japan by Toyota to reduce the costs of carrying inventory.

In a JIT system, materials are produced "just in time" for the next step in the supply chain to use it. For a JIT system to be successful, each company in the supply chain must coordinate each activity and be flexible when necessary. When JIT works well, both manufacturers and retailers can save time and money.

Copyright Goodheart-Willcox Co., Inc.

A retail business using JIT tracks sales and only orders the least amount of stock necessary for any given point in time. A manufacturing company using JIT makes sure raw materials are delivered right before they are needed in the assembly process. Ideally, it would finish producing goods just before they are shipped to customers.

Advantages of JIT are increased efficiency, reduced waste, reduced storage space, and freed up cash for other purposes. Another advantage of a JIT system is that it reduces losses and possible damage to products sitting on shelves or with expiration dates.

A disadvantage of JIT is when products arrive late, products are not available when they should be. The lack of product on hand would mean sales could be lost. If raw materials are late in arriving for any reason, a manufacturing production line may even be shut down. For companies needing smaller amounts of goods, they may not meet the minimum order amount or shipping costs may be too high. Also, if projected sales are too low, then the advantages of JIT are not achieved.

Sales Forecasting

The business owner is responsible for determining the correct amount of money to invest in inventory each year. Sales forecasting based on previous sales history is one way to plan for upcoming inventory needs to meet demand for the goods and services of the

Social Entrepreneurs

Jodie Wu

Jodie Wu has a mechanical engineering degree from the Massachusetts Institute of Technology (MIT). On a trip to Tanzania, Wu visited farmers who needed help in their fields. The staple crop of Tanzania, maize, was being harvested by beating it with a stick. Technology could help the farmers, but they lacked fuel and electricity. Wu knew there had to be a better way. Working with fellow students, Wu and her team created add-ons to bicycles that would help the farmers' level of efficiency. The company she started to produce the add-ons is Global Cycle Solutions (GCS). GCS' products attach to the backs of bicycles and use pedal power to function. One of the inventions is the corn sheller, which shells corn 40 times faster than by hand. With no dependence on fuel or electricity, the corn sheller changed the lives of Tanzanians with small maize farms. GCS continues to create technologies to help farmers take a step out of poverty, without dependency on electricity or fuel.

Copyright Goodheart-Willcox Co., Inc.

business. It is usually done a year in advance, depending on the type of business. Most businesses then review actual weekly sales and adjust the sales projections, which will also impact inventory orders.

A typical sales projection may look like the one shown in Figure 15-4 for Raj's Computer Shack. This forecast is for the projected number of units sold per month for one year. The year's sales projection is 16,885 laptop units and 3,380 desktop computer units. Raj knows that if the sales forecast is accurate, there must be at least that number of units available for sale.

To gather information to make your business' initial sales forecast, use your marketing research. Review your research data on potential markets, industry trends, and demand for your product. Analyze the information you learned about the competition and similar companies to determine how much they invest in their inventory. Sales forecasts after the first year in business are based on the previous sales history and current market conditions.

80/20 Inventory Rule

Many businesses use the 80/20 rule to forecast sales to have enough inventory on hand. The **80/20 inventory rule** states that 80 percent of a business' sales come from 20 percent of its inventory. The **productive inventory** is 20 percent of a business' inventory that produces the most sales. The 80/20 rule helps a business determine which merchandise to keep in stock at higher levels and which products to keep at a minimum. The business will then need to decide how much to purchase in advance and when to place the orders.

Turnover Rate

When forecasting inventory, another factor to consider is the turnover rate of stock. A **turnover rate**, or *turnover ratio*, is the number of times inventory has been sold during a time period, usually one year. A *ratio* is a way to see how two numbers compare with each other.

Raj's Computer Shack Unit Sales Forecast for 20--												
	Jan.	**Feb.**	**Mar.**	**Apr.**	**May**	**June**	**July**	**Aug.**	**Sep.**	**Oct.**	**Nov.**	**Dec.**
Laptops	1,000	1,200	1,250	1,300	1,320	1,111	1,345	1,450	1,454	1,460	1,975	2,020
Desktops	300	200	210	210	225	175	200	250	250	300	500	560

Goodheart-Willcox Publisher

Figure 15-4. Sales Projection for One Year

Copyright Goodheart-Willcox Co., Inc.

For example, as shown in Figure 15-5, a business has a cost of merchandise sold of $120,000 for the previous year. The cost of merchandise sold includes beginning inventory, plus any inventory purchased during the year, minus ending inventory. The business has stated that the average inventory of merchandise on hand at the end of the year was $50,000. To calculate turnover rate, use the following:

$$\frac{\text{cost of goods sold}}{\text{average inventory}} = \text{turnover rate}$$

$$\frac{\$120,000}{\$50,000} = 2.4 \text{ times}$$

This ratio indicates that inventory has been turned around a total of 2.4 times during the year. A turnover rate is a good indicator of how effectively a business is managing its inventory. A high turnover rate generally indicates higher sales and productive inventory. Depending on the industry, a business may benefit from ordering high-turnover products in larger quantities to save shipping costs and lower the price per unit. Merchandise with a low turnover rate means it is sitting on the shelves and is nonproductive inventory.

Once a business' turnover rate is known, it is possible to project how many months of productive inventory to have on hand. The turnover rate for the above business is 2.4. Is that number good? It depends on the business.

SBA Tips

The SBA provides average turnover rates for various industries so you can compare your business' turnover rate to the industry average.
www.sba.gov

Figure 15-5. Determining the cost of merchandise sold helps the business calculate the turnover rate of its inventory.

Cost of Merchandise Sold for One Year	
Merchandise inventory January 1, 20--	$80,000
Plus purchases during the year	75,000
Total merchandise available for sale	155,000
Less ending inventory, December 31, 20--	30,000
Cost of merchandise sold	$125,000

Goodheart-Willcox Publisher

Copyright Goodheart-Willcox Co., Inc.

You Do the Math   Communication and Representation

When solving an equation, it is important to make sure the units match. For example, when calculating fuel economy in miles per gallon (MPG), the final unit must be miles over gallons. So, the equation must be the number of miles divided by the number of gallons. If the equation is incorrectly expressed as the number of miles times the number of gallons, the final unit would be mile-gallons, not miles/gallon.

Solve the following problems.

1. A business must calculate the number of sales dollars generated per sales representative. Is the following equation correct for this calculation: dollars × reps? If this is not the correct equation, what is?

2. A shipping box is rated to hold 65 pounds. The company ships products that weigh 1.3 pounds each. It uses the following formula to determine how many products can be placed in one box: pounds per product × pound per box. Is this the correct equation? If this is not the correct equation, what is?

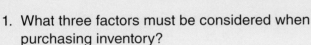

Section 15.2 Review

Check Your Understanding ➦

1. What three factors must be considered when purchasing inventory?

2. Explain the concept of sales forecasting. How is marketing research used in sales forecasting?

3. What percentage of inventory is considered productive inventory?

4. List at least five features of a computerized inventory-control system.

5. State the equation used to calculate turnover rate.

Build Your Vocabulary ➦

As you progress through this text, develop a personal glossary of key terms. This will help you build your vocabulary and prepare you for a career. Write a definition for each of the following terms and add them to your personal glossary.

inventory
    management
lead time
buffer stock
stockout
physical inventory
perpetual inventory-
    control system
manual-tag system
unit-control system
point-of-sale (POS)
    software

radio frequency
    identification
    (RFID)
periodic inventory-
    control system
just-in-time (JIT)
    inventory-control
    system
80/20 inventory
    rule
productive
    inventory
turnover rate

Copyright Goodheart-Willcox Co., Inc.

Chapter Summary

Section 15.1 **Purchases**

- The purchasing process involves having technical knowledge about product and an understanding of what the market wants. Purchasing management is the processes involved in purchasing inventory.
- There are eight steps in the purchasing process: 1. Identify inventory needs. 2. Identify vendors. 3. Select the vendor. 4. Negotiate the purchase. 5. Make the purchase. 6. Receive the order. 7. Pay the invoice. 8. Evaluate the vendor.

Section 15.2 **Inventory**

- Inventory management is the process of acquiring and tracking product orders, keeping adequate supplies of products, and organizing products in warehouses or retail locations.
- The most widely used inventory systems are perpetual inventory and periodic inventory. Perpetual inventory-control systems track merchandise on a continuous basis. A periodic inventory system is taking a physical count of merchandise on a regular or periodic basis.
- Using the 80/20 inventory rule and turnover rate for sales forecasting purposes help determine inventory needs.

Online Activities

Complete the following activities to help you learn, practice, and expand your knowledge and skills.

Posttest. Now that you have finished the chapter, see what you learned by taking the chapter posttest.

Key Terms. Practice vocabulary for this chapter using the e-flash cards, matching activity, and vocabulary game until you are able to recognize their meanings.

Review Your Knowledge

1. Why is purchasing management important to a business?
2. Explain the different methods used to keep track of inventory.
3. Why is inventory management important to a business?
4. Describe the importance of lead time.
5. List five costs directly related to carrying or holding inventory.
6. State the equation that represents carrying costs.
7. What are the two inventory systems that are commonly used?
8. What is the difference between perpetual and periodic inventory?

Copyright Goodheart-Willcox Co., Inc.

9. Explain the 80/20 inventory rule.

10. Why is turnover rate used in deciding how much to purchase?

Apply Your Knowledge

1. Each business has different inventory needs. If your chosen business is one that requires inventory, make a list of the inventory you will need.

2. Managing the purchasing process requires steps to help make wise decisions. Using the eight steps defined in this chapter, write a few lines for each as to how you will apply these steps to your business.

3. As an entrepreneur, it will be very important to have vendors on whom you can depend. Make a list of vendors who might be able to provide inventory for your business. List each product you will need and the potential vendor who could supply that product.

4. Every business needs a purchase order that is specific to the business. Research purchase orders on the Internet and find several examples that might work for you. Create your own purchase order.

5. Every business needs a receiving record that is specific to the business. Research receiving records on the Internet and find several examples that might work for you. Create your own receiving record.

6. Conduct research on the Internet to determine the average carrying cost for businesses in your field. What steps do you think you can take to minimize those costs for your business?

7. Certain considerations must be made before purchasing goods or services that will meet the operational needs of a business. The type and quality of merchandise must be evaluated. List the merchandise that you would need for the operation of your business. Next, create a list of quality standards that you would require for your business.

8. Create a sales forecast for one line of merchandise you might want to sell in your business. Use your marketing research data as reference for your initial sales forecast. Remember to take into consideration whether your business is seasonal or steady throughout the year.

9. Analyze the services you would require from a vendor based on the operational needs of your business. List some of the vendor services that you think will be important for your business.

10. For your business, list the items that you anticipate will have a low turnover rate and items you feel will turn over quickly. What steps can you take to increase your turnover rate while keeping inventory at adequate levels?

Teamwork

Working with your team, list the business that each team member would like to pursue. Select one of the businesses and research sales forecasting for that industry. What common methods are used? Report your findings to the class.

Copyright Goodheart-Willcox Co., Inc.

Internet Research

Purchasing Inventory. As the owner of a business, you will likely be making the purchasing decisions for inventory. Research the term *purchasing management*. Based on what you read, describe how it will apply to your business.

College and Career Readiness

Communication Skills

Reading. Analyze the structure of the relationship of sales forecasting and its dependence on various aspects of sales history. What roles do the turnover rate and the 80/20 rule play when a business is forecasting inventory?

Writing. Conduct research on effective inventory management strategies. Write an informative report, consisting of several paragraphs, to describe your findings. Include the positive or negative inventory management strategies for a small business in your report.

CTSOs

Communication Skills. Entrepreneurship competitive events may also judge participants' communications skills. Presenters must be able to exchange information with the judges in a clear, concise manner. The evaluation will include all aspects of effective writing, speaking, and listening skills as applied to the entrepreneurial environment. To prepare for the business communications portion of the event:

1. Visit the organization's website and determine specific communication skills that will be evaluated.

2. Spend time reviewing the essential principles of business communication, such as grammar, spelling, and punctuation.

3. If you are making a written presentation, ask a teacher to evaluate your writing. Review and apply the feedback so that your writing sample appears professional and correct.

4. Ask a teacher to review your presentation and listen for errors in grammar or sentence structure. After you have received comments, adjust and make the presentation several times until you are comfortable.

5. Review the Communication Skills activities that appear at the end of each chapter of this text as a way to practice your reading, writing, listening, and speaking skills using topics in entrepreneurship.

6. To practice listening skills, ask your teacher to give you a set of directions. Then, without assistance, repeat those directions to your teacher. Did you listen closely enough to do what was instructed?

Copyright Goodheart-Willcox Co., Inc.

Building Your Business Plan—Putting the Puzzle Together

Purchases and Inventory Management

Inventory is perhaps the most important asset for a business. With too little inventory, there may not be enough product available to meet customer needs. This means customers may go elsewhere and sales would be lost. Too much inventory means more money is tied up in product and cannot be used for other purposes. Purchasing and managing inventory is a balancing act for any business, large or small.

Goals

- Create a purchase order form.
- Select possible vendors to use for purchasing inventory.
- Describe the business' inventory management process.
- Create business plan notes.

Directions

Access the *Entrepreneurship* companion website at www.g-wlearning.com ↗. Download each data file for the following activities. A complete sample business plan is available on the companion website to use as a reference. The name of the file is BusPlan_Sample.RetroAttire. docx.

Preparation

Activity 15-1. Purchase Order. Create a purchase order form to use when purchasing from vendors.

Activity 15-2. Vendor Selection. Research possible vendors to use for materials to create your products, deliver your services, or purchase your inventory. Explain their advantages to your business.

Activity 15-3. Inventory Management. Describe your inventory management process.

Activity 15-4. Business Plan Notes. Create notes about the research you did when determining an inventory management system for your business. Keep your notes and research sources here to reference in the Bibliography section of the plan.

Business Plan—Operations

In this chapter, you learned about purchasing and maintaining adequate levels of merchandise for your business. Now, you will work on the Marketing Strategies subsection of the Operations section of the business plan. In specific, you will complete the place strategy.

1. Open your saved business plan document.

2. Locate the Operations section of the business plan and the Marketing Strategies subsection. Finish writing the place strategies portion. Include the vendors you plan to use and describe your inventory management system. Use the suggestions and questions listed in each section of the template to help you generate ideas. Delete the instructions and questions when you are finished writing each section. Make sure to proofread your document and correct any errors in keyboarding, spelling, and grammar.

3. Save your document.

CHAPTER

16 Risk Management

Good business is not all about making money; it also involves being prepared in case of a disaster. On May 22, 2011, Joplin, Missouri, experienced a tornado that claimed 160 lives and destroyed more than 8,000 homes and businesses. Fortunately, Jason Ingermason, the owner of the Freddy's Frozen Custard and Steakburgers franchise in Joplin took steps to prepare his business for emergency situations. Ingermason's plan included: 1. create a disaster plan; 2. train employees how to use the plan; 3. store important business documents off-site; 4. have insurance coverage for business interruptions; and 5. plan to provide for employees after a disaster. Since Ingermason was prepared, he was able to rebuild his business. Having a risk-management plan may mean the difference between saving your business and closing its doors.

"Entrepreneurs are risk takers, willing to roll the dice with their money....They willingly assume responsibility for the success or failure of a venture and are answerable for all its facets."

—Victor Kiam, entrepreneur and former owner of the New England Patriots

College and Career Readiness

Reading Prep. As you read this chapter, think about what you are learning. How does this compare and contrast with similar information you have learned in other classes?

Sections

Picture Yourself Here
Michael Evangelista-Ysasaga

Michael Evangelista-Ysasaga is the CEO of The Penna Group, a construction contractor located in Fort Worth, Texas. Michael has been working in construction for most of his life. Both of his grandfathers were general contractors. By age 8, Michael was painting the inside of closets for his maternal grandfather. At age 18, he started his own general-contracting firm to pay his way through college.

The Penna Group is a contractor for the US military and government. It conducts excavation and site preparation; water, sewer, road, and other infrastructure installations; and construction of commercial, institutional, and residential buildings.

Michael earned his bachelor degree and went to law school. Even while working at a law firm, he continued working at his general-contracting firm as a side job. By 2006, the contracting business outpaced the functions of sole proprietorship, so Michael incorporated the business as The Penna Group, LLC.

Photo © The Penna Group

Check Your Entrepreneurship IQ

Before you begin the chapter, see what you already know about entrepreneurship by taking the chapter pretest. The pretest is available at www.g-wlearning.com

SECTION 16.1 Identify Risk

Objectives

After completing this section, you will be able to:
- **Explain** why it is important to plan for risk.
- **List** and describe the four types of risk.

Essential Question

How can a business identify and plan for risks?

Key Terms

controllable risk
uncontrollable risk
natural risk
human risk
shoplifter
burglary
robbery

employee theft
fraud
embezzlement
economic risk
market risk
product obsolescence
planned obsolescence

Critical Thinking

All businesses face some type of risk. Identify the various risks an entrepreneur might anticipate. Make a list of the top-ten risks entrepreneurs could face at some point in their business operations.

Plan for Risk

As discussed in chapter 2, *business risk* is the possibility of loss or injury that might occur while running a business. Whenever possible, it is important to plan for the different risks that may affect your business. Once you have identified possible risks, assess the seriousness of the risks and the likelihood of loss. Risks fall into different categories.

Controllable risk is one that cannot be avoided, but can be minimized by purchasing insurance or implementing a risk plan. For example, the risks of fire or storm damage are controllable because they are covered by insurance.

Uncontrollable risk is a situation that cannot be predicted or covered by purchasing insurance. For example, an economic recession or a price war started by competitors is an example of uncontrollable risks. There are no insurance plans to cover those types of financial losses.

In addition, risk can be identified as either speculative or pure. A *speculative risk* carries with it the chance of a profit or loss. For example, becoming an entrepreneur is a speculative risk because the

Copyright Goodheart-Willcox Co., Inc.

business may be successful or unsuccessful. A *pure risk* is the threat of loss with no chance for profit. If someone steals from the business or a natural disaster happens, for example, there is no possibility of gain from these events. Such events can also be a *liability risk* that has the possibility of losing money or other property as a result of legal proceedings.

Types of Risk

As shown in Figure 16-1, there are four basic types of risk: natural, human, economic and political, and market. Each type of risk will cost a business money if or when that situation happens.

Natural Risk

Natural risk is a situation caused by nature. Extreme weather conditions like floods, tornadoes, hurricanes, and earthquakes may damage or demolish a business. Many businesses may never recover from these natural disasters. However, natural risks are considered controllable because insurance can help recover the losses from damage.

All business owners, as well as individuals, should have a disaster plan. Storms, earthquakes, and other unexpected events can happen without warning. It is important to have a plan for protecting business records, equipment, people, etc., from unexpected natural disasters.

- Develop a communication plan to instruct and notify employees of evacuation procedures should a hurricane, tornado, or other natural disaster occurs.

- Hold fire drills and practice sessions with employees using fire extinguishers.

- Protect assets by storing pictures of each and an accurate inventory backed up at another location in case of fire.

SBA Tips

Getting back to business after a disaster depends on preparedness planning done today. For small business owners, being prepared can mean the difference between staying open following a disaster or closing. The SBA offers information to help entrepreneurs plan for doing business after disasters.
www.sba.gov

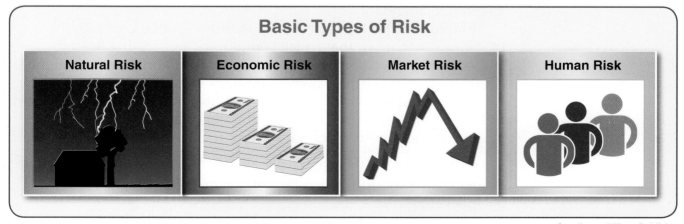

Basic Types of Risk

Natural Risk   Economic Risk   Market Risk   Human Risk

Goodheart-Willcox Publisher

Figure 16-1. The four basic types of risk can cause loss, damage, or injury.

Copyright Goodheart-Willcox Co., Inc.

Human Risk

Human risk is a situation caused by human actions. Employees and customers pose potential risks of theft, fraud, or accidental injury. *Shrinkage* is the term that identifies inventory losses due to shoplifting, employee theft, paperwork errors, and vendor fraud. Paperwork errors are unavoidable and unintentional. They are usually found through accounting and inventory procedures.

Theft

There are several different ways that theft that can impact any business. They include shoplifting, burglary, robbery, and employee theft.

Shoplifting. A **shoplifter** is a person, posing as a customer, who takes goods from the store without paying for them. In 2010, shoplifting worldwide accounted for approximately $115 billion of lost sales. Shoplifting tends to happen when there are not enough employees to observe people coming into a business. Creating false distractions is a common method of fraud. One customer may distract an employee while another person steals cash or causes confusion with numerous exchanges of cash in order to get more money in return.

Burglary. A **burglary** occurs when a person breaks into a business to steal merchandise, money, valuable equipment or take confidential information. There are many different ways for burglars to enter a building. Picking locks, hiding in the business after closing, using stolen or duplicated keys, or breaking windows or doors are all common methods.

Robbery. A **robbery** is a theft involving another person, often by using force or with the threat of violence. Robbers typically approach employees who have access to cash. Robbers usually target businesses that have large sums of money and have few employees, such as a convenience store or bank. However, robbers may also steal from employees with little access to cash, such as pizza delivery people or gas station attendants.

Employee Theft. It is never fun to think about the possibility of **employee theft**, or that trusted employees are stealing from the business. However, employee theft is more common than you might think. It can cost business owners millions of dollars each year.

Many employees handle money and inventory, and the temptation to steal it may be great. There are numerous ways for employees to steal, so make sure to watch for signs of theft.

- Abuse of employee-discount privileges.

- Excessive voiding of sales, which may mean an employee is pocketing cash sales.

Copyright Goodheart-Willcox Co., Inc.

- Customers complaining of being overcharged, which may mean an employee is pocketing the difference between the ticket price and the amount paid.

- Repeated shortages on an employee's cash drawer.

- Inventory records not matching sales on an employee's shift.

- Friends hanging around an employee who is working may be a distraction so the employee can take products or cash.

Fraud

Fraud is cheating or deceiving a business out of money or property. Employees, vendors, and customers can commit fraud. Some of the more common types of fraud include embezzlement, vendor theft, writing bad checks, using expired or stolen credit cards, using counterfeit money, and hacking electronic data.

Embezzlement. Embezzlement is a type of fraud that occurs when somebody entrusted with confidential company information, financial records, money, or other valuables takes it for personal gain. There are many ways to embezzle business funds, such as diverting

Property theft is the number one crime in the United States. It is estimated that in North America there are 600,000 cases of shoplifting each day.

Employee theft becomes a risk when you have several people handle money.

Christy Thompson/Shutterstock.com

Copyright Goodheart-Willcox Co., Inc.

Focus on Finance

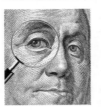

Diminishing Returns

Diminishing returns is the economic principle that putting more effort into creating a good or service may not necessarily generate more revenue. As an owner, you want your product to be perfect for your customer. However, the time comes when you must say, "I have done my best," and move on to the next product or task. Any additional time or effort will not generate more revenue. It will be important to know when you have reached the point of diminishing returns to put your efforts to moving the company forward. Flat or declining sales will most likely be a good indicator.

money or products and changing sales or bookkeeping records. For example, employees may create fake entries in ledgers and transfer business funds into personal bank accounts.

Vendor Theft. Dishonest vendors will deliver less than what was ordered but charge for the full order. These vendors may or may not change records. The loss is absorbed by the business.

Bad Checks. Dishonest customers may try to pay with fake checks printed for the purpose of fraud. They may also attempt to pay with checks from bank accounts with insufficient funds to cover the purchase. If a business accepts bad checks, the bank will not honor the check and the business will lose that amount of money. The business may also be charged a fee by the financial institution for trying to deposit bad checks.

Expired or Stolen Credit Cards. Some customers try to pay with a credit card knowing the card is no longer valid. This can be avoided by using a credit card authorizing machine linked to a central source where the credit cards are validated. Avoid accepting stolen credit cards by always asking for a photo ID of the person trying to use the card.

Counterfeit Money. Counterfeit money is fake and not legal tender. Banks will not accept counterfeit money. Businesses that accept counterfeit money as payment for goods or services will lose that amount of money as well as the cost of the product.

Data Security. Every business storing electronic data runs the risk of data security violations. Businesses that use e-commerce are vulnerable to computer hackers attempting to steal sensitive customer and credit card information. Business owners must be concerned with maintaining security on their Internet sites to prevent identity theft and unauthorized use of credit cards.

Copyright Goodheart-Willcox Co., Inc.

Accidental Injury

Accidents can happen easily in the workplace. Employees and customers run the risk of falling or becoming involved in other situations leading to injury. For example, a customer may break a leg by tripping over a bucket left in an aisle by an employee. Or, an employee may be injured while using heavy equipment. The business is responsible for all associated costs of injuries happening on the premises and may even face a negligence lawsuit.

Economic and Political Risk

Economic risk is a situation that occurs when the economy suffers due to negative business conditions in the United States or the world. Economic risk is hard to predict and is uncontrollable. During a stable or expanding economy, customers are purchasing enough goods and services to keep most businesses open and profitable.

However, every economy has both good and bad business cycles. One example is the financial crises that started in 2008. The US economy fell into a deep recession and many people lost their jobs. These economic crises created a negative impact on consumer spending over a long period of time. Some businesses were forced to close their doors, lay off employees, or find other ways of earning revenue.

Political conditions in the United States or other countries may create risk for global businesses. Countries without free trade agreements with the United States can change their import and export policies at any time. This may negatively affect the ability of US businesses to sell products.

During an economic recession or depression, customers have less money to spend.

Kzenon/Shutterstock.com

Copyright Goodheart-Willcox Co., Inc.

Market Risk

Businesses create goods and services based on projected consumer needs and wants. However, these wants and needs can change very quickly. All businesses have some type of market risk. **Market risk** is the potential that the target market for new goods or services is much less than originally thought.

Products that could be sold yesterday may be obsolete and unsellable today. When customers no longer want to buy a product, an owner might be stuck with merchandise that will not sell. This is known as **product obsolescence**. Some products have short life cycles, which are discussed in chapter 10. **Planned obsolescence** is evaluating and updating current products or adding new ones to replace older ones.

Competitors can also contribute to the market risk of a business. For example, a direct competitor may choose to drastically reduce prices and put pressure on your business.

Section 16.1 Review

Check Your Understanding ⤷

1. What is a business risk?
2. What is risk management?
3. What are the four types of risks an entrepreneur should anticipate?
4. What types of risks are posed by employees and customers?
5. Explain product obsolescence.

Build Your Vocabulary ⤷

As you progress through this text, develop a personal glossary of key terms. This will help you build your vocabulary and prepare you for a career. Write a definition for each of the following terms and add them to your personal glossary.

controllable risk	fraud
uncontrollable risk	embezzlement
natural risk	economic risk
human risk	market risk
shoplifter	product
burglary	obsolescence
robbery	planned
employee theft	obsolescence

SECTION 16.2 | Manage Risk

? **E**ssential **Q**uestion

What can businesses do to manage risks?

Objectives

After completing this section, you will be able to:

- **Summarize** the importance of risk management.
- **Describe** ways to avoid or reduce risk.
- **Explain** how a business can transfer some forms of risk.
- **Discuss** why a business may assume some risk.

Key Terms

surveillance
insurance
business owner's policy insurance
worker's compensation
premium

insurable interest
guarantee
surety bond
uninsurable risk

Critical Thinking

You have identified the types of risk that your business may encounter. Which of these risks can be managed by purchasing insurance? What are the best types of insurance for your business?

Risk-Management Techniques

Risk management, as defined in chapter 2, is the process for identifying, assessing, and reducing risks of different kinds. Depending on the type of risk, there are several risk-management techniques. Through proper risk management, risks may be avoided, reduced, transferred, or assumed by the business.

Successful entrepreneurs also learn to become skilled risk managers. They can identify risks before they happen. As the business grows, there will probably be other managers who, as part of the leadership team, participate in creating and maintaining a risk-management plan.

Avoid or Reduce the Risk

Putting the business in a situation that could bring negative results is not a good business decision. The best way to manage risk is to prevent a risky situation from happening in the first place.

Copyright Goodheart-Willcox Co., Inc.

However, risk cannot always be avoided, so the strategy of reducing or minimizing risk is just as important.

It is nearly impossible to avoid natural or economic and political risk. Some human risk and market risk may be avoided or reduced, though, by using simple proactive strategies.

Human Risk

Reducing human risk takes many forms and depends on the nature of each risk. The different forms of theft and fraud may be hard to detect; so, there can never be enough prevention or detection activities. The number of accidents can be reduced through education and employee-safety policies.

External Theft

Funds may not be available to create a security department or hire a security officer. However, there are ways to reduce the chance of someone shoplifting in, robbing, or burglarizing a business.

Cash-Handling Policies. To help reduce the financial loss from robberies, have cashiers periodically turn in cash or put money in a secure drop box. Employees who make bank deposits should change the times they go and the routes taken often. Post signs indicating the business does not keep cash on the premises.

Structural Security. Providing security measures on the structure of the building is a good option to protect business assets. Examples of structural security include outside lighting, burglar alarms, extra locks, fire exits, and security systems.

To help reduce the risk of theft, some businesses install security systems.

aodaodaodaod/Shutterstock.com

Copyright Goodheart-Willcox Co., Inc.

Global Entrepreneurs

Ray Zuckerman

Ray Zuckerman established ServerLIFT in 2002 when he was in his early 60s, an age when most people are thinking about retirement. However, Zukerman is still the chief executive of the company. ServerLIFT manufactures lifting units designed specifically for computer data centers.

ServerLIFT is located in Phoenix and has only 10 employees. Yet, its sales are about $3 million annually. One-third of sales are from customers in 20 countries other than the United States, including Australia and China. The company saw growth of about 50 percent a year from 2009 to 2010. Zuckerman is confident the market will continue to grow.

One uncontrollable risk of selling globally is the changing value of the US dollar. As the value of the dollar rises, international customers cannot buy as much product. However, Zuckerman feels customers in other countries think of US products as having high quality. He believes the perception of quality drives international sales for ServerLIFT more than a decrease in the value of the US dollar would. "We've always offered a money-back guarantee with paid return freight, and we've never had a product returned," says Zuckerman. The first unit ServerLIFT produced, which was in 2005, is still in service.

Surveillance. Surveillance is the process of observing everything going on in the business to detect and prevent crimes. Having enough employees on the sales floor to monitor every customer is a key to preventing shoplifting. Posting *shoplifters will be prosecuted* signs may help deter some theft as well.

Businesses might hire security guards, use two-way mirrors, or have video and closed-circuit monitoring devices. Camera and video surveillance are good security measures, but surveillance is not enough to catch all shoplifters or dishonest employees.

Theft Deterrents. Place valuable merchandise in locked display cases with limited access. Electronic tags on merchandise may also prevent theft. The electronic tags will set off an alarm if they are removed from the store.

Security Policies. Security policies are rules for employees to follow to help protect the business and ensure security. Many businesses address security situations and how to handle them in their employee handbooks. Topics covered may include how to handle money when working alone and how to secure the business when closing. The risk can also be reduced by having enough employees in the establishment so that customers are not unattended.

The National Retail Federation says organized retail crime costs US businesses an estimated $30 billion each year in stolen property and lost revenue. It is estimated that worldwide businesses lose $115 billion or more each year.

Employee Theft

The best way to prevent employee theft is by hiring honest employees. Conduct background checks on applicants to discover criminal records or other negative issues. It is also important to verify that the applicant is eligible to work in the United States. The US government runs a free program called E-Verify that confirms applicants' work status.

Since there are no guarantees that even the most honest employee will not steal, it is also wise to create employee-theft deterrents. Have specific employee policies in place with the penalties for violating them stated in clear terms. These policies are especially important for those handling cash. When reviewing surveillance video, look for signs of employee theft in addition to customer activities.

Fraud

Managing the risk of fraud takes some very specific steps to reduce the potential losses. Fraud can be difficult to prove.

Bad Checks. Verify that all checks will clear. Call the financial institution issuing the check to verify there are sufficient funds in the account to cover the purchase. Some financial institutions and companies offer check-verification services that electronically identify whether the check is from an account with previous problems. However, the only way to learn if the account has sufficient funds is to call the financial institutions directly. The financial institution may charge a fee to perform the service.

It is a good practice to ask for customer identification. Write the driver's license number or other identification on the check for future reference. Many businesses also have a policy to only accept checks written up to a certain amount, such as $100, to lessen the loss if the check is bad.

Employee Fraud. Make sure employees are not in the position to commit fraud. Maintain a system of checks and balances by separating purchasing and recordkeeping duties. Also, have more than one person check the incoming inventory shipments for errors.

Vendor Fraud. Before using a vendor, check its status with the Better Business Bureau. Have employees check in deliveries while the delivery person is present. If possible, set the delivery schedule with the vendor at down times for the business. Instruct employees to only accept deliveries when they have time to physically check them in.

Data Security. Firewalls and strong passwords can reduce the risk from hackers stealing a business' electronic proprietary information. Use updated virus-protection software to reduce the risk of malware and viruses.

For a business conducting e-commerce, set up a secure order-taking website. A URL that starts with https:// indicates the website is secure. Make sure that credit card or other sensitive customer information is only taken through the secure site. Secure sites use sophisticated encryption techniques to prevent hacking.

Copyright Goodheart-Willcox Co., Inc.

Data security often begins with a secure password.

EDHAR/Shutterstock.com

Accidents

As the saying goes, "accidents will happen." However, many can be prevented with safety policies and techniques. The Occupational Safety and Health Administration (OSHA) enforces safety and health regulations in the workplace. Since it was established in the 1970s, OSHA's efforts have greatly reduced workplace injuries and deaths.

Learn and follow the OSHA rules and regulations that apply to your business. Some OSHA rules are simply common sense and are good preventative techniques, while others are required by law. It is also wise to ensure employees follow the safety and ergonomic suggestions discussed in greater detail in chapter 14.

Provide periodic accident-prevention education for all employees. Inspect equipment on a regular basis for employee safety. Make sure the interior and exterior of the business location is free from obstructions and safe for both customers and employees.

Market Risk

Market risks are a part of doing business. No owners can control their competition or foresee all changes in consumer buying behaviors. It is important to be aware of the competition and have a marketing plan in place to keep competitors at a distance. Conduct extensive market research before offering or creating new products to ensure there is enough demand.

Copyright Goodheart-Willcox Co., Inc.

Transfer the Risk

Both *natural risk* and *human risk* can be transferred or shifted to other companies so the business owner does not bear the losses alone. Purchasing insurance is the most common way to transfer risk. For example, a business may purchase insurance to cover damages from natural disasters or losses due to theft or workplace accidents.

Insurance

Insurance is a form of risk management that spreads individual risk among a large group, thereby reducing the cost of losses to a single member of the group. Most people purchase personal insurance to protect themselves and their families from unforeseen events. By purchasing insurance, risk is transferred to the insurance company.

A business can also purchase insurance to protect itself and its employees. For example, commercial general liability and commercial property insurance are the most common forms of commercial insurance. **Business owner's policy insurance** provides low-cost property and liability coverage for small business owners.

Worker's compensation insurance is a state-mandated business insurance program. It is intended to provide medical and financial support for workers who are injured or made ill due to the job.

Some owners choose to buy additional personal insurance that covers them in the case of financial loss. Figure 16-2 shows examples of risk and the types of insurance that a business might need to purchase.

An individual or business buying an insurance policy is the *policyholder.* Each insurance policyholder is sharing the risk by paying a fee called a **premium**. The insurance company earns money, in part, by investing the premiums. Premiums and earnings are used to pay claims. A *claim* is submitted by a policyholder for payment related to a covered loss.

Businesses spend billions of dollars annually on insurance. The greater the insured risk, the higher the cost of insurance. An insurance professional can recommend the appropriate amount of insurance coverage for a business. Professional organizations such as the SBA can provide a list of agents in a specific area. In order to obtain insurance, some conditions must be met.

Insurable Interest

The policyholder must have an insurable interest. **Insurable interest** means the policyholder is at risk of suffering a loss. For example, a business cannot purchase fire insurance on a neighboring business and then collect money if that business is destroyed by fire.

Entrepreneur Ethics

Filing false insurance claims is unethical and illegal. It is important to file accurate information and only request assistance from an insurance company when a claim can be proven. Filing false or misleading claims can result in insurance coverage being canceled.

Copyright Goodheart-Willcox Co., Inc.

Insurance Coverage Available to Business Owners	
Commercial Insurance	**How It Protects the Business**
General liability	Provides protection for businesses and individuals against losses resulting from personal injuries or damage to the property of others for which the insured is responsible
Product liability	Provides protection for injuries or damage resulting from faulty products
Professional liability	Protects from suits stemming from mistakes made or bad advice given in a professional situation
Automobile liability	Covers property damage, bodily injury, collision, fire, theft, vandalism, and other related vehicle losses
Fire and theft	Covers losses to buildings and their contents from fire and theft
Business interruption	Provides compensation for loss due to fire, theft, or similar disasters that close a business; covers loss of income, continuing expenses, and utility expenses
Fidelity bonds	Covers costs incurred from employee dishonesty
Surety bonds	Covers losses resulting from a second party's failure to fulfill a contract
Employee Insurance	**How It Protects the Employees**
Group health insurance	Covers losses due to sickness or accidents
Group life insurance	Provides compensation in the event of an employee's death
Workers' compensation	Guarantees payment of wages, medical care, and rehabilitation services for employees injured on the job
Owner Insurance	**How It Protects the Owner**
Personal disability	Covers earnings while the insured is disabled as a result of accident or illness
Key person insurance	Enables business with the loss of a key executive/partner to pay bills and continue operation of the business
Basic health insurance	Covers losses due to sickness or accidents
Medical insurance	Protects against catastrophic losses by covering expenses beyond the limits of basic policies
Life insurance	Provides compensation in the event of death

Goodheart-Willcox Publisher

Figure 16-2. There are many different types of insurance coverage available for business owners.

Measurable Loss

The insured loss must be measurable. There must be a specific value to determine the amount of loss. It is important to document insured items with pictures, copies of inventory records, and costs and dates when items were purchased. If damage occurs, the insurance company is able to calculate loss from the documentation. Keep these documents in a safe place, preferably off-site.

Copyright Goodheart-Willcox Co., Inc.

The chance of loss must also be measurable. Insurance companies anticipate the percentage of losses that might occur and base the premium amounts on their calculations.

Unexpected

The loss must be accidental and unexpected. For example, general liability insurance covers property damage if it happens. However, property damage is not actually expected.

Contracts

As discussed in chapters 6 and 8, contracts are legally binding agreements. Lease and rental agreements, guarantees or warranties, and surety bonds are some common contracts that transfer business risk.

When starting a business, it may be too costly to purchase or construct a building. A business may lease or rent property to lower expenses. When leasing or renting a building, the risk of property ownership is transferred to the owner of the property. The property owner is responsible for maintenance and upkeep.

Warranties and guarantees are promises by the seller or manufacturer made to the buyer about the performance or quality of products. *Warranties* are promises to repair or replace faulty products. **Guarantees**, however, ensure product quality and promise to give customers their money back on faulty products. If a customer has a guarantee or warranty on a product, the risk of defects is transferred to the provider of the product.

Surety bonds are three-party contracts that guarantee one party fulfills its obligation to a second party. However, if the obligation is not met, the payment is made by the third party, which is the company issuing the surety bond. Surety bonds are similar to buying short-term insurance to guarantee performance.

Surety bonds are often required in the construction industry to guarantee a project is completed on time and as the contract specified. The surety bond protects the receiving business against losses resulting from the other party's failure to meet the obligation. When purchasing a surety bond, the risk of fulfilling the contract is transferred to the insurance company issuing the surety bond.

Assume the Risk

Unfortunately, insurance may not be available for all of the risks that need to be covered. An **uninsurable risk** is one that an insurance company will not cover. When that is the case, the business must assume the full risk and be responsible for losses associated with those risks. Some examples of uninsurable risks are losses due to market risk, economic and political risk, and personal risk. For example, losing a job is an uninsurable risk.

Copyright Goodheart-Willcox Co., Inc.

In addition, a business may choose to self-insure some risk to keep insurance premiums low and save money. One way is to self-insure by setting up a bank account for that purpose. This could be a designated account where money is deposited each month to plan ahead for a possible loss. In a way, it would be much like paying a premium to an insurance company, except the premium is paid to your own business and your business assumes 100 percent of the risk. That way, if something happens, self-insurance money is available to draw on to cover losses. State regulations may require a business to prove it can finance self-insurance before allowing it.

jcjgphotography/Shutterstock.com

Certain types of products, such as video game systems, usually come with a manufacturer's warranty.

Copyright Goodheart-Willcox Co., Inc.

Section 16.2 Review

Check Your Understanding ➦

1. List five things business owners can do to reduce the risk of loss resulting from external theft.
2. What is OSHA?
3. What is the most common way to transfer risk?
4. What type of low-cost policy provides property and liability coverage for small business owners?
5. Explain under what circumstances a surety bond is required.

Build Your Vocabulary ➦

As you progress through this text, develop a personal glossary of key terms. This will help you build your vocabulary and prepare you for a career. Write a definition for each of the following terms and add them to your personal glossary.

surveillance
insurance
business owner's policy insurance
worker's compensation
premium
insurable interest
guarantee
surety bond
uninsurable risk

Copyright Goodheart-Willcox Co., Inc.

Essential Question

How can businesses manage credit risks?

Objectives

After completing this section, you will be able to:

- **Define** the types of credit risk.
- **Explain** the risks and rewards of extending credit.
- **Identify** the costs of credit for a business.
- **Identify** how to reduce credit risk.

Key Terms

debtor
creditor
debtor-creditor relationship
credit risk
consumer credit
installment loan

trade credit
customer loyalty
collection agency
credit report
credit bureau
accounts receivable aging report

Critical Thinking

Determine what the costs of credit might be for your business. Are these costs going to help your business to grow or will they simply eat away at your profits? Explain why.

Types of Credit Risk

Credit is an agreement or contract to receive goods or services before actually paying for them. The **debtor** is the individual or business who owes money for goods or services received. The **creditor** is the individual or business to whom money is owed for goods or services provided.

The **debtor-creditor relationship** is a legal relationship existing between the two parties. This relationship is based on good faith that both parties will uphold their end of the agreement. The debtor must repay the creditor based on the terms. This relationship can be enforced by law because it is a contract.

Credit risk is the potential of credit not being repaid. Businesses or consumers that cannot pay their credit debts may risk legal action being taken against them.

Creating debt for the business is similar to creating debt for an individual. If the business does not have cash to pay what is owed, the owner could get in financial trouble and have to close the business. A business' credit card debt will show up on personal credit reports and affect the credit rating of the owner. In a recession or depression, businesses may face closure due to an inability to pay credit card or trade credit debts.

There are benefits for a business to use credit for purchases. As with individuals, cash flow is a benefit of using credit. Credit enables cash to be used for more immediate needs where credit cannot be used. Being able to use credit allows goods and services to be used while they are being paid for. Credit, especially for a small business, can help keep the operation going.

Consumer Credit

Consumer credit is credit given to individual consumers by a retail business. Consumer credit can be in the form of a loan or the business' proprietary credit card, such as Macy's or Dillard's. Proprietary credit cards may only be used in the stores issuing them.

Each credit card transaction costs the business money.

Edyta Pawlowska/Shutterstock.com

Copyright Goodheart-Willcox Co., Inc.

Green Entrepreneurs

Green Insurance

When purchasing insurance for the business, consider buying from an insurance company that supports sustainable resources. One way insurance companies help protect the environment is by providing electronic billing rather than paper billing, helping to save tons of paper each year. When seeking insurance coverage, ask the agent about the company's commitment to sustainability and how it is demonstrated in the business.

If the business sells big-ticket items like appliances or cars, consumer credit may be offered in the form of an installment loan. An **installment loan** is a loan paid in regular payments, or installments, with interest until the loan is paid in full. Installment loans are called *secured loans.* Secured loans require *collateral,* an asset pledged to guarantee the loan will be repaid. If the loan is not repaid, the asset can be taken by the creditor and sold to recoup the cost of the loan.

Some businesses extend credit by accepting debit or credit cards from their customers. It is sometimes preferable to accept bank cards, such as MasterCard and Visa. An advantage of accepting these cards is that the retailer transfers the responsibility for collecting the money owed to the financial institution. The bank collects the money owed for the sale directly from the customer and then pays the business. This service is not free for the retailer or the customer. For the retailer, the bank adds a service charge to each purchase made on one of its debit or credit cards. For the customer, he or she must pay monthly interest on unpaid balances to the bank issuing the credit card.

Trade Credit

Trade credit is granting a line of credit to another business for a short period of time to purchase its goods and services. Trade credit is often used by established businesses. The line of credit extended is most often 30 or 60 days. This means that the negotiated purchase price is interest free for 30 or 60 days. Full payment is expected at the end of the time period. If the bill is paid in full by the specified date, no interest is charged. However, if the bill is not paid or not paid in full by the specified date, interest charges begin to accumulate. The negotiated purchase price is due plus interest charges, which increases the cost of the purchase. Due dates for trade credit repayment must be carefully monitored to maintain adequate cash flow and avoid interest charges.

Copyright Goodheart-Willcox Co., Inc.

Rewards and Risks of Extending Credit

When credit is extended to customers, there are obvious rewards. The most obvious reward is the generation of sales. Research shows that people will often spend more when using a credit card than if they are paying cash. The risks, of course, revolve around the inability to pay a debt.

Rewards

Offering credit through credit cards, installment loans, or trade credit can create a steady income for the business. Another reward of extending credit to customers is building customer loyalty. **Customer loyalty** is the continued and regular patronage of a business even when there are other places to purchase the same or similar products. There are many reasons that customers are loyal to a business, but one of them is convenience. Customers appreciate using a bank card for in-store or Internet purchases. Businesses that offer other businesses credit tend to generate more sales than if they only accepted cash.

Risks

FYI

Businesses that cannot pay their credit bills risk the possibility of bankruptcy that can lead to either restructuring the business or closing its doors.

While there are many rewards to offering consumer or trade credit, there are also risks. If a customer fails to pay a bill on time, it may cause a cash flow problem for the business. For example, many people lost their jobs during the recession of the early 21st century. The number of unemployed people who could not repay their credit bills put many business owners at risk.

For those customers who do not eventually pay their debts, it may be necessary for the creditor to incur costs and hire a collection agency. A **collection agency** is a company that collects past-due bills for a fee. Businesses may also attempt to get payment for debt under a certain amount of money through small claims court, depending on the state. Collecting bad debts, however, creates additional expenses for the business and, in turn, decreases income.

Costs of Credit

There are multiple costs involved when businesses extend or accept credit. These costs may directly affect profit. These are only a few of the costs of extending credit.

- If credit or debit cards are accepted, the business will have to pay transaction fees to the institution that issued the card.

- If trade credit is extended to businesses, cash is tied up that could be used to operate the business.

Copyright Goodheart-Willcox Co., Inc.

- Some customers may not pay their credit, which means that the net income for the business will be decreased.

- Credit requires additional paperwork, which takes management or employee time to process.

For these reasons, many businesses add an additional percentage, or markup, to the sales price of products to cover the cost of credit. *Cost of credit* includes a variable expense that influences the pricing decisions for products, as discussed in chapter 10. It is part of the overhead necessary for doing business.

Reducing Credit Risk

Each business must decide if extending credit to customers is a good business decision. Some businesses choose to only accept cash or checks to avoid the associated transaction fees. When granting credit to customers, it is important to establish a credit process that reduces risk.

Create a Credit Policy

Having a credit policy in place can help guide the process of extending credit. Credit policies vary by the type of credit extended to businesses or individual customers. It may be wise to seek professional financial advice when creating a credit policy. Once the best plan is established for your business, stick with it.

Before extending credit, establish dollar figures for the amount of credit that will be extended for installment loans and trade credit. Establish specific terms of repayment, interest rates, late fees, penalties, and actions for nonpayment. Make sure employees always ask for customer identification when accepting credit cards to help avoid credit card fraud. Set limits and guidelines for how much credit the business can afford to extend. Most importantly, when extending credit, carefully monitor the business' cash flow.

Require a Credit Application

If providing credit to customers through installment loans or with your proprietary credit card, it is important to check applicants' financial backgrounds. Customers should complete an application that shows credit history, work history, and other information necessary to qualify for credit. Depending on the loan amount or trade credit extended, you may also request financial statements that show net worth and financial status. Bank statements should also be requested.

Before extending credit to customers, customers should complete an application for credit.

bikeriderlondon/Shutterstock.com

Obtain a Credit Report

Before extending credit, it is important to learn an applicant's credit history. A person's credit history may provide information about his or her likelihood of repaying the credit. A **credit report** is a record of a business or person's credit history and financial behavior. It shows:

- the number and types of credit accounts and indicates any that are past due;

- how promptly credit cards statements and loans were paid off in full;

- if other bills, such as rent, taxes, or utilities, were paid on time;

- current total outstanding debts; and

- the available credit left on credit cards and home equity loans.

Credit reports are issued by credit bureaus. A **credit bureau** is a private firm that maintains consumer credit data and provides credit information to businesses for a fee. There are three national credit-reporting agencies: Equifax, Experian, and TransUnion LLC.

Copyright Goodheart-Willcox Co., Inc.

Evaluate the Information

Once information is obtained about the customer, evaluate the applicant's creditworthiness based on the *three Cs of credit.* The three Cs of credit are:

- character; the individual or business has a good record of repaying bills on time;

- capacity; the individual or business has a good employment history or business earnings; and

- capital; the individual or business has a positive net worth.

If approved for credit, give the customer a copy of your credit policies. This is necessary so that the customer knows what his or her responsibilities are to pay off the credit. Included may be payment schedule, interest, and late payment penalties. The Truth in Lending Act requires that businesses convey information to customers before the first transaction. If the customer is *not* approved for credit, convey that message as well.

If your business is going to extend credit to customers, be aware of consumer credit laws.

Manage Accounts Receivable

One very important financial-management task is to keep track of when the accounts receivable are due or overdue. The accounts receivable are the individuals or businesses that owe the company money. This activity is critical to keeping cash flow at the level that will pay bills so the business can remain open. Customers who are late making payments should be sent reminders urging them to pay.

You Do the Math   Problem Solving and Reasoning

Insurance is a financial service used to protect against loss. The insurance company charges its customers to assume their risk. The charge is called a *premium*. When a claim is made, the policyholder is responsible to pay a certain amount toward the loss before the insurance company begins to pay. This amount is called a *deductible*. Once the deductible is met, the insurance company begins to pay for covered losses above the deductible amount.

Solve the following problems.

1. The business auto insurance for Scott's printing company has a deductible of $500. One of the delivery drivers is in an accident that affects only the company truck. The truck requires $3,000 worth of repairs. How much will both Scott and the insurance company pay toward the repairs?

2. Angela's business owner's policy premium is $1,500 annually. She wants to increase the business property coverage limit from $150,000 to $250,000. Her insurance agent says this change will raise her premium by 6 percent. How much is Angela's new annual premium for this policy?

Copyright Goodheart-Willcox Co., Inc.

An **accounts receivable aging report** shows when accounts receivables are due as well as length of time accounts have been outstanding. An aging report typically shows receivables as current, 30 days, 60 days, 90 days, and 120 days and over. The purpose of an aging report is to indicate which receivables are more urgent to collect because they have been past due longer.

Section 16.3 Review

Check Your Understanding ➡

1. What is consumer credit? Identify and explain the types of consumer credit that a business might extend to customers.
2. Installment loans are taken out to finance what types of purchases?
3. Why should the due dates for trade credit repayment be carefully monitored?
4. Why would a business risk extending credit? Explain the cost of credit to a business owner. Describe how credit affects profit.
5. List five ways business can reduce credit risk.

Build Your Vocabulary ➡

As you progress through this text, develop a personal glossary of key terms. This will help you build your vocabulary and prepare you for a career. Write a definition for each of the following terms and add them to your personal glossary.

- debtor
- creditor
- debtor-creditor relationship
- credit risk
- consumer credit
- installment loan
- trade credit
- customer loyalty
- collection agency
- credit report
- credit bureau
- accounts receivable aging report

Copyright Goodheart-Willcox Co., Inc.

Chapter Summary

Section 16.1 Identify Risk

- Being an entrepreneur means taking some risks. A risk is the possibility that an unfavorable situation could happen to you or your business. This situation could cause an injury or loss. As an entrepreneur, you would need to identify risks that might occur and to be proactive in anticipating them. This is called risk management.

- There are several types of risk with which an entrepreneur needs to be concerned. These include natural, human, economic and political, and market risks.

Section 16.2 Manage Risk

- It is very important for an entrepreneur to first identify then manage risk to himself or herself as well as the business. All businesses need to create a risk management plan.

- The first risk management strategy to use is to avoid a risk. By using safeguards, such as a sprinkler system or security alarms, business owners might be able to avoid loss from fire and theft.

- Insurance is the most common way to transfer risk. By transferring risk, a business owner limits his or her risk of loss to what is paid for a premium and the amount of the deductible.

- One technique for risk management is to assume the risk. Some businesses choose to self-insure.

Section 16.3 Credit Risk

- Credit risk can come in the form of a business taking on more debt than it can pay back. It can also come from those to whom the business has extended credit. If they do not pay the debt back in a timely manner, or at all, the business loses the use of that money and may have to go out of business.

- Although extending credit to customers can be risky, it can also be in the business' best interest to do so. A potential reward for a business that extends credit is a customer may make a purchase on credit they would not otherwise be able to make. In addition, customers may tend to shop more where they have credit than where they do not. This helps build a customer base and customer loyalty.

- The cost of credit to a business is a variable expense. The more credit costs a business, the more it needs to charge for a good or service to recoup the credit costs.

- Creating a credit policy is a good way for businesses to reduce credit risk.

Online Activities

Complete the following activities to help you learn, practice, and expand your knowledge and skills.

➨ **Posttest.** Now that you have finished the chapter, see what you learned by taking the chapter posttest.

➨ **Key Terms.** Practice vocabulary for this chapter using the e-flash cards, matching activity, and vocabulary game until you are able to recognize their meanings.

Review Your Knowledge

1. How can an entrepreneur plan for risks?
2. Describe the four types of risks an entrepreneur might anticipate encountering in a business.
3. Name and describe the two classifications of risks.
4. How can an entrepreneur avoid risk? Reduce risk?
5. What does it mean to transfer the risk?
6. How does trade credit affect the negotiated price of a purchase?
7. Describe the purpose of a guarantee.
8. Explain a contractual agreement.
9. Explain the importance of purchasing insurance for a business.
10. Explain the concept of self-insuring.

Apply Your Knowledge

1. You have identified your business and the goods and services you will be providing your customers. Identify each risk you might encounter and label each as controllable or uncontrollable.
2. List the natural risks that you might face in your business as an entrepreneur.
3. Describe human risks which you might face in your business.
4. Which economic and political risks might be challenging for your business?
5. Describe the market risks you might face in your business.
6. Risks may be speculative risks or pure risks. Give examples of each that you might face in your business. Identify which risks are insurable and those that are uninsurable.
7. Describe your plan for reducing risks that pertains to the employees in your business.

Copyright Goodheart-Willcox Co., Inc.

8. Describe your plan for reducing risks from burglary or robbery.

9. How will you protect your technology assets from risks?

10. Describe your plan for transferring risks in your business.

Teamwork

Working with your team, discuss credit and debtor-creditor relationships. What risks and benefits do entrepreneurs encounter when they use credit for their business? What risks and benefits do entrepreneurs encounter when they extend credit to customers? Create a chart with two columns. Label the first column *Entrepreneurs Using Credit* and the second column *Entrepreneurs Extending Credit*. Record your team's discussion comments in each column of the chart.

Internet Research

Human Risks. Search the Internet for statistics on shoplifting and the impact on businesses. What is the financial impact that shoplifting has on businesses in your industry? Find an estimated dollar amount of losses related to shoplifting. What have businesses in your industry done to protect themselves from this type of risk?

Communication Skills

College and Career Readiness

Listening. Engage in a conversation with someone you have not spoken with before. Ask the person how he or she manages risk in personal circumstances and more formal circumstances such as at school or a job. Actively listen to what that person is sharing. Build on his or her ideas by sharing your own. Try this again with other people you have not spoken to before. How clearly were the different people able to articulate themselves? How do you think having a conversation with someone you do not normally speak to is different from a conversation you might have with a friend or family member you speak with every day?

Speaking. The way you communicate with and to customers and vendors will have a lot to do with the success of the relationships you build with them. There are different ways you communicate with different people in your life. There are formal and informal ways of communicating your message. Create two short speeches that will introduce your business. The audience for the first speech should be your friends who you hope will also be your customers. Design the second speech for a bank's loan committee. Deliver each speech to your class. How did the words, phrases, and tone you used change in the different speeches?

Copyright Goodheart-Willcox Co., Inc.

CTSOs

Entrepreneurship Project. Some Career and Technical Student Organizations (CTSOs) have competitive events where the chapter develops and executes a plan for a real business. A school store would be an example of this type of activity. The store would sell products, generate revenue, and operate as a small business.

For the competition, the chapter is required to prepare a report detailing: how the business contributes to the community, a business plan, and how the plan was implemented. There is a written document and a presentation to the judges.

To prepare for a chapter project on entrepreneurship marketing campaigns, complete the following activities.

1. Read the guidelines provided by your organization. Make certain that you ask any questions about points you do not understand. It is important to follow each specific item that is outlined in the competition rules.

2. Contact the association immediately at the end of the state conference to prepare for next year's event. The activity may begin any time after the state conference.

3. As a team, select a project that will involve the members of the chapter.

4. Decide which roles are needed for the team. If a school store is selected, there will be an accountant, inventory person, etc. Ask your instructor for guidance in assigning roles to team members.

5. Identify your target audience, which may include business, school, and community groups.

6. Make a decision as to how the business will be set up, where it will be located, how the revenues will be distributed, and all other details on how to run a profitable business.

7. This project will span the school year. During regular chapter meetings, create a draft of the report based on direction from the CTSO. Write and refine drafts until the final report is finished.

Copyright Goodheart-Willcox Co., Inc.

Building Your Business Plan—Putting the Puzzle Together

Risk Management

Risk is part of owning and operating a business. While the threat of losses from some risk can be avoided or reduced, there are many other risks that simply must be managed. Successfully managing the different forms of natural, human, economic and political, and market risk is critical to any business owner's success. Some risk can be transferred through insurance, while other risks may have to be assumed by the business. The risks of offering and receiving credit must also be taken into consideration for pricing and cash flow management purposes.

Goals

- Write a risk management plan for the first year of operation.
- Create a credit policy for your business.
- Create business plan notes.

Directions

Access the *Entrepreneurship* companion website at www.g-wlearning.com ➡. Download each data file for the following activities. A complete sample business plan is available on the companion website to use as a reference. The name of the file is BusPlan_Sample.RetroAttire. docx.

Preparation

Activity 16-1. Risk Management Plan. Identify the types of risk you expect to face in your business. Write a risk management plan that shows how you plan to avoid, reduce, transfer, or assume those risks in the first year of operation.

Activity 16-2. Credit Policy. Write a short initial credit policy you think might work well for your business. Include policies for both offering credit and receiving credit. If your business will not be offering or receiving credit, write a short policy for the possibility of that situation changing in the future.

Activity 16-3. Business Plan Notes. Create notes about risks your business may encounter and how to manage them. These risks will be addressed in the business plan. Keep your notes and resources here.

Business Plan—Operations

In this chapter, you learned about the different types of risk that businesses may face and how to manage them. In this activity, you will complete Risk Management, the last subsection of the Operations section of the business plan. Use the information you learned about risk and how to avoid, reduce, transfer, or assume your business' risk.

1. Open your saved business plan document.

2. Locate the Operations section of the business plan and the subsection called Risk Management. Use the suggestions and questions listed in the template to help you generate ideas. Delete the instructions and questions when you are finished writing the section. Make sure to proofread your document and correct any errors in keyboarding, spelling, and grammar.

3. Save your document.

CHAPTER

17 Financial Management

As a small business owner, it can be difficult to manage finances. Lance Bloyd, owner of Bucking Bull Pro, faced more challenges than most small business owners. A former rodeo rider, Bloyd provides custom goods and services for professional bucking bull breeders and contractors. He does not have a traditional store. A portion of his business results from website exposure and another part is from on-site sales at bull-riding events. Originally, Bloyd shipped the product and an invoice and simply trusted people to pay. He found that getting the invoice paid was troublesome. So, he started requiring up-front payment and ended up losing some sales. Bloyd realized he needed a way to accept credit card payments and a system that could travel with him to events. He found a mobile app that met his needs. The app also helps him manage his finances and track sales.

> *"It is not the employer who pays the wages. He only handles the money. It is the product that pays the wages."*

—Henry Ford, founder of Ford Motor Company

College and Career Readiness

Reading Prep. As you read this chapter, think about what you are learning. How can this information apply to the other classes you are taking?

Sections

Picture Yourself Here
Megan Faulkner Brown

Megan Faulkner Brown embraced the foundations of baking and entrepreneurship at an early age. Some of Brown's earliest memories are of sitting at the kitchen counter helping her mom make cookies. The Sweet Tooth Fairy is a gourmet bake shop specializing in all things sweet. After operating out of her home kitchen for several years, Megan opened her first retail location in January of 2009. With the help of family, friends, business mentors and partners, and investors, there are now more than 10 locations.

Once crowned champion of the Food Network's Cupcake Wars, Megan continues to lead the company as Chief Visionary Officer. In addition, she trains employees, finds new locations, and has introduced her signature Cakebites™ on the Rachael Ray Show, QVC, and the Gayle King Show. Before any product hits the shelves of the Sweet Tooth Fairy locations, it is first refined in Megan's kitchen. Megan also launched the Bake a Difference initiative, which actively supports causes to improve and inspire communities.

Photo © Megan Faulkner Brown, The Sweet Tooth Fairy

Check Your Entrepreneurship IQ

Before you begin the chapter, see what you already know about entrepreneurship by taking the chapter pretest. The pretest is available at www.g-wlearning.com

Accounting 101

Essential Question

What are basic accounting procedures that businesses should practice?

Objectives

After completing this section, you will be able to:

- **Explain** the basics of accounting.
- **Summarize** types of daily business transactions.
- **Describe** double-entry accounting procedures.

Key Terms

accounting
GAAP
audit
fiscal period
business entity
cash basis
accrual basis
sale on account

purchase on account
account
chart of accounts
double-entry accounting
journal
journalizing
ledger
posting

Critical Thinking

As a small business owner, you may have to take care of your financial records yourself rather than hire outside accounting help. Make a list of all business transactions that you will need to track in the operation of your business.

Accounting Basics

Accounting is the system of recording business transactions and analyzing, verifying, and reporting the results. The function of accounting is to keep a record of transactions and create regular financial statements.

Accounting functions are the financial recordkeeping activities for a business. They include recording, summarizing, analyzing, and interpreting financial information. Daily transactions must be *recorded* so that written evidence exists of business that has transpired. These records are then *summarized* to create financial statements. Financial statements are *analyzed* and *interpreted* to report the progress of the business.

Accounting is called the *language of business.* No matter the type of business or its form of ownership, the accounting process is an established standard for communicating financial information. All businesses large and small follow the *generally accepted accounting principles,* or **GAAP**. These are the rules, standards, and practices that businesses follow to record and report financial information.

Businesses use *internal controls* to make sure financial information is accurate and honest, as well as to safeguard the financial information. Controls can be preventive or detective. An example of an internal control that is preventative is limiting access of financial information to specific persons within an organization. Another example is conducting a review process of the financial information to ensure that processes follow GAAP.

In addition, audits are usually performed on a regular basis as a detective control. An **audit** is a review of the financial statements of a business and the accounting practices that were used to produce them. Most businesses hire an outside firm to conduct an audit.

Some businesses hire an accountant or bookkeeper to keep track of sales, expenses, and other accounting activities. However, hiring someone may not be feasible when the business is just beginning; so, the owner may take on this responsibility. A paper system is acceptable and used by many small business owners. However, most businesses use automated accounting packages and spreadsheets to streamline the process. The IRS and SBA provide free counseling services that can help an owner set up a proper accounting system.

Establish the Fiscal Period

A **fiscal period** is the period of time for which a business summarizes accounting information and prepares financial statements. It may also be called an *accounting period.* Fiscal periods may be for one month, one quarter, or one year. Newly established businesses may select monthly or quarterly fiscal periods so that they may evaluate progress more frequently. However, for tax purposes, most businesses use a year as the fiscal period, which is called the *fiscal year.* Businesses often use the *calendar year* of January 1 through December 31 as a fiscal year. However, a fiscal year can be any consecutive 12-month period.

FYI

Accountants plan, summarize, analyze, and interpret financial information for the business. A *bookkeeper* is trained to do general accounting activities, such as summarizing accounting information. A *tax accountant* specializes in tax preparation.

Green Entrepreneurs

Tax Advantages

Participating in green practices can bring the small business owner tax advantages. The federal and state governments may offer tax incentives for businesses that purchase energy-efficient products. It is beneficial for business owners to learn more about which tax breaks might be available for their businesses.

Copyright Goodheart-Willcox Co., Inc.

Using the accrual basis accounting method, you must record a sale the day it happens.

auremar/Shutterstock.com

Keep Personal Records Separate

Each business, whether it is a sole proprietorship, partnership, or corporation, is considered a business entity. A **business entity** is an organization that exists independently of the owner's personal finances. This means that personal financial records must be kept separate from the business records. For example, personal possessions, like a house and car, are not reported in business financial reports. If the business owns a building and vehicles that are used for the business, they will be only listed on the business' financial records, not the owner's personal records.

Establish the Accounting Method

There are two alternative accounting methods that are used to keep track of business transactions: cash basis of accounting and accrual basis of accounting. The **cash basis** of accounting recognizes revenue when it is received and expenses when they are paid. For example, a business sells $1,000 worth of DVDs to a customer. The invoice for that sale may request payment in 30 days. Under the cash basis, the sale is not recorded when it happened, but when the business receives the check from the customer. Usually, only very small businesses use the cash method.

The **accrual basis** of accounting records revenues and expenses when they occur. For example, under the accrual basis, that sale for $1,000 worth of DVDs is recorded the day the sale happens, regardless of when the check is received. Most businesses use the accrual method.

Copyright Goodheart-Willcox Co., Inc.

Keep Accurate Records

If the business does not keep accurate financial records, it may not be able to remain open for the long term. Also, records are necessary for accurate tax reporting. It is important to accurately maintain checking accounts, source documents, inventory, record of assets, and payroll.

Checking Account

Give the business checking account undivided attention. It is important to have adequate money in the account to pay the bills. Reconcile the account each month so that there are no penalties for overdrawn checks.

Source Documents

Create a system for tracking source documents for all transactions. This means keeping copies of all sales receipts as well as purchase orders and invoices.

Inventory

Keep all merchandise inventory records up to date. Each inventory item should have a record of the number of units, cost per unit, and reorder point. Depending on the business, other detailed information about the inventory may be included.

All businesses must know exactly how much merchandise is in stock and needed at all times to keep the business running. The value of merchandise inventory must also be calculated. The IRS recognizes alternative accounting for assigning costs to inventory. A business should use the method that is most advantageous to its situation.

Assets

Keep a list of all assets that the business owns. Create a record that describes each asset, its purchase price, where it was purchased, and date of purchase. This information is required for tax and insurance purposes.

Depreciation must also be recorded for assets. *Depreciation* is a method of distributing the cost of assets over the life of the assets that can be recorded on tax returns. The IRS recognizes alternative accounting for depreciation of assets. A business should use the method that is most advantageous to its situation.

Payroll

If there are employees, maintain accurate payroll information. The *payroll* is a list of the employees working for the business, their earnings, taxes withheld, and other deductions. Employers must understand the Federal Insurance Contribution Act (FICA) and other

SBA Tips

In 1979, the SBA created the Office of Women's Business Ownership to encourage more women to become entrepreneurs. The office now oversees more than 100 Women's Business Centers (WBCs) throughout the United States and its territories. The WBCs provide counseling and general business training in many languages specifically tailored for new female entrepreneurs. Staff at WBCs are trained in finance, management, marketing, and Internet use and have access to all of the SBA's financial-assistance and loan programs. The SBA found that businesses helped through the WBCs have a better survival rate than those that did not work with them.
www.sba.gov

payroll taxes so that they are properly deducted from the payroll and forwarded to the appropriate agencies. The business sends the tax withholdings for employees to the local, state, and federal governments. Other deductions, such as insurance premiums, are forwarded to the insurance company or other institutions that should receive the amounts.

Payroll records also include personal information about the employee such as Social Security number, employee address, number of dependents, and other specifics related to compensation. Employers are required by law to file various payroll forms for employees. Contact the IRS for rules and regulations about employer requirements for employee payroll records.

The Internal Revenue Service (IRS) has strict rules about which business records must be kept, such as W-2 and W-4 forms. It also dictates which forms employees must receive by certain dates for their own tax purposes. The IRS may assess fines for failure to comply with the rules.

FYI

All payroll information is summarized yearly for employee tax purposes.

Use the Accounting Equation

The accounting equation is necessary to begin recording financial information for the business. It is the foundation of all accounting records. The accounting equation is stated as:

$$\text{assets} = \text{liabilities} + \text{owner's equity}$$

As discussed in chapter 9, *assets* are the property or items of value a business owns. Examples of assets are cash, inventory, buildings, and office and manufacturing equipment.

A business also generally has *liabilities,* which are its debts owed to others. Examples of liabilities are accounts payable.

The difference between a business' assets and its liabilities is called *owner's equity.* Owner's equity is also known as *net worth.*

Daily Transactions

A business transaction is any activity that impacts the business. However, it does not always have to be a cash sale. A transaction could be issuing a purchase order or processing a customer return. A typical business will have transactions every day.

All transactions must be documented with a physical source document, such as a receipt, purchase order, or invoice. The IRS requires that a business maintain proper documentation. Source documents are necessary to prove the transaction actually happened. There are a variety of transactions that happen each day. Plan to keep records for cash sales, credit sales, sales on account, and purchases on account.

Copyright Goodheart-Willcox Co., Inc.

Source documents, like receipts, provide the documentation required by the IRS.

Golden Pixels LLC/Shutterstock.com

Cash Sales

Some customers will pay cash or write a check for their purchases. Give a copy of the sales receipt to the customer. Keep a copy for the business records.

Credit Sales

If a purchase is made using a proprietary card, credit card, or debit card, give the customer a sales receipt. The sales receipt includes details of the purchase and the last four digits of the card number used for payment. The business also keeps a copy of the same receipt.

The business uses these daily credit and debit sales receipts to calculate how much will be received from the credit card companies. The business also uses these records to calculate the monthly service charges owed to the credit card companies.

Sales on Account

A **sale on account** is a transaction for which cash for the sale will be received at a later date. A sales invoice will be sent to the customer and a copy will be kept for the business. The customer account is known as an account receivable. Accounts receivable are considered assets.

Copyright Goodheart-Willcox Co., Inc.

Purchases on Account

A **purchase on account** is a transaction for which merchandise purchased will be paid to the vendor at a later date. A purchase invoice will be sent to the vendor and a copy will be kept for the business. The vendor account is known as an account payable. Accounts payable are considered liabilities.

Double-Entry Accounting

The first step in recording a transaction is to identify which accounts are affected. An **account** is an individual record that summarizes information for a single category, such as cash or sales. The name of the account is called the *account title*. A list of all accounts in the business is called the **chart of accounts**, as shown in Figure 17-1.

Every transaction has at least two parts, or two accounts. For example, if a customer buys CDs, the business not only has a sale, but it also receives money. The two accounts involved for this transaction are Sales and Cash. At least one account will be debited and one account will be credited. *Debit* is the left side of an account and *credit* is the right side of an account, as shown in Figure 17-2.

Figure 17-1. Example of a chart of accounts.

Sophia's Web Design Co.
Chart of Accounts

ASSETS
101   Cash
102   Accounts Receivable
103   Equipment

LIABILITIES
201   Accounts Payable
202   Notes Payable

OWNER'S EQUITY
301   Sophia Nguyen, Capital
302   Sophia Nguyen, Drawing

REVENUE
401   Sales

EXPENSES
501   Advertising Expense
502   Rent Expense
503   Insurance Expense
504   Supplies Expense
505   Utilities Expense

Goodheart-Willcox Publisher

Copyright Goodheart-Willcox Co., Inc.

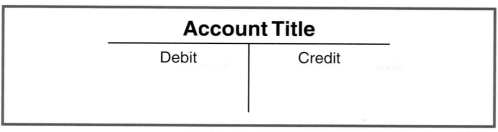

Account Title

Debit	Credit

Goodheart-Willcox Publisher

Figure 17-2. Placement of debits and credits in an account.

Recording the debit and credit parts of a transaction is called **double-entry accounting**. In addition, at least one account will be increased and one account will be decreased by the transaction. Increases are recorded on the balance side of an account.

- Asset and expense account types have debit balances; for these accounts, debits increase the balance and credits decrease the balance.

- Liability, revenue, and owner's equity account types have credit balances; for these accounts, credits increase the balance side and debits decrease the balance.

After a transaction is analyzed to determine the debits and credits, it is then recorded in a journal.

Journals

A **journal** is a form used to record business transactions in chronological order. **Journalizing** is the process of recording business transactions in a journal.

A business will select the journals that best fit its needs. Some businesses use special journals. A *special journal* is used to record only one type of transaction. For a business with a large number of transactions, special journals are an efficient way to journalize. There are four special journals:

- *Cash receipts journals* are used for all receipts of cash.

- *Cash payments journals* are used for all payments of cash.

- *Sales journals* are used for all sales on account transactions.

- *Purchases journals* are used for all purchases on account transactions.

If a business uses special journals, there will still be some transactions that will not fit in one of those journals. For example, when a customer returns merchandise, that transaction does not fit in a special journal. A return is not a cash receipt, cash payment, sale, or purchase. Instead, it is categorized as a return. In that situation, another journal is needed. The journal used for any transaction that does not belong in a special journal is called a *general journal*. A general journal can also be used to record all business transactions.

Entrepreneur Ethics

Business expenses are those costs necessary to keep the business running. Necessary expenses for the business may be deducted on the business' income tax returns. These deductions will decrease the amount of taxable income reported and lower the amount of taxes owed. It is unethical and illegal to report expenses that were not actually used for the operation of the business. Personal expenses such as meals and purchases may not be legally deducted on a business income tax return.

Some businesses choose to use only a general journal rather than special journals. Because the general journal requires the account name of the debit and credit to be written, it can accommodate any type of transaction. An example of a general journal is shown in Figure 17-3.

Ledgers

A group of accounts is called the **ledger**. The general ledger has individual accounts for each asset, liability, and owner's equity accounts.

Businesses also create individual accounts for customers who owe money as well as accounts for the vendors to whom the business owes money. Individual accounts for customers and vendors are called *subsidiary ledgers*.

After transactions are recorded in the journals, the information is transferred to the general ledger and the subsidiary ledgers, as shown in Figure 17-4. The transferring of information from the journals to the ledger is called **posting**. By posting to the ledgers, the business can obtain specific information about each account in the business. For example, if the business wants to know how much it owes for supplies expenses, the Supplies Expense account will show the current balance. Businesses generally post at the end of each business day so that the accounts are up to date.

	DATE		ACCOUNT TITLE	DOC. NO.	POST. REF.	GENERAL DEBIT	GENERAL CREDIT	
1	Mar	1	Cash			100 00		1
2			Sales				100 00	2
3			Receipt 101					3
4								4
5								5
6								6

GENERAL JOURNAL   **PAGE 3**

Goodheart-Willcox Publisher

Figure 17-3. Example of a general journal.

ACCOUNT SALES					ACCOUNT NO. 410		
		POST.				BALANCE	
DATE	ITEM	REF.	DEBIT	CREDIT	DEBIT	DEBIT	CREDIT
Mar 1		G1		100 00			100 00

Goodheart-Willcox Publisher

Figure 17-4. Example of a posting to the Cash account in a general ledger.

Section 17.1 | Review

Check Your Understanding

1. Define and explain basic accounting functions.
2. Analyze and differentiate the two alternative accounting methods of cash basis of accounting and accrual basis of accounting.
3. List five record types that are important for a business to accurately maintain.
4. When the debit and credit parts of a transaction are recorded, what type of accounting is being used?
5. What is the relationship between a journal and journalizing?

Build Your Vocabulary

As you progress through this text, develop a personal glossary of key terms. This will help you build your vocabulary and prepare you for a career. Write a definition for each of the following terms and add them to your personal glossary.

accounting	account
GAAP	chart of accounts
audit	double-entry
fiscal period	accounting
business entity	journal
cash basis	journalizing
accrual basis	ledger
sale on account	posting
purchase on account	

Copyright Goodheart-Willcox Co., Inc.

SECTION 17.2 Financial Statements

?E ssential Question

How do businesses use financial statements?

Objectives

After completing this section, you will be able to:

- **Explain** the importance of financial statements for a business owner.
- **Describe** the importance of financial statement analysis for making business decisions.

Key Terms

stakeholder
income statement
financial ratio
working capital

current ratio
debt ratio
net profit ratio
operating ratio

Critical Thinking

Recordkeeping is a timely and important task for any business. It may be your preference to hire someone to do your accounting tasks for you. However, you may not be able afford this service right away. List the pros and cons of stretching your budget to include professional accounting services.

Financial Statements

Financial statements are important to those who have invested in the business as well as those who own the business. Investors want to see how their investments are doing. Lenders want to know their loans will be repaid on time. Financial statements give stakeholders, or the people with interests in the business, updates about the status of the business.

Owners use financial statements to determine the business' profitability and to help plan future business activities. Financial statements are also used when completing tax returns. Accurate statements will make the tax process go smoothly and efficiently.

Chapter 9 discussed four pro forma statements—balance sheet, cash flow, income, and owner's equity. Pro forma statements are projections of future business transactions. After the business is operating, financial statements will be created to reflect the actual transactions that have occurred in the business.

Financial statements will vary depending on the type of ownership and if the business is a proprietorship, partnership, or corporation. However, for all businesses, financial statements will

Copyright Goodheart-Willcox Co., Inc.

Focus on Finance

Budgeting

A *budget* is a plan to estimate how much revenue will be earned and expenses will be incurred for a fiscal period. A budget is usually based on previous income and expense history from previous periods. By creating a budget, a business can be prepared to make decisions for future transactions. Compare the budget with your financial statements to review actual numbers and see how successful the budget is. Creating a budget is useful for cash-management purposes.

be created on a regular basis, either monthly or quarterly. Financial statements will also be prepared at the end of the fiscal year.

Balance Sheet

The balance sheet reports the assets, liabilities, and owner's equity. The difference between the assets and liabilities is the owner's equity. The information on the balance sheet is expressed as the accounting equation:

$$\text{assets} = \text{liabilities} + \text{owner's equity (net worth)}$$

The balance sheet gives a snapshot of the financial condition of the business for a specific date. An example of a balance sheet is shown in Figure 17-5.

FYI

After the business is open and running, the financial statements are no longer pro forma statements because they reflect actual business transactions, not estimates.

Sophia's Web Design Co.
Balance Sheet
December 31, 20--

ASSETS

Cash	$36,000	
Accounts Receivable	22,000	
Equipment	10,000	
Total Assets		$68,000

LIABILITIES

Accounts Payable	$24,000	
Notes Payable	13,000	
Total Liabilities		$37,000

OWNERS' EQUITY

Sophia Nguyen, Capital		31,000
Total Liabilities and Owner's Equity		$68,000

Figure 17-5. A sample balance sheet.

Goodheart-Willcox Publisher

Copyright Goodheart-Willcox Co., Inc.

Figure 17-6. A sample cash flow statement.

Sophia's Web Design Co.		
Cash Flow Statement		
June 31, 20--		
Cash Receipts		$10,000
Cash Disbursements		
Advertising Expense	$ 500	
Rent Expense	1,000	
Insurance Expense	500	
Supplies Expense	25	
Utilities Expense	250	
Total Disbursements		2,275
Net Cash Flow		$ 7,725

Goodheart-Willcox Publisher

Cash Flow Statement

A *cash flow statement* reports how cash moves in and out of a business. If the business is receiving more cash than it is spending, that is a positive cash flow. The reverse is negative cash flow. A cash flow statement indicates how well a business is managing its expenses as they relate to income. An example of a cash flow statement is shown in Figure 17-6.

Income Statement

An **income statement** reports the revenue and expenses of a business for a specific time period and shows a net income or net loss. The income statement is also known as a *profit and loss statement (P & L).* The income statement in Figure 17-7 is an example of an income statement for a service business.

Owner's Equity Statement

The *owner's equity statement* summarizes changes in the owner's equity during a fiscal period. It is important for business owners to know what the equity was at the beginning of the accounting period as well as the end. An owner's equity statement is shown in Figure 17-8.

Financial Statement Analysis

Financial statements are used to report information for the business. The information is also used to analyze the business by calculating financial ratios. **Financial ratios** evaluate a business' overall financial condition by showing the relationships between certain figures on financial statements.

FYI

Cash management is the process a company uses to ensure that it collects all cash owed to it. Effective cash management is vital to the success of any business because if enough cash does not come in, bills cannot be paid, and the business may close.

Copyright Goodheart-Willcox Co., Inc.

Sophia's Web Design Co.
Income Statement
Year Ended December 31, 20--

Revenue		
Sales		$68,000
Operating Expenses		
Advertising Expense	$ 5,000	
Rent Expense	20,000	
Insurance Expense	6,000	
Supplies Expense	200	
Utilities Expense	1,800	
Total Expenses		33,000
Net Income		$35,000

Figure 17-7. A sample income statement.

Goodheart-Willcox Publisher

Sophia's Web Design Co.
Owner's Equity Statement
December 31, 20--

Sophia Nguyen, Capital, January 1		$10,000
Plus Net Income	35,000	
Less Withdrawals	14,000	
Net Increase in Capital		21,000
Sophia Nguyen, Capital, December 31		$31,000

Figure 17-8. A sample owner's equity statement.

Goodheart-Willcox Publisher

By knowing the financial ratios, owners can identify in which areas the business is strong and where improvements need to be made. Financial ratios provide a benchmark of company performance to earlier years of the business. Ratios are also a good way to show comparisons with competitors in the same business.

Balance Sheet

The balance sheet shows the financial strength of the business. In order to plan for the future, a business must have enough resources to pay debts and still have money to invest in the business. A business can measure its financial strength by analyzing the balance sheet.

An important analysis for a business is to determine working capital. **Working capital** is the amount of money a business has after the liabilities are paid. This amount is the available capital for the operation of the business.

current assets – current liabilities = working capital
$68,000 – $37, 000 = $31,000

Copyright Goodheart-Willcox Co., Inc.

Social Entrepreneurs

Jason Aramburu

As part of a Princeton University research project, student Jason Aramburu worked with poverty-stricken farmers in rural Panama and realized he could help them. At age 25, Aramburu created a low-cost kiln that makes a product called biochar and founded the company re:char. Re:char's mission is to help subsistence farmers in the developing world. Biochar is a type of charcoal created from biomass, such as corn husks, wood, and animal waste. It is also a soil enrichment and can be used as cooking fuel. Farming has been improved in areas where re:char has provided kilns. Re:char manufactures locally in the areas it helps, cutting down on waste and distribution cost and increasing the need for local workers. Biochar is carbon-negative; so, it can help fight global climate change. More than 750 farmers in Kenya are using biochar, and the process is moving to Haiti to produce biochar for heating and cooking fuel.

The **current ratio** shows the relationship of assets to liabilities. This ratio shows how capable a company is to pay its liabilities.

current assets ÷ current liabilities = current ratio

$68,000 ÷ $37,000 = 1.8:1

The current ratio of 1.8:1 shows that assets are 1.8 times larger than liabilities. The business can compare this ratio with those of other similar businesses to see if it meets industry norms. Knowing this

You Do the Math   Probabilistic Reasoning

The fundamental counting principle is a way to calculate the sample space for multiple independent events. The sample space is the set of all possible outcomes when determining probability. To use the fundamental counting principle, simply multiply the total possible outcomes of all events to find the sample space. For example, if a printing company offers five types of printed banner material in one of seven sizes and four choices of fonts:

5 × 7 × 4 = 140 possible combinations

Solve the following problems.

1. The owner of a construction company must purchase a new work truck. The dealership offers three choices for engine size, 14 choices for paint color, two choices for drive train, five choices for wheels and tires, and three choices for seat configuration. How many total combinations are possible for the work truck?

2. A marketing company specializes in promotional items. It offers a package in which a company's logo is printed as stickers in one of three sizes, magnets in one of five shapes, key chains in two styles, and water bottles in one of four styles. How many different packages are available?

Copyright Goodheart-Willcox Co., Inc.

information can help the owner determine if the business is doing well or needs improvement.

A **debt ratio** shows the percentage of dollars owed as compared to assets owned.

$$\text{total liabilities} \div \text{total assets} = \text{debt ratio}$$
$$\$37,000 \div \$68,000 = .54{:}1$$

This ratio shows that for every dollar of assets, the business owes creditors 54 cents. The business can compare this ratio with the industry guidelines to see if the ratio is healthy.

Income Statement

A business must analyze its progress on a regular basis to see if it is performing to industry standards and meeting the company's goals. Profit margin ratios are an important indicator of progress.

Net profit ratio illustrates how much profit is generated per dollar of sales.

$$\text{net income} \div \text{sales} = \text{net profit ratio}$$
$$\$35,000 \div \$68,000 = .52{:}1$$

This ratio shows that for every dollar of sales, the business is producing 52 cents in profit.

Comparing expenses to sales is another important ratio. **Operating ratio** shows the relationship of expenses to sales.

$$\text{expenses} \div \text{sales} = \text{operating ratio}$$
$$\$33,000 \div \$68,000 = .49{:}1$$

This ratio shows that for every dollar of sales, 49 cents goes toward expenses.

Section 17.2 Review

Check Your Understanding

1. What does an income, or profit and loss, statement report? How does analyzing this statement help a business evaluate its performance?

2. Why is a cash flow statement important when applying for a loan?

3. What does the cash flow statement report?

4. What does the owner's equity statement report?

5. What does the balance sheet report? How does the accounting equation apply to the information on the balance sheet?

Build Your Vocabulary

As you progress through this text, develop a personal glossary of key terms. This will help you build your vocabulary and prepare you for a career. Write a definition for each of the following terms and add them to your personal glossary.

stakeholder
income statement
financial ratio
working capital
current ratio
debt ratio
net profit ratio
operating ratio

Chapter Summary

Section 17.1 Accounting 101

- All businesses follow the generally accepted accounting principles, which are known as GAAP. These principles guide how transactions are recorded.
- All daily business transactions must have a source document to prove it happened.
- Businesses use double-entry accounting to record transactions.

Section 17.2 Financial Statements

- Financial statements are important to all the stakeholders in a business. These statements provide information about the financial status of the business.
- Financial statement analysis provides benchmarks for making decisions about the business.

Online Activities

Complete the following activities to help you learn, practice, and expand your knowledge and skills.

➡ **Posttest.** Now that you have finished the chapter, see what you learned by taking the chapter posttest.

➡ **Key Terms.** Practice vocabulary for this chapter using the e-flash cards, matching activity, and vocabulary game until you are able to recognize their meanings.

Review Your Knowledge

1. Why is accounting called the *language of business?*
2. What are two common accounting methods?
3. What is the difference between the two common accounting methods?
4. Why is good recordkeeping important?
5. What are daily transactions?
6. When is a purchase order used?
7. Name the four common types of special journals that are used in business.
8. What is an account payable?
9. How are financial statements different from pro forma statements?
10. Which four financial statements will most businesses create on a regular basis?

Copyright Goodheart-Willcox Co., Inc.

Apply Your Knowledge

1. Good accounting practices dictate that personal records be kept separate from your business records. Outline a plan to keep your personal and business records separate. Will you have separate files? Separate computer? What practices can you put into place to help abide by this rule?

2. What type of recordkeeping system do you think you will use—cash or accrual? Explain how you made your choice.

3. Pay a visit to the accounting teacher in your school. Ask for examples of each of the basic journals. Which one do you think you will use for your business? Why?

4. Research SBA income statement templates on the Internet. Download the form. Practice entering various numbers for each of the lines. Save the template for future planning for your business. Continue downloading templates for the other financial statements.

5. Research financial ratios that are used in your selected industry. What are the five most common ratios? What do they tell about the business?

6. You may decide to keep your records using pencil and paper. However, you may decide to use an automated system. What are the names of some financial recordkeeping software that might be appropriate for your business?

7. Financial forms are crucial to managing the finances of a business. Review Figures 17-5, 17-6, 17-7, and 17-8. Demonstrate your understanding by summarizing the function that each of these financial statements serves for a business.

8. In the last activity, you summarized the function of the financial statements shown in Figures 17-5, 17-6, 17-7, and 17-8. What is the financial result or outcome each statement provides? How does a business owner use the information shown on each of the financial statements?

9. Outline the steps that you can take to make sure your cash flow is healthy. You may need to do some research for advice on managing cash flow.

10. Tax laws require that you keep you tax records for a certain amount of time in the event that you are audited. What does the IRS recommend as an acceptable number of years to maintain your records?

Teamwork

This chapter discussed the importance of following the generally accepted accounting principles (GAAP). Working with your team, research the GAAP. List each and describe how these principles impact the way a company operates.

Copyright Goodheart-Willcox Co., Inc.

Internet Research

Accounting Controls. Conduct an Internet search for *internal accounting controls*. Create a list of common accounting controls used in business. Analyze why they are needed for an effective organization.

Communication Skills

College and Career Readiness

Reading. Carefully review this chapter. How does the author structure the text in a way that the reader can see the relationship between accounting principles and financial statements? What structure can you discern for the organization of this chapter? Is there any other way the chapter could have been structured to increase meaning?

Writing. Conduct a short research project on generally accepted accounting principles (GAAP) for small businesses. Select one principle and write several paragraphs about its importance. Ask others to review early drafts and incorporate their suggestions where appropriate.

CTSOs

Proper Attire. Some Career and Technical Student Organizations (CTSOs) require appropriate business attire from all entrants and those attending the competition. This requirement is in keeping with the mission of CTSOs: to prepare students for professional careers in business. To be certain that the attire you have chosen to wear at the competition is in accordance with event requirements, complete the following.

1. Visit the organization's website and look for the most current dress code.
2. The dress code requirements are very detailed and gender specific. Some CTSOs may require a chapter blazer to be worn during the competition.
3. Do a dress rehearsal when practicing for your event. Are you comfortable in the clothes you have chosen? Do you present a professional appearance?
4. In addition to the kinds of clothes you can wear, be sure the clothes are clean and pressed. You do not want to undermine your appearance or event performance with wrinkled clothes that may distract judges.
5. Make sure your hair is neat and worn in a conservative style. If you are a male, you should be clean shaven. Again, you do not want anything about your appearance detracting from your performance.
6. As far in advance of the event as is possible, share your clothing choice with your organization's advisor to make sure you are dressed appropriately.

Copyright Goodheart-Willcox Co., Inc.

Building Your Business Plan—Putting the Puzzle Together

Financial Management

You were successful in raising start-up capital for your business. Now the business is operating, and an accounting system is needed. It is necessary to have a system in place to track how much you make, how much you spend, and other business transactions that keep things flowing. Keeping accurate records is only a part of managing your business finances, however. Financial statements are necessary for any business, no matter the size. For business owners, financial statements are extremely important to help them make good business decisions as well as to obtain additional funding.

Goals

• Create a chart of accounts for your business.
• Create business plan notes.

Directions

Access the *Entrepreneurship* companion website at www.g-wlearning.com ➡. Download each data file for the following activities. A complete sample business plan is available on the companion website to use as a reference. The name of the file is Bus Plan_Sample.RetroAttire. docx.

Preparation

Activity 17-1. Chart of Accounts. Create the chart of accounts for your business. Indicate which charts are assets, liabilities, owner's equity, revenue, or expense accounts.

Activity 17-2. Business Plan Notes. Make notes on accounting software packages that might relieve you from some of the accounting duties for your business. Investigate accounting software packages, their features and benefits, and their cost. Keep your notes as reference information for your business plan.

Business Plan—Financial Plans

In this chapter, you learned about accounting procedures and the importance of maintaining accurate financial records. Now, you will continue refining the Financial Plans section of the business plan.

1. Open your saved business plan document.

2. Locate the Financial Plans section of the business plan. Finish writing the Introduction section. Explain your business' accounting method, fiscal period, and fiscal year. Who will be in charge of recordkeeping? Discuss how you plan to budget to manage cash flow. Use the suggestions and questions listed in each section of the template to help you generate ideas. Delete the instructions and questions when you are finished writing each section. Make sure to proofread your document and correct any errors in keyboarding, spelling, and grammar.

3. Save your document.

©iStock.com/Yuri

Unit 6
Expanding and Exiting

Your Business Plan—Putting the Puzzle Together

It is time to put the remaining puzzle pieces in place. Next, you will project what the business will look like in the upcoming three to five years. How much will it grow and how will you achieve that growth? Additionally, there will come a time for you to leave the business. Who will run it after you? Will you sell it or keep it in the family? In this unit, you will:

Describe strategies to grow the business.

Determine possible exit strategies for leaving the business.

Unit Overview

Every entrepreneur wants to know his or her business will grow and remain profitable. There are a number of ways to achieve growth. Choosing the right growth strategies is part of the planning process. Exiting a business is also something that should be considered long before it finally happens. Leaving a prosperous business to your family or selling it to reap the profits are both viable options, among others. Which might you choose?

Chapters

18 Business Growth
19 Exit Strategies

Entrepreneurs and the Economy

Did you know that entrepreneurial start-up businesses created nearly all of the new jobs since the late 1970s? That is how important entrepreneurs are to the US economy. Without entrepreneurs and their ideas and innovations, the economy would not function as well as it does.

In his recent book *The Microtheory of Innovative Entrepreneurship,* author William Baumol explains how the activities of entrepreneurs and inventors play a vital role in microeconomics. Baumol is the director of the Berkley Center for Entrepreneurial Studies at New York University and CEO of the Kauffman Foundation.

Microeconomics is the study of the economy as related to individual buyer and seller interactions and the factors influencing their choices. In particular, microeconomics focuses on patterns of supply and demand and the pricing and production decisions in different markets.

In contrast, *macroeconomics* is the study of the economy at the national level. Factors at the macroeconomic and microeconomic levels often have an effect on each other. For example, a low national unemployment rate may determine how many skilled workers are available for jobs in small businesses.

Baumol analyzes the influence of innovative entrepreneurs on the US economy. *Innovative entrepreneurs* are those who invent or create new products. His research suggests that microeconomists have tended to overlook the impact of innovative entrepreneurs despite the fact that most disruptive innovations came from innovative entrepreneurs. *Disruptive innovations* are those that radically change society. Perhaps this is due to the fact that most innovative entrepreneurs go on to form large companies

alphaspirit/Shutterstock.com

to bring their products to the public. For example, the airplane, car, computer software, Internet search engine, and air conditioning are just a few disruptive innovations created by entrepreneurs.

The value of entrepreneurs and the entrepreneurial spirit in the United States cannot be overestimated. Every business starts as a small business. The only differences are in how fast they grow.

While studying, look for the activity icon 📲 for:

- Chapter pretests and posttests
- Key terms activities
- Section reviews
- Building Your Business Plan activities

G-WLEARNING.com

18 Business Growth

It is important to have a plan for growing the business. It is just as important to be ready to adjust that plan. In 2009, 24-year-old Shama Kabani founded The Zen Marketing Group to offer social media marketing services. She quickly realized clients wanted comprehensive marketing services. That required an adjustment to the business plan, but a bigger challenge loomed. She had created a plan for slow and steady growth. But, in late 2009, Kabani was named by *Business Week* as one of its top 25 entrepreneurs under 25. The article appeared on the Yahoo home page, and her plan for slow and steady growth was no longer adequate. She had to hire additional staff and make other investments to keep up with demand.

"You have to be open-minded when those early opportunities present themselves; take advantage of them whether they're going to make you a lot of money or not."

—Rachael Ray, entrepreneur, talk-show host, and celebrity chef

College and Career Readiness

Reading Prep. Before reading this chapter, page through the text taking note of how the headings signal the central ideas and themes in the chapter. As you read, focus on how the key details support the central ideas presented.

Sections

18.1 Growth Strategies

18.2 Business Growth Funding

Picture Yourself Here
Marie Diaz

In 1994, Marie Diaz founded the Dallas-based company Pursuit of Excellence, which partners with other companies to serve as their human resources (HR) specialist. Pursuit of Excellence offers two solutions to assist businesses with outsourcing their HR needs. The first provides administrative services and payroll and tax administration. The other provides more integrated services, including employee benefits, payroll, and worker's compensation.

Marie is an advocate for small business growth and entrepreneurship. She also values giving back to the community. Consequently, she is on the board of directors and a member of advisory committees for a variety of organizations. These include the Dallas Theater of Arts, Boys & Girls Clubs of America, and St. Jude's Children's Research Hospital.

Pursuit of Excellence has been consistently recognized as one of the fastest growing private companies by *Inc.* magazine. Maria has earned many awards recognizing women business leaders. She was also a finalist for the Ernst & Young Entrepreneur of the Year® award in the Southwest Area, North Program in 2010.

Photo © Marie Diaz

Check Your Entrepreneurship IQ

Before you begin the chapter, see what you already know about entrepreneurship by taking the chapter pretest. The pretest is available at www.g-wlearning.com

Growth Strategies

Objectives

After completing this section, you will be able to:

- **Explain** the concept of growing a business.
- **Describe** how to achieve organic growth.
- **Describe** how to achieve inorganic growth.

How can a business plan for growth?

Key Terms

recession
organic growth
intensive growth strategies
market penetration
market development
initial public offering (IPO)
inorganic growth
diversification

synergistic diversification
horizontal diversification
integrative growth strategies
merger
acquisition
backward integration
forward integration
horizontal integration

Critical Thinking

You have written a business plan and have considered all aspects of how to establish the business. Now list and describe some of the ways you would consider growing your company as a long-term goal.

Plan for Growth

Turning a small business into a large business is not an easy task. Most businesses start small and stay that way. Only 0.1 percent of all businesses will ever reach annual revenues of $250 million. Less than 0.036 percent of businesses will ever reach annual revenues of $1 billion. But some businesses do—and your business could be the next one if growth is one of your objectives.

Controlling growth can be a challenge. If a business grows too quickly, there is a chance of overextension. This can have a negative impact on a business. Creating and managing a growth plan is important for any business. A growth plan should be approached in the same way as a plan for opening a business. Set goals that are realistic and can be attained. Determine what needs to expand in terms of employees and space. Then, look at ways to fund the expansion. Stick to the growth plan to prevent overextending the expansion.

Copyright Goodheart-Willcox Co., Inc.

Concept of Growing a Business

An entrepreneur usually starts with little or nothing, so growth is expected. In fact, it is necessary for the business to succeed. However, in most cases, the business will only be able to grow sales to a certain point before they level off. In some cases, sales may reach a peak then decline. Figure 18-1 shows sales growth for a company. Notice how sales steadily increase until about the fifth year and then remain at that level. To increase sales beyond this plateau, the business may need to consider expansion.

Growth for an organization usually means that business operations will be changed or modified in some way. *Business operations* are the activities involved in the day-to-day functions of a business, which are conducted for the purpose of generating profits. Operations include location, labor, equipment, and processes. As an organization grows, there is a chance that the location of the business might need to change. The number of employees may increase and the equipment they use may need to be updated. To continue being productive, processes are always subject to modification.

Organization plays a great role in the effectiveness of any business. From the start-up to growth phase, the human resources of a business can take many forms. They may grow, change, or even decrease in a time of expansion. In chapter 13, organization was discussed as a management function and illustrated in Figure 13-3. In the process of growing an organization, this organizational chart will typically change. Levels of management may increase or decrease and the number of employees may do the same. The first step is to identify

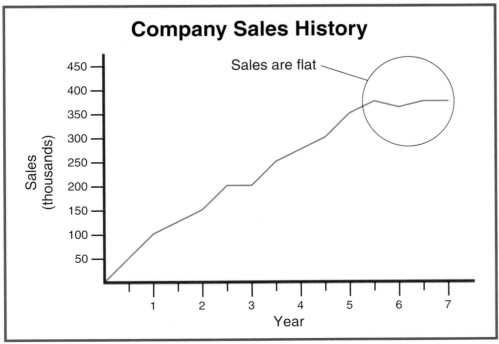

Figure 18-1. Sales have reached a peak for this company.

Goodheart-Willcox Publisher

Copyright Goodheart-Willcox Co., Inc.

needs. Then, create a job analysis to make sure the right positions are identified. Having an effective organization of staff is important to be efficient in an organization.

There are many ways to expand or grow a business. There may be new ways to sell existing products. Maybe it is possible to introduce new products into the market. Sometimes a reorganization of the company can better serve the market. In some cases, buying another business is the answer. Each of these options can be classified as one of the two concepts for growing a business: organic growth and inorganic growth. These concepts are discussed later in this chapter.

Growth During Economic Downturns

Think about growing your business even when the economy is experiencing a downturn. If you do so, you may be ahead of other businesses that wait for better economic times. Here are some reasons growing during an economic downturn may be a good idea.

- Resources may cost less.

- Better-qualified people may be looking for employment.

- Credit may be easier to obtain.

- There may be less competition.

The price of land, equipment, supplies, and buildings may decline during an economic downturn. Employees may be willing to work for a lower wage. You may be able to buy relatively low-priced equipment and furniture at auctions for businesses that have closed their doors.

Businesses suffer and vendors lose customers during a slow economy. Many vendors will be looking for new business-to-business opportunities and may be willing to offer more-favorable credit terms.

In a recession, it is likely that many businesses will decrease their staff. You may be able to hire more-qualified people than you would when the unemployment rate is low.

A **recession** occurs when the country experiences negative economic growth for at least a six-month stretch. During recessions, many businesses close. This may mean some of your competitors disappear. Customers of those businesses will need to find other places to purchase goods or services. So, an economic downturn might be a great time to grow your business to increase market share.

The Great Recession started in December of 2007 and lasted until June of 2009. It had a major impact on the economy. Many recessions last about 16 months followed by an expansion time that might last for five years. The Great Recession lasted 20 months.

Growing your business can have a positive impact on job creation for the country during an economic downturn. Of the approximately 12 million new jobs added in the first year after the Great Recession, young firms were responsible for nearly 8 million of those jobs.

Copyright Goodheart-Willcox Co., Inc.

Organic Growth

Many businesses begin expanding through organic growth. Organic growth occurs by expanding the current business. This can be done by increasing the number of locations, number of customers, or other growth that comes from the current business rather than buying another business.

Part of growing a company is to create a growth strategy that gets the best results with an acceptable amount of risk. Think about growth strategies as climbing a mountain. The strategies at the bottom of the mountain represent the least amount of risk, but also bring less change, as shown in Figure 18-2. The bottom of the mountain is where the intensive growth strategies are located. Intensive growth strategies are ways of growing by taking advantage of the opportunities in the current market. These include market penetration, market development, and product development. At the top of the mountain are integrative growth strategies, which are discussed later in this chapter.

Market Penetration

Market penetration involves increasing sales in the existing target market. This is also called *vertical growth* and focuses on current

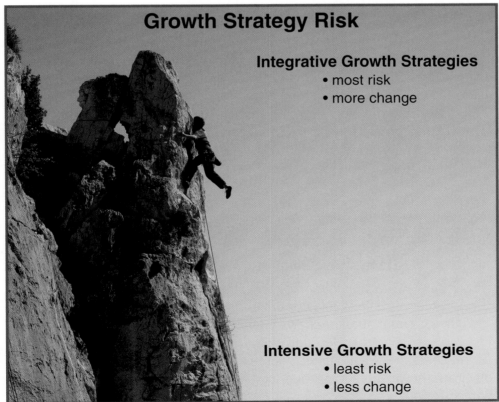

Growth Strategy Risk

Integrative Growth Strategies
- most risk
- more change

Intensive Growth Strategies
- least risk
- less change

Figure 18-2. Business growth strategies vary in the amount of risk involved and how much change results.

Alex Emanuel Koch/Shutterstock.com; Goodheart-Willcox Publisher

Copyright Goodheart-Willcox Co., Inc.

customers, rather than acquiring new customers. It is a relatively low-risk growth strategy. Market penetration may include:

- convincing customers to buy your product more often;

- working to take away business from competitors;

- increasing advertising;

- increasing promotional offers; and

- continuing to develop relationships with existing customers.

One way to convince customers to buy the product more often is to explain the benefits of doing so. This may be promoting the benefits of having an extra supply of the product on hand for when the customer runs out. Or, you may recommend a shorter amount of time between using your service.

To take away business from competitors, develop a strategy that makes your product more attractive than theirs. Lower price, better service, and flexible shopping hours are examples of ways you can attract customers to your business. For example, some restaurants are open 24 hours a day. This may make them more attractive to some people than restaurants that close overnight.

Make sure customers know who you are by increasing advertising. Place advertisements in strategic places that will capture your target market. Do your research before placing advertisements to be sure your target market will be reached. An advertisement does no good if it targets a market that is not the one you want to target.

Promotional offers include such things as customer-loyalty programs, discounts, and other incentives. These offers are often good at attracting new customers. Many times, a promotion will allow the customer to buy something at a loss to the business to get the customer in the door. This is called a *loss leader*. The hope is, once inside the business, the customer will purchase more.

To continue developing relationships with existing customers, show your appreciation for them. Learn the names of regular customers. When they come into your store, greet them by name. Offer excellent customer service. Sometimes you may not be able to help

Green Entrepreneurs

Electronic Newsletters

One valuable marketing strategy is to send monthly newsletters to current and potential customers. Consider turning paper newsletters into electronic newsletters. The electronic format can cut printing and paper costs and decreases paper waste. In fact, some companies only use interactive electronic newsletters to provide a greater level of content and customer participation.

Copyright Goodheart-Willcox Co., Inc.

the customer with your own goods or services. However, if you refer the customer to another business that can, you will probably make a lasting impression.

Market Development

Another intensive growth strategy is market development. **Market development** is expanding existing products to new physical locations or target markets. This is also called *horizontal growth* and focuses on finding new customers for existing products.

Add Another Location

Many small business owners expand their businesses by adding a new location. If you are in a large community, you may decide to open a second location across town. If you have a fishing-guide business, for example, you might have one location in the north that operates during the summer and a second location in the south that operates during the winter months. This way, the business can remain open all year long.

Promote Different Product Benefits

A business might expand its target market by promoting different benefits of its product to different markets. For example, today Arm & Hammer baking soda is promoted not only as a baking product, which was its original market, but also a cleaning product, a tooth whitener, and an odor eliminator. During the Great Depression, Church & Dwight, the company that produces Arm & Hammer baking soda, advertised the money-saving aspect of using its baking soda for personal care. In the 1950s and 1960s, the company distributed quick reference "use wheels" to promote the many ways to use its baking soda.

One way to grow a business is to franchise it.

viki2win/Shutterstock.com

Copyright Goodheart-Willcox Co., Inc.

Add New Channels

Another growth strategy is to sell current products through new channels. If you sell products through other companies, maybe it is time to open your own outlets. If you do not have an online store, opening one may increase sales. If you currently have only an online store, you may consider opening a brick-and-mortar store.

Franchise the Business

You learned about becoming a franchisee in chapter 6, but what about becoming the franchisor? There are many examples of large franchises that started out as a single store. The US Census Bureau reported in 2010 that franchises accounted for 10.5 percent of all businesses. In terms of revenue, franchises accounted for $1.3 trillion in revenue and $153.7 billion in wages and salaries for 7.9 million workers.

Create a Public Corporation

Your business may have been started as a sole proprietorship, partnership, or private corporation. Maybe it is time to take the company public and offer shares of public stock to investors. Facebook did just that in 2012. To become a public corporation, there are a number of steps you will need to complete, including:

- forming a board of directors;

- filing a letter of incorporation;

- creating bylaws; and

- filing an initial public offering.

An **initial public offering (IPO)** is the first time shares of stock are available for public purchase. Seek professional assistance if you choose to take your company public. Check with the state in which you plan to file for incorporation to make sure to follow the state laws.

FYI

Taking a company public is very complicated and expensive. It requires a lot of time and outside professional expertise.

Product Development

Another intensive growth strategy is to engage in product development. This may mean creating new products to sell to the current market. It may also mean replacing older products with updated ones. Updating a product may simply mean improving a current product to make it more appealing. It could also mean redesigning the product to meet a change in the market.

Inorganic Growth

Inorganic growth occurs when a company buys a new product line, buys another business, or merges with another company. This

Copyright Goodheart-Willcox Co., Inc.

can be a good option if you are interested in expanding the types of offerings. For example, if you sell computers and want to expand into the office furniture business, it might be easier to buy an office furniture company than start one from scratch. Inorganic growth may involve diversification or integrative growth strategies.

Diversification Growth Strategies

When a company has reached its limit on current product sales, it may choose to diversify. **Diversification** is a way to reduce risk that involves adding different products, services, locations, or markets. Diversification can help reduce the risk to a company. If one product line experiences slow sales, the other product lines may still be selling steadily. Sales may even continue to increase. This can help balance the ups and downs of sales cycles. There are two basic types of diversification: synergistic and horizontal.

Synergistic Diversification

When they first begin, many companies only have one or two products to offer. As the business grows, it may decide to expand the number of goods and services. *Synergy* is the increased effectiveness of two or more things working together. **Synergistic diversification** is adding new product lines or businesses compatible with yours. This strategy can help you get into a new market quickly. For example, if you sell bicycles, you may add a line of skateboards. These products complement each other because the target markets are similar.

Horizontal Diversification

Horizontal diversification is adding new products to your company that are not related to your current product line. For example, if you own a gas station, you might add a sandwich shop in an unused space. The two products—gasoline and sandwiches—have nothing to do with each other. The target markets are very different. However, when people purchase gas, many are also looking for a bite to eat. So, the sandwich shop can increase sales to the current customer base.

Integrative Growth Strategies

Integrative growth strategies are the riskiest. These strategies are at the top of the mountain: most risk and most change. **Integrative growth strategies** occur when one company buys another company. There are three types of integrative growth strategies: backward integration, forward integration, and horizontal integration.

Integrative growth strategies can occur either through mergers or acquisitions. A **merger** occurs when two companies agree to combine as a new company. The two companies may create a new name for the

Entrepreneur Ethics

It is unethical and illegal for a business to participate in acts of collusion. Collusion occurs when competing businesses work together to eliminate competition by misleading customers, setting prices, or other fraudulent activities. Unethical businesses sometimes collude with other businesses so that they can dominate the marketplace. Collusion is not only unethical, it is also illegal.

new company. Or, the new company might take the name of one of the two companies involved in the merger. A merger can be thought of as a partnership of sorts. On the other hand, an **acquisition** occurs when one company purchases another company. Often, the company that is purchased in an acquisition ceases to exist. Sometimes it continues to operate as a subsidiary.

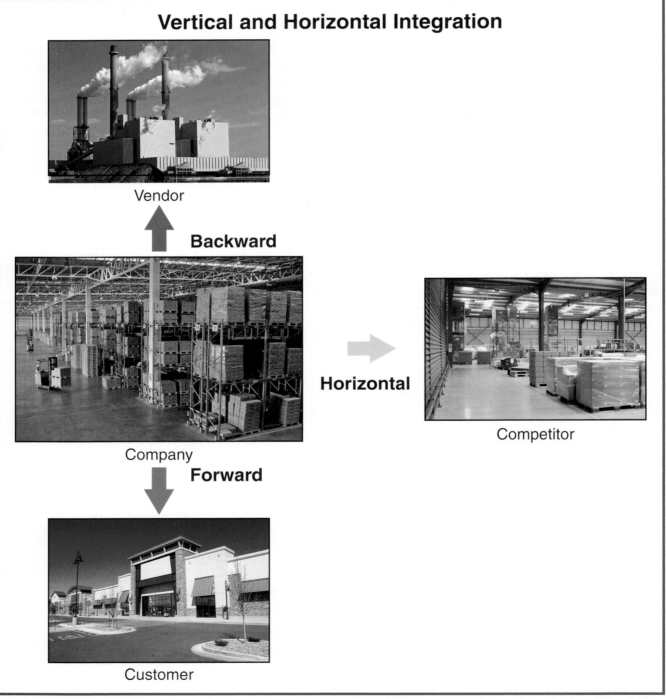

Bram van Broekhoven/Shutterstock.com; Champiofoto/Shutterstock.com; Rihardzz/Shutterstock.com; Steve Rosset/Shutterstock.com; Goodheart-Willcox Publisher

Figure 18-3. Integrative growth strategies can be effective ways to quickly grow an established business.

Copyright Goodheart-Willcox Co., Inc.

Backward Integration

Backward integration occurs when a company buys one of its vendors, as shown in Figure 18-3. Vendors are the businesses that supply companies with goods and services. Buying a vendor can reduce production costs. The profit the vendor would have made selling products to the business is eliminated. This strategy can also increase the number of products the business can offer because it can become a vendor to other companies.

Forward Integration

Forward integration is the opposite of backward integration. **Forward integration** occurs when a company buys one of the businesses for which it serves as a vendor. Forward integration allows control over the products that are offered by the company.

Horizontal Integration

Horizontal integration occurs when a company buys one of its competitors. This is a way to grow market share by eliminating some of the competition. It is also a way to increase the number of products offered to current customers.

FYI

Together, backward and forward integration are called *vertical integration* because they deal with the vertical line between producer and consumer.

Section 18.1 Review

Check Your Understanding 📲

1. Why would a company choose to grow organically?
2. List three intensive growth strategies.
3. Name two ways of penetrating the current market.
4. Give an example of synergistic diversification.
5. Name three integrative growth strategies.

Build Your Vocabulary 📲

As you progress through this text, develop a personal glossary of key terms. This will help you build your vocabulary and prepare you for a career. Write a definition for each of the following terms and add them to your personal glossary.

recession
organic growth
intensive growth
   strategies
market penetration
market development
initial public offering
   (IPO)
inorganic growth
diversification

synergistic
   diversification
horizontal diversification
integrative growth
   strategies
merger
acquisition
backward integration
forward integration
horizontal integration

Copyright Goodheart-Willcox Co., Inc.

SECTION 18.2 Business Growth Funding

? **Essential Question**

How can an entrepreneur fund business growth?

Objectives

After completing this section, you will be able to:
- **Explain** business cycles.
- **Identify** ways to fund growth.

Key Terms

inflation
business cycle
growth phase
peak phase
contraction phase
trough phase

retained earnings
cash on delivery (COD)
Farm Services Agency (FSA)
Export-Import Bank of the United States
World Bank Group (WBG)

Critical Thinking

Obtaining funding for growing the business is similar to obtaining funding for starting a business. Review the funding strategies you used when you wrote the funding section of your business plan. Which funding strategies do you think you could use to grow the business?

Monitor Economic Business Cycles

There can be difficult times in a market economy such as the US economy. One of the most difficult times was the Great Depression. It started in 1929 and lasted until the beginning of World War II. During the Great Depression, the unemployment rate was as high as 25 percent. Additionally, there have been times when inflation was high. **Inflation** is the increase in the price of goods and services over time. The 1970s and 1980s had relatively high inflation. By contrast, the 1990s and the first part of the 21st century had average or relatively low inflation.

The Great Depression would not have been a good time to grow a business, or would it? During tough economic times, businesses may close so there may be fewer competitors. If a business can survive during hard economic times, then the other business cycles probably will not be as difficult.

The **business cycle** refers to the rise and fall of an economy over several months or years, as shown in Figure 18-4. These fluctuations

Copyright Goodheart-Willcox Co., Inc.

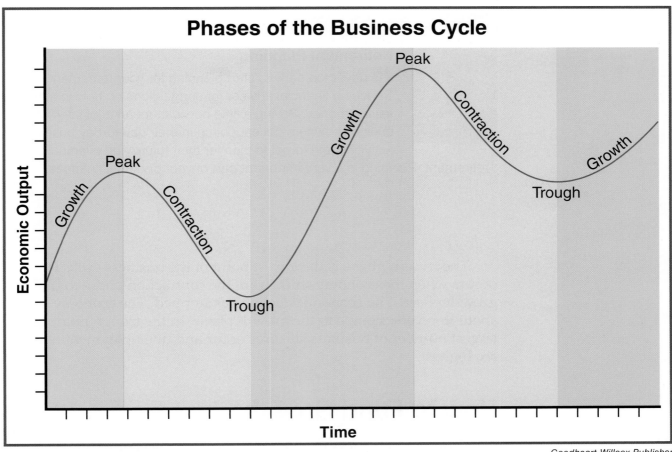

Phases of the Business Cycle

Economic Output / Time

Growth — Peak — Contraction — Trough — Growth — Peak — Contraction — Trough — Growth

Goodheart-Willcox Publisher

Figure 18-4. The specific effects of the economy's business cycle differ, depending on the type of business.

are due to many factors, including changes in production, spending, interest rates, employment rate, and consumer confidence. The four phases of the business cycle are growth, peak, contraction, and trough. There is no timeline to a phase. A phase can last a few months or a few years.

The **growth phase** of the business cycle is characterized by expansion of the economy. This phase may be called *growth, expansion,* or *recovery.* Businesses are spending more money, hiring, and expanding. Governmental spending increases. Consumers feel confident about the economy and are spending money.

The **peak phase** occurs when the economy shifts from the growth phase to the contraction phase. This phase is the highest point of the business cycle. It is characterized by slowing economic growth. There is also a slowdown in spending.

The **contraction phase** occurs when the economy is in decline. This phase may be called *contraction* or *recession.* Workers are laid off, businesses close, spending slows, demand for expensive products declines, and fewer people buy houses. If a contraction lasts more than two quarters (six months), it is called a recession. If contraction continues for a long time, it could turn into a depression.

Copyright Goodheart-Willcox Co., Inc.

Focus on Finance

Retirement Planning

It is never too early to start planning for your retirement. Consult a financial advisor for suggestions on how to start saving money. Saving a little now can mean a lot later. Many business owners get caught up in their day-to-day business activities and forget to plan for their future and eventual retirement. Planning is a very important part of your personal finances.

The **trough phase** is the lowest point of the business cycle. It occurs when the economy shifts from the contraction phase to the growth phase. The economic decline has stopped. The economy is about to reverse course to the growth phase. In the trough phase, the largest number of business closures occur and unemployment rates are highest.

How to Fund Growth

Growing a business usually requires money. Whether the plan is for organic or inorganic growth, cash will likely be needed to take the business to the next level. Entrepreneurs probably obtained financing when they started their businesses. They can use the same channels or open new ones to fund expansion. Before making the decision about how to finance growth, make sure some basic questions are answered.

- Can money from the business be used to finance the expansion without having to find additional investors or borrow money?

- How quickly is the money needed?

- Can expansion be started without an additional investment, borrowing money as needed later?

- Are the risks associated with growth high, in which case interest on borrowed money will be high?

- Does the company have a financial track record with great credit and stable growth?

- If outside money is needed, why and how will it be used?

- How strong is the management team, and will investors see it as a plus or minus?

- How does financing fit into the company's mission statement and business plan?

Copyright Goodheart-Willcox Co., Inc.

Once these questions are answered, it is time to seek funding to finance the company's growth. There are a number of ways to fund growth. The following sections discuss some of the more common ways to fund a company's expansion. Be sure to review the business plan and current financial statements to make sure the business is ready to expand.

Company-Generated Funds

One of the best ways to finance growth is through the business' retained earnings. **Retained earnings** are profits put aside from the operation of the company. The advantage to using company-generated funds is that they already exist. There is no application paperwork, interest to pay, or monthly payments to make. A disadvantage is the opportunity cost: giving up the interest that could have been earned on the money if it had been invested. Do not use too much of the retained earnings when expanding. If retained earnings are depleted, an unexpected event, such as an economic downturn, could cause the business to close due to lack of funds.

Small businesses usually borrow money for four principle reasons: starting the business, purchasing inventory, expanding the business, and strengthening the financials of the business.

Dragon Images/Shutterstock.com

Discuss the timing of and funding options for expansion with your financial advisor before making any decisions.

Copyright Goodheart-Willcox Co., Inc.

Self-Financing

Self-financing is similar to using company-generated funds in that you use existing cash to finance the expansion. Self-financing may include using credit cards, a home-equity loan, the cash value of a life insurance policy, redeemed investments, or savings. The advantage of financing the expansion yourself is that you do not take on a loan or give up part of the business ownership. The disadvantage of self-financing is that if the expansion does not work, you may not have any personal reserves to live on after the business closes.

Trade Credit

When a business first opens, most of its vendors probably require COD payment for products. **Cash on delivery (COD)**, also called *collect on delivery*, means payment must be made when the product is delivered, not invoiced for later payment. This may be by credit card or cash.

Once a business is established, it might be offered trade credit. *Trade credit* is when a vendor allows a business it serves to receive goods or services and pay for them after a specified term. The term is often 30, 60, or 90 days. Trade credit can temporarily free up money to expand the company by delaying payment for products.

The advantage to trade credit is that the products can be sold before payment for them is due. The disadvantage is that if the products are not sold, they must still be paid for at the end of the specified term. This could leave the business short on cash.

Social Entrepreneurs

Lauren Bush and Ellen Gustafson

Lauren Bush and Ellen Gustafson met while both were involved with the United Nations World Food Programme. The two wanted to do more for world hunger than they were. Bush, who had studied fashion design, and Gustafson, who was a communications officer, teamed up and created simple, reusable bags. Proceeds from sales would go directly to World Food Programme. However, many legal and logistical problems that come with working with the United Nations nearly doomed the program. The two decided to start their own company called FEED Projects to sell the bags. FEED Projects funds antihunger programs across the world. The company distributes its bags through Whole Foods, Bergdorf Goodman, Gap, Nordstrom, other stores, and Internet sales. FEED Projects has sold around 600,000 bags, providing over 70 million meals to children around the world. FEED Projects has also started a program to address hunger in the United States.

Copyright Goodheart-Willcox Co., Inc.

Family or Friends

Family or friends may be a source of money to finance an expansion of your company. The advantage of borrowing from someone you know is that you might receive a lower interest rate and a more-flexible repayment plan. The disadvantage is that if you cannot repay the loan, you may permanently ruin the relationship.

Equity Financing

Equity financing is money raised by the business owner in exchange for part ownership in the company. There are two sources of equity financing: angel investors and venture capitalists. These types of investors are discussed in chapter 9.

The advantage of equity financing is that larger sums of money can be obtained from a single or just a few investors. They are usually willing to take more risk than a bank, and the business is not taking on more debt. The disadvantage is that a percentage of the company is given to the investor. If the investor requires more than 50 percent of the company, then the investor takes control of the company.

Lenders

Lenders, such as banks, are usually more willing to loan money to an established company with a proven credit history. Banks loan money for a set interest rate. Interest rates vary. Shopping around for the best rates can save a great deal of money over the long term. The advantage of borrowing from a bank is that it eliminates the risk of using your own money or that of your company. The disadvantages are paying interest and the expense of monthly payments.

Public Incorporation

The business may not have been started as a corporation, but becoming a public corporation might be a good way to fund expansion. The advantage of becoming a public company is that doing so can very quickly raise a lot of money. This money is not a loan. It does not need to be repaid. A disadvantage is that a publicly traded company must have a board of directors, which in turn must answer to shareholders. Also, by selling shares of stock in the company, part of the ownership is given to stockholders. However, as long as you retain more than 50 percent of the stock, you will still have control of the company. You will have to answer to the board of directors, however.

Governmental Agencies

The Small Business Administration (SBA) has a number of loan and grant programs for established businesses. While the SBA does

SBA Tips

The SBA is committed to their Small/Rural Lender Advantage initiative. This program stimulates the economies of local and rural communities through increased lending and quick loan turn-around times for small businesses. Communities facing the issues of population loss, disaster recovery, and high unemployment are eligible. www.sba.gov

Copyright Goodheart-Willcox Co., Inc.

not loan money, it guarantees loans made by banks and other financial institutions. Research SBA-backed loans and grants to determine which one will be best for your business. The advantage of the SBA loan or grant is that it is backed by the federal government and usually offers a lower interest rate than traditional loans. The disadvantages include the amount of paperwork to complete and that these loans and grants may be more difficult to obtain than a traditional loan.

In addition to the SBA, there are other governmental agencies dedicated to helping businesses. The **Farm Services Agency (FSA)** provides assistance to commercial farms. The **Export-Import Bank of the United States**, better known as *Ex-Im Bank,* is set up to help US businesses export goods and services. The **World Bank Group (WBG)** provides assistance to developing countries, which can help provide a market for goods and services from US companies.

Small Business Investment Company Program

The SBA licenses and regulates companies participating in the Small Business Investment Company (SBIC) Program. These private companies receive matching funds from the SBA for money they invest in other businesses. A company in the SBIC program must invest in firms with a net worth under $18 million and after-tax earnings over a two-year period of less than $6 million. The

The World Bank Group provides technical and financial resources to support growth in developing countries.

Source: www.usaid.gov

Copyright Goodheart-Willcox Co., Inc.

advantages and the disadvantages of using investment companies in the SBIC program are the same as those for angel investors and venture capitalists as detailed in chapter 9. The only difference is that the SBA monitors the investment companies in the SBIC program.

Section 18.2 Review

Check Your Understanding ➦

1. What are the stages of the business cycles?
2. Why would using retained earnings be a good method for financing business expansion?
3. List any disadvantage to self-financing business expansion.
4. What is the advantage of using trade credit?
5. What role does the government play in promoting and supporting entrepreneurship?

Build Your Vocabulary ➦

As you progress through this text, develop a personal glossary of key terms. This will help you build your vocabulary and prepare you for a career. Write a definition for each of the following terms and add them to your personal glossary.

inflation
business cycle
growth phase
peak phase
contraction phase
trough phase
retained earnings
cash on delivery
   (COD)

Farm Services
   Agency (FSA)
Export-Import
   Bank of the
   United States
World Bank Group
   (WBG)

 ## You Do the Math   Probabilistic Reasoning

Probability is the likelihood of an event occurring. In general, probability is stated as the number of ways an event can happen over the total number of outcomes. Flipping a coin, for example, can result in either heads or tails. The probability of the result being heads is one in two (1/2). There is only one side of the coin with heads, and there are two total possible outcomes. Probability can be expressed as a percentage. In the case of a flipped coin: $1/2 = .5 \times 100 = 50\%$ chance of being heads.

Solve the following problems.

1. A local office supply store offers a random discount to its regular customers. The discount may be 2 percent, 4 percent, 6 percent, or 25 percent. The discount is randomly selected by the cash register computer. What is the probability that a customer will receive the 25 percent discount?

2. At a combination supermarket and retail store, 47 customers purchased only groceries, 13 customers purchased groceries and items from the retail area, and 62 customers purchased items only from the retail area. What is the probability that a customer will purchase groceries?

Copyright Goodheart-Willcox Co., Inc.

Chapter Summary

Section 18.1 Growth Strategies

- Having a plan for growing a business is just as important as having a plan for opening a business. Growth and expansion must be managed carefully; otherwise, expansion can actually have a negative impact on a business.

- Organic growth of a business may be achieved by expanding the current business. Increasing the number of locations and customers or optimizing business operations are all organic growth strategies.

- Business growth can also be achieved through inorganic means. Inorganic growth is achieved when one business buys a new product line, another business, or merges with or acquires another business.

Section 18.2 Business Growth Funding

- Business cycles are fluctuations in the economy that can be caused by production, spending, interest rates, employment rate, and consumer confidence. The four phases of the business cycle are the growth phase, the peak phase, the contraction phase, and the trough phase.

- There are many ways to fund growth of a business. Entrepreneurs can use some of the same ways to fund the growth of a business as they used to fund its start-up.

Online Activities

Complete the following activities to help you learn, practice, and expand your knowledge and skills.

Posttest. Now that you have finished the chapter, see what you learned by taking the chapter posttest.

Key Terms. Practice vocabulary for this chapter using the e-flash cards, matching activity, and vocabulary game until you are able to recognize their meanings.

Review Your Knowledge

1. What is the difference between organic and inorganic growth?
2. Explain the idea of market penetration, also known as vertical growth, as a potential growth strategy for a business.
3. Explain the idea of market development, also known as horizontal growth, as a potential growth strategy for a business.
4. Why is diversification considered a way to reduce risk?

Copyright Goodheart-Willcox Co., Inc.

5. Why are integrative growth strategies so risky?

6. List three integrative growth strategies.

7. List three factors that can cause fluctuations in the economy.

8. During what two decades in the past 50 years had relatively high rates of inflation?

9. During what phase of the business cycle does the economy usually expand?

10. What company-generated funding source is one of the best ways to finance business growth?

Apply Your Knowledge

1. Project five years into the future. Your business has been profitable and it is now time for growth. Would organic growth strategies work for you? Why or why not?

2. What are some ways you could increase market penetration for your business?

3. What are some ways you could develop your market and grow your business?

4. Project five years into the future. Your business has been profitable and it is now time for growth. Would inorganic growth work for you? Why or why not?

5. Would it make sense for you to grow your business through synergistic diversification or horizontal diversification? Why or why not?

6. Name one integrative growth strategy that could work for your business.

7. Research the current economy. How will the business cycles in the United States impact your growth strategies?

8. When you started your business, you probably obtained funding from outside sources. Describe the funding strategies that would work for you to grow the business. How would these differ from the strategy used for original funding?

9. Some companies consider public incorporation as a growth strategy. Would this make sense for your company? Why or why not?

10. Summarize the three overall growth strategies that will work for your business.

Teamwork

Working with your team, list all of the growth strategies that were presented in this chapter. Use a spreadsheet to record your responses. Next, rank the strategies in order of preference of your team. Compare with other teams in the class. What strategies were ranked in the top-ten responses?

Internet Research

Comparing Growth Strategies. Growth strategies will be included as part of your business plan. Using the Internet, research strategies for both organic and inorganic business growth. List the pros and cons of each.

Communication Skills

College and Career Readiness

Speaking. To be an effective speaker, it is important to identify the purpose of the presentation and the audience. Prepare a speech about the importance of growing a business. Make use of visual displays to enhance the audience's understanding.

Listening. Active listeners know when to comment and when to remain silent. Practice your active listening skills while listening to your teacher present a lesson. Participate when appropriate and build on his or her ideas.

CTSOs

Preparing for an Event. No matter what competitive events you will participate in for a Career and Technical Student Organization (CTSO), you will have to be well organized and prepared. Of course, you will have studied the content exhaustively before the event, but you also have to prepare by making sure all the tools you need for the event, or for travel to the event, are taken care of. Finalizing all the details well in advance of an event will decrease stress and leave you free to concentrate on the event itself. To prepare for a competition:

1. Pack appropriate clothing, which includes shoes and proper garments. See the Event Prep feature in chapter 17.

2. Double-check to make sure that any presentation material that is saved electronically is done so on media that is compatible with the machines that will be available to you at the event.

3. If the event calls for visuals, make sure you have them prepared in advance, packed, and ready to take with you.

4. Bring registration materials, including a valid form of identification.

5. Bring study materials, including the flash cards and other materials you have used to study for the event.

6. At least two weeks before you go to the competition, create a checklist of what you need for the event.

Copyright Goodheart-Willcox Co., Inc.

Building Your Business Plan—Putting the Puzzle Together

Business Growth

Growing a business is not an easy challenge. You are probably wondering how to project growth plans when your business plan has not yet been completed. However, growth is part of the business plan strategy. Lenders and investors are always looking to see how they will recoup their investments when they become involved in a business venture. A business that has growth potential will be evaluated favorably when seeking financing.

Goals

- Identify growth strategies for your business.
- Create business plan notes.

Directions

Access the *Entrepreneurship* companion website at www.g-wlearning.com . Download each data file for the following activities. A complete sample business plan is available on the companion website to use as a reference. The name of the file is BusPlan_Sample.RetroAttire. docx.

Preparation

Activity 18-1. Growth Strategies. Select several growth strategies that would be feasible for your business. As you develop these strategies, consider that business operations must evolve as a business grows. Identify potential changes in location, labor, equipment, and processes that will change as a result of growth. Next, identify what will change in the organization of your business— identify positions and job descriptions. Then, create a new organization chart that will fit the new phase of your business.

Activity 18-2. Business Plan Notes. Create notes about the sources of your growth opportunities. Keep your notes and resources here.

Business Plan—Financial Plans

The financial plans portion of the business plan is nearly complete. In this activity, you will write the Future Plans subsection of the Financial Plans section.

1. Open your saved business plan document.

2. Locate the Financial Plans section of the plan. Based on the information in this chapter, begin writing the Future Plans subsection of your plan.

3. Locate the Executive Summary section of the plan and begin writing it based on the other plan sections. Use the suggestions and questions listed to help you generate ideas. Delete the instructions and questions when you are finished recording your responses. Make sure to proofread your document and correct any errors in keyboarding, spelling, and grammar.

4. Save your document.

19 Exit Strategies

Many entrepreneurs begin the same way that Kevin O'Leary started his business: with a great idea and no money. In the early 1990s, using $10,000 loaned to him by his mother, O'Leary started Softkey in his basement. Softkey was a software publisher. From that humble beginning, O'Leary grew his company into a multibillion dollar business, buying many of its competitors in the process. Then, in 1999, O'Leary sold the company to Mattel for about $3.7 billion and he eventually left the company. As an entrepreneur, when is it time to let go? Some entrepreneurs eventually sell the business, while others pass on the business to a family member. When you start a business, be prepared to let go at some time in the future.

> "My interest is in the future because I am going to spend the rest of my life there."

—Charles Kettering, American inventor and industrialist

College and Career Readiness

Reading Prep. Before you begin reading the last chapter of this text, consider how the author developed and presented information. How does the information in one chapter provide the foundation for the next? Why do you think the author decided to make this chapter the last chapter?

Sections

19.1 Exit the Business

19.2 Legal Obligations

Picture Yourself Here
Warner Cruz

Warner Cruz is the owner and president of JC Restoration, a company his father founded in 1982. Warner earned a bachelor degree in international business and finance from Augustana University. Warner began working in various positions in his father's company.

When Warner took over the business in 2002, he combined his business acumen and his father's work ethic to increase the company's annual sales from just under $1 million a year to more than $20 million today.

JC Restoration repairs and rebuilds homes and businesses after they have been substantially damaged by storms, fire, water, or mold. As part of Warner's commitment to helping the community, JC Restoration participated in creating an environmentally friendly home for a deserving family as part of the ABC series Extreme Makeover: Home Edition.

JC Restoration received the International Torch Award for Marketplace Excellence by the Better Business Bureau. Warner Cruz was recognized as Illinois' Small Business Person of the Year for "embodying the spirit of entrepreneurship" by the Small Business Administration. He has also previously been named Entrepreneur of the Year by the Chicago Latino Network. Warner continues to grow the business while improving the lives of his workers and those for whom JC Restoration comes to the rescue when disaster strikes.

Photo © Warner Cruz

Check Your Entrepreneurship IQ

Before you begin the chapter, see what you already know about entrepreneurship by taking the chapter pretest. The pretest is available at
www.g-wlearning.com

Exit the Business

Objectives

After completing this section, you will be able to:

- **Identify** ways an entrepreneur may leave a business he or she started.
- **Explain** harvest strategies as they relate to exiting a business.

Why would an owner need exit strategies for a business?

Key Terms

succession plan
buy-sell agreement
harvest strategy
outright sale
gradual sale

lease agreement
employee buyout (EB)
employee stock option plan (ESOP)
liquidation

Critical Thinking

Think ahead 30 years from now. You had a prosperous business, but now want to exit and pursue other interests. What do you think would be the best exit strategy for you?

Exit Strategies

You have been successfully running your business for years. Doing anything other than running your business seems silly. However, a wise business owner looks ahead to the future of the company. What will happen to the company if you decide to leave some day or can no longer run the business?

There comes a time when every entrepreneur leaves the business. This does not always mean something bad has happened. Exiting the business may not mean it is closing. Many successful entrepreneurs retire early and exit the business. Exiting the business might mean:

- passing the business on to your children;

- selling your share to your partners;

- developing a harvest strategy;

- taking the company public;

- merging with or being acquired by another company;

- ending a brand that you created;

Copyright Goodheart-Willcox Co., Inc.

- closing some of your locations; or

- liquidating the business.

Ending a business can be emotionally and financially painful, but it can also be a time of great joy as you look to the future. Many business owners close or transfer ownership of their business so they can pursue other interests, open another business, or retire. No matter why you might exit your business, be sure you have a plan in place well before you make the decision to exit.

Succession Plan

A **succession plan** details who will run the company in the event the owner leaves the company, retires, or dies. It helps ensure that the owner's company will continue. Hopefully, the owner's vision for the company also continues. The succession plan describes how the ownership of the business will be transferred when the owner exits the business.

FYI

Succession plans, like other legal documents, should be created by a professional and regularly reviewed.

Marcin Balcerzak/Shutterstock.com

As an entrepreneur, have a plan for exiting your business.

Copyright Goodheart-Willcox Co., Inc.

Family

Some owners transfer the business to family members. Transferring ownership to a family member can have both emotional and economic impacts.

For the person transferring the company, there is an emotional attachment that may be difficult to sever. It is sometimes difficult to step back and let the family make the decisions about the business.

For the family members taking over the business, there may be emotional ties that prevent them from making changes that need to be made. Taking over a business from parents or other relatives sometimes creates hesitancy to do what is best for the business.

Nonfamily

In some cases, family members may not be interested in the business, may not be capable of running a business, or there are no family members to take over the business. In these cases, a business owner may appoint a trusted individual who is not a family member to take over the company. Often, this is someone who has been successful in the operation of the business.

If there are no family members, transferring the business to someone else can be seamless. However, if there are family members who want the business, but were not selected to take over the business, problems can arise.

Partners

Exiting a business that is a partnership is more complicated than exiting a sole proprietorship. The partners have to agree on the decisions. The written partnership agreement should detail a buy-sell

Focus on Finance

Personal Assets

When exiting your business, you may have a large transfer of cash into your personal assets. Have a plan for how to deal with this transfer of wealth. Consult a financial advisor before exiting the business. There may be ways to reduce or defer your tax liabilities related to transferring cash and other assets to your personal wealth. Additionally, you should have a plan for how to use the transferred wealth. While the lump sum may seem large, that wealth may need to last for the rest of your life. Or, perhaps you plan to use the acquired wealth to start a new business. Having a plan is the only way to go.

Copyright Goodheart-Willcox Co., Inc.

agreement. **Buy-sell agreements**, sometimes called *buyout agreements*, are legally binding contracts that control when an owner can sell interest in the partnership, who can buy the owner's interest, and what price will be paid. These agreements are critical to the business if one of the partners wants to leave, retires, or dies.

Harvest Strategies

A harvest strategy is another way to exit a business, or take cash out after the business has become a success. A **harvest strategy** is a plan for extracting the cash from a business, brand, or product line. This can be a way to repay investors as well as provide an exit for the owner. A harvest strategy might include selling the company or allowing employees to buy the company.

Sell the Company

Selling the company is one of the most obvious harvesting strategies. There are three basic types of sale.

- outright sale

- gradual sale

- lease agreement

Outright Sale

In an **outright sale**, the business is sold in full. Ownership is transferred immediately. The seller receives payment for the assets of the business. An advantage for the seller is receiving a single payment for the business. An advantage for the buyer is immediately receiving complete ownership of the business.

Gradual Sale

A **gradual sale** occurs when the new owner finances the purchase with a long-term payment plan, making payments to the seller, while the seller transitions out of the business. It is a flexible option that can benefit the buyer and the seller. The seller receives money for the business and is able to pursue another career. The buyer can receive expertise and advice when needed from the seller for an agreed on period of time.

Lease Agreement

A **lease agreement** is a contract that provides the lessee the temporary rights to the business. The agreement details the conditions and payments the owner receives in return. An advantage to this option for the owner is he or she retains the business and can later sell

Entrepreneur Ethics

Before exiting your business, clear up any outstanding debts or obligations for the business. It is unethical to take new orders from customers that you know you will not be able to complete before the business closes. It is also unethical to order products from vendors when you know you will not be able to pay the bills before closing the business.

Copyright Goodheart-Willcox Co., Inc.

Goodluz/Shutterstock.com

One way to exit your business is to gradually transfer ownership to a new owner.

it. An advantage to the lessee is being able to run the business with the expertise and advice of the owner. This option can also be used as a trial run for both the owner and lessee to see if the match is good.

Initiate an Employee Buyout

With any type of business, an employee buyout is always an option. In an **employee buyout (EB)**, the owner sells the company to its employees. The most common form of employee ownership is through an employee stock option plan. An **employee stock option plan (ESOP)** is a trust fund set up to contribute new shares of stock or cash to purchase existing shares of the company on behalf of the employees. Employees, or the ESOP, must own at least 50 percent of the company for it to be considered an employee-owned business.

An ESOP is a way an owner can exit the business without dissolving the corporation, motivate and reward employees, and take advantage of incentives to borrow money using pretax dollars.

An ESOP can be set up for both privately and publicly held companies. If the business is a privately held corporation, employees must sell their shares back to the ESOP if they leave the company. In a

Copyright Goodheart-Willcox Co., Inc.

publicly held company, employees may keep their shares if they leave the company or they may choose to sell them back to the ESOP.

Take the Company Public

When a business becomes a public corporation, the private owner gives up some of the control of the company to others. Taking the company public allows the sale of shares of stock in the company, which provides the company with cash. It requires that a board of directors be selected. The first time the public can buy shares of stock in a company it is called an initial public offering (IPO).

Merge or Be Acquired

Another way of transferring ownership of a business is through merger or acquisition. A merger is combining two companies into one new company. For example, Company X merges with Company Y to form a new company, Company Z. If your company merges with another, this may be a way for you to exit the company instead of staying with the new company.

An acquisition is the outright purchase of one business by another business. For example, you sell your business to another company. This allows you to keep the business going while you exit the company.

SBA Tips

You may wish to leave your business for a variety of reasons. For example, you may be ready to retire and wish to hand your business to a relative. Or perhaps your business did not live up to your expectations. Whatever the reason, be smart about how you make your exit. The SBA offers advice on how to exit a business.
www.sba.gov

Social Entrepreneurs

Jeffrey Skoll

Jeffrey Skoll was born in Canada. When Skoll was a teenager, his father was diagnosed with cancer. His father's regrets for things not accomplished led Skoll to strive harder to meet his goals at an earlier age than most. In 1996, Skoll met eBay founder Pierre Omidyor and became eBay's first full-time employee and its president. In 1999, he founded the Skoll Foundation to pursue his vision of a sustainable world of peace and prosperity. It has grown to be one of the world's most prominent foundations for social entrepreneurs.

Skoll Foundation is still creating major change by investing in, connecting, and celebrating social entrepreneurs and other innovators dedicated to solving the world's pressing problems. By asset size, the Skoll Foundation ranks as the largest foundation for social entrepreneurship in the world. Skoll is still currently involved in the foundation as well as operating an independent movie production company called Participant Media. He has won numerous Academy Awards, acknowledgments, and nominations for his work.

Copyright Goodheart-Willcox Co., Inc.

Goodluz/Shutterstock.com

In some cases, when you exit your business you may need to liquidate its assets.

Liquidate the Business

For some business owners, transferring ownership or selling the business are not options. For these owners, the plan is to close the business. **Liquidation** refers to the sale of all assets of a business, including inventory, equipment, and buildings. A business owner may decide to close the business because he or she wants to retire, sales are down and the business can no longer pay its expenses, or the owner wishes to pursue another opportunity. No matter what the reason, the business ceases to exist. The next section discusses legal obligations of closing a business.

Copyright Goodheart-Willcox Co., Inc.

Check Your Understanding ➡

1. What does it mean to *exit a business*? List eight different ways an entrepreneur can exit a business.
2. How does an outright sale differ from a gradual sale?
3. Name three benefits of using an employee stock option plan as an exit strategy.
4. What is the difference between a merger and an acquisition?
5. Under what circumstances might an entrepreneur choose to liquidate his or her business?

Build Your Vocabulary ➡

As you progress through this text, develop a personal glossary of key terms. This will help you build your vocabulary and prepare you for a career. Write a definition for each of the following terms and add them to your personal glossary.

succession plan
buy-sell agreement
harvest strategy
outright sale
gradual sale
lease agreement
employee buyout (EB)
employee stock option plan (ESOP)
liquidation

SECTION 19.2   Legal Obligations

Essential Question

What are the legal issues an owner must consider when exiting a business?

Objectives

After completing this section, you will be able to:

- **Identify** the steps needed to exit a business.
- **Explain** legal implications of exiting a business.

Key Terms

Workers Adjustment and Retraining Notification Act (WARN)
dissolution documents

Critical Thinking

Fast forward your life; do you have an idea of how you would like to stop your entrepreneurial venture? Make a table of options for discontinuing your business. List the advantages and disadvantages of each option. From this table of options, what is the best choice for you, and why?

What to Do When Exiting the Business

When an owner exits a business, there are important steps to take to make sure everything is done legally. If you are a sole proprietor with no employees and you are closing the business, the process is straightforward. However, if the business has employees, specific steps must be followed.

- Obtain advice from experts.
- File, change, or cancel appropriate business documents.
- Follow labor and employment laws.
- Pay your taxes.
- Pay your creditors.
- Collect debts owed to you.
- Close company accounts.

Other considerations will be made if you are transferring ownership to another individual or company.

Copyright Goodheart-Willcox Co., Inc.

Goodluz/Shutterstock.com

When exiting your business, obtain advice from experts so you can fulfill all legal obligations.

Obtain Advice from Experts

Transferring ownership or closing a business requires following the laws in the state in which the business operates. It is highly recommended that professional help be enlisted. Expert advice is available from a number of sources, including lawyers, accountants, business brokers, auctioneers, bankers, and the IRS.

File, Change, or Cancel Appropriate Business Documents

If you are fully exiting the business, remove your name from all legal documents. If you will continue to participate in some capacity, make sure your role is clearly defined on all documents. If you are transferring ownership of the company, make sure that all licenses and permits are transferred to protect your name and your finances. If you are closing the company, cancel licenses, permits, and the business-name registration.

Copyright Goodheart-Willcox Co., Inc.

Green Entrepreneurs

Power Savers

Saving money is at the top of the list for many business owners. Up to 25 percent of energy costs can be saved by simply turning equipment off at the end of the workday. Use a power strip for all equipment so that one flip of the switch turns off all devices. Turn all computers and printers off each evening to save energy. Make sure the lights are off whenever you leave a room or if there is enough natural light to brighten the room.

Follow Labor and Employment Laws

The **Workers Adjustment and Retraining Notification Act (WARN)** requires that employees be given a 60-day written notice if their company is going to close. WARN protects employees who work for a company that employs more than 100 workers. Final paychecks must be issued according to state laws, and W-2s must be sent to employees the following January.

Pay Your Taxes

When filing the last income tax return for the business, check the box that indicates the return is the final one for the company. If the business has employees, make sure the payroll tax obligations are met. Notify the IRS that the business' employer identification number (EIN) needs to be closed. Also, consult the IRS for what other actions the business needs to take when closing. These vary, depending on the type of business structure.

Pay Your Creditors

Make sure all vendors are notified that ownership of the business is being transferred or the business is closing. Make final payments on any debts. Some business owners also make a public announcement that they are exiting the business and will no longer be responsible for any debts of the business.

Collect Debts Owed to You

Debtors are individuals or businesses that owe you money. Notify all debtors that you are transferring ownership of or closing the business. Provide a date by which debtors must make payment in full.

Copyright Goodheart-Willcox Co., Inc.

Close Company Accounts

Close all accounts the business has. This includes bank accounts and credit accounts. Also, be sure to cancel all business credit cards. If ownership of the business is being transferred, the new owner will need to open new accounts.

Legal Implications

Even after the business is closed or ownership is transferred, you may still have legal obligations. Company records must be maintained even after your business has closed or ownership has been transferred. This is especially true of tax and employment records. Records should be kept for at least three years. However, many experts recommend keeping records for a minimum of seven years.

You must also file dissolution documents. **Dissolution documents** are filed in a court of law to notify everyone that you plan to end your business.

Use the checklist in Figure 19-1 to help ensure you have met your legal obligations. This checklist may need to be altered to match your specific business structure. The checklist also helps ensure you meet financial obligations to your employees, shareholders, and state and local governments.

FYI

If a customer does not pay a debt, check with the local consumer protection agency first to learn about debt-collection options and state laws. Some options may include contacting the police, employing a collection agency, or attempting to work with the customer to pay the bill.

You Do the Math   Functions

A function involves relating an input to an output. Each value in a *discrete function* is one of a specified set, usually a whole number. For example, the number of children in a family must be a whole number, so the function for how many children are in a family is a discrete function. The values in a *continuous function* do not have to be one of a specific set; they can include fractions, decimals, or irrational values. For example, the average age of students in a class does not need to be a whole number, so the function for average age is a continuous function.

Solve the following problems.

1. The amount a vendor charges for delivery. Is this a discrete or continuous function?

2. The average age of a business' accounting staff. Is this a discrete or continuous function?

Copyright Goodheart-Willcox Co., Inc.

Checklist for Legal and Financial Obligations	
Final state and federal tax deposits made	You may need to pay sales tax, employment taxes, or other taxes up to and including the date the business is closed or ownership transferred.
Final wage and withholding information (W-2s) issued to employees; information reported to appropriate governmental agencies	This is usually done in January, but can be done when the business closes.
Final tip income and allocated tips information return filed	If you own a company where your employees are paid tips, report the information.
Capital gains or losses reported	Be sure to report any gains or losses you have made from the transfer or sale of the business.
Partner and shareholder shares reported	If your business is a partnership or corporation, report the number of shares and selling price of the final shares.
Final employee pension or benefit plan filed	If you have a pension (retirement) plan or a benefit plan (such as health insurance), file plans for how these will be handled after the transfer or closing of the business.
Payment information issued to subcontractors or vendors	Make final payments to any subcontractors or vendors.
Information from issued 1099s reported	A 1099 is similar to a W-2 for employees; it is issued to someone like a consultant who does work for the company, but is not an employee.
Corporate dissolution or liquidation reported	If your business is an LLC or a corporation, file the appropriate paperwork notifying the state of the dissolution.
S corporation election held to close the business or change owners	If your business is an S corporation, you may want to hold a formal vote of the shareholders to terminate the business or transfer ownership.
Business asset sales reported	Report the sale of all business assets; there may be tax implications.
Sale or exchange of property reported	Report the sale or exchange of any property; there may be tax implications.
All documents reviewed by lawyer or accountant	Pay experts to review all of the documents to ensure everything is legal and you do not miss something.

Goodheart-Willcox Publisher

Figure 19-1. Customize this checklist to fit your business' needs.

Copyright Goodheart-Willcox Co., Inc.

Section 19.2 Review

Check Your Understanding ↪

1. List seven actions an entrepreneur should take when closing a business.
2. Which professionals can help you with an exit strategy?
3. What is a debtor?
4. How long do experts suggest company documents should be kept?
5. What are dissolution documents?

Build Your Vocabulary ↪

As you progress through this text, develop a personal glossary of key terms. This will help you build your vocabulary and prepare you for a career. Write a definition for each of the following terms and add them to your personal glossary.

Workers Adjustment and Retraining Notification Act (WARN)
dissolution documents

Chapter Summary

Section 19.1 Exit the Business

- There are many options available for an entrepreneur should he or she want to leave the business. These include passing the business on to family members; selling shares to partners; developing a harvest strategy; taking the company public; merging with or being acquired by another company; ending a brand that you created; closing some locations; or liquidating the business.
- Harvest strategies are ways an owner can extract money from a business he or she owns. Two harvest strategies are selling the business or having employees buy the company.

Section 19.2 Legal Obligations

- In most cases, a business owner cannot just cease doing business and walk away. There are still some actions that must be taken. Just as entrepreneurs sought expert advice when starting their businesses, expert advice is needed when closing a business.
- Many laws at the state and federal level exist regarding the conduct of business. There are also many laws dealing with what a business must do when it closes. Dissolution documents must be filed in a court of law to notify everyone when a business closes.

Online Activities

Complete the following activities to help you learn, practice, and expand your knowledge and skills.

➦ **Posttest.** Now that you have finished the chapter, see what you learned by taking the chapter posttest.

➦ **Key Terms.** Practice vocabulary for this chapter using the e-flash cards, matching activity, and vocabulary game until you are able to recognize their meanings.

Review Your Knowledge

1. Why would a business owner choose to exit a business?
2. Why is having a succession plan important for the business as well as the business owner?
3. What role does a buy-sell agreement play in a partnership agreement?
4. Why would an entrepreneur want to use a harvest strategy?
5. What two things might a harvest strategy include?
6. What are the advantages of leasing a business?

Copyright Goodheart-Willcox Co., Inc.

7. When transferring ownership to another individual or company, why is it important to file, change, or cancel appropriate business documents?

8. What are the unique challenges involved in transferring ownership of selling a business to a family member?

9. Why is it important to consult an expert when closing a business?

10. What are the three different ways a business can be sold?

Apply Your Knowledge

1. Do an Internet search for a succession plan for owners who are exiting a business. Make notes on important points that will help you write this portion of your business plan. What features of a succession plan do you think are the most essential?

2. Do an Internet search for harvest strategies for a small business. Make notes on important points that will help you write this portion of your business plan.

3. There may be a time in your business when you decide to offer an employee stock option plan (ESOP). Research these plans and make notes about the advantages and disadvantages to offering an ESOP. What do you think are the pros and cons of instituting such a plan for your business?

4. You may eventually go public with an initial public offering (IPO) for your company. Explain what it means to go public with a business. Make a list of five other well-known companies who went public. What did you learn about this process?

5. Some owners of companies decide to sell their brand when they leave their business. What would be the advantages for you in selling your brand?

6. Make a checklist of things that should be done if you decide to sell your business.

7. Explain what it means to liquidate a business. Do a search for local businesses that have liquidated. What types of strategies did they use?

8. Make a checklist of things that should be done if you liquidate your business.

9. Are there any local laws you need to be aware of if you decide to cease doing business in your community?

10. You have completed the last part of your business plan. Write several paragraphs about what you have learned through this experience.

Teamwork

Together with a teammate, research different buy-sell agreements and the laws governing these in your state. Create a buy-sell agreement for each of your businesses—imagining that each is the other's partner in the business. What conditions were important for each individual to include in the agreement? Make sure your agreements are fair to each side.

Copyright Goodheart-Willcox Co., Inc.

Internet Research

Closing a Business. Use the Internet to research closing a business or how to close a business. Compose a summary of the information you find. Is there a standard procedure to follow when closing a business? What are the legal documents involved?

College and Career Readiness

Communication Skills

Reading. Read a magazine, newspaper, or online article about a business that recently transferred ownership to a family member. What logical inferences can you make about whether the transfer was a negative or positive thing for the family members and the business? What evidence can you point to in the text that would support your inference? Provide a summary of the material as well as what you were able to infer from it.

Writing. Research the relative merits of the different exit strategies presented in this chapter. Write a persuasive essay in which you argue for one strategy being better than the rest. Use valid reasons and cite evidence from your research to back up your contention.

CTSOs

Day of the Event. You have practiced all year for this competition, and now you are ready. Whether it is for an objective test, written test, report, or presentation, you have done your homework and are ready to shine. To prepare for the day of the event, complete the following activities.

1. Be sure to get plenty of sleep the night before the event so that you are rested and ready to go.

2. Use your event checklist before you go into the presentation so that you do not forget any of your materials that are needed for the event.

3. Be early for the room where the competition will take place. If you are late and the door is closed, you will be disqualified.

4. If you are making a presentation before a panel of judges, practice what you are going to say when you are called on. State your name, your school, and any other information that has been requested. Be confident, smile, and make eye contact with the judges.

5. When the event is finished, thank the judges for their time.

Copyright Goodheart-Willcox Co., Inc.

Building Your Business Plan—Complete the Puzzle

Exit Strategies

While it may be difficult to think about how to leave, sell, or close a business in the early stages of starting it, planning for the future is wise for any entrepreneur. Letting a business go can be a positive experience for an owner, though. A new business venture, retirement, or passing the business on to family members are all things to look forward to. The exit or harvest strategy you choose will depend on your goals, which may change over time. Before making any decisions, also investigate the legal obligations for each strategy you are considering.

Goals

- Identify exit or harvest strategies for your business.
- Create business plan notes.

Directions

Access the *Entrepreneurship* companion website at www.g-wlearning.com ➦ . Download each data file for the following activities. A complete sample business plan is available on the companion website to use as a reference. The name of the file is BusPlan_Sample.RetroAttire. docx.

Preparation

Activity 19-1. Exit or Harvest Strategies. Write a short exit or harvest strategy for your business and include it in the Appendices.

Activity 19-2. Business Plan Notes. Create notes about the sources of plans for a future exit strategy from your business.

Business Plan—Financial Plans

In this chapter, you learned about various ways a business owner can let go of his or her business. Use the information you learned about leaving a business to help you finish the Financial Plans section of the business plan. This is also the time to complete the Conclusion and Executive Summary sections.

1. Open your saved business plan document.
2. Locate the Financial Plans section of the plan. Based on the information in this chapter, finish writing the Future Plans subsection of the Financial Plans section. Use the suggestions and questions listed to help you generate ideas. Delete the instructions and questions when you are finished recording your responses.
3. Locate the Executive Summary section of the plan and complete it now. It should be two pages or less.
4. Locate the Conclusion section of the plan and write it.
5. Locate the Title Page section of the plan and finalize.
6. Locate the Table of Contents section of the plan and finalize.
7. Finalize the Appendices section of the plan.
8. Proofread your entire business plan document. Make any final additions or corrections.
9. Save your document.
10. Print the document, print the attachments, and assemble.

Congratulations. You have finished your business plan.

Math Skills Handbook

Table of Contents

Copyright Goodheart-Willcox Co., Inc.

Getting Started

Math skills are needed in everyday life. You will need to be able to estimate the cost of purchases, calculate sales tax, and large quantities of materials. This section is designed to help develop your math proficiency for better understanding of the concepts presented in the textbook. Using the information presented in the Math Skills Handbook will help you understand basic math concepts and their application to the real world.

Using a Calculator

There are many different types of calculators. Some are simple and only perform basic math operations. Become familiar with the keys and operating instructions of your calculator so calculations can be made quickly and correctly.

Shown below is a scientific calculator that comes standard with the Windows 8 operating system. To display this version, select the **View** pull-down menu and click **Scientific** in the menu.

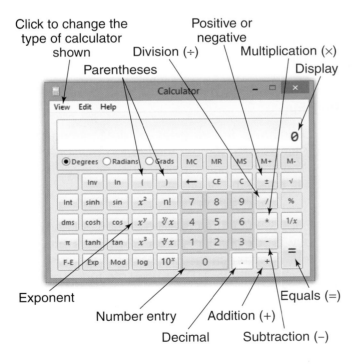

Solving Word Problems

Word problems are exercises in which the problem is set up in text, rather than presented in mathematical notation. Many word problems tell a story. You must identify the elements of the math problem and solve it.

There are many strategies for solving word problems. Some common strategies include making a list or table; working backward; guessing, checking, and revising; and substituting simpler numbers to solve the problem.

Strategy	How to Apply
List or table	Identify information in the problem and organize it into a table to identify patterns.
Work backward	When an end result is provided, work backward from that to find the requested information.
Guess, check, revise	Start with a reasonable guess at the answer, check to see if it is correct, and revise the guess as needed until the solution is found.
Substitute simpler information	Use different numbers to simplify the problem and solve it, then solve the problem using the provided numbers.

Number Sense

Number sense is an ability to use and understand numbers to make judgments and solve problems. Someone with good number sense also understands when his or her computations are reasonable in the context of a problem.

Example
Suppose you want to add three basketball scores: 35, 21, and 18.
- First, add $30 + 20 + 10 = 60$.
- Then, add $5 + 1 + 8 = 14$.
- Finally, combine these two sums to find the answer: $60 + 14 = 74$.

Example
Suppose your brother is 72 inches tall and you want to convert this measurement from inches to feet. You use a calculator to divide 72 by 12 (number of inches in a foot) and the answer is displayed as 864. You recognize immediately that your brother cannot be 864 feet tall and realize you must have miscalculated. In this case, a multiplication operation was entered instead of a division operation. The correct answer is 6.

Copyright Goodheart-Willcox Co., Inc.

Numbers and Quantity

Numbers are more than just items in a series. Each number has a distinct value relative to all other numbers. They are used to perform mathematical operations from the simplest addition to finding square roots. There are whole numbers, fractions, decimals, exponents, and square roots.

Whole Numbers

A whole number, or integer, is any positive number or zero that has no fractional part. It can be a single digit from 0 to 9, or may contain multiple digits, such as 38.

Place Value

A digit's position in a number determines its *place value.* The digit, or numeral, in the place farthest to the right before the decimal point is in the *ones position.* The next digit to the left is in the *tens position,* followed by the next digit in the *hundreds position.* As you continue to move left, the place values increase to thousands, ten thousands, and so forth.

Example

Suppose you win the lottery and receive a check for $23,152,679. Your total prize would be *twenty-three million, one hundred fifty-two thousand, six hundred seventy-nine dollars.*

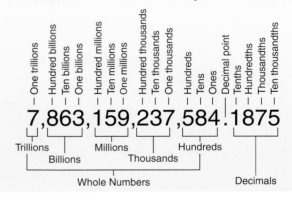

Addition

Addition is the process of combining two or more numbers. The result is called the *sum.*

Example

A plumber installs six faucets on his first job and three faucets on his second job. How many faucets does he install in total?

$$6 + 3 = 9$$

Subtraction

Subtraction is the process of finding the *difference* between two numbers.

Example

A plumber installs six faucets on her first job and three faucets on her second job. How many more faucets did she install on the first job than the second? Subtract 3 from 6 to find the answer.

$$6 - 3 = 3$$

Multiplication

Multiplication is a method of adding a number to itself a given number of times. The multiplied numbers are called *factors,* and the result is called the *product.*

Example

Suppose you are installing computers and need to purchase four adapters. If the adapters are $6 each, what is the total cost of the adapters? The answer can be found by adding $6 four times:

$$\$6 + \$6 + \$6 + \$6 = \$24$$

However, the same answer is found more quickly by multiplying $6 times 4.

$$\$6 \times 4 = \$24$$

Division

Division is the process of determining how many times one number, called the *divisor,* goes into another number, called the *dividend.* The result is called the *quotient.*

Example

Suppose you are installing computers and buy a box of adapters for $24. There are four adapters in the box. What is the cost of each adapter? The answer is found by dividing $24 by 4:

$$\$24 \div 4 = \$6$$

Decimals

A decimal is a kind of fraction with a denominator that is either ten, one hundred, one thousand, or some power of ten. Every decimal has three parts: a whole number (sometimes zero), followed by a decimal point, and one or more whole numbers.

Copyright Goodheart-Willcox Co., Inc.

Place Value

The numbers to the right of the decimal point indicate the amount of the fraction. The first place to the right of a decimal point is the tenths place. The second place to the right of the decimal point is the hundredths place. As you continue to the right, the place values move to the thousandths place, the ten thousandths place, and so on.

Example

A machinist is required to produce an airplane part to a very precise measurement of 36.876 inches. This measurement is *thirty-six and eight hundred seventy-six thousandths* inches.

36.876

Addition

To add decimals, place each number in a vertical list and align the decimal points. Then add the numbers in each column starting with the column on the right and working to the left. The decimal point in the answer drops down into the same location.

Example

A landscaper spreads 4.3 pounds of fertilizer in the front yard of a house and 1.2 pounds in the backyard. How many pounds of fertilizer did the landscaper spread in total?

```
  4.3
+ 1.2
-----
  5.5
```

Subtraction

To subtract decimals, place each number in a vertical list and align the decimal points. Then subtract the numbers in each column, starting with the column on the right and working to the left. The decimal point in the answer drops down into the same location.

Example

A landscaper spreads 4.3 pounds of fertilizer in the front yard of a house and 1.2 pounds in the backyard. How many more pounds were spread in the front yard than in the backyard?

```
  4.3
- 1.2
-----
  3.1
```

Multiplication

To multiply decimals, place the numbers in a vertical list. Then multiply each digit of the top number by the right-hand bottom number. Multiply each digit of the top number by the bottom number in the tens position. Place the result on a second line and add a zero to the end of the number. Add the total number of decimal places in both numbers you are multiplying. This will be the number of decimal places in your answer.

Example

An artist orders 13 brushes priced at $3.20 each. What is the total cost of the order? The answer can be found by multiplying $3.20 by 13.

```
   $ 3.20
 ×     13
 --------
      960
 +   3200
 --------
  $41.60
```

Division

To divide decimals, the dividend is placed under the division symbol, the divisor is placed to the left of the division symbol, and the quotient is placed above the division symbol. Start from the *left* of the dividend and determine how many times the divisor goes into the first number. Continue this until the quotient is found. Add the dollar sign to the final answer.

```
      3.20
   3)9.60
     9↓       Product of 3 × 3
    ----
     06|      Bring down the 6
      6↓      Product of 2 × 3
    ----
      0       No remainder
```

Example

An artist buys a package of three brushes for $9.60. What is the cost of each brush?

```
      3.20
   3)9.60
    -9 ↓
    ----
      06↓
    ----
      00
```

The quotient is found by dividing $9.60 by 3.

Copyright Goodheart-Willcox Co., Inc.

Rounding

When a number is rounded, some of the digits are changed, removed, or changed to zero so the number is easier to work with. Rounding is often used when precise calculations or measurements are not needed. For example, if you are calculating millions of dollars, it might not be important to know the amount down to the dollar or cent. Instead, you might *round* the amount to the nearest ten thousand or even hundred thousand dollars. Also, when working with decimals, the final answer might have several more decimal places than needed.

To round a number, follow these steps. First, underline the digit in the place to which you are rounding. Second, if the digit to the *right* of this place is 5 or greater, add 1 to the underlined digit. If the digit to the right is less than 5, do not change the underlined digit. Third, change all the digits to right of the underlined digit to zero. In the case of decimals, the digits to the right of the underlined digit are removed.

Example

A company's expense for utilities last year was $32,678.53. The owner of the company is preparing a budget for next year and wants to round this amount to the nearest 1,000.

Step 1: Underline the digit in the 10,000 place.

$$\$3\underline{2},678$$

Step 2: The digit to the right of 2 is greater than 5, so add 1.

$$2 + 1 = 3$$

Step 3: Change the digits to the right of the underlined digit to zero.

$$\$33,000$$

Fractions

A fraction is a part of a whole. It is a numerator that is divided by a denominator.

$$\frac{\text{numerator}}{\text{denominator}}$$

The *numerator* specifies the number of equal parts that are in the fraction. The *denominator* shows how many equal parts make up the whole.

Proper

In a *proper fraction,* the numerator is less than the denominator.

Example

A lumber yard worker cuts a sheet of plywood into four equal pieces and sells three of them to a carpenter. The carpenter now has 3/4 of the original sheet. The lumber yard has 1/4 of the sheet remaining.

Improper

An *improper fraction* is a fraction where the numerator is equal to or greater than the denominator.

Example

A chef uses a chili recipe that calls for 1/2 cup of chili sauce. However, the chef makes an extra-large batch that will serve three times as many people and uses three of the 1/2 cup measures. The improper fraction in this example is 3/2 cups of chili sauce.

Mixed

A mixed number contains a whole number and a fraction. It is another way of writing an improper fraction.

Example

A chef uses a chili recipe that calls for 1/2 cup of chili sauce. However, the chef makes an extra-large batch that will serve three times as many people and uses three of the 1/2 cup measures. The improper fraction in this example is 3/2 cups of chili sauce. This can be converted to a mixed number by dividing the numerator by the denominator:
The remainder is 1, which is 1 over 2. So, the mixed number is 1 1/2 cups.

$$2\overline{\smash)3} \atop \underline{-2} \atop 1$$ with quotient 1

Copyright Goodheart-Willcox Co., Inc.

Reducing

Fractions are reduced to make them easier to work with. Reducing a fraction means writing it with smaller numbers, in *lowest terms.* Reducing a fraction does not change its value.

To find the lowest terms, determine the largest number that *evenly* divides both the numerator and denominator so there is no remainder. Then use this number to divide both the numerator and denominator.

Example

The owner of a hair salon asks ten customers if they were satisfied with the service they recently received. Eight customers said they were satisfied. So, the fraction of satisfied customers is 8/10. The largest number that evenly divides both the numerator and denominator is 2. The fraction is reduced to its lowest terms as follows.

$$\frac{8}{10} = \frac{8 \div 2}{10 \div 2} = \frac{4}{5}$$

Addition

To add fractions, the numerators are combined and the denominator stays the same. However, fractions can only be added when they have a *common denominator.* The *least common denominator* is the smallest number to which each denominator can be converted.

Example

A snack food company makes a bag of trail mix by combining 3/8 pound of nuts with 1/8 pound of dried fruit. What is the total weight of each bag? The fractions have common denominators, so the total weight is determined by adding the fractions.

$$\frac{3}{8} + \frac{1}{8} = \frac{4}{8}$$

This answer can be reduced from 4/8 to 1/2.

Example

Suppose the company combines 1/4 pound of nuts with 1/8 pound of dried fruit. To add these fractions, the denominators must be made equal. In this case, the least common denominator is 8 because $4 \times 2 = 8$. Convert

1/4 to its equivalent of 2/8 by multiplying both numerator and denominator by 2. Then the fractions can be added as follows.

$$\frac{2}{8} + \frac{1}{8} = \frac{3}{8}$$

This answer cannot be reduced because 3 and 8 have no common factors.

Subtraction

To subtract fractions, the second numerator is subtracted from the first numerator. The denominators stay the same. However, fractions can only be subtracted when they have a *common denominator.*

Example

A snack food company makes a bag of trail mix by combining 3/8 pound of nuts with 1/8 pound of dried fruit. How much more do the nuts weigh than the dried fruit? The fractions have common denominators, so the difference can be determined by subtracting the fractions.

$$\frac{3}{8} - \frac{1}{8} = \frac{2}{8}$$

This answer can be reduced from 2/8 to 1/4.

Example

Suppose the company combines 1/4 pound of nuts with 1/8 pound of dried fruit. How much more do the nuts weigh than the dried fruit? To subtract these fractions, the denominators must be made equal. The least common denominator is 8, so convert 1/4 to its equivalent of 2/8. Then the fractions can be subtracted as follows.

$$\frac{2}{8} - \frac{1}{8} = \frac{1}{8}$$

This answer cannot be reduced.

Multiplication

Common denominators are not necessary to multiply fractions. Multiply all of the numerators and multiply all of the denominators. Reduce the resulting fraction as needed.

Copyright Goodheart-Willcox Co., Inc.

Example
A lab technician makes a saline solution by mixing 3/4 cup of salt with one gallon of water. How much salt should the technician mix if only 1/2 gallon of water is used? Multiply 3/4 by 1/2:

$$\frac{3}{4} \times \frac{1}{2} = \frac{3}{8}$$

Division

To divide one fraction by a second fraction, multiply the first fraction by the reciprocal of the second fraction. The *reciprocal* of a fraction is created by switching the numerator and denominator.

Example
A cabinetmaker has 3/4 gallon of wood stain. Each cabinet requires 1/8 gallon of stain to finish. How many cabinets can be finished? To find the answer, divide 3/4 by 1/8, which means multiplying 3/4 by the reciprocal of 1/8.

$$\frac{3}{4} \div \frac{1}{8} = \frac{3}{4} \times \frac{8}{1} = \frac{24}{4} = 6$$

Negative Numbers

Negative numbers are those less than zero. They are written with a minus sign in front of the number.

Example
The number −34,687,295 is read as *negative thirty-four million, six hundred eighty-seven thousand, two hundred ninety-five.*

Addition

Adding a negative number is the same as subtracting a positive number.

Example
A football player gains nine yards on his first running play (+9) and loses four yards (−4) on his second play. The two plays combined result in a five yard gain.

$$9 + (−4) = 9 − 4 = 5$$

Suppose this player loses five yards on his first running play (−5) and loses four yards (−4) on his second play. The two plays combined result in a nine yard loss.

$$−5 + (−4) = −5 − 4 = −9$$

Subtraction

Subtracting a negative number is the same as adding a positive number.

Example
Suppose you receive a $100 traffic ticket. This will result in a −$100 change to your cash balance. However, you explain the circumstance to a traffic court judge and she reduces the fine by $60. The effect is to subtract −$60 from −$100 change to your cash balance. The final result is a −$40 change.

$$−\$100 − (−\$60) = −\$100 + \$60 = −\$40$$

Multiplication

Multiplying an odd number of negative numbers results in a *negative* product. Multiplying an even number of negative numbers results in a *positive* product.

Example
If you lose two pounds per week, this will result in a −2 pound weekly change in your weight. After five weeks, there will be a −10 pound change to your weight.

$$5 \times (−2) = −10$$

Suppose you have been losing two pounds per week. Five weeks ago (−5) your weight was 10 pounds higher.

$$(−5) \times (−2) = 10$$

Division

Dividing an odd number of negative numbers results in a *negative* quotient. Dividing an even number of negative numbers results in a *positive* quotient.

Example
Suppose you lost 10 pounds, which is a −10 pound change in your weight. How many pounds on average did you lose each week if it took five weeks to lose the weight? Divide −10 by 5 to find the answer.

$$−10 \div 5 = −2$$

Suppose you lost 10 pounds. How many weeks did this take if you lost two pounds each week? Divide −10 by −2 to find the answer.

$$−10 \div −2 = 5$$

Copyright Goodheart-Willcox Co., Inc.

Percentages

A percentage (%) means a part of 100. It is the same as a fraction or decimal.

Representing Percentages as Decimals

To change a percentage to a decimal, move the decimal point two places to the left. For example, 1% is the same as 1/100 or 0.01; 10% is the same as 10/100 or 0.10; and 100% is the same as 100/100 or 1.0.

Example

A high school cafeteria estimates that 30% of the students prefer sesame seeds on hamburger buns. To convert this percentage to a decimal, move the decimal point two places to the left.

$$30\% = 0.30$$

Representing Fractions as Percentages

To change a fraction to a percentage, first convert the fraction to a decimal by dividing the numerator by the denominator. Then convert the decimal to a percentage by moving the decimal point two places to the right.

Example

A high school cafeteria conducts a survey and finds that three of every ten students prefer sesame seeds on hamburger buns. To change this fraction to a percentage, divide 3 by 10, and move the decimal two places to the right.

$$3 \div 10 = 0.30 = 30\%$$

Calculating a Percentage

To calculate the percentage of a number, change the percentage to a decimal and multiply by the number.

Example

A car dealer sold ten cars last week, of which 70% were sold to women. How many cars did women buy? Change 70% to a decimal by dividing 70 by 100, which equals 0.70. Then multiply by the total number (10).

$$0.70 \times 10 = 7$$

To determine what percentage one number is of another, divide the first number by the second. Then convert the quotient into a percentage by moving the decimal point two places to the right.

Example

A car dealer sold 10 cars last week, of which seven were sold to women. What percentage of the cars were purchased by women? Divide 7 by 10 and then convert to a percentage.

$$7 \div 10 = 0.70$$

$$0.70 = 70\%$$

Ratio

A ratio compares two numbers through division. Ratios are often expressed as a fraction, but can also be written with a colon (:) or the word *to*.

Example

A drugstore's cost for a bottle of vitamins is $2.00. It sells the bottle for $3.00. The ratio of the selling price to the cost can be expressed as follows.

$$\frac{\$3.00}{\$2.00} = \frac{3}{2}$$

$$\$3.00{:}\$2.00 = 3{:}2$$

$$\$3.00 \text{ to } \$2.00 = 3 \text{ to } 2$$

Measurement

The official system of measurement in the United States for length, volume, and weight is the US Customary System of measurement. The metric system of measurement is used by most other countries.

US Customary Measurement

The following are the most commonly used units of length in the US Customary System of measurement.

- 1 inch
- 1 foot = 12 inches
- 1 yard = 3 feet
- 1 mile = 5,280 feet

Example

An interior designer measurers the length and width of a room when ordering new floor tiles. The length is measured at 12 feet 4 inches (12′ 4″). The width is measured at 8 feet 7 inches (8′ 7″).

Example

Taxi cab fares are usually determined by measuring distance in miles. A recent cab rate in Chicago was $3.25 for the first 1/9 mile or less, and $0.20 for each additional 1/9 mile.

Metric Conversion

The metric system of measurement is convenient to use because units can be converted by multiplying or dividing by multiples of 10. The following are the commonly used units of length in the metric system of measurement.

- 1 millimeter
- 1 centimeter = 10 millimeters
- 1 meter = 100 centimeters
- 1 kilometer = 1,000 meters

The following are conversions from the US Customary System to the metric system.

- 1 inch = 25.4 millimeters = 2.54 centimeters
- 1 foot = 30.48 centimeters = 0.3048 meters
- 1 yard = 0.9144 meters
- 1 mile = 1.6093 kilometers

Example

A salesperson from the United States is traveling abroad and needs to drive 100 kilometers to meet a customer. How many miles is this trip? Divide 100 kilometers by 1.6093 and round to the hundredth place.

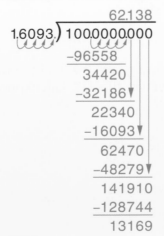

Estimating

Estimating is finding an *approximate* answer and often involves using rounded numbers. It is often quicker to add rounded numbers, for example, than it is to add the precise numbers.

Example

Estimate the total miles a delivery truck will travel along the following three segments of a route.

- Detroit to Chicago: 278 miles
- Chicago to St. Louis: 297 miles
- St. Louis to Wichita: 436 miles

The mileage can be estimated by rounding each segment to the nearest 100 miles.

- Detroit to Chicago: 300 miles
- Chicago to St. Louis: 300 miles
- St. Louis to Wichita: 400 miles

Add the rounded segments to estimate the total miles.

$$300 + 300 + 400 = 1{,}000 \text{ miles}$$

Accuracy and Precision

Accuracy and precision mean slightly different things. *Accuracy* is the closeness of a measured value to its actual or true value. *Precision* is how close measured values are to each other.

Example

A machine is designed to fill jars with 16 ounces of peanut butter. The machine is considered accurate if the actual amount of peanut butter in a jar is within 0.05 ounces of the target, which is a range of 15.95 to 16.05 ounces. A machine operator tests a jar and measures the weight to be 16.01 ounces. The machine is accurate.

Suppose a machine operator tests 10 jars of peanut butter and finds the weight of each jar to be 15.4 ounces. The machine is considered precise because it fills every jar with exactly the same amount. However, it is not accurate because the amount differs too much from the target.

Copyright Goodheart-Willcox Co., Inc.

Algebra

An *equation* is a mathematical statement that has an equal sign (=). An *algebraic* equation is an equation that includes at least one variable. A *variable* is an unknown quantity.

Solving Equations with Variables

Solving an algebraic equation means finding the value of the variable that will make the equation a true statement. To solve a simple equation, perform inverse operations on both sides and isolate the variable.

Example

A computer consultant has sales of $1,000. After deducting $600 in expenses, her profit equals $400. This is expressed with the following equation.

$$\text{sales} - \text{expenses} = \text{profit}$$
$$\$1,000 - \$600 = \$400$$

Example

A computer consultant has expenses of $600 and $400 in profit. What are her sales? An equation can be written in which sales are the unknown quantity, or variable.

$$\text{sales} - \text{expenses} = \text{profit}$$
$$\text{sales} - \$600 = \$400$$

Example

To find the value for sales, perform inverse operations on both sides and isolate the variable.

$$
\begin{array}{r}
\text{sales} - \$600 = \$400 \\
+ \$600 + \$600 \\
\hline
\text{sales} = \$1,000
\end{array}
$$

Order of Operations

The order of operations is a set of rules stating which operations in an equation are performed first. The order of operations is often stated using the acronym *PEMDAS*. PEMDAS stands for parentheses, exponents, multiplication and division, and addition and subtraction. This means anything inside parentheses is computed first. Exponents are computed next. Then, any multiplication and division operations are computed. Finally, any addition and subtraction operations are computed

to find the final answer to the problem. The equation is solved from left to right by applying PEMDAS.

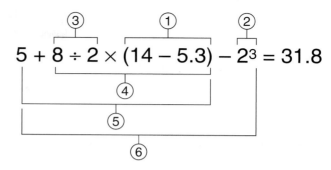

$$5 + 8 \div 2 \times (14 - 5.3) - 2^3 = 31.8$$

Recursive Formulas

A *recursive formula* is used to determine the next term of a sequence, using one or more of the preceding terms. The terms of a sequence are often expressed with a variable and subscript. For example, a sequence might be written as a_1, a_2, a_3, a_4, a_5, and so on. The subscript is essentially the place in line for each term. A recursive formula has two parts. The first is a starting point or seed value (a_1). The second is an equation for another number in the sequence (a_n). The second part of the formula is a function of the prior term (a_{n-1}).

Example

Suppose you buy a car for $10,000. Assume the car declines in value 10% each year. In the second year, the car will be worth 90% of $10,000, which is $9,000. The following year it will be worth 90% of $9,000, which is $8,100. What will the car be worth in the fifth year? Use the following recursive equation to find the answer.

$$a_n = a_{n-1} \times 0.90$$

$$\text{where } a_1 = \$10,000$$

$$a_n = \text{value of car in the } n^{th} \text{ year}$$

Year	Value of Car
n = 1	$a_1 = \$10,000$
n = 2	$a_2 = a_{2-1} \times 0.90 = a_1 \times 0.90 = \$10,000 \times 0.90$ $= \$9,000$
n = 3	$a_3 = a_{3-1} \times 0.90 = a_2 \times 0.90 = \$9,000 \times 0.90$ $= \$8,100$
n = 4	$a_4 = a_{4-1} \times 0.90 = a_3 \times 0.90 = \$8,100 \times 0.90$ $= \$7,290$
n = 5	$a_5 = a_{5-1} \times 0.90 = a_4 \times 0.90 = \$7,290 \times 0.90$ $= \$6,561$

Copyright Goodheart-Willcox Co., Inc.

Geometry

Geometry is a field of mathematics that deals with shapes, such as circles and polygons. A *polygon* is any shape whose sides are straight. Every polygon has three or more sides.

Parallelograms

A *parallelogram* is a four-sided figure with two pairs of parallel sides. A *rectangle* is a type of parallelogram with four right angles. A *square* is a special type of parallelogram with four right angles (90 degrees) and four equal sides.

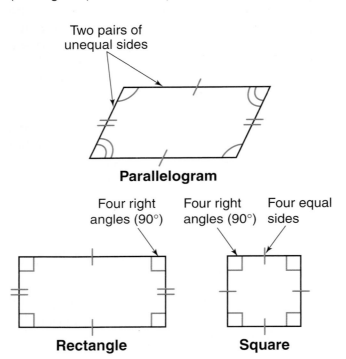

Parallelogram

Rectangle   **Square**

Example
Real-life examples of squares include ceramic floor and wall tiles. Real-life examples of a rectangle include a football field, pool table, and most doors.

Triangles

A three-sided polygon is called a *triangle.* The following are four types of triangles, which are classified according to their sides and angles.

- *Equilateral:* Three equal sides and three equal angles.
- *Isosceles:* Two equal sides and two equal angles.

- *Scalene:* Three unequal sides and three unequal angles.
- *Right:* One right angle; may be isosceles or scalene.

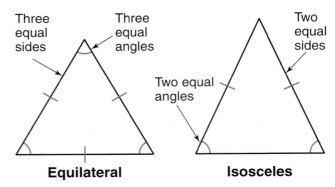

Equilateral   **Isosceles**

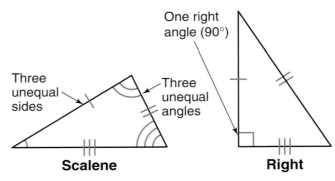

Scalene   **Right**

Example
Real-life examples of equilateral triangles are the sides of a classical Egyptian pyramid.

Circles and Half Circles

A *circle* is a figure in which every point is the same distance from the center. The distance from the center to a point on the circle is called the *radius.* The distance across the circle through the center is the *diameter.* A half circle is formed by dividing a whole circle along the diameter.

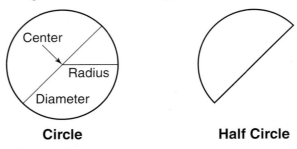

Circle   **Half Circle**

Example
Real-life examples of circles include wheels of all sizes.

Copyright Goodheart-Willcox Co., Inc.

Perimeter

Perimeter is a measure of length around a figure. Add the length of each side to measure the perimeter of any figure with sides that are all line segments, such as a parallelogram or triangle. The perimeter of a circle is called the *circumference*. To measure the perimeter, multiply the diameter by pi (π). Pi is approximately equal to 3.14. The following formulas can be used to calculate the perimeter of various figures.

Figure	Perimeter
parallelogram	2 × width + 2 × length
square	4 × side
rectangle	2 × width + 2 × length
triangle	side + side + side
circle	π × diameter

Example

A professional basketball court is a rectangle 94 feet long and 50 feet wide. The perimeter of the court is calculated as follows.

2 × 94 feet + 2 × 50 feet = 288 feet

Example

A tractor tire has a 43 inch diameter. The circumference of the tire is calculated as follows.

43 inches × 3.14 = 135 inches

Area

Area is a measure of the amount of surface within the perimeter of a flat figure. Area is measured in square units, such as square inches, square feet, or square miles. The following formulas can be used to calculate the area of the corresponding figures.

Figure	Area
parallelogram	base × height
square	side × side
rectangle	length × width
triangle	1/2 × base × height
circle	π × radius^2 = π × radius × radius

Example

An interior designer needs to order decorative tiles to fill the following spaces. Measure the area of each space in square feet.

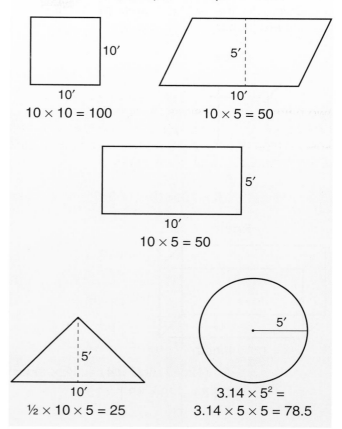

10 × 10 = 100

10 × 5 = 50

10 × 5 = 50

½ × 10 × 5 = 25

3.14 × 5^2 =
3.14 × 5 × 5 = 78.5

Surface Area

Surface area is the total area of the surface of a figure that occupies three-dimensional space, such as a cube or prism. A *cube* is a solid figure that has six identical square faces. A *prism* has bases or ends that have the same size and shape and are parallel to each other, and each of whose sides is a parallelogram. The following are formulas to find the surface area of a cube and a prism.

Object	Surface Area
cube	6 × side × side
prism	2 × [(length × width) + (width × height) + (length × height)]

Copyright Goodheart-Willcox Co., Inc.

Example

A manufacturer of cardboard boxes wants to determine how much cardboard is needed to make the following size boxes. Calculate the surface area of each in square inches.

Cube

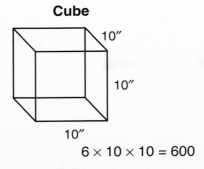

$6 \times 10 \times 10 = 600$

Prism

7" = width

4" = height

12" = length

$2 [(12 \times 7) + (7 \times 4) + (12 \times 4)] =$
$2 [84 + 28 + 48] = 320$

Volume

Volume is the three-dimensional space occupied by a figure and is measured in cubic units, such as cubic inches or cubic feet. The following formulas can be used to calculate the volume of the corresponding figures.

Solid Figure	Volume
cube	side^3 = side × side × side
prism	length × width × height
cylinder	π × radius^2 × height = π × radius × radius × height
sphere	4/3 × π × radius^3 = 4/3 × π × radius × radius × radius

Example

Find the volume of packing material needed to fill the following boxes. Measure the volume of each in cubic inches.

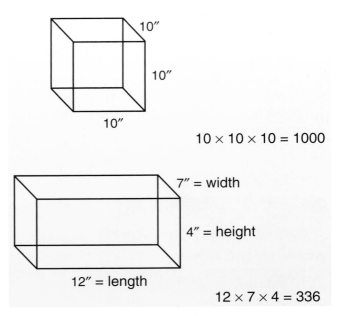

$10 \times 10 \times 10 = 1000$

7" = width

4" = height

12" = length

$12 \times 7 \times 4 = 336$

Example

Find the volume of grain that will fill the following cylindrical silo. Measure the volume in cubic feet.

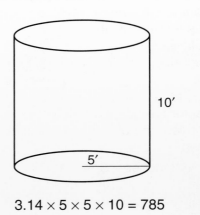

$3.14 \times 5 \times 5 \times 10 = 785$

Example

A manufacturer of pool toys wants to stuff soft material into a ball with a 3 inch radius. Find the cubic inches of material that will fit into the ball.

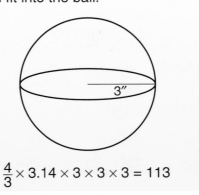

$\frac{4}{3} \times 3.14 \times 3 \times 3 \times 3 = 113$

Copyright Goodheart-Willcox Co., Inc.

Data Analysis and Statistics

Graphs are used to illustrate data in a picture-like format. It is often easier to understand data when shown in a graphical form instead of a numerical form in a table. Common types of graphs are bar graphs, line graphs, and circle graphs.

A *bar graph* organizes information along a vertical axis and horizontal axis. The vertical axis runs up and down one side and the horizontal axis runs along the bottom.

A *line graph* also organizes information on vertical and horizontal axes. However, data are graphed as a continuous line rather than a set of bars. Line graphs are often used to show trends over a period of time.

A *circle graph* looks like a divided circle and shows how a whole object is cut up into parts. Circle graphs are also called *pie charts* and are often used to illustrate percentages.

Example

A business shows the following balances in its cash account for the months of March through July. These data are illustrated below in the line graph.

Month	Account Balance	Month	Account Balance
March	$450	June	$800
April	$625	July	$900
May	$550		

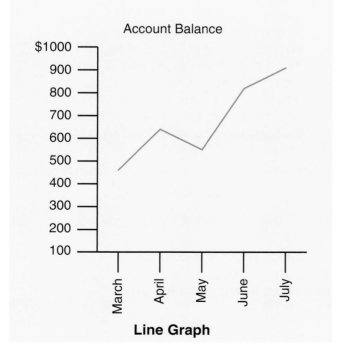

Line Graph

Example

A business lists the percentage of its expenses in the following categories. These data are displayed in the following circle graph.

Expenses	Percentage
Cost of goods	25
Salaries	25
Rent	21
Utilities	17
Advertising	12

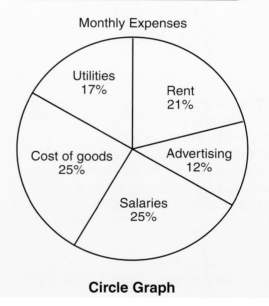

Circle Graph

Math Models for Business

Math skills used in business are the same math skills required in everyday life. The ability to add, subtract, multiply, and divide different types of numbers is very important. However, this type of math is often focused on prices, taxes, profits, and losses.

Markup

Markup is a term for the amount by which price exceeds the cost. One way to express markup is in dollars. Another way to express markup is percentage. The *markup percentage* is the amount of the markup as a percentage of the cost.

Copyright Goodheart-Willcox Co., Inc.

Example

A retailer pays $4 for a pair of athletic socks and prices them for sale at $7. The dollar markup is $3.

selling price − cost = dollar markup

$$\$7 - \$4 = \$3$$

Example

A pair of athletic socks costs $4 and is priced at $7. The dollar markup is $3. To find the markup percentage, divide $3 by $4. The markup percentage is 75%.

markup dollars ÷ cost = markup percentage

$$\$3 \div \$4 = 0.75 = 75\%$$

Percentage Markup to Determine Selling Price

The selling price of an item can be determined if you know the markup percentage and the cost. First, convert the markup percentage to a decimal. Next, multiply the cost by the decimal. Then, add the markup dollars to the cost to determine the selling price. Another way to find the selling price is to convert the markup percentage to a decimal and add 1.0. Then, multiply this amount by the cost.

Example

A pair of athletic socks costs $4, which the retailer marks up by 75%. Find the selling price.

1. Convert the markup percentage to a decimal.

$$75\% = 0.75$$

2. Multiply the cost by the markup.

cost × markup = dollar markup

$$\$4 \times 0.75 = \$3$$

3. Add the $3 markup to the $4 cost to find the selling price. The selling price is $7.

$$\$4 + \$3 = \$7$$

Example

A pair of athletic socks costs $4, which the retailer marks up by 75%. Find the selling price.

1. Convert the 75% markup percentage to 0.75 and add 1.0.

$$0.75 + 1.0 = 1.75$$

2. Multiply 1.75 by the $4 cost to find the selling price.

$$\$4 \times 1.75 = \$7$$

Markdown

A *markdown* is the amount by which the selling price of an item is reduced. Sometimes a markdown is also called a *discount.* To find the amount of a markdown, subtract the new or discounted price from the original price. A markdown can also be expressed as a percentage of the original price. Sometimes this is called a *percentage discount.*

Example

A package of meat at a supermarket is originally priced at $10. However, the meat has not sold and is nearing its expiration date. The supermarket wants to sell it quickly, so it reduces the price to $6. This is a markdown of $4.

selling price − discounted price = dollar markdown

$$\$10 - \$6 = \$4$$

Example

A package of meat at a supermarket is originally priced at $10. However, the meat has not sold and is nearing its expiration date. The supermarket wants to sell it quickly, so it marks down the price by $4. The markdown percentage is determined by dividing the $4 markdown by the original $10 price.

markdown ÷ selling price = markdown percentage

$$\$4 \div \$10 = 40\%$$

Gross Profit

Gross profit is a company's net sales minus the cost of goods sold. *Gross margin* is often expressed as a percentage of revenue.

Copyright Goodheart-Willcox Co., Inc.

Example

A wristband manufacturer generated net sales of $100,000 last year. The cost of goods sold for the wristbands was $30,000. The net sales of $100,000 minus the $30,000 cost of goods sold leaves a gross profit of $70,000.

net sales − cost of goods sold = gross profit

$$\$100,000 - \$30,000 = \$70,000$$

Example

The gross profit of $70,000 divided by the net sales of $100,000 is 0.70, or 70%.

gross profit ÷ net sales = gross margin percentage

$$\$70,000 \div \$100,000 = 0.70 = 70\%$$

Net Income or Loss

Net income or loss is a company's revenue after total expenses are deducted from gross profit. Total expenses include marketing, administration, interest, and taxes. A company earns a *net income* when gross profit exceeds expenses. A *net loss* is incurred when expenses exceed gross profit.

Example

A wristband manufacturer had a gross profit of $70,000. In addition, expenses for marketing, administration, interest, and taxes were $50,000. Net profit is calculated by subtracting the total expenses of $50,000 from the gross profit of $70,000. The net profit was $20,000.

gross profit on sales − total expenses = net income or loss

$$\$70,000 - \$50,000 = \$20,000$$

Break-Even Point

A *break-even point* is the number of units a company must sell to cover its costs and expenses and earn a zero profit. Use the following formula to find a company's break-even point.

total costs ÷ selling price = break-even point

Sales Tax

Sales tax is a tax collected on the selling price of a good or service. The sales tax rate is usually expressed as a percentage of the selling price. Sales tax is calculated by multiplying the sale price by the tax rate.

Example

Suppose you buy a T-shirt for $10.00. How much is the sales tax if the tax rate is 5%? Convert 5% to a decimal (.05) and multiply it by the sale price.

sale price × sales tax rate percentage = sales tax

$$\$10 \times 0.05 = \$0.50$$

Return on Investment

Return on investment (ROI) is a calculation of a company's net profit as a percentage of the owner's investment. One way to determine ROI is to divide net profit by the owner's investment.

Example

Suppose you start a dry-cleaning business with a $100,000 investment, and you earn a $20,000 net profit during the first year. Divide $20,000 by $100,000, which equals a 20% return on your investment.

net income ÷ owner's investment = return on investment (ROI)

$$\$20,000 \div \$100,000 = 0.20 = 20\%$$

Glossary

80/20 inventory rule. Business guideline stating that 80 percent of a business' sales come from 20 percent of its inventory. (15)

A

account. Individual record that summarizes information for a single category, such as cash or sales. (17)

accounting. System of recording business transactions and analyzing, verifying, and reporting results. (17)

accounts payable. Money that a business owes to suppliers for goods or services received. (9)

accounts receivable. Money owed to a business by customers for goods or services delivered. (9)

accounts receivable aging report. Document that shows when accounts receivables are due, as well as the length of time accounts have been outstanding. (16)

accrual basis. Accounting method that records revenue and expenses when they occur. (17)

acquisition. When one company purchases another company, and the purchased company ceases to exist. (18)

action plan. Includes a detailed timeline, budget, and metrics to evaluate the effectiveness of marketing campaigns. (12)

administrative law. Body of law that governs the activities of administrative agencies of government. (4)

aesthetics. Ideas or opinions about beauty. (7)

agency law. Laws regulating the relationship between a business owner, or *principal*, and another party working on his or her behalf as an agent. (8)

agent. Someone contracted to work on behalf of another party. (8)

AIDA. Model for the four stages of a customer's buying process before making a purchase. Stands for *attention, interest, desire,* and *action.* (11)

angel investor. Private investor who wants to fund promising start-up businesses. Also known as an *angel.* (9)

aptitude. Natural ability to do or learn something. (1)

assets. Property or items of value owned by a business. Assets may be fixed or liquid. (9)

attitude. Feelings that a person has about people or things. (1)

audit. Review of the financial statements of a business and the accounting practices that were used to produce them. (17)

autocratic style. Management style characterized by a leader who makes all of the decisions without input from others. (13)

B

backward integration. When a company buys one of its vendors. (18)

barter. Exchange of goods or services for other goods or services with no money changing hands. (9)

behavioral segmentation. Dividing the market by the relationships between customers and the product. (5)

benefits. Extras over and above regular pay given to employees by employers, such as vacation time and health insurance. (14)

Better Business Bureau (BBB). Nonprofit organization that evaluates and monitors businesses and charities, and provides consumers with reliability reports about companies. (4)

bonus. Cash award given to an employee who reaches certain performance goals. (14)

Copyright Goodheart-Willcox Co., Inc.

bootstrapping. Cutting all unnecessary expenses and operating a business on as little cash as possible. (9)

brand. Name, term, or design that sets a product or business apart from its competitors. (10)

branding. Using a product's personality, image, and history to position it favorably in the minds of consumers. (10)

breach of contract. When one or both parties involved in a contract choose not to fulfill the contract's terms. (8)

break-even point. Amount of revenue a business must generate to equal its expenses. (9)

brick-and-mortar business. Company with a physical store or facility for at least a portion of its operation. (7)

buffer stock. Additional stock that is kept above the minimum amount required to meet forecasted sales. (15)

bulk-breaking. Process of separating a large quantity of goods into smaller quantities for resale. (10)

Bureau of Economic Analysis (BEA). An agency within the US Department of Commerce that calculates gross domestic product (GDP) quarterly to evaluate economic trends.

Bureau of Labor Statistics (BLS). Surveys the prices of a cross section of 80,000 goods and services to create the monthly consumer price index.

burglary. Theft that occurs when a person breaks into a business to steal merchandise, money, valuable equipment, or to take confidential information. (16)

business. Term for all the activities involved in developing and exchanging products. (2)

business cycle. Rise and fall of an economy over several months or years. (18)

business entity. Organization that exists independently of its owner's finances. (17)

business laws. Promote fair business practices and protect the best interests of employers, employees, consumers, and the government. (8)

business operations. Day-to-day activities necessary to keep a business up and running. (2)

business owner's policy (BOP) insurance. Risk management product that provides low-cost property and liability coverage for small business owners. (16)

business plan. Written document that describes in detail the strategy for creating a new business. (2)

business risk. Possibility of loss or injury that might occur while running a business. (2)

business to business (B2B). Companies that sell to other businesses. (5)

business to consumer (B2C). Companies that sell primarily to consumers. (5)

buying status. Describes when a customer will buy a product. (5)

buy-sell agreement. Legally binding contract that controls when an owner can sell interest in a partnership, who can buy the owner's interest, and what price will be paid. Also known as a *buyout agreement*. (19)

C

C corporation. Corporation that pays taxes on profits and provides personal liability protection for its owners. (6)

capacity. The ability of a person to legally enter into a binding agreement. (8)

capital. Money and other assets owned by a business or person. (6)

career and technical student organizations (CTSO). National student organizations with local school chapters that are related to career and technical education (CTE) courses. (1)

career clusters. Sixteen groups of occupational and career specialties. (1)

career pathways. Subgroups within the career clusters that reflect occupations requiring similar knowledge and skills. (1)

Copyright Goodheart-Willcox Co., Inc.

career plan. List of steps on a timeline to reach each established career goal. Also known as a *postsecondary plan*. (1)

cash basis. Accounting method that recognizes revenue when it is received and expenses when they are paid. (17)

cash flow. Money moving into and out of a business. (2)

cash on delivery (COD). Payment option where payment for goods and services must be made upon delivery. Also called *collect on delivery*. (18)

census. Count of the people living in a country. (5)

certified development corporation (CDC). Nonprofit corporation that stimulates economic growth in a community through small business lending. (9)

chain of command. Organization's structure of decision-making responsibilities, from highest to lowest levels of authority. (13)

chamber of commerce. Association of business people that promote the commercial interests of a community. (4)

channel of distribution. Path that goods take through the supply chain. (10)

chart of accounts. List of all accounts in a business. (17)

charter. Legal document describing the purpose, place of business, and other details of a corporation. Also called the *articles of incorporation*. (6)

circulation. Number of copies distributed to subscribers and other outlets. (11)

code of conduct. Acceptable behavior for specific business situations based on a company's code of ethics. (3)

code of ethics. General principles or values, often social or moral, that guide an organization. (3)

collaboration skills. Interpersonal skill that enables individuals to work with others to achieve a common goal. (13)

collateral. Asset pledged that will be claimed by the lender if the loan is not repaid. (9)

collection agency. Company that collects past-due bills for a fee. (16)

command economy. Economic system in which most industries are owned by the government. The government decides what goods are produced, how much is produced, and the prices. (2)

commission. Method of compensation where an employee is paid a percentage of what he or she sells. (14)

compensation. Wages or salaries, incentives, and benefits that employees are paid. Also called a *compensation package*. (14)

compensation-and-benefits laws. Laws that address fair wages and benefits for all employees. (8)

competition-based pricing. Pricing strategy based primarily on what the competitors charge. (10)

competitive advantage. Giving customers greater value, better products, or something not offered by the competition. (5)

confidentiality agreement. Document that states an employee will not share any company information with outsiders. (3)

conflict of interest. When an employee has competing interests or loyalties. (3)

conflict resolution. Solving problems that usually arise when people or groups have different goals or needs. (14)

consideration. Something of value involved in the conditions of a contract. (8)

consulting style. Management style characterized by a leader who combines both democratic and autocratic styles. (13)

consumer credit. Credit given to individual consumers by a retail business. (16)

consumer goods. End-use products bought by the public for personal use, such as clothing, appliances, or sporting equipment. (2)

consumer price index (CPI). Average change in prices for goods and services purchased by households as surveyed by the Bureau of Labor Statistics (BLS).

Copyright Goodheart-Willcox Co., Inc.

consumer protection laws. Laws that keep people safe from harmful goods and services. (8)

contingency plan. Written plan of action to ensure a positive and rapid response to a changing situation. (2)

contract. Legally binding agreement. (6)

contraction phase. Phase of the business cycle that occurs when the economy is in decline. Also called *contraction* or *recession*. (18)

controllable risk. Risk that cannot be avoided, but can be minimized by purchasing insurance or implementing a risk plan. (16)

controlling. Business management function of monitoring the progress a business has made in meeting its goals at any given time and making needed corrections. (13)

convenience goods. Items bought with little effort for immediate use, such as grocery items and gasoline.

copyright. Protects music, writings, paintings, and other original works of authorship. (8)

corporate culture. How a company's owners and employees think, feel, and act as a business. (3)

corporate formalities. Records and procedures that corporations are required by law to complete. (6)

corporate social responsibility. Actions of a business to further social good. (3)

corporation. As defined by the US Supreme Court: "an artificial being, invisible, intangible, and existing only in contemplation of the law." A legal entity. (6)

cosigner. Person who signs a loan with the applicant and takes equal responsibility for repaying it. (9)

cost-based pricing. Pricing strategy that uses the cost of a product to set the product's selling price. (10)

credit bureau. Private firm that maintains consumer credit data and provides credit information to businesses for a fee. (16)

credit report. Record of a business' or individual's credit history and financial behavior. (16)

credit risk. Potential of credit not being repaid. (16)

creditor. Individual or business to whom money is owed for goods or services provided. (16)

critical thinking skills. Ability to analyze a situation, interpret information, and make reasonable decisions. (13)

current ratio. Shows the relationship of assets to liabilities. (17)

customer loyalty. Continued and regular patronage of a business even when there are other places to purchase the same or similar products. (16)

customer profile. Detailed description of target market customers based on demographic, geographic, psychographic, and behavioral information. (5)

D

data analysis. Involves studying raw data to find patterns and organizing the data into graphs and charts. (5)

data mining. Practice of searching through large amounts of computerized data to find useful patterns or trends. (5)

database. Collection of data that is organized. (5)

DBA license. License needed to officially register a business. Also known as a *doing business as license*. (6)

debt financing. Borrowing money for business purposes. (9)

debt ratio. Percentage of dollars owed compared to assets owned. (17)

debtor. Individual or business who owes money for goods or services received. (16)

debtor-creditor relationship. Legal relationship existing between a debtor and a creditor based on a good faith agreement that both parties will uphold their end of the agreement. (16)

Copyright Goodheart-Willcox Co., Inc.

demand-based pricing. Pricing strategy that is based on what customers are willing to pay. Also called *value-based pricing*. (10)

democratic style. Management style characterized by a leader who allows and encourages all members of the group to participate and share ideas. Also called *participatory style*. (13)

demographic segmentation. Dividing the market by customers' personal statistics. (5)

demographics. Qualities, such as age, gender, and income, of a specific group of people. (5)

digital citizen. Someone who regularly and skillfully engages in the use of technology. (3)

digital citizenship. Standard of appropriate behavior when using technology to communicate. (3)

digital communication. Exchange of information through electronic means. (3)

digital literacy. Ability to use technology to locate, evaluate, communicate, and create information. (3)

diminishing marginal utility. Principle that there is a point at which having more of something becomes less desirable. This is also called the *threshold of demand* or the *law of diminishing marginal utility*.

direct channel. Distribution channel in which goods or services go directly from the manufacturer to the end user. (10)

direct competitor. Company that sells goods or services that are identical or very similar to the ones another business sells. (5)

dissolution documents. Documents filed in a court notifying everyone that the business is closing. (19)

diversification. Way to reduce risk that involves adding different goods, services, locations, or markets. (18)

division of labor. Breaking complex processes into more simple, specialized tasks that can be assigned to various workers. (7)

double-entry accounting. Recording the debit and credit parts of a transaction. (17)

E

e-business. Any business process conducted through electronic networks using the Internet. Short for *electronic business*. (7)

e-commerce. Buying and selling goods or services through the Internet. (7)

economic indicators. Statistics about the economy indicating how it is performing, which can include the gross domestic product (GDP), consumption expenditures, unemployment rate, inflation rate, new home sales, and stock prices. (7)

economic resources. The natural resources, human resources, and capital resources with which a country creates goods and provides services. Also known as *factors of production*. (2)

economic risk. Situation that occurs when the economy suffers due to negative business conditions in the United States or the world. (16)

economics. Science that deals with examining how goods and services are produced, sold, and used. Focuses on how people, governments, and companies make choices about using limited resources to satisfy unlimited wants. (2)

economy of scale. Decrease in unit cost of a product resulting from large-scale manufacturing operations. (15)

elastic market. When a small change in price produces a relatively large change in the amount of the items demanded.

electronic data interchange (EDI). Standard transfer between organizations of electronic data for business transactions, such as orders, confirmations, and invoices. (15)

electronic promotion. Any promotional effort carried out on the Internet or other technology that uses digital information. (11)

embezzlement. Type of fraud that occurs when somebody entrusted with confidential company information, financial records, money, or other valuables takes them for personal gain. (16)

emotional buying motives. Motives for buying products based on feelings. (11)

Copyright Goodheart-Willcox Co., Inc.

employee buyout (EB). Owner sells the company to its employees. (19)

employee-complaint procedure. Formal process for employees to share their issues with management. (14)

employee handbook. Translates the policies of the business into day-to-day information that the employees need to know. (14)

employee stock option plan (ESOP). Trust fund set up to contribute new shares of stock or cash to purchase existing shares of the company on behalf of the employees. (19)

employee theft. Employees stealing from the business for which they work. (16)

empower. Give employees the authority to make decisions. (13)

enterprise zone. Geographic area where businesses receive favorable tax credits, financing, or other incentives. (4)

entrepreneur. Person who starts a new business. (1)

entrepreneurship. Taking on both the risks and the responsibilities of starting a new business. (1)

Environmental Protection Agency (EPA). Governmental agency that provides information about environmental compliance rules and regulations. (3)

equal-employment opportunity laws. Laws that ensure all workers are given an equal opportunity for employment. (8)

equity. Amount of ownership a person has in a business. (9)

equity financing. Raising money for a business in exchange for a percentage of ownership. (9)

ergonomics. Science of adapting a workstation to fit the needs of the worker and lessen the chance of injury. (14)

ethics. Rules of behavior based on ideas about what is right and wrong. (3)

exchange rate. Rate at which one currency can be converted to another. (4)

expenses. Costs involved in operating a business. (2)

Export-Import Bank of the United States. Governmental agency that helps US businesses export goods and services. Known as *Ex-Im Bank*. (18)

exporting. Shipping products made in one country to another country for future sale. (4)

F

factors of production. Economic resources, including natural resources, human resources, and capital resources. (2)

Farm Services Agency (FSA). Governmental agency that provides assistance to commercial farms. (18)

feasible. Something can be done successfully. (2)

features. Facts about a good or service. (10)

Federal Reserve System. Central bank for the United States charged with keeping the economy stable and able to grow. Also known as the *Fed*.

Federal Trade Commission (FTC). Department of the federal government dedicated to consumer protection. (6)

finance. As a function of business, includes all the business activities that involve money. (2) Funding through a loan. (9)

financial ratio. Shows the relationship between certain figures on financial statements. (17)

fiscal period. Period of time for which a business summarizes accounting information and prepares financial statements. (17)

fixed assets. Items of value that may take time to sell. (9)

fixed expenses. Type of operating expenses that remain the same every month. (9)

floor plan. Scale drawing showing how an overall space will be divided. (7)

forward integration. When a company buys one of the businesses for which it serves as a vendor. (18)

four Cs of communication. Standards that apply to all types of written communication: clarity, conciseness, courtesy, and correctness. (13)

Copyright Goodheart-Willcox Co., Inc.

franchise. Right to sell a company's goods or services in a particular area. (2)

franchise disclosure document. Legal document that includes detailed information that a franchisee must know before purchasing a franchise. (6)

fraud. Cheating or deceiving a business out of money or property. (16)

free enterprise system. Economic system that allows privately owned businesses to operate and make a profit with limited government regulation. Also known as a *market economy*. (2)

freeware. Software available at no charge that can be used at any time. (3)

freight forwarder. Company that organizes shipments. (10)

functions of business. Basic activities of a business, which include production, finance, marketing, and management. (2)

G

GAAP. Acronym for generally accepted accounting principles. (17)

geographic segmentation. Dividing a market based on where customers live. (5)

goal. Something a person wants to achieve in a specified time period. (1)

goods. Physical, or tangible, items that can be touched and used. (2)

goodwill. Advantage a business has due to its good reputation. (3)

gradual sale. Sale of a company in which the new owner finances the purchase with a long-term payment plan, making payments to the seller, while the seller transitions out of the business. (19)

gross domestic product (GDP). A measure of the value of all goods and services produced inside a nation's borders used to indicate a country's economic strength and stability.

gross national product (GNP). A measure of the value of a nation's goods and services, even those produced outside its borders.

growth phase. Phase of the business cycle characterized by expansion of the economy. Also called *growth*, *expansion*, or *recovery*. (18)

guarantee. Promise that a product has a certain quality or will perform in a specific way. (10) Statement of product quality and promise to compensate customers for faulty products. (16)

H

harvest strategy. Planned method for extracting the cash from a business, brand, or product line in order to exit a business. (19)

health and safety laws. Laws that establish regulations to eliminate illness and injury in the workplace. (8)

horizontal diversification. Diversification through adding new products to a company that are not related to the current product line. (18)

horizontal integration. When a company buys one of its competitors. (18)

human resources (HR). Employees who work for the company. (14)

human resources management. Facilitating and managing employees in an organization. (14)

human risk. Situations caused by human actions. (16)

hybrid business. Blend of two or more business location types. (7)

hypothesis. Statement that can be tested and proved to be either true or false. (5)

I

illiquid asset. Item that cannot be sold quickly without suffering a loss. (9)

imperfect competition. Actual realistic market structure under which many small businesses operate. Also known as *monopolistic competition*. (2)

importing. Bringing products made in one country into another country for future sale. (4)

income statement. Reports the revenue and expenses of a business for a specific time

Copyright Goodheart-Willcox Co., Inc.

period and shows a net income or net loss. Also called a *profit and loss (P & L) statement*. (17)

indirect channel. Distribution channel that uses intermediaries to get a product from the producer to the end user. (10)

indirect competitor. Company that offers different, but similar, goods or services that could also meet customer needs. (5)

industrial goods. Products or components made for manufacturing other products, such as steel beams, computer hardware, or fabrics. (2)

inelastic market. When the price of a product has no effect on the demand for it.

inflation. Increase in the price of goods and services over time. (18)

infringement. Any use of intellectual property without permission. (8)

initial public offering (IPO). The first time shares of a company's stock are available for public purchase. (18)

inorganic growth. Business growth that occurs when a business buys a new product line, buys another business, or merges with another company. (18)

insider trading. When an employee uses private company information to purchase company stock or other securities for personal gain. (3)

installment loan. Loan paid in regular payments, known as *installments*, with interest until the loan is paid in full. (16)

institutional promotion. Promoting the business rather than a specific product. (11)

insurable interest. Insurance provision that requires a policyholder to be the party at risk of suffering a loss. (16)

insurance. Form of risk management that spreads individual risk among a large group for a fee. (16)

integrative growth strategies. Occur when one company buys another company. (18)

integrity. Quality of being honest and fair. (3)

intellectual property. Something that comes from a person's mind, such as an idea, invention, or process. (8)

intellectual-property laws. Laws that protect a person's or company's inventions, artistic works, and other intellectual property. (8)

intensive growth strategies. Growing a business by taking advantage of opportunities in the current market. (18)

intermediaries. People or business in between the manufacturers or producers and the end users of a product. (10)

International Franchise Association (IFA). Organization that regulates the franchising industry. (6)

interpersonal skills. Skills used to communicate with those around you. (1)

intranet. Internal computer network. (14)

intrapreneur. Person who works for a company and uses skills, knowledge, and company resources to create new products, make improvements, or develop ideas that benefit the company. (1)

inventory. Assortment or selection of items that a business has on hand to sell to customers at a particular point in time. Also known as *goods on hand* or *inventory on hand*. (9, 10)

inventory management. Process of tracking product orders, keeping an adequate supply and assortment of products, and storing products in warehouses and retail locations. (15)

invoice. Vendor's bill requesting payment for goods shipped or services provided. (15)

J

job analysis. Process that identifies a new position's job requirements, employee qualifications, and how success will be evaluated. (14)

job description. Written definition of a position and the expectations of a specific job. (14)

job posting. Advertisement for an open position. (14)

Copyright Goodheart-Willcox Co., Inc.

joint venture (JV). Partnership in which two or more companies join together for a specific business purpose. (4)

journal. Form used to record business transactions in chronological order. (17)

journalizing. Process of recording business transactions in a journal. (17)

just-in-time (JIT) inventory control system. Keeping a minimal amount of production materials or sales inventory on hand at all times. (15)

K

keystone pricing. Pricing strategy in which the total cost of a product is doubled to determine its selling price. (10)

L

labor relations. How the employer and employees behave toward each other, particularly during contract negotiations. (14)

labor relations laws. Laws that give employees the right to organize and collectively bargain with their employers. (8)

laissez-faire style. Management style characterized by a leader who allows employees to make their own decisions about how to complete tasks. (13)

law of diminishing returns. Economic concept explaining that at a certain point, the benefits generated from investing more revenue or effort decrease and no longer justify the continued investment. (7)

layout. Physical arrangement of a business. (7)

lead time. Total time it takes from placing an order until it is received. (15)

leader. Someone who influences others in a positive way and makes things different or makes things better. (1)

lease. Legal contract to use property owned by another person or company for a specific amount of time. (7)

lease agreement. Contract that provides a lessee the temporary rights to the business. (19)

ledger. Group of accounts. (17)

lessee. Person paying to rent the property. (7)

lessor. Owner of a rental property. (7)

liabilities. Business debts, or what it owes to others. (9)

liability. Legal responsibility. (6)

licensing. When a business sells the right to manufacture its products or use its trademark to another company. (4)

limited partnership (LP). Type of partnership where there is one managing partner and at least one limited partner. (6)

line of credit. Specific dollar amount that a business can draw against as needed. (9)

liquid assets. Items that are easily turned into cash. (9)

liquidation. Sale of all assets of a business, including inventory, equipment, and buildings. (19)

list price. Established price printed in a catalog or on a price tag. (10)

listening. Evaluating what is heard. (13)

listening skills. The ability of an individual to hear what a person says and understand what is being said. (13)

logistics. Planning and managing the flow of goods, services, and people to a destination. (4)

logo. Graphic symbol closely associated with a brand. (10)

long-term liabilities. Business debts that extend beyond the current year. (9)

M

macroeconomics. Study of the economy at the national level.

management. Process of controlling and making decisions about a business. (13)

management style. Way in which a person leads employees or a group. (13)

manual-tag system. Type of manual perpetual inventory control system in which sales are tracked by removing the price tags when products are sold. (15)

Copyright Goodheart-Willcox Co., Inc.

manufacturer. Business that turns raw materials from natural resources or product components into new products for sale. (2)

manufacturer's suggested retail price (MSRP). List price recommended by a manufacturer. (10)

marginal benefit. Point at which having more of something becomes less desirable. Also known as *marginal utility.*

marginal cost. Relates to quantity and economy of scale; the decrease in unit cost resulting from producing more than one item.

market development. Intensive growth strategy that involves expanding existing products to new locations or target markets. Also called *horizontal growth.* (18)

market economy. System that allows privately owned businesses to operate and make a profit with limited government regulation. Also known as a *free enterprise system.* (2)

market penetration. Intensive growth strategy that involves increasing sales in the existing target market. Also called *vertical growth.* (18)

market research. Gathering and analyzing information about a business. (5)

market risk. Potential that the target market for new goods or services is much less than originally thought. (16)

market segment. Group of people, families, businesses, or organizations with common characteristics or needs. (5)

market segmentation. Process of dividing a large market into smaller groups. (5)

market share. Percentage of the total sales in a given market that one business conducts. (10)

market structure. How a market is organized; is based on the number of businesses competing for sales in an industry. (2)

marketing. Function of business that consists of customer-focused activities intended to generate a transaction; comprised of product, price, place, and promotion. (12)

marketing information system. Consists of the processes involved in collecting, analyzing, and reporting marketing research information, usually through technology. (5)

marketing objective. Goals a business wants to achieve during a given time by implementing the marketing plan. (12)

marketing plan. Document describing a business' marketing objectives and the strategies and tactics to achieve them. (12)

marketing strategy. Decisions about product, price, place, and promotion. (12)

marketing tactics. Specific activities used to carry out the marketing strategies. (12)

markup. Desired amount of profit added to the cost of a product to determine the final price. (10)

mass market. Entire large market of potential customers with no segmentation. (5)

merger. When two companies agree to combine as a new company. (18)

metrics. Standards of measurement that provide ways to measure the effectiveness of a promotion. (11)

microeconomics. Study of the economy as related to individual buyer and seller interactions and the factors influencing their choices.

mission statement. Message to the customer as to why a business exists; included in the business plan. (2)

mixed economy. System practiced by most developed countries in which both the government and the private sector make decisions about providing goods and services. (2)

mobile app. Application software developed for use on mobile devices, such as smartphones and tablets. (11)

monopolistic competition. Market structure in which a large number of small businesses sell similar, but not identical, products at different prices. Also known as *imperfect competition.* (2)

monopoly. Market structure with one business that has complete control of the entire supply of goods or services in a market. (2)

mutual acceptance. When both parties agree to the terms of an agreement or contract. (8)

N

NAFTA. North American Free Trade Agreement (NAFTA) established in 1994 removed all trade restrictions among Canada, the United States, and Mexico. (4)

natural resources. A factor of production that includes land, water, minerals, forests, and sunlight. (2)

natural risk. Situation caused by nature. (16)

nature of business. General category of business operations that generate profit. (2)

need. Something that is necessary for survival, such as food, clothing, and shelter. (2)

net profit ratio. Illustrates how much profit is generated per dollar of sales. (17)

nonprice competition. Competition between businesses that is based on the features and benefits of a good or service, not the price. (5)

nonprofit corporation. Company set up to accomplish a specific mission rather than generate a profit. (6)

O

offer. Proposal to provide a service or good. (8)

oligopoly. Market structure with a small number of large companies selling the same or similar products. (2)

open-door policy. Practice of allowing employees to speak with a manager at any time. (13)

operating capital. Money needed to support day-to-day business operations. (9)

operating ratio. Shows the relationship of expenses to sales. (17)

operational planning. Process of setting the day-to-day goals for a company. (13)

opportunity cost. Cost of passing up the next best choice when making a decision. (2)

organic growth. Business growth that occurs through expansion of the current business. (18)

organizational chart. Diagram of employee positions showing how the positions interact within the chain of command. (13)

orientation. Beginning stage of employee training in which a new hire becomes familiar with the business, fellow employees, and job duties. (14)

outright sale. Business is sold in full and ownership is transferred immediately. (19)

overtime pay. Employee wages that are typically 1 1/2 times the normal hourly rate of pay. (14)

owner's equity. Difference between a business' assets and its liabilities. Also known as the owner's *net worth*. (9)

P

packaging. Protects products until customers are ready to use them. (10)

packing slip. Document included in a shipment of goods that lists the contents of the box or container. (15)

partnership. Relationship between two or more people who join to create a business. (6)

patent. Legal protection that gives a person or company the right to be the sole producer of a product for a defined period of time. (8)

peak phase. Highest point in the business cycle; occurs when the economy shifts from growth to contraction. (18)

peer-to-peer lending. Borrowing money from investors via a website. Also called *social lending*. (9)

perfect competition. Market structure characterized by a large number of small businesses selling identical products for the same prices. (2)

performance appraisal. Assessment of an employee's job performance and the progress made toward achieving set goals. (14)

periodic inventory-control system. Taking a physical count of merchandise on a regular basis. (15)

perpetual inventory-control system. Method of counting inventory that shows the quantity on hand at all times. (15)

Copyright Goodheart-Willcox Co., Inc.

personal information management (PIM). System that individuals use to acquire, organize, maintain, retrieve, and use information. (13)

personal selling. Direct contact between a salesperson and a prospective customer with the objective of selling a good or service. (11)

philanthropy. Promoting the welfare of others, usually through volunteering, protecting resources, or donating money or products. (3)

physical inventory. Actual count of items in inventory. (15)

place. Activities involved in getting a good or service to the end user. (10)

place strategy. Decisions about how and where products will be sold, including how goods or services move through the distribution channel. (12)

plagiarism. Using another's words without giving credit to the person who wrote them. (3)

planned obsolescence. Evaluating and updating current products or adding new products to replace older ones. (16)

point-of-sale (POS) software. Computerized perpetual inventory control system that records each sale as it happens. (15)

policy manual. Outlines company policies and procedures. (14)

posting. Transferring information from the journals to a ledger. (17)

premium. Amount paid for insurance by the policyholder. (16)

press conference. Meeting arranged by a business or organization in which the media is invited to attend. (11)

press kit. Packet of information distributed to the media about a new business opening or other major business events. (11)

press release. Media communication written by the company's PR contact to announce new products, locations, businesses, or community events. Also called a *news release*. (11)

price competition. Occurs when price is the main reason that customers choose to buy from one business over another. (5)

price strategy. Decisions about the markup, profit margin, discounts offered, and list price versus selling price. (12)

pricing objectives. Goals defined in the business and marketing plans for the overall pricing policies of the company. (10)

pricing strategies. Business decisions about pricing and how prices are set to make a profit. (10)

primary data. Pieces of information personally collected by an organization or individual. (5)

private corporation. Corporation that does not sell company stock publicaly to investors on stock exchanges. (6)

pro forma balance sheet. Reports a business' assets, liabilities, and owner's equity. (9)

pro forma cash flow statement. Reports the anticipated flow of cash into and out of the business. (9)

pro forma financial statements. Financial statements based on the best estimate of the business' future sales and expenses. (2)

pro forma income statement. Projects the financial progress of the business. Also called the *pro forma profit and loss (P & L) statement.* (9)

product. Anything that can be bought or sold, which includes both goods and services. (2)

product life cycle. Stages a product goes through from the beginning to the end. (10)

product line. Group of closely related products within the product mix. (10)

product mix. All of the goods and services that a business sells. (2, 10)

product obsolescence. When customers no longer want to buy a product and a business owner is stuck with merchandise that will not sell. (16)

Copyright Goodheart-Willcox Co., Inc.

product planning. Process of deciding which product elements to include that will appeal to the target market. (10)

product positioning. Distinguishing your products from competing products. (10)

product promotion. Promoting specific goods or services offered by the business. (11)

product specification sheet. Document that provides product facts, including sizes, colors, materials, and weights. (15)

product strategy. Decisions about the goods or services a business offers, including quantities, sizes, packaging, warranties, brand names, image, and design. (12)

production. All the activities required to make a product. (2)

production workflow. Sequence of assembly, which greatly influences a facility layout. (7)

productive inventory. The 20 percent of a business' inventory that produces the most sales. (15)

productivity. Measure of a worker's production in a specific amount of time. (7)

professional development. Training on the skills and knowledge that contribute to employees' personal development and career advancement. (14)

profit. Difference between the income earned and expenses incurred by a business during a specific period of time.

profit margin. Amount by which revenue from sales exceeds the costs of making a product and selling it. (10)

profit sharing. Type of employee compensation where a percentage of the company profits is distributed to employees, usually on an annual basis. (14)

promotion. Moving an employee to a higher-level position. (14)

promotion strategy. Decisions about which advertising, sales promotions, personal selling, and public-relations activities to pursue. (12)

promotional mix. Combination of different promotional methods to motivate customers to purchase goods or services. (11)

proprietary information. Information a company wishes to keep private. Also known as *trade secrets*. (3)

prospecting. Process of finding potential customers. (11)

prototype. Working model of a new product for testing purposes. (10)

psychographic segmentation. Dividing the market by lifestyle choices. (5)

psychological pricing. Pricing technique used by retailers to influence buying decisions. (10)

public corporation. Corporation that sells its stock on stock exchanges to any investor who wants to buy it. (6)

publicity. Unpaid media coverage for a newsworthy business, person, or product. (11)

purchase on account. Transaction for which merchandise purchased will be paid to the vendor at a later date. (17)

purchase order (PO). Form completed by a buyer and sent to a vendor listing the quantity, variety, and price of the products ordered. (15)

purchasing. Purchasing is the process of buying goods and materials from other businesses for resale to customers. (15)

purchasing management. Purchasing management includes ordering the merchandise that is needed, receiving the merchandise into stock once it arrives, and paying the vendor for the order. (15)

Q

qualitative data. Type of primary data that provide insight into what people think about a topic. (5)

quality control. Activity of checking goods as they are produced or received to ensure the quality meets expectations. (15)

Copyright Goodheart-Willcox Co., Inc.

quantitative data. Type of primary data that are the facts and figures from which conclusions can be drawn. (5)

quick response (QR) code. Bar codes that connect the user to a website or other digital information when scanned with a smartphone. (11)

R

radio frequency identification (RFID). Computerized inventory control system that uses computer chips attached to inventory items and radio frequency receivers to track inventory. (15)

rational buying motives. Motives for buying products based on reason. (11)

real GDP. Gross domestic product numbers corrected for inflation.

recall. Action that removes unsafe products from the market. (8)

receiving record. Form on which all merchandise received is listed as it comes into the place of business. (15)

recession. Negative economic growth within an economy that lasts at least six months. (18)

recruiting. Process of finding suitable people and getting them to join a company. (14)

regulation. Rule that has the force of law and is issued by an agency of government. (4)

research plan. Specific steps to take for testing a hypothesis. (5)

retailer. Business that buys products from wholesalers or directly from manufacturers and resells them to consumers. (2)

retained earnings. Profits set aside from the operation of the company. (18)

retainer. Fee paid to a lawyer or other professional in advance for his or her services. (8)

return on investment (ROI). Common measure of profitability for a business; based on the amount earned from the investment in the business. (10)

return on sales (ROS). Measure of a company's profitability; is equal to the net income divided by total sales. (10)

revenue. Earnings that a business receives for the goods and services it sells. Also called *income.* (2)

risk management. Process for identifying, assessing, and reducing risks of different kinds. (2)

robbery. Theft involving another person, often by using force or the threat of violence. (16)

royalty payment. Fee that franchisees must continually pay the franchisor to keep operating the franchise. (6)

S

sale on account. Transaction for which cash for a sale will be received at a later date. (17)

sales force. Team of employees involved in personal selling for a business. (11)

sales quota. Expected sales for a certain time period as assigned to each salesperson. (11)

sample size. Number of people in the group from which the data are collected. (5)

scarcity. Demand is higher than the available resources. (2)

search engine optimization (SEO). Process of indexing a website to rank it higher on the results list when a search is conducted. (11)

secondary data. Information that already exists. (5)

self-assessment. Tool that helps an individual understand his or her personal preferences and identify strengths and weaknesses. (1)

selling price. Price a customer actually pays for a product after discounts and coupons. (10)

selling process. Organized method or approach to product sales. (11)

service. Intangible action or task that is performed, usually for a fee. (2)

service business. Business that earns income by providing its services and expertise to businesses or consumers. (2)

Service Corps of Retired Executives (SCORE). Nonprofit association helping small business start-ups and entrepreneurs. (4)

Copyright Goodheart-Willcox Co., Inc.

Copyright Goodheart-Willcox Co., Inc.

sexual harassment. Unwanted sexual attention. (8)

shareware. Copyrighted software that is available free of charge on a trial basis. (3)

shoplifting. Theft that occurs when a person posing as a customer takes goods from a store without paying for them. (16)

shopping goods. Items usually purchased after making the effort to compare price, quality, and style in more than one store; includes more expensive, durable items such as appliances and furniture.

short-term liabilities. Business debts expected to be paid within the current year. (9)

silent partner. Business partner who invests money, but is not involved in the business' daily operations or management. (6)

situation analysis. Snapshot of the environment in which a business has been operating during a given time. (12)

situational management. Changes in a manager's behavior and management style according to individual situations. (13)

skill. An ability that a person learned over time and can do well. (1)

small business. Business that is independently owned and operated, organized for profit, and not dominant in its field. (2)

Small Business Administration (SBA). Governmental agency dedicated to helping small businesses and entrepreneurs succeed. (4)

small business development center (SBDC). Program administered by the SBA that gives a wide variety of information and small business guidance. (4)

SMART goal. Goal that is specific, measurable, attainable, realistic, and timely. (1)

socially responsible. Behaving with sensitivity to social, economic, and environmental issues. (3)

sole proprietor. Person who owns a business and is personally responsible for its debts. (6)

sources of funds. Document summarizing where the start-up funding comes from for a new business. (2)

sourcing. Process of finding suppliers of materials needed for the production of a product. (15)

spam. Electronic messages sent in bulk to people who did not give a company permission to e-mail them. (3)

speaking. Verbal communication with others. (13)

specialization. Performing a particular task within a larger process on a regular basis. (7)

specialty goods. Unique items consumers are willing to spend considerable time, effort, and money to buy, such as unique sports cars or rare antiques.

staffing. Business management function of hiring people and matching them to the best position for their talents. (13)

stakeholder. Person with an interest, usually financial, in a business. (17)

start-up capital. Initial sum of money needed to open a business and cover start-up expenses. (2, 9)

start-up companies. Newly created businesses. (1)

start-up costs. Initial expenses necessary to open the doors of a business. (9)

statistical analysis. Mathematical technique for analyzing collected data. (5)

stock. Shares of ownership in a company. (6)

stock option. Share of company stock that employees can purchase at a discount as a form of compensation. (14)

stockholders. People who own stock in a company. (6)

stockout. When a business runs out of inventory. (15)

strategic planning. Process of determining the long-term goals of a company. (13)

Subchapter S corporation. Corporation that provides limited liability to its owners and is taxed like a partnership. (6)

succession plan. Exit strategy that details what will happen to the company in the event of the owner's death, retirement, or decision to leave the company. (19)

supply and demand. Economic principle relating the quantity of products available to meet consumer demand. (2)

supply chain. Businesses, people, and activities involved in turning raw materials into products and delivering them to end users. (4)

supply chain management. Coordinating the events happening throughout the supply chain. (10)

surety bond. Three-party contract that guarantees one party will fulfill its obligation to a second party. (16)

surveillance. Process of observing everything going on at a business to detect and prevent crimes. (16)

SWOT analysis. Analyzing the goods and services of a business to determine the company's *strengths, weaknesses, opportunities,* and *threats.* (5)

synergistic diversification. Diversification through adding new product lines or businesses that are compatible with an existing business. (18)

T

tactical planning. Process of determining the short-term goals for a company. (13)

tagline. Phrase or sentence that summarizes some essential part of a product. Also known as a *slogan.* (10)

target market. Specific group of consumers at which a company aims its goods and services. (5)

tariff. Tax on imported goods. (4)

tenant improvement. Cost to remodel existing interior space for a new business. (7)

time-management skills. Ability to use time wisely by setting priorities. (13)

tort. Civil wrong, as opposed to a criminal wrong. (8)

trade area. Area from which a business expects to draw most of its customers. (7)

trade barriers. Governmental regulations that restrict trade with other countries. (4)

trade credit. Granting a line of credit to another business for a short time to finance the purchase of the first business' goods or services. (9, 16)

trademark. Protects taglines, slogans, names, symbols, or any unique method to identify a product or company. (8)

traditional economy. System used by countries with primarily rural populations in which citizens make just enough to survive and barter for most goods or services. (2)

traits. Behavioral and emotional characteristics that make each person unique. (1)

transportation. Physical movement of products through the channel of distribution. (10)

trough phase. Lowest point of the business cycle; occurs when the economy shifts from contraction to growth. (18)

turnover rate. Number of times inventory has been sold during a specific time period. Also known as *turnover ratio.* (15)

U

uncontrollable risk. Situation that cannot be predicted or covered by purchasing insurance. (16)

uniform resource locator (URL). Unique address of a document, web page, or website on the Internet. (11)

uninsurable risk. Risk that an insurance company will not cover. (16)

unique selling proposition (USP). Statement that lists a business' or product's special features or benefits that highlight its competitive advantage. (5)

Copyright Goodheart-Willcox Co., Inc.

unit-control system. Type of manual perpetual inventory control system in which a visual determination is made when more stock is needed. (15)

usage rate. How often a customer buys or uses a good or service. (5)

utility. Attribute that makes a product capable of satisfying a need or want; four types include place, time, possession, and form. (10)

V

value. Relative worth of something to a person. (10)

values. Beliefs of a person or a culture. (1)

variable expenses. Type of operating expenses that can change on a monthly basis. (9)

vendor. Company that sells products to other businesses. (15)

venture capitalist (VC). Professional investor or investing group looking to fund new startups or expansions of existing companies. (9)

vision statement. Overall goal for a company's future; included in the business plan. (2)

visual merchandising. Process of creating floor plans and displays to attract customer attention and encourage purchases. (7)

W

want. Something that a person desires, but can function without. (2)

warranty. Written document that states the quality of a product with a promise to correct certain problems that might occur. (10)

wholesaler. Business that purchases large amounts of goods directly from manufacturers for resale to various retailers. (2)

Workers Adjustment and Retraining Notification Act (WARN). Law that requires employees be given 60 days written notice that their company is going to close. (19)

worker's compensation. State-mandated business insurance program intended to provide medical and financial support for workers who are injured or made ill at the workplace. (16)

working capital. Amount of money a business has after its liabilities are paid. (17)

workplace discrimination. Occurs when a person is denied a job based on age, race, sex, religion, or nationality. (8)

World Bank Group (WBG). Agency that provides assistance to developing countries, which can help provide a market for goods and services from US companies. (18)

World Trade Organization (WTO). An international organization formed in 1995 working to reduce trade barriers and solve trade problems among its 153 member countries. (4)

writing. Communicating using visible words and characters. (13)

Copyright Goodheart-Willcox Co., Inc.

Index

7(a) loan program, 229
80/20 inventory rule, 409
80/20 rule, 114

A

ability tests, 373
Abt, David, 338
accidental injury, 423
account, 456
account credit, 456
account debit, 456
account title, 456
accounting, 450
accounting basics, 450–454
accounting equation, 242, 454
accounting functions, 450
accounting period, 451. *See also* fiscal period
accounts payable, 242
accounts receivable, 241, 441
accounts receivable aging report, 442
acquisition, 482
accrual basis of accounting, 452
action plan, 329–331
   budget, 330
   metrics, 330–331
   time line, 329
active listening, 355
ad, 293
administrative law, 99
advertising, 293–296
   broadcast media, 295–296
   print media, 293–295
aesthetics, 183
agency law, 200
agency relationships, 200
agent, 200
AIDA, 309
   action, 310
   attention, 309

desire, 310
interest, 309
Allen, Paul, 4
alternative forms of ownership, 163–164
Altmann, Cecil, 56
angel investors, 225
angular floor plan, 186–187
anticipation stock, 403
appendices, 55
aptitude, 11
Aramburu, Jason, 464
Arora, Nikhil, 74
articles of incorporation, 160
assets, 240, 453, 454
assume risk, 432–433
attitude, 11, 113
audit, 451
autocratic management style, 348
avoid risk, 425–429

B

backward integration, 483
bad checks, 422, 428
bait and switch, 264
balance sheet, 461, 463
bartering, 223
behavioral segmentation, 114–115
   benefits sought, 114
   brand loyalty, 114
   buying status, 114
   special occasions, 115
   usage rate, 114
benefits, 311, 365
Better Business Bureau (BBB), 88
bibliography, 55
bin ticket, 405
blind taste test, 123
blog, 299

Bloyd, Lance, 448
blue collar, 112
Blumenthal, Neil, 220
bonuses, 373
bootstrapping, 222–224
Bordenave Jr., Darryl, 363
brainstorming, 35
brand, 255
brand loyalty, 256
brand mark, 256. *See* also logo
branding, 255–256
breach of contract, 203
break-even point, 233, 268
brick-and-mortar business, 177
Brin, Sergey, 4
Brindak, Juliette, 107
broadcast media, 295–296
   radio, 295–296
   television, 295
brokers, 277
Brown, Justin, 370
Brown, Megan Faulkner, 449
budget, 32, 240, 330
buffer stock, 403
Building Your Business Plan
   Business Growth, 495
   Business Ownership, 169
   Business Plan, 61
   Entrepreneurial Careers, 27
   Ethics and Social Responsibility, 81
   Exit Strategies, 515
   Finance the Business, 247
   Financial Management, 469
   Human Resources Management, 391
   Legal Issues, 219
   Local and Global Opportunities, 105
   Management Functions, 361
   Marketing Plan, 335

Copyright Goodheart-Willcox Co., Inc.

Copyright Goodheart-Willcox Co., Inc.

Copyright Goodheart-Willcox Co., Inc.

Copyright Goodheart-Willcox Co., Inc.

Copyright Goodheart-Willcox Co., Inc.

Copyright Goodheart-Willcox Co., Inc.

Copyright Goodheart-Willcox Co., Inc.